GENDER-BASED VIOLENCE IN CANADIAN POLITICS IN THE #METOO ERA

Edited by Tracey Raney and Cheryl N. Collier

Gender-based violence in politics is a significant and growing problem that threatens the democratic process in Canada. Despite its prevalence, little academic research has been conducted on this topic to date.

Gender-Based Violence in Canadian Politics in the #MeToo Era raises awareness of and presents new innovative research on this timely and pressing public issue. Here, leading experts from across Canada uncover critical new insights and identify potential solutions that would help address gender-based violence in politics, improve gender equality, and strengthen Canadian democracy. Using an intersectional lens, chapters range in their approaches; offer new concepts and measures of gender-based violence in online political spaces, political media coverage and cartoons, campaigns, municipal politics, and legislatures; and explore Indigenous ways of knowing about gender-based violence in Canadian politics. Additionally, the volume presents recommendations for decision-makers, policymakers, anti-violence advocates, and the academic community on how to best address the problem of gender-based violence in the political sphere.

TRACEY RANEY is a professor in the Department of Politics and Public Administration at Toronto Metropolitan University.

CHERYL N. COLLIER is a professor of political science and dean of the Faculty of Arts, Humanities, and Social Sciences at the University of Windsor.

Gender-Based Violence in Canadian Politics in the #MeToo Era

EDITED BY TRACEY RANEY
AND CHERYL N. COLLIER

UNIVERSITY OF TORONTO PRESS
Toronto Buffalo London

© University of Toronto Press 2024
Toronto Buffalo London
utorontopress.com

ISBN 978-1-4875-4001-2 (cloth)   ISBN 978-1-4875-4004-3 (EPUB)
ISBN 978-1-4875-4002-9 (paper)   ISBN 978-1-4875-4003-6 (PDF)

Library and Archives Canada Cataloguing in Publication

Title: Gender-based violence in Canadian politics in the #MeToo era /
   edited by Tracey Raney and Cheryl N. Collier.
Names: Raney, Tracey, editor. | Collier, Cheryl N., 1967– editor.
Description: Includes bibliographical references and index.
Identifiers: Canadiana (print) 2023062278X | Canadiana (ebook)
   20230622836 | ISBN 9781487540012 (cloth) | ISBN 9781487540029 (paper) |
   ISBN 9781487540036 (PDF) | ISBN 9781487540043 (EPUB)
Subjects: LCSH: Gender-based violence – Canada. | LCSH: Women –
   Political activity – Canada. | LCSH: Women – Violence against – Canada.
Classification: LCC HV6250.4.W65 G46 2024 | DDC 362.88082 – dc23

Cover design: Jennifer Stimson
Cover image: ivanastar / iStockphoto.com

We wish to acknowledge the land on which the University of Toronto Press operates. This land is the traditional territory of the Wendat, the Anishnaabeg, the Haudenosaunee, the Métis, and the Mississaugas of the Credit First Nation.

This book has been published with the help of a grant from the Federation for the Humanities and Social Sciences, through the Awards to Scholarly Publications Program, using funds provided by the Social Sciences and Humanities Research Council of Canada.

University of Toronto Press acknowledges the financial support of the Government of Canada, the Canada Council for the Arts, and the Ontario Arts Council, an agency of the Government of Ontario, for its publishing activities.

 Canada Council for the Arts   Conseil des Arts du Canada

Funded by the Government of Canada   Financé par le gouvernement du Canada

Contents

List of Figures and Tables ix

Acknowledgments xi

Introduction: Gender-Based Violence in Canadian Politics – A Threat to Gender Equality and Democracy 3
TRACEY RANEY AND CHERYL N. COLLIER

Part One: Violence against Women in Politics on Social Media in Canada

1 Online Violence against Women in Politics: Canada in a Comparative Perspective 25
GABRIELLE BARDALL AND CHRIS TENOVE

2 Digital Dangers: Theorizing Online Violence against Politicians 45
ANGELIA WAGNER AND TAYLER YOUNG

3 Ringing an Early Alarm Bell: Image-Based Sexual Violence against Political Actors 65
DIANNE LALONDE

Part Two: Violence against Women in Politics Reporting in Canadian Mainstream Media

4 Psychological Violence, Media Effects, Counter-Speech, and Political Attitudes 87
MELANEE THOMAS AND SCOTT PRUYSERS

5 Gender-Based Violence towards Political Women:
   Did Print News Coverage Shift after #MeToo?   109
   ELIZABETH GOODYEAR-GRANT

6 Gender-Based Violence, Humour, and Frontier Masculinity
   in Alberta Political Cartoons   130
   RISSA REIST

Part Three: Experiences of Violence against Women in Politics

7 Blurred Lines: Boundaries and Consequences for Indigenous
   Women in Politics in the Era of #MeToo   151
   REBECCA MAJOR AND CYNTHIA NIIOO-BINEH-SEH-KWE STIRBYS

8 Who Calls Foul? Gender-Based Violence on the Municipal
   Campaign Trail   170
   KATE GRAHAM

9 The Dark Side of Working in Politics: A Study of MP Staff
   in Canada   188
   MEAGAN CLOUTIER

Part Four: Assessing "Solutions" to Violence against Women in Politics in Canada

10 Just Bad Apples? Political Accountability and Canadian MPs
   Accused of Gender-Based Violence   211
   BAILEY GERRITS

11 Can MP Anti-harassment Training Combat Gender-Based Violence
   in the House of Commons? A Comparative Analysis of Canada
   and the United Kingdom   229
   LOUISE COCKRAM

12 Fixing the Upper House: A Gender and Intersectional Analysis
   of the Canadian Senate's 2021 Harassment and Violence
   Prevention Policy   246
   TRACEY RANEY

13 Provincial and Territorial Legislature-Based Sexual Harassment
   Policies for Elected Members: Variation in Approaches but
   Commonality in Ineffectiveness   265
   CHERYL N. COLLIER AND TRACEY RANEY

Conclusion: Canadian Experiences of Gender-Based Violence
in Politics – Key Learnings, Action Items, and Avenues for
Further Research   285
   CHERYL N. COLLIER AND TRACEY RANEY

Contributors   297

Index   301

Figures and Tables

Figures

1.1 Framework of analysis for online gender-based violence in politics (GBV-P) 27
2.1 Theoretical model of continuum of online discourse with or about a political actor 48
4.1 Headline highlighting threats against Catherine McKenna 88
4.2 Political attitudes by condition 97
4.3 Political attitudes by condition (women only) 98
5.1 Print media coverage of violence and abuse towards women in politics 117
13.1 Elected women in provincial and territorial legislatures, 2022 269

Tables

3.1 Percentage of sexual deepfakes of the top two US politically active men and women featured on the Sensity platform 73
4.1 Perceptions of the victims of psychological violence 99
6.1 Hostile humour themes in representations of the premier 139
6.2 Perpetrators of physical violence directed at the premier 141
9.1 The gender gap in harassment 193
10.1 Type of accountability pursued 219
13.1 Provincial and territorial legislature member-based sexual harassment policies 272
13.2 Provincial and territorial sexual harassment policy content analysis 277

Acknowledgments

This volume draws on research supported by the Social Sciences and Humanities Research Council. The editors wish to thank Rachel Russell, master's student in public policy and administration at Toronto Metropolitan University, for her excellent research assistance and University of Windsor bachelor of interdisciplinary arts and science student Jacob Collier for editing assistance. We also thank Mona Lena Krook, Ethel Tungohan, and Erin Tolley who served as discussants and provided all authors with extremely helpful comments when the chapters were workshopped as part of the Canadian Political Science Association Annual Conference in 2021. Thanks as well to Chris Tenove, Gabrielle Bardall, and Bailey Gerrits who provided input into earlier versions of the introductory chapter. A special thank you to our two anonymous reviewers for providing us with superb feedback on the volume. We would also like to thank our editor at the University of Toronto Press, Daniel Quinlan, for his support and guidance throughout the process. Finally, we thank all our contributors for sharing their important research work in the pages that follow.

GENDER-BASED VIOLENCE IN CANADIAN POLITICS
IN THE #METOO ERA

Introduction: Gender-Based Violence in Canadian Politics – A Threat to Gender Equality and Democracy

TRACEY RANEY AND CHERYL N. COLLIER

In June 2021, member of Parliament (MP) Mumilaaq Qaqqaq delivered a farewell speech in the Canadian House of Commons – a space she called a "colonial house on fire I am willingly walking into" (Qaqqaq 2021). Qaqqaq reported that she had been racially profiled in politics and that, as an Inuit woman, she never felt safe or protected. Her speech is a powerful testimony of the experiences that women – particularly Indigenous, Black, and women of colour – face today in the Canadian political arena and in settler colonial institutions. Unfortunately, violence – including harassment, assault, and harmful threats – has been a persistent and increasing feature of the political process. Many women political actors, including federal, territorial, and provincial leaders, political staffers, as well as party volunteers, journalists, and activists, have reported sexist, racist, and/or homo- or transphobic harassment and violence through their engagement in politics, sometimes online and other times in person, at every level of government.

These experiences are not new or rare in the political process, but they have become an increasing threat to democratic governance in Canada and around the world. This book contributes to the growing global study of gender-based violence in politics (GBV-P) by investigating this problem in the Canadian context for the first time (see Bardall, Bjarnegård, and Piscopo 2020; Krook 2020; Bjarnegård and Zetterberg 2023). It contributes to multiple fields, including Canadian politics and women's political representation, and expands our understanding of gender-based violence as an additional barrier to women entering into, and staying engaged in, the political process. The book is framed around three broad research questions: How have political actors in Canada experienced GBV-P? What does the prevalence of GBV-P tell us about the state of democracy in Canada and the goal of increasing women's representation in the public sphere? What does the Canadian case tell us about how GBV-P should be tackled globally? The chapters that follow address these questions in turn.

In this introduction, we offer a brief overview of the broader global context of GBV-P. We then highlight the volume's theoretical and empirical contributions to the literature from this Canadian case study. Despite being one of the world's most enduring democracies, Canada has yet to reach gender parity in its public offices; it is also the site of increasing reports of sexism, racism, homo- and transphobia, and violence across the spectrum, including ongoing colonial violence against Indigenous peoples. Taken together, the volume's findings demonstrate that GBV-P is a serious and ongoing threat to gender equality and democracy in Canada and that solutions are urgently needed to address it. Drawn from our authors' research, the book concludes with a summary of actionable steps that can be taken to prevent further democratic erosion on this issue.

A Global Problem: Gender-Based Violence in Politics

Attention to the problem of violence against women in politics (VAWIP) was first garnered in the late 1990s and early 2000s by a network of politicians, activists, practitioners, and academics predominantly located in Latin America (Valverde 2010; Piscopo 2016; Biroli 2016; Restrepo Sanín 2018, 2020, 2023; Krook 2019, 2021). Around this time in Bolivia, the Association of Locally Elected Women of Bolivia (ACOBOL) began to systematically collect data on violence perpetrated against local women politicians. ACOBOL was the first organization globally to define the problem and organize to draft a national bill on political harassment and violence based on gender (Restrepo Sanín 2018; Krook 2019, 79). As a result, the Quito Consensus, agreed at the 10th Regional Conference of Women in Latin American and the Caribbean in 2007, became the first international call to United Nations member states to adopt legislative measures that would "prevent, sanction, and eradicate political and administrative harassment against women to accede to elected and appointed decision-making positions" (cited in Krook 2020, 14). Similarly, in the early to mid-2000s women activists in other regions of the Global South, including South Asia and Kenya, also began organizing to address the problem of VAWIP (see Krook 2020).

Non-governmental organizations and human rights activists have contributed to the creation and establishment of a broad, international normative rights framework on gender equality and VAWIP (Ballington and Borovsky 2023). Calls affirming this framework include the United Nations 1948 Declaration of Human Rights, the 1979 Convention on the

Elimination of All Forms of Discrimination against Women (CEDAW), and the 1993 Declaration on the Elimination of Violence against Women (DEVAW; United Nations 1993). In 2007, iKNOW Politics, the first cross-regional joint project, was established: it is a joint project of International IDEA, the Inter-Parliamentary Union, the United Nations Development Programme, and UN Women, which has as one of its goals the elimination of VAWIP (iKnow Politics n.d.; Krook 2020, 17). In 2011, the United Nations called for a "zero tolerance" policy for violence against women candidates and election officials (Resolution 66/130; see United Nations 2011; Bjarnegård and Zetterberg 2023). In a 2015 resolution, the United Nations further adopted the *2030 Agenda for Sustainable Development* (Resolution 70/1). Goal 5 of the resolution's seventeen sustainable development goals, "Achieve gender equality and empower all women and girls," included two provisions intended to encourage states to eliminate all forms of violence against women and girls in private and public spaces (Goal 5, Target 5.2) and to seek to ensure the full and effective political participation of women in decision-making spaces (Goal 5, Target 5.5; United Nations 2015, 18; see also Ballington and Borovsky 2023). In 2017, CEDAW adopted General Recommendation 35 on gender-based violence against women, updating its previous 1992 commitments. Updates included calling for the repeal of all laws and policies that directly or indirectly condone and facilitate violence and emphasizing the need for approaches that promote and respect women's autonomy and decision-making in all spheres of life (CEDAW 2017). Together, these and other international human rights mechanisms have sought to raise awareness that all countries have an obligation to prevent and address GBV-P.

Global awareness campaigns have also ensued. In 2016, the National Democratic Institute launched its #NotTheCost campaign to stop VAWIP, outlining steps that local, national, and international actors could take to address it (National Democratic Institute 2016; Krook 2019). The same year, the Inter-Parliamentary Union published a report that found 82 per cent of women politicians had experienced some form of psychological abuse, while 44 per cent had experienced beating, abduction, and rape or received death threats globally (Inter-Parliamentary Union 2016). Even though the survey sample of women-identified political actors is small, these findings signalled that GBV-P is widespread and similar across several countries and political systems. In her 2018 report, the United Nations Special Rapporteur on violence against women and girls recognized and condemned gender-based violence as a deterrent to women's participation in the political realm globally (Šimonović 2018). In late 2022, the Office for Democratic Institutions and Human Rights (ODIHR) of the Organization for Security and Co-operation in Europe (OSCE) launched a global toolkit to prevent GBV-P, which aims to raise awareness and strengthen knowledge and capacities among OSCE countries (of which Canada is a member). The toolkit is designed for politicians, parliaments, political parties, and civil society representatives (ODIHR 2022).

A Canadian Problem: GBV-P in an Established Liberal Democracy

This book builds on the global scholarship and activism identified above by providing an in-depth investigation of GBV-P in a well-established liberal democracy, Canada. In a 2018 *Social Politics* article, we examine the Westminster liberal legislatures in Canada, the United Kingdom, and Australia, and show how violence and harassment against women are widespread and the result of historically entrenched patriarchal institutional norms (Collier and Raney 2018b). In this edited book, our authors centre the Canadian case to deeply interrogate the motives, forms, and impacts of gender-based violence in this country. As Canada is one of the world's most established democracies, some might assume that Canada's political process is relatively safe, equitable, and inclusive. Canada has a generally positive global reputation for gender equality, particularly under the Liberal government of self-identified feminist Prime Minister Justin Trudeau, who has held power since 2015. This book raises questions about the validity of this reputation.

In terms of women's descriptive (or "numerical") representation, Canadian women, racialized minorities, and 2SLGBTQQIA+[1] people have seen a steady, albeit slow, increase in their representation in elected offices across the country (Black and Griffith 2022). However, political power is far from being equitably shared in the country. In the House of Commons, women currently hold just 30 per cent of seats. This percentage is a historic high and places Canada sixty-second in the world for women's representation to elected office (Inter-Parliamentary Union 2022). Among the current MPs, there are twelve (4 per cent) Indigenous, eight (2 per cent) Black, and eight (2 per cent) who identify as 2SLGBTQQIA+. As Canada's population continues to be over-represented by white, cis-gendered, heterosexual men in most decision-making spaces, democracy or rule by the people is left to only "some" people who form the majority. Existing research explains that women's political under-representation is due to several factors, including barriers erected by political parties and the media (Trimble, Arscott, and Tremblay 2013; Bashevkin 1993, 2019; Thomas and Bodet 2013; Goodyear-Grant 2013; Trimble 2017). Immigrants, racialized minorities, and 2SLGBTQQIA+

people also face unique obstacles in Canada's political process (Andrew et al. 2008; Tolley 2016; Tremblay 2019; Wagner and Everitt 2019).

This book seeks to provide a clearer picture of the scope and nature of gendered political violence as an *additional* key barrier to inclusive political representation in Canada. Outside Canada, studies highlight how violence and harassment pose a threat to women's and racial and sexual minority members' political representation, undermining their effective participation in the public sphere. For Krook, VAWIP is linked to women's numerical gains in politics in that the *motivation* for violence is to curtail these gains and to "exclude women as women from participating in political life" (2020, 65). Similarly, Berry, Bouka, and Kamuru, in their study on backlash against gender quotas in Kenya, find that, as women begin to occupy previously male-dominated spaces, they can be subjected to renewed gendered subordination. This "reactivation of patriarchal efforts" manifests in efforts to police women's bodies through any means possible, including violence and harassment (2021, 645).

Comparative research further sets out to examine the linkages between violence, harassment, and gender specifically. Using a gendered lens, Bardall, Bjarnegård, and Piscopo (2020) suggest that political violence is gendered when perpetrators use it to uphold men's hegemonic control over the political system (*gendered motives*); when gender structures how men and women perpetrate and experience violence through such things as gendered scripts (*gendered forms*); and when audiences understand violent acts to include gendered dimensions (*gendered impacts*). In her book *Violence against Women in Politics*, Krook takes a "bias event" approach and argues that violence in politics and VAWIP are distinguished from one another by the gendered motivations of violence. While the former can include acts directed at women, the latter are concerted efforts that are aimed at driving women out of public life (Krook 2020, 104).

Contributing to this broader global research agenda, the authors in this book apply the concept of gender-based violence in politics (GBV-P) to the Canadian context for the first time.[2] We define GBV-P as harmful actions that are directed at an individual because of their gender, gender expression, gender identity, or perceived gender and are designed to discourage or restrict them from being active in informal (for example, movement, advocacy, online) or formal (for example, elections, political parties, legislatures) political spaces. GBV-P is rooted in, and perpetuated by, systems of domination and exclusion that seek to punish those who participate in the political process but do not conform to traditional gendered norms.

GBV-P is shown in this volume to be an *additional* barrier that impacts not only the number of women in politics but also their capacity to engage meaningfully and substantively in issues of importance to themselves and to their communities. It exists across multiple spaces of public life – in elections and campaigns, media (both traditional and online), and political institutions, as well as in informal political spaces such as in community-based and movement organizations.

We further draw on Krook's (2020) conceptualization of violence as a continuum, which includes physical, psychological, sexual, economic, and semiotic violence. *Physical violence* might include acts such as murder, attempted murder, mutilation, and torture. *Psychological violence* includes death and rape threats, intimidation, coercion, or intrusive disruptions to political work. *Sexual violence* encompasses unwanted behaviours that focus on a person's sexual characteristics and can include rape, sexual assault, sextortion, and sexual harassment. *Economic violence* imposes economic hardship on targets and can include vandalism, property destruction, theft, threats to terminate employment, and withholding or restrictions of funds or financial support (177). *Semiotic violence* refers to the use of words or images to injure, subjugate, or discipline members of marginalized groups (188). It might include attempts to "invisibilize" women's achievements or "presence" in politics, to silence or ignore them, to "masculinize" them, to subject them to emotional ridicule, or to challenge their competencies through microaggressions such as "manterruptions" and "mansplaining." Chapters in this volume describe violence along all these categories, save for examples of physical violence, which are less common in Canada (although physical violence threats are certainly common). Accordingly, chapter authors offer insights (to varying degrees) on why these types of violence are being perpetrated and against whom, how the violence is being perpetrated, and the repercussions of the violence on its targets and wider society (Bardall, Bjarnegård, and Piscopo 2020).

The concept of GBV-P encourages and facilitates an understanding of violence as a collective, rather than an individual, problem, where gender is understood as a social structure that enables violence that is rooted in historically unequal power relations between women (and 2SLGBTQQIA+) and men (True 2020). While some authors in this volume focus on violence that is directed primarily at women targets (see, for example, Lalonde, Major and Stirbys, Graham, and Cockram), each uses a gender-based violence framework with a focus on gender (rather than sex) to ultimately explain the gendered causes and consequences of violence. They further query how violence is used with the intent to reproduce, maintain, and reassert pre-existing gendered hierarchies, asymmetries, and inequalities in the political realm (True 2020). A gender-based violence perspective also allows us to reflect on how perceptions of masculinity (and femininity) shape experiences of, and attitudes towards, violence that is perpetrated against political actors other than those who identify as women. Thomas and Pruysers's chapter 4, for example, investigates public attitudes towards women and men politicians who experience violence, while Bardall and Tenove's chapter 1 analyses men and women politicians who experience online harassment. Additionally, Reist's discussion in chapter 6 of "frontier masculinity" in editorial cartoons examines both men and women former premiers. These chapters open the door to future research on the gendered dimensions of violence perpetrated against gender non-conforming men political actors more generally.

This volume also contributes to global research on GBV-P through its intersectional approach to the topic. In 2018, Kuperberg argued persuasively for intersectional approaches to VAWIP. Future analyses should consider not only how the identities of women politicians motivate violence but also how the motivations and forms of such violence reflect different structures of oppression (Kuperberg 2018). Applying an intersectional lens to violence requires attention to characteristics beyond individual social identities (for example, an individual's race or sex), incorporating the interlocking systems of domination and oppression that perpetuate racism, colonialism, sexism, cisgenderism, and so on (Dhamoon 2011; Hill Collins and Bilge 2020). In her work on violence against women, Crenshaw (1991, 1245) reminds us that "structural intersectionality" or "the ways in which the location of women of color and the intersection of race and gender makes [their] actual experience of domestic violence, rape, and remedial reform qualitatively different than that of white women."

Intersectional perspectives on violence are necessary to ensure that proposed solutions do not assume that women are a "homogenous mass" or that only men are perpetrators (Hill Collins and Bilge 2020). Some chapters here highlight how traditional and technologically assisted (online) media frame the violence perpetrated against women of colour and 2SLGBTQQIA+ political actors (see chapters 1, 2, and 5), while others offer intersectional approaches to address violence and harassment within political institutions (see chapters 11, 12, and 13). More work needs to be done to address the intersecting ways in which political actors experience violence. In the book's conclusion, we suggest some directions that an intersectional approach to research on GBV-P could take in the future.

This volume also contributes to broader discussions about gender representation and democracy globally. The research by our authors makes clear that violence and harassment are serious, ongoing threats to gender political equality and pose a critical challenge to women's descriptive and substantive representation *inside an established liberal democracy* (Childs and Krook 2008). GBV-P should not be understood as a phenomenon that occurs only in weak or emerging democracies; it is also a significant threat in established democracies. The prevalence of GBV-P challenges the notion that liberal democratic countries – in this case Canada – are safe spaces for women and other marginalized political participants. Moreover, as Thomas and Pruysers's chapter 4 observes, GBV-P may dampen political ambition and engagement among the public, undermining the health and vibrancy of democratic politics. This contribution echoes earlier research by Weldon, who conducted a cross-country comparison on state-level policy aimed at combating violence against women. In her 2002 study, she found that Scandinavian democracies performed worse than Latin American countries in terms of responsiveness to the problems of gender-based violence.

GBV-P research from a Canadian vantage point allows for broader insights on how this pressing problem should be tackled globally. At a time when significant threats to democracies have emerged worldwide (for example, increasing partisanship and polarization, mis- and disinformation campaigns), violence and harassment against marginalized political actors need to be understood as democratic threats in their own right. GBV-P inflicted upon individual targets can result in physical, psychological, and emotional harm to their well-being and safety. When GBV-P occurs in public spaces, it also sends a wider message to members of the public that they could also be subjected to the same treatment should they have political aspirations, potentially suppressing the pipeline of future leaders (Krook 2018). If left unchecked, GBV-P has the potential to further erode public trust in the political process more broadly, thus contributing to additional democratic backsliding.

This research is timely as lawmakers worldwide – including in the Global North – grapple with how to combat this problem in the #MeToo era, with mixed results to date. Researchers have queried the responsiveness of global parliaments to sufficiently address sexism and sexual misconduct, ranging from more positive developments (such as the Parliament of Catalonia) to less encouraging (the European, Swedish, British, Canadian, and Australian Parliaments; see Krook 2018; Collier and Raney 2018a; Erikson and Josefsson 2019; Verge 2021, 2022; Berthet and Kantola 2021; Cox 2022; Julios 2022; Raney and Collier 2021, 2022). Although Canadian decision-makers have taken some steps to address this problem, prior research shows that these attempts have been insufficient and that more action is needed (Collier and Raney 2018a, 2018b).

This book should serve as a cautionary note for global leaders that efforts to safeguard democratic principles and values must include addressing violence and harassment in the political sphere as a matter of urgency. Moreover, these measures should include serious and systematic action to address the underlying gendered, colonial, and other inequities historically embedded in the political foundations of established democracies. As the research in this book demonstrates, global activists and comparative scholars should therefore use caution in using Canada as a "best practices" case in dealing with GBV-P.

Structure and Organization of the Book

As the first edited volume on this topic in Canada, this collection offers new theoretical and empirical contributions to GBV-P in the Canadian context and beyond. It introduces novel conceptualizations of GBV-P, typologies, and comparative research frameworks (chapters 1 and 13), as well as centring an interdisciplinary approach to the realm of violence in politics (chapter 3). The book also makes inroads by incorporating intersectional concepts and methods into the study of GBV-P. As a settler society, Canada's colonial history requires us to pay particular attention to Indigenous women's experiences of political violence. Major and Stirbys's chapter 7 applies an intersectional lens to understanding Indigenous women political actors, revealing the embeddedness of the effects of colonization, both past and present, in their lived experiences of violence. Other chapters explore how questions of race (chapter 5) and gender identity (chapter 2) should be incorporated into our understandings of GBV-P.

On the empirical side, the book offers new Canadian evidence of GBV-P. Some chapters apply feminist, intersectional policy analyses to institutional responses to GBV-P (chapters 12 and 13), while others use innovative experimental methodologies (chapter 4), in-depth, single-case study analyses (chapter 8), quantitative data analyses of news articles on GBV in Canadian politics (chapter 5), and harassment and violence against staffers, an oft-overlooked set of political actors (chapter 9). Labelling and applying a GBV-P lens to Canadian politics, we suggest, will additionally provide feminist political science researchers another tool to frame this problem, to better understand how violence permeates the experiences of women and marginalized political actors, and to consider the actions that are needed to address it.

The volume also considers the role of the #MeToo movement in spurring change and action on issues of violence and harassment in Canadian politics. While some chapters deal explicitly with the question of #MeToo (chapters 5 and 10), others reflect on it as a frame for analysis (chapter 7). Nonetheless, we view this book as representative and a product of a unique moment in the global women's movement where increased attention to, and concerns about, the violence against and harassment of women, BIPOC,[3] and 2SLGBTQQIA+ people are ongoing. As Macdonald and Dobrowolsky (2020) observe, this time period coincides with increasing turbulence and uncertainty around questions of inequality and the political, economic, and social rights of marginalized groups globally, within which conversations about gender and feminism are crucial. The #MeToo movement, as well as the #SayHerName campaign that seeks to create awareness of police brutality and anti-Black violence, brings possibilities for transformative change as well as renewed threats to, and backlash against, democratic progress. Resistance to gender and racial justice campaigns have been spotlighted by the MeToo movement since 2006, when Tarana Burke, a US Black feminist, first founded it. Since the #MeToo hashtag exploded on social media in fall 2017 (and in light of the allegations against Harvey Weinstein), some media commentators have suggested that the movement is ostensibly "over" (Garber 2018) or that it has spurred a "cancel culture" that unfairly penalizes white, cisgender, heterosexual men (Lewis 2020). To the contrary, evidence in this volume indicates that backlash continues and is part of the normal cycles of social movement contestation, which affirms the continued relevance, timeliness, and energy of the #MeToo movement (Tarrow 2011).

Authors in this book seek to contribute to broader advocacy, policy, and public debates on GBV-P. In Canada, non-profit organizations such as Equal Voice and Platform (formerly the Young Women's Leadership Network) have sounded the alarm on violence against women and BIPOC political actors, and have proposed various solutions (Young Women's Leadership Network 2018; Raney et al. 2019). In 2019, the Standing Committee on the Status of Women recommended that the government of Canada "develop and fund awareness campaigns and training programs to counter the negative effects of gender-biased treatment and harassment of female politicians, both in traditional and social media" (Recommendation 13; Standing Committee on the Status of Women 2019, 71); and that it "support data collection on the barriers faced by minority women and women from diverse backgrounds in electoral politics, and that this data be publicly available" (Recommendation 14; Standing Committee on the Status of Women 2019, 74). To our knowledge, many of these recommendations have not been adopted, and a broader national dialogue on how to address gender-based violence in Canadian politics has yet to take place. Applying a gender-based violence lens to Canadian politics allows us to speak to and with women's movement actors in support of stronger, evidence-informed policy solutions. As previous research shows, national government responses to address gender-based violence are correlated with strong domestic feminist movements that utilize international and regional networks to pressure governments into action (Htun and Weldon 2018).

In the pages that follow, each chapter offers a dedicated list of actions on how to address GBV-P. These might include policy proposals or calls for future research to address particular areas of concern. In so doing, each author not only provides their expertise in identifying and analysing different forms and spaces of GBV-P in Canada, but they also extend this expertise towards improving the situation. In the concluding chapter, we summarize these action agendas for future consideration. We argue that more needs to be done to create safer, more inclusive democratic spaces in electoral processes and on the campaign trail, in legislatures, and in traditional and social media spaces in Canada and beyond. In her farewell speech to federal politics, Inuit MP Qaqqaq said: "I shouldn't be afraid to go into work. No one should be afraid to go into work. It is possible to create change" (Qaqqaq 2021). We could not agree more.

The volume is organized thematically into four sections – all of which map onto different public spaces within which democratic processes occur. The first section investigates the growing – and increasingly complex – manifestations of GBV-P in online spaces, the new democratic frontier of political discourse that in many cases threatens democracy by spreading and legitimizing disinformation, toxicity, and hate. At the same time, social media has enabled new forms of advocacy against gender and race-based violence, including campaigns like #MeToo, #SayHerName, #TIMESUP, and #BelieveSurvivors. Additionally, social media and other digital communication technologies have created new opportunities to tackle GBV-P. The three chapters in this section develop unique analytical frameworks to better understand and address what they commonly refer to as "technology-facilitated gender-based violence." They thus avoid the simplistic notion that what happens online is not "real life" or is distinct from offline, historical, or institutionalized forms of violence and inequality. They explore the diverse harms that may result from online GBV-P, ranging from violations of individuals' safety or sexual autonomy to undermining or delegitimizing political participation by groups that already face gender-based marginalization.

In chapter 1, Gabrielle Bardall and Chris Tenove situate Canadian experiences of GBV-P inside global trends in online violence. This chapter marks the first systematic comparison of online GBV-P in Canada to other jurisdictions globally. They argue that, even though there are unique aspects of online GBV-P in Canada, there is much we can learn from other countries about successfully combating the problem. They call for transnational collective responses moving forward, as opposed to a country-by-country piecemeal approach.

Chapter 2 by Angelia Wagner and Tayler Young introduces a unique intersectional, gender-based conceptual framework to measure and typify the increasing occurrences of technology-facilitated harassment against political actors in Canada. Being able to recognize, name, and categorize these forms of GBV-P is a crucial step in addressing the growing toxic online environment for women, BIPOC, and 2SLGBTQ-QIA+ political actors.

Chapter 3 by Dianne Lalonde introduces readers to the growing use and emerging threat of image-based sexual violence in the United States and Canada. Her cautionary tale highlights the destructive nature of image-based sexual violence online and the ways in which Canadian political actors and social media companies can combat it before it becomes more widespread.

The book's second section examines the reporting of GBV-P in Canada in the mainstream media – paying particular attention to print and online large-scale national and provincial newspapers. Media shape, and are shaped by, public attitudes to phenomena in Canadian society, and thus media analyses can tell us a lot about how an issue is characterized and recognized in the larger public consciousness. This knowledge can help us understand how the problem is popularly understood, and what type of pressure, if any, can be placed on democratically elected decision-makers to address the issue at all levels of government. Chapter 4 by Melanee Thomas and Scott Pruysers kicks off this analysis by considering the psychological impact of GBV-P, not only directly on its targets but also on how reporting of this violence impacts voters' assessments of harassment targets. Their study employs a unique experimental survey method to assess voters' reactions to mainstream media reports of GBV-P, showing that, while perceptions of one GBV-P incident may not discourage political involvement, the impact may be cumulative. They also point to the importance of counter-speech in framing the issue inside of media reports.

Elizabeth Goodyear-Grant in chapter 5 employs an intersectional gender-based analytical lens to examine the impact of the #MeToo movement on mainstream print media reporting of GBV-P. Goodyear-Grant's research determines that media have reported about GBV-P more often post-#MeToo than prior and that this reporting often identifies the gendered nature of these incidents. Recognition of intersectional impacts of GBV-P, while somewhat present, is not well-explored in media accounts. In particular, she notes that reports on BIPOC women's experiences of GBV-P do not fully recognize the racist forms of sexism or the gendered forms of racism that underpin these experiences in Canada.

This section ends with a contribution by Rissa Reist in chapter 6 that examines the impact of GBV-P via political cartoons in mainstream print media in the province of Alberta. Reist's research shows the increase in violent imagery in political cartoons published to depict political critiques of the province's first two women premiers – Alison Redford and Rachel Notley – as well as of a male premier, Ed Stelmach. Her chapter queries the impact of partisanship and a masculinized "frontier" provincial political culture on these leaders from a gendered lens.

The third section of the book examines diverse experiences of GBV-P in Canada across social movement/local community, local politics, and inside public office spaces. Chapter 7 by Rebecca Major and Cynthia Stirbys chronicles Indigenous women political actors' experiences of GBV-P. The authors note that the political spaces in which Indigenous women experience GBV-P are varied and the causes rooted in intergenerational trauma following historic and ongoing colonial practices. This chapter makes an important contribution to understanding how GBV-P impacts Indigenous women specifically and contributes essential theoretical insights into the existing comparative literature.

Kate Graham in chapter 8 examines a much different context of GBV-P, offering an in-depth, "thick" description and analysis of a woman-identified municipal councillor running for re-election in London, Ontario. Her analysis illustrates the broad range of negative psychological violence women can experience on the campaign trail when subjected to a gendered disinformation campaign. She also notes that electoral GBV-P can be more acute and intense, especially when a woman takes the "rightful" place of a man who is an expected incumbent.

In chapter 9, Meagan Cloutier focuses on GBV-P experienced by political staff on Parliament Hill. Her inside look at the issues of violence from MP staffers' perspectives adds much to our understanding of the experiences of political actors with some of the least power inside of the political process. Using original survey data, she finds that, despite the existence of a 2014 Canadian federal staffing policy that was supposed to prevent and address harassment on Parliament Hill, staffers – and especially women – continue to experience harassment.

The book's final section examines existing policy and informal actions aimed at addressing GBV-P perpetrated against different political actors in Canada in legislative spaces. Seven years on from the 2017 wave of the #MeToo movement, a common theme in this section is the need for better policy, improved actions, and a deeper public awareness of, and reckoning for, those who commit GBV-P. Chapter 10 by Bailey Gerrits assesses political accountability of accused perpetrators of GBV-P pre- and post-#MeToo. Her chapter documents eleven cases of sexual harassment involving MPs and finds that attention to the problem of GBV-P increased post-#MeToo. However, she also finds that perpetrators of GBV-P are still largely viewed as "bad apples," masking the systemic nature of the problem and its underlying institutional causes. This chapter notes that accountability for GBV-P has been inconsistently applied and varied even in the post-#MeToo era.

Louise Cockram in chapter 11 compares the anti-harassment training and orientation of MPs in Canada and the United Kingdom. Her research uncovers that this training, while a good first step, is plagued by challenges related to party control in both countries. If training has any hope of being effective in curbing sexual and non-sexual harassment, her chapter suggests the need for party buy-in and support.

Chapter 12 by Tracey Raney turns our attention to GBV-P in appointed office with her analysis of an anti-harassment policy adopted by the Canadian Senate. This chapter constitutes the first assessment of gender-based violence in Canada's upper house. Her analysis shows that, while the most recent attempt to address sexual harassment in 2021 held promise, the final result was more symbolic than substantive and that more work needs to be done to tackle the underlying gendered and raced causes and consequences of harassment and violence inside this political institution.

Chapter 13 takes the examination of policies aimed at addressing sexual harassment between elected members of the legislature to the thirteen provincial and territorial jurisdictions in Canada. This comparative chapter by Cheryl Collier and Tracey Raney finds a variety of responses across the cases, including jurisdictions with little to no direction to guide sexual harassment prevention and adjudication between elected members. Despite attention following the federal lead in 2015, as well as the #MeToo movement, little policy improvement at this level has occurred, even though the provinces and territories can potentially act as policy "laboratories of experimentation." The resulting patchwork of protections unfortunately replicates several shortcomings of previous federal policies and leaves many instances of GBV-P outside of an adjudicative framework.

The volume concludes with a collation of, and reflection on, the collective avenues for action on GBV-P in Canada. It highlights what we can learn from the Canadian case, as well as identifies areas for further investigation and research in the future.

NOTES

1 2SLGBTQQIA+ refers to those who identify as two-spirit, lesbian, gay, bisexual, transgender, queer, questioning, intersex, androgynous, and asexual. "Two-spirit" is a term used by some Indigenous people to reflect the complex (and non-binary) nature of gender roles and identities in Indigenous communities.
2 Women and Gender Equality Canada (2022) defines gender-based violence as "violence based on gender norms and unequal power dynamics, perpetrated against someone based on their gender, gender expression, gender identity, or perceived gender. It takes many forms, including physical, economic, sexual, as well as emotional (psychological) abuse."
3 BIPOC refers to Black, Indigenous, and people of colour.

REFERENCES

Andrew, Caroline, John Biles, Myer Siemiatycki, and Erin Tolley, eds. 2008. *Electing a Diverse Canada: The Representation of Immigrants, Minorities, and Women.* Vancouver, BC: UBC Press.

Ballington, Julie, and Gabriella Borovsky. 2023. "A Normative Foundation for Ending Violence against Women in Politics." In *Gender and Violence against Political Actors*, edited by Elin Bjarnegård and Pär Zetterberg, 191–200. Philadelphia, PA: Temple University Press.

Bardall, Gabrielle, Elin Bjarnegård, and Jennifer M. Piscopo. 2020. "How Is Political Violence Gendered? Disentangling Motives, Forms, and Impacts." *Political Studies* 68 (4): 916–35. https://doi.org/10.1177/0032321719881812.

Bashevkin, Sylvia. 1993. *Toeing the Lines: Women and Party Politics in English Canada.* 2nd ed. Toronto, ON: Oxford University Press.

–, ed. 2019. *Doing Politics Differently? Women Premiers in Canada's Provinces and Territories.* Vancouver, BC: UBC Press.

Berry, Marie, Yolande Bouka, and Marilyn Muthoni Kamuru. 2021. "Implementing Inclusion: Gender Quotas, Inequality, and Backlash in Kenya." *Politics & Gender* 17 (4): 640–64. https://doi.org/10.1017/S1743923X19000886.

Berthet, Valentine, and Johanna Kantola. 2021. "Gender, Violence, and Political Institutions: Struggles over Sexual Harassment in the European Parliament." *Social Politics: International Studies in Gender, State & Society* 28 (1): 143–67. https://doi.org/10.1093/sp/jxaa015.

Biroli, Flávia. 2016. "Political Violence against Women in Brazil: Expressions and Definitions." *Revista Direito e Práxis* 7 (15): 557–89. https://www.redalyc.org/pdf/3509/350947688018.pdf.

Bjarnegård, Elin, and Pär Zetterberg, eds. 2023. *Gender and Violence against Political Actors.* Philadelphia, PA: Temple University Press.

Black, Jerome, and Andrew Griffith. 2022. "Do MPs Represent Canada's Diversity?" *Policy Options*, 7 January 2022. https://policyoptions.irpp.org/magazines/january-2022/do-mps-represent-canadas-diversity/.

CEDAW (Committee on the Elimination of Discrimination against Women). 2017. *General Recommendation No. 35 on Gender-Based Violence against Women, Updating General Recommendation 19*. United Nations. CEDAW/C/GC/35. https://tbinternet.ohchr.org/_layouts/15/TreatyBodyExternal/Download.aspx?symbolno=CEDAW/C/GC/35&Lang=en.

Childs, Sarah, and Mona Lena Krook. 2008. "Critical Mass Theory and Women's Political Representation." *Political Studies* 56 (3): 725–36. https://doi.org/10.1111/j.1467-9248.2007.00712.x.

Collier, Cheryl N., and Tracey Raney. 2018a. "Canada's Member-to-Member Code of Conduct on Sexual Harassment in the House of Commons: Progress or Regress?" *Canadian Journal of Political Science* 51 (4): 795–815. https://doi.org/10.1017/S000842391800032X.

– 2018b. "Understanding Sexism and Sexual Harassment in Politics: A Comparison of Westminster Parliaments in Australia, the United Kingdom, and Canada." *Social Politics: International Studies in Gender, State & Society* 25 (3): 432–55. https://doi.org/10.1093/sp/jxy024.

Cox, Dame Laura. 2022. "A Woman's Place is in the House: Reclaiming Civility, Tolerance and Respect in Political Life." *The Political Quarterly* 93 (1):17–24. https://doi.org/10.1111/1467-923X.13069.

Crenshaw, Kimberlé. 1991. "Mapping the Margins: Intersectionality, Identity Politics, and Violence against Women of Color." *Stanford Law Review* 43 (6): 1241–99. https://doi.org/10.2307/1229039.

Dhamoon, Rita Kaur. 2011. "Considerations on Mainstreaming Intersectionality." *Political Research Quarterly* 64 (1): 230–43. https://doi.org/10.1177/1065912910379227.

Erikson, Josefina, and Cecilia Josefsson. 2019. "The Legislature as a Gendered Workplace: Exploring Members of Parliament's Experiences Working in the Swedish Parliament." *International Political Science Review* 40 (2): 197–214. https://doi.org/10.1177/0192512117735952.

Garber, Megan. 2018. "Is #MeToo Too Big?" *The Atlantic*, 4 July 2018. https://www.theatlantic.com/entertainment/archive/2018/07/is-metoo-too-big/564275/.

Goodyear-Grant, Elizabeth. 2013. *Gendered News: Media Coverage and Electoral Politics in Canada*. Vancouver, BC: UBC Press.

Hill Collins, Patricia, and Sirma Bilge. 2020. *Intersectionality*. 2nd ed. Cambridge: Polity Press.

Htun, Mala N., and S. Laurel Weldon. 2018. *The Logics of Gender Justice: State Action on Women's Rights around the World*. Cambridge: Cambridge University Press.

iKnow Politics. n.d. Violence Against Women in Politics. https://www
.iknowpolitics.org/en/issues/violence-against-women-politics.
Inter-Parliamentary Union. 2016. *Sexism, Harassment and Violence against Women Parliamentarians.* Issues Brief, October 2016. https://www.ipu
.org/resources/publications/reports/2016-10/sexism-harassment-and
-violence-against-women-parliamentarians.
– 2022. "Monthly Ranking of Women in Parliaments." IPU Parline, 11 November 2022. https://data.ipu.org/women-ranking?month=11&year=2022.
Julios, Christina. 2022. *Sexual Harassment in the UK Parliament: Lessons from the #MeToo Era.* Cham, CH: Palgrave Macmillan.
Krook, Mona Lena. 2018. "Westminster Too: On Sexual Harassment in British Politics." *The Political Quarterly* 89 (1): 65–72. https://doi.org/10.1111
/1467-923X.12458.
– 2019. "Global Feminist Collaborations and the Concept of Violence against Women in Politics." *Journal of International Affairs* 72 (2): 77–94. https://
www.iknowpolitics.org/sites/default/files/jia_2019_1.pdf.
– 2020. *Violence against Women in Politics.* New York: Oxford University Press.
– 2021. "A Global Movement to End Violence against Women in Politics and Public Life." *E-International Relations,* 25 April 2021. https://www.e-ir.info/2021/04/25
/a-global-movement-to-end-violence-against-women-in-politics-and-public-life/.
Kuperberg, Rebecca. 2018. "Intersectional Violence against Women in Politics." *Politics & Gender* 14 (4): 685–90. https://doi.org/10.1017
/S1743923X18000612.
Lewis, Helen. 2020. "Why I've Never Believed in 'Believe Women.'" *The Atlantic,* 14 May 2020. https://www.theatlantic.com/international
/archive/2020/05/believe-women-bad-slogan-joe-biden-tara-reade/611617/.
Macdonald, Fiona, and Alexandra Dobrowolsky, eds. 2020. *Turbulent Times, Transformational Possibilities? Gender and Politics Today and Tomorrow.* Toronto, ON: University of Toronto Press.
National Democratic Institute. 2016. "#NotTheCost: Stopping Violence against Women in Politics." https://www.ndi.org/not-the-cost.
Office of Democratic Institutions and Human Rights (ODIHR), Organization for Security and Co-operation in Europe (OSCE). 2022. *Addressing Violence against Women in Politics in the OSCE Region: Toolkit.* https://www.osce.org
/odihr/530272.
Piscopo, Jennifer. 2016. "State Capacity, Criminal Justice, and Political Rights: Rethinking Violence against Women in Politics." *Política y Gobierno* 23 (2): 437–58. https://uva.theopenscholar.com/files/pvi/files/1665-2037-pyg
-23-02-00437-en.pdf.
Qaqqaq, Mumilaaq. 2021, 15 June. "Farewell Speech to the House of Commons by Mumilaaq Qaqqaq (Nunavut, NPD)." In *House of Commons*

Debates, vol. 150, no. 118, 43rd Parliament, 2nd Session (Hansard 118), 8511–13. https://www.ourcommons.ca/DocumentViewer/en/43-2/house/sitting-118/hansard#11397663.

Raney, Tracey, and Cheryl N. Collier. 2021. "A Question of Ethics: Addressing Sexual Harassment in the Legislatures of the United States, the United Kingdom, and Canada." In *Women, Power, and Political Representation: Canadian and Comparative Perspectives*, edited by Roosmarijn de Geus, Erin Tolley, Elizabeth Goodyear-Grant, and Peter John Loewen, 89–100. Toronto: University of Toronto Press.

– 2022. "Privileged and Gendered Violence in the Canadian and British Houses of Commons: A Feminist Institutionalist Analysis." *Parliamentary Affairs* 75 (2): 382–99. https://doi.org/10.1093/pa/gsaa069.

Raney, Tracey, Cheryl N. Collier, Grace Lore, and Andrea Spender. 2019. *Democracy during #MeToo: Taking Stock of Violence against Women in Canadian Politics: A Comprehensive Scope Report Prepared for Equal Voice*. https://equalvoice.ca/wp-content/uploads/2022/01/VAW-P_Scope_report_-_FINAL.pdf.

Restrepo Sanín, Juliana. 2018. "The Law and Violence against Women in Politics." *Politics & Gender* 14 (4): 676–80. https://doi.org/10.1017/S1743923X18000594.

– 2020. "Violence against Women in Politics: Latin America in an Era of Backlash." *Signs* 45 (2): 302–10. https://doi.org/10.1086/704954.

– 2023. "Measures to Address Violence against Women in Politics in Bolivia and Mexico." In *Gender and Violence against Political Actors*, edited by Elin Bjarnegård and Pär Zetterberg, 223–301. Philadelphia, PA: Temple University Press.

Šimonović, Dubravka. 2018. *Report of the Special Rapporteur on Violence against Women, Its Causes and Consequence on Violence against Women in Politics*. Presented to the United Nations General Assembly, 73rd Session, 6 August 2018. A/73/301. https://undocs.org/A/73/301.

Standing Committee on the Status of Women. 2019. *Elect Her: A Roadmap for Improving the Representation of Women in Canadian Politics: Report of the Standing Committee on the Status of Women*. House of Commons, Canada, 42nd Parliament, 1st Session, April 2019. https://www.ourcommons.ca/Content/Committee/421/FEWO/Reports/RP10366034/feworp14/feworp14-e.pdf.

Tarrow, Sidney G. 2011. *Power in Movement: Social Movements and Contentious Politics*. 3rd ed. New York: Cambridge University Press.

Thomas, Melanee, and Marc André Bodet. 2013. "Sacrificial Lambs, Women Candidates, and District Competitiveness in Canada." *Electoral Studies* 32 (1): 153–66. https://doi.org/10.1016/j.electstud.2012.12.001.

Tolley, Erin. 2016. *Framed: Media and the Coverage of Race in Canadian Politics*. Vancouver, BC: UBC Press.

Tremblay, Manon, ed. 2019. *Queering Representation: LGBTQ People and Electoral Politics in Canada*. Vancouver, BC: UBC Press.
Trimble, Linda. 2017. *Ms. Prime Minister: Gender, Media, and Leadership*. Toronto, ON: University of Toronto Press.
Trimble, Linda, Jane Arscott, and Manon Tremblay, eds. 2013. *Stalled: The Representation of Women in Canadian Governments*. Vancouver, BC: UBC Press.
True, Jacqui. 2020. *Violence against Women: What Everyone Needs to Know*. New York: Oxford University Press.
United Nations. 1993, 20 December. *Declaration on the Elimination of Violence against Women*. General Assembly Resolution 48/104. A/Res/48/104. https://www.ohchr.org/en/instruments-mechanisms/instruments/declaration-elimination-violence-against-women.
– 2011. *Women and Political Participation*. General Assembly Resolution 66/130. https://daccess-ods.un.org/access.nsf/Get?OpenAgent&DS=A/RES/66/130&Lang=E.
– 2015. *Transforming Our World: The 2030 Agenda for Sustainable Development*. General Assembly Resolution 70/1. https://undocs.org/en/A/RES/70/1.
Valverde, María Eugenia Rojas. 2010. "Gender-Based Political Harassment and Violence: Effects on the Political Work and Public Roles of Women." *New Solutions: A Journal of Environmental and Occupational Health Policy* 20 (4): 527–35. https://doi.org/10.2190/NS.20.4.i.
Verge, Tània. 2021. "Legislative Reform in Europe to Fight Violence against Women in Politics." *European Journal of Politics and Gender* 4 (3): 459–61. https://doi.org/10.1332/251510821X16149579296781.
– 2022. "Too Few, Too Little? Parliaments' Response to Sexism and Sexual Harassment." *Parliamentary Affairs* 75 (1): 94–112. https://doi.org/10.1093/pa/gsaa052.
Wagner, Angelia, and Joanna Everitt, eds. 2019. *Gendered Mediation: Identity and Image Making in Canadian Politics*. Vancouver, BC: UBC Press.
Weldon, S. Laurel. 2002. *Protest, Policy, and the Problem of Violence against Women: A Cross-National Comparison*. Pittsburgh, PA: University of Pittsburgh Press.
Women and Gender Equality Canada. 2022. "Gender-Based Violence." https://women-gender-equality.canada.ca/en/gender-based-violence/gender-based-violence-glossary.html#G.
Young Women's Leadership Network. 2018. "It's Time: Addressing Sexual Violence in Political Institutions." https://issuu.com/ywln/docs/ywln_itstime_0930.

PART ONE

Violence against Women in Politics on Social Media in Canada

1 Online Violence against Women in Politics: Canada in a Comparative Perspective

GABRIELLE BARDALL AND CHRIS TENOVE

Canadian women's experiences of online violence are part of a global trend. From Alberta to Azerbaijan, Shawinigan to Sri Lanka, the online vitriol directed at political women builds on broader patterns of gendered exclusion, discrimination, and violence. The harms of online abuse and violence are gendered in significant ways, such as driving women out of political spaces and reinforcing patriarchal political institutions and policies.

This chapter explores how Canada fits key global patterns of gender-based violence in politics (GBV-P) using digital technologies. We present research on the causes, forms, and consequences of online violence against women in politics, drawing primarily on Bardall's findings from ten country case studies and Tenove and colleagues' research on the Canadian context. This comparative research enables us to consider key questions: How might online GBV-P be conceptualized and studied across diverse contexts, and what are the challenges in doing so? Are some global patterns more or less prevalent in Canada? What are the implications of these findings for action in Canada and globally in addressing the role of digital technologies in GBV-P?

This chapter proceeds in four sections. The first discusses key terms and approaches for understanding online abuse of women in politics and proposes a framework for looking at the motives, forms, and impacts of GBV-P. The second explains the methods used in our respective research projects and discusses some of the methodological challenges and paths forward for comparative research. The third presents comparative findings, such as the presence of high levels of GBV-P targeting prominent women politicians across cases, as well as counter-mobilizations against online abuse of women in politics. We conclude with brief proposals for research and policy responses to address online abuse of women in politics, both within Canada and internationally.

Conceptualizing a Global Problem: Key Terms and Frameworks

The online abuse of women and girls is increasingly recognized as a global human rights problem and an obstacle to women's full participation in politics (Amnesty International 2018; Bardall 2019; Inter-Parliamentary Union 2016; OHCHR 2018). Despite this attention, or perhaps because of it, there is a tangle of competing terms and approaches. In this chapter, we focus on online abuse as a form of GBV-P, emphasize the need to consider online abuse in contexts of systemic and intersectional discrimination and vulnerability, and draw upon a framework that attends to the motives, forms, and impacts of online abuse.

Our approach, shown in Figure 1.1, builds on Bardall, Bjarnegård, and Piscopo's (2020) framework identifying three dimensions of gendered violence in politics: *motives* (whether actions are explicitly intended to promote hegemonic men's control of the political system), *forms* (how gender is expressed in violent acts themselves), and *impacts* (how gender affects the consequences of acts for individuals and broader audiences). Gendered forms are present in all manifestations of online GBV-P, from seemingly low-intensity incivility (use of gendered tropes in uncivil comments) to disinformation (campaigns exploiting gender biases) to more severe forms (for example, threats of sexual violence). Gendered motives can be revealed in explicit expressions of gendered violence (for example, hate speech against women) or when it is very unlikely that a hegemonic male politician in the same position and under the same circumstances would be similarly targeted (Bardall, Bjarnegård, and Piscopo 2020). Gendered impacts can result from gendered motives or forms as well as from contexts of gendered vulnerability and political disempowerment. For instance, both men and women in politics face online death threats, but targeted women and broader audiences may interpret a death threat against a prominent woman as a threat against all women in politics. Gendered impacts may be experienced by targeted individuals, secondary victims (such as associates and family members), and broader audiences.

Two complementary bodies of research, on incivility and on technology-facilitated gender-based violence (TFGBV), further inform our framework.

Research on online incivility highlights how it can undermine the quality and inclusiveness of public discourse and can intimidate, shame, or otherwise silence targeted individuals and broader audiences (Jamieson et al. 2017; Rossini 2022). Incivility exists on a spectrum, from violations of politeness norms to more explicit expressions of disrespect and threat (Chen 2017; Rossini 2022). In this vein, Wagner and Young (chapter 2, this volume) propose a spectrum from "tolerable" to

Figure 1.1. Framework of analysis for online gender-based violence in politics (GBV-P)

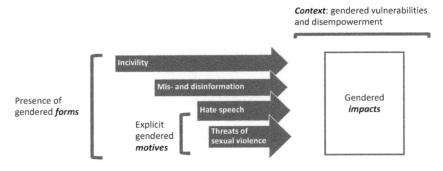

"delegitimizing" to "abusive" discourses. Using the motives/forms/impacts approach enables us to overcome some of the limitations in literature on incivility, such as being overly broad in its operationalization (see Wagner and Young, chapter 2, this volume; Sydnor 2019, 15), inconsistently used to delegitimize some voices (Jamieson et al. 2017), or neglectful of relationships between online content and targets' offline context. For instance, attending to gendered motives when manually reviewing social media data helps us distinguish between "uncivil" gendered language used to consolidate gendered power dynamics and counter-speech (including repeating gendered terms of disrespect to bring attention and condemnation).

Research on TFGBV highlights the fact that harms of online communication frequently arise through interactions between online communication and offline activities (Dunn 2020). As Tenove and Tworek observe, the impact of online abuse for women, and especially racialized women, is significantly due to their personal experiences of hostility and discrimination offline, as well as to their shared exposure to "the poisonous environment created by gendered and racist attacks – most conspicuously, targeting women and racialized individuals who seek or hold the most senior positions in public life" (2020, 24). We draw on TFGBV to assess gendered mechanisms of harm and impacts.

Methodology

Our framework requires methods capable of revealing motives, forms, and impacts of online GBV-P. In this section, we describe our efforts to negotiate the challenges of applying this nuanced framework in comparing cross-national research. We first detail the methodological approaches used by the authors in multi-country comparative research (Bardall) and in Canada (Tenove), and then explain how we compare these findings. We acknowledge that our projects arose from different research imperatives. The incongruences in this chapter's comparative analysis reflect those in the broader literature, illustrating the need for greater coordination on frameworks and methods.

The global comparative findings are drawn from an analysis of cross-national data from ten country cases: Afghanistan, Bougainville, Haiti, Myanmar, Papua New Guinea, Sri Lanka, Syria, Ukraine, Zambia, and Zimbabwe (studies led or supported by Bardall); published case studies on Australia, India, Indonesia, Colombia, Kenya, Nigeria, the United Kingdom, and the United States; and a cross-national study covering thirty countries.[1] The studies were conducted primarily by international non-profit organizations and focused on gender-specific violence against women in elections and politics. Most cases focused on online violence, although some covered offline GBV-P as well. Studies used mixed methods: All drew on qualitative interviews and focus groups conducted in local languages; several employed data analytics, including AI-based sentiment analysis based on tailored, multilingual lexicons. Cases focused primarily on women candidates or elected officials but also included other women leaders (civil society, journalists, electoral officials) as well as comparative data with male counterparts.

The second research stream was conducted by Chris Tenove and colleagues, overseen by Heidi Tworek.[2] This team used a mixed-methods approach to investigate online incivility directed at candidates in Canada's 2019 federal election. Thirty-one interviews were conducted with candidates and campaign staff belonging to four national parties (Conservative, Green, Liberal, and New Democratic [NDP]). About 60 per cent of the candidates identified as women, and about 40 per cent were Indigenous or otherwise racialized individuals. Interviews focused on how candidates and staff interpreted, responded to, and were affected by online incivility, including abuse focused on gender or race. The team also analysed tweets directed at candidates during the campaign period, including manual analysis of over 3,000 tweets and computational analysis of over one million tweets using a novel machine learning model.

Direct comparisons of quantitative findings between the Canadian and other country studies are not possible, as they used significantly different algorithmic models to quantify online incivility and violence. Moreover, while computational social media analysis can identify broad patterns, algorithms regularly miss or misinterpret abuse that is gendered or racialized (see, for example, Davidson, Bhattacharya, and Weber 2019). Quantitative studies tend to focus on Twitter (now X), since the necessary data are not available for other key platforms like Facebook or private messaging apps like WhatsApp. In addition, measurements of online GBV-P can reflect a circular problem: when attacks are successful, they can silence women or deter women seeking leadership positions.[3] Thus, places where online GBV-P is most potent may be those places with the lowest absolute volumes of measurable online abuse of women. A relatively low volume of online GBV-P can reflect women's overall marginalization from political life rather than a safer online environment.

More nuanced qualitative analysis of social media can highlight forms that might otherwise be missed, such as othering, essentializing, and authenticating narratives (Harmer and Southern 2021; Reddi, Kuo, and Kreiss 2023) that are essential to evaluating gendered impacts. Interviews and surveys can better reveal experiences of online abuse that are hard to detect (because they are coded or occur in hidden spaces of communication) as well as the consequences of online abuse.

For these reasons, we emphasize the forms as well as the frequency of online GBV-P, its targeting and potential motives, its social and political context, and its impacts. We draw on evidence that includes large-scale social media analysis, discourse analysis of select social media samples, representative surveys, and in-depth qualitative interviews.

Comparative Findings Globally and in Canada

Online GBV-P: Frequency and Content

In every country studied, including Canada, we found that women were systematically subject to gender-based online aggression linked to the exercise of their political and civil rights and expression of free speech. Online GBV-P is pervasive: In Sri Lanka, nearly 94 per cent of women leaders studied were targeted by online abuse. Between 60 and 75 per cent of online abuse was targeted at women leaders in Zimbabwe and Sri Lanka. Women leaders in Afghanistan, Haiti, Ukraine, Zambia, and many other countries reported that personal experience of online abuse and/or the threat of online harassment had negatively impacted their work.

Online GBV-P was widespread in Canada during the 2019 election. In Tenove and colleagues' sample, about 40 per cent of over one million tweets aimed at 692 candidates employed negative language (Tenove et al. 2023). The tweets ranged from high negativity (1 per cent of sample, which included misogynistic slurs and other threats or hateful remarks towards groups, indicating gendered motives), medium negativity (15 per cent, including personal insults or group stereotypes, which sometimes took explicit gendered forms), and low negativity (25 per cent, such as dismissive remarks or milder insults of candidates).[4] Only a fraction of negative tweets had gendered content, but in interviews, twelve of thirteen women candidates in the 2019 Canadian election reported facing some sexist online messaging during the campaign.

Worldwide, both men and women experience GBV-P. In Ukraine and Zimbabwe, online harassment involving sexual themes more frequently targeted men, primarily with homophobic content designed to maintain hegemonic male control of political space (IFES 2020). In Tenove and colleagues' research, none of the twelve male candidates claimed to face sexist abuse, but qualitative analysis of tweets revealed that men frequently faced gendered incivility, such as derogatory remarks claiming Justin Trudeau does not meet certain models of masculinity (Tenove et al. 2023).

While it is pervasive, online GBV-P exists in a broad universe of other kinds of online incivility and violence. It is not the only – or even the most common – form of online abuse. Consistent with other findings (see, for example, Gorrell et al. 2020; Theocharis et al. 2020), the frequency of online abuse in Canada was not correlated with gender. Canadian male candidates received the majority of all tweets and all uncivil tweets in Tenove and colleagues' sample (Tenove and Tworek 2020). This finding reflects gendered differences in power, since four of five national party leaders were men. The finding is also true in other global contexts where men dominate political contests.

The relative proportion of abusive content directed at men and women varied in each case. Countries like Sri Lanka and Zimbabwe reported significantly greater relative frequency of online harassment against women. In Canada, no statistically significant differences were found between the proportion of abusive tweets directed at men and women candidates.

Globally, the frequency of online abuse of politicians tends to be "spiky" rather than consistent over time (Gorrell et al. 2020; Theocharis et al. 2020). Across our case studies, we found that attacks on women often went "viral," concentrating a high volume of abuse into condensed time periods. Women face greater constraints around social norms and behaviour. When women break with those norms (or are accused of breaking norms), the shock factor is much greater, and shocking or sensational content is associated with faster and broader dissemination on social media. Furthermore, viral moments sometimes trigger cycles of online GBV-P lasting for years.

Overall, we believe that frequency counts of uncivil or violent messaging are unlikely to be a reliable standard for comparisons across genders or across countries. At a practical level, different levels of internet penetration, digital literacy, access to electricity/cell phones, and other factors create fundamentally different bases of comparison. At a conceptual level, profound cultural differences shape the expression of violence in different countries (including social norms that affect the expression of gendered motives or forms and the context-specificity of intersectional power dynamics that determine different gendered impacts).

Beyond frequency, analysis of thematic content (gendered forms) reveals important consistencies across case studies. We routinely found online abuse of a sexual nature across case studies in Canada and abroad, ranging from sexualizing women leaders as a means of degrading their image or depicting them as unfit for public office to direct threats of sexual attack. Similar to Sobieraj (2020), we saw aggressors draw upon three overlapping approaches: intimidating, shaming, and discrediting women in politics. These approaches are sometimes expressed in culturally specific terms. In countries where conservative religion dominates norms for women's behaviour among large segments of the population (for example, Poland, Afghanistan, and Syria), online abuse tends to target political women for violating faith-based principles, especially the incompatibility of politics and motherhood (IFES 2020). In countries such as Haiti, Zimbabwe, and Zambia, online vitriol against political women can reflect culturally specific themes such as witchcraft and/or voodoo. Where machismo prevails in politics, such as in Russia, Ukraine, Brazil, and the United States, online GBV-P is rife with themes depicting women as too weak, soft, or emotional for political leadership (see Biroli 2016; IFES 2020; Jankowicz et al. 2021).

In Canada, manual content analysis of over 3,000 tweets found that women more commonly received messages that were apparently gender-motivated (explicitly sexist), were gendered in their form (contained dismissive gendered insults like "climate bimbo"), or used inappropriately sexualized language. This difference in message content was frequently flagged in interviews with Canadian candidates. Furthermore, all racialized women candidates we interviewed described online abuse directed at intersections of their multiple identities.

Targeting and Motives of Online GBV-P

Globally, online violence and harassment is concentrated around high-profile women. All global case studies found that high-profile political women are much more likely to be targeted by high-intensity violence (Rheault, Rayment, and Musulan 2019; see also Håkansson 2021). In Canada, high-profile women in politics have faced particularly high levels of online and offline vitriol, most prominently former Ontario premier Kathleen Wynne, former Alberta premier Rachel Notley, as well as federal and provincial cabinet members (Burke 2019; Dawson 2017; Trynacity 2018). Both Rheault, Rayment, and Musulan (2019) and Tenove and Tworek (2020) found that prominent female candidates (including those with high follower numbers) tend to receive higher proportions of abuse in their Twitter mentions than less prominent male or female candidates.

However, women may face online GBV-P even if they do not have national or regional prominence. For example, in Sri Lanka's 2018 local elections, women candidates studied received substantially higher amounts of online abuse, including rape threats and sexual harassment.

Politicians with intersectional identities are targeted, suggesting motives at play. In Canada, interviews revealed that racialized candidates felt particularly under attack, facing comments with anti-Black, anti-Indigenous, anti-immigrant, Islamophobic, and misogynistic content. For 2SLGBTQQIA+[5] candidates, attacks sometimes included explicit expressions of homophobia or transphobia. Online abuse did not limit itself to a single aspect of candidates' identities. One candidate, reflecting on insults targeted at her, said: "Why me? I'm a woman of colour, I am a minority on two fronts ... It's a package."

Interviewees noted that racialized women politicians are most likely to be abused online when they publicly take a stand on issues related to their identities, such as on abortion or when former member of Parliament (MP) Celina Caesar-Chavannes spoke publicly about facing racism in Canada's Parliament (Tenove and Tworek 2020, 31). Such targeting suggests attackers' motivation to silence and exclude issues of gender or racial inequality. Similarly, Al-Rawi, Chun, and Amer (2022) found that MP Iqra Khalid faced intense levels of online abuse in 2017 when she promoted a parliamentary resolution to address racism and Islamophobia. Findings suggest that members of minority communities may also face "lateral violence," including attacks from community members for not representing their group "properly" (Reddi, Kuo, and Kreiss 2023). For example, interviewees of South Asian descent described receiving gender-based abuse from within the diaspora in Canada. This finding aligns with the comparative studies that indicated diasporas may be active in abusive online commentary against women in politics in their country of origin (see discussion below).

Some interviewees interpreted attacks on high-profile female or racialized politicians as an attack on their own social identities. In other words, attacks on prominent women and racialized politicians may be experienced as motivated attempts to intimidate, denigrate, and silence women and non-white politicians more broadly.

Finally, the geography of online GBV-P targeting is relevant. Online violence targeting an individual can spread across geographic regions and borders. In the global cases where data were available, online abuse often spread outward from urban centres, including outside national borders. High-density population centres are natural hubs for information and communication technology (ICT)–facilitated abuse because they tend to have greater levels of access to technology, wealth, connectivity, and techno-literacy. Violent or degrading themes and abusive messages that dominate urban-centric platforms (for example, Twitter [now X] or Instagram) fan out across the country via private messaging applications. Traditional media platforms such as radio and print media pick up on online narratives and echo them in rural areas where internet and data coverage are less accessible.

Relatedly, online GBV-P content does not respect national borders, and individuals who belong to diaspora communities may be particularly vulnerable to abuse. Bardall's research finds that diaspora hubs outside of the originating country are often "hotspots" for online violence. For example, aggressive and abusive posts against Zimbabwean women were linked to accounts in the United States, South Africa, and the United Kingdom, common destinations of Zimbabwean immigrants and expatriates. In Afghanistan, abusive online posts were linked to accounts in Pakistan, India, the United States, and the United Kingdom. Finally, in the Ukraine and the United States, we see online GBV-P potentially being spread as a tool of disinformation by hostile states that use gendered forms with the motive of meddling in foreign elections (Bardall 2019). This practice aligns with an analysis for Global Affairs Canada (Bradshaw and Henle 2021), which found that some hostile foreign actors use narratives around gender identity to influence, polarize, and disrupt online discussions of feminism.

Social and Political Context

Global comparative research suggests that the consequences of online GBV-P vary according to the broader social context of the status of women, along with the narrower political context such as the type of electoral system, the design of applicable gender electoral quotas, and the prominence of women politicians in high-profile electoral races.

One hypothesis for these observed trends is related to understanding GBV-P (offline and online) as a form of backlash (Rheault, Rayment, and

Musulan 2019; Banet-Weiser 2018; Okimoto and Brescoll 2010). Backlash can be generated by institutional arrangements in which women are perceived as challenging control of male-dominated spaces by threatening to replace male incumbents, disrupting male discourse and policy, or diminishing the public image of a male leader. Conversely, processes and institutional arrangements where women are absent or marginalized may exhibit lower levels of backlash.

For example, the selected quota formula and the process of consensus building around quota introduction may impact the degree of gendered backlash. Where consensus is lacking and/or quotas are viewed as imposed from outside or as a zero-sum game for men, backlash may be stronger. By contrast, backlash may be less likely if quota systems fail to disrupt hegemonic power structures, such as where quota formulas are structured in such a way as to ghettoize women candidates into spaces with little or no popular constituency base or meaningful access to power. These scenarios suggest that the absence of backlash can be an indicator of both negative *and* positive progress towards breaking structured inequality and that more attention must be paid to the policy processes surrounding quota adoption.

Research has not examined similar institutional factors impacting online GBV-P in Canada, and further studies are needed on this topic. Other aspects of the political and social context affect the extent and consequences of online abuse for women and racialized politicians. Candidates and politicians explained that incivility and abuse can have a greater impact when they amplify other experiences of violence or systemic discrimination (Tenove and Tworek 2020; Tenove et al. 2023). Those more likely to experience or fear threats, violence, and discrimination are also those under-represented in Canadian politics: Indigenous, women, visible minorities, Black, and 2SLGBTQQIA+ Canadians (Cotter and Savage 2019). Individuals living at the intersections of these identities are disproportionately affected. For instance, an Indigenous candidate noted that sexualized posts about her fit into a context: "We have 5,700 Indigenous women who have gone murdered or missing, and part of the reason is because of hyper-sexualization of Indigenous women ... It's hard to separate my identity from my online experience. It's a lived experience that also shows up online."

Impacts on Targeted Individuals and Broader Society

The impacts of online GBV-P are complex and diverse, as are responses to the problem. The global case studies reveal that online abuse can silence individual women and have broader chilling effects on political participation by some groups. It can also spark outrage, activate advocacy, and drive change by bringing injustice to the surface.

Physical, psychological, and social harms. Research on TFGBV has identified myriad direct harms from online abuse, including coordinated attacks, non-consensual surveillance, psychological and emotional harms, and damage to economic livelihood or social relationships due to false allegations and efforts to shame women (Amnesty International 2018; Bailey and Mathen 2019; Dunn 2020; OHCHR 2018). Our research in Canada and beyond finds that women in politics – as well as their families, staff, and associates – experience all these harms when targeted by online campaigns. The comparative cases suggest that online GBV-P causes terror, depression, anxiety, sleep loss, and panic attacks. It is often a deterrent to pursing political ambition (IFES 2019). One interviewee from Afghanistan stated: "We are afraid of being defamed [online], this is why we don't dare to run for office."

In Canada, women politicians describe harms ranging from online death threats to the psychological strain that politicians and their staff face due to reading and addressing large volumes of insulting and hostile online discourse (Tenove and Tworek 2020). Furthermore, social media often does not begin or end online. In our interviews, candidates and staff described facing abusive language, misogyny, homophobia, racism, and anti-immigrant sentiments by email, mail, telephone, while door-knocking, at campaign events, and at campaign and constituency offices.

Political silencing and exclusion. It is well established that online abuse, and the fear of online abuse, can prevent women from fully participating in political activities or online discourse (NDI 2019; Sobieraj 2020). Some research suggests that women are more likely than men to practise self-censorship in the face of online harassment (Citron and Penney 2019; Nadim and Fladmoe 2021). The psychological and logistical burdens of addressing online harassment can exacerbate obstacles to women and marginalized groups achieving equal representation in elected bodies. For instance, Lalonde (chapter 3, this volume) argues that fears of being targeted by image-based sexual violence may reduce women's willingness to seek office, especially racialized women and 2SLGBTQQIA+ folks. Collignon and Rüdig (2021) show that in the 2019 UK election, women candidates were more likely to react to harassment by reducing in-person canvassing and other campaign modifications, in turn lowering their likelihood of being elected.

Harming democratic discourse. Online abuse can damage the inclusiveness and quality of democratic discourse. Online GBV-P is often visible to larger audiences and not just the target, exposing them to efforts to delegitimize members of identity groups (see Wagner and

Young, chapter 2, this volume). The denigration of individuals and groups not only undermines their full inclusion in public discourse, it "degrades speech norms and is toxic to mutual respect," which is needed for productive discussion across political divides (McKay and Tenove 2021, 709). Furthermore, online GBV-P may be particularly damaging to inclusive and productive discussion of some issues. For instance, women appear more likely to face online attacks when they take strong positions on issues such as climate change (Raney and Gregory 2019).

Motivating resistance and activism. While online GBV-P may reduce women's voice or leadership in politics, it can also have the effect of prompting women and their supporters to push back, speak out, and enhance solidarity. For instance, women in focus groups in Sri Lanka (IFES 2020) said that outrage at their treatment online made them more determined to speak out. Di Meco (2019) finds that, despite facing hostility online, women find inspiration and empowerment through their online engagement and would not forego their political ambitions or social media presence due to the threat of online GBV-P. Although its perpetrators often hide behind anonymous identities, online GBV-P brings misogyny and gender-based violence out into the open in unprecedented ways, making one of the most historically private, hidden forms of violence visible to broad public audiences. Social media offers a space for women to amplify their voice and activate networks of support. Social media has offered important networks for women internationally to connect with one another and provide resources and support to address online GBV-P (Di Meco 2019; Hodson et al. 2018; Bardall 2013).

Findings in Canada, too, suggest that online abuse often prompts women to become more resolute in their political participation. As Wagner observes, harassment "succeeds in making women feel they are in a hostile political environment even as it fails to deter them from engaging in politics" (2022, 2). Similarities can further be drawn to Thomas and Pruysers's findings in chapter 4 of this book, which demonstrate that depictions of psychological violence against politicians do not appear to suppress citizens' political interests. Several interviewees noted that sexist or racialized abuse prompted supporters, including many they were unaware of, to express their outrage and solidarity. Many said that the online backlash to their views, particularly those that address questions of identity, reminded them of the importance of addressing these social problems. As one federal MP put it, the abuse she receives "pushes me to a place where I will stand even firmer" (Tenove and Tworek 2020, 9).

Conclusion

Findings and Gaps in Comparative Research

Online gender-based violence in politics is pervasive and a severe global problem. Comparative research can lead to a better understanding of how online GBV-P manifests itself in different cultural and political contexts, including its targeting of people of different genders, and how to develop strategies to address it. Such research is in its infancy and comes with significant challenges. To conclude this chapter, we offer methodological suggestions for pursuing comparative research on online GBV-P; we highlight some of the insights and gaps that come from our preliminary comparison of Canada to other country cases; and we sketch some implications for action in Canada and beyond.

How might online GBV-P be conceptualized and studied across diverse contexts? Our framework suggests that gendered online violence needs to be understood not only in terms of the motives of its perpetrators but also through its gendered forms and impacts. It is significantly shaped by broader contextual factors, ranging from the prevalence of offline GBV-P to the inclusiveness of political and media institutions. Future research on online GBV-P should examine patterns such as the targeting of prominent women or gender non-conforming politicians; the speed and scope of the spread of harmful messaging; the motivation and organization of the perpetrators involved; and the impacts on targeted politicians, secondary victims, and broader public discourse. To better understand and compare these different dimensions requires methodological diversity so that the dynamics and consequences of online GBV-P can be understood in their particular social and political contexts.

What global patterns of GBV-P appear more or less prevalent in Canada? Our initial comparisons reveal several similarities, as well as gaps and opportunities for future research. First, across all cases, gendered online abuse came from actors with the explicit aim of excluding women from political power, as well as from individuals drawing on gendered terms, tropes, or narratives to advance other political aims. While we see both in Canada, the explicit, motivated GBV-P does not appear to be significantly driven by political parties or mainstream civil society institutions, compared to other countries. Further comparative research could explore the varying extent and impact of these two general sources of online GBV-P.

Second, in Canada and other countries we see frequent, extensive, and often viral online abuse of women who challenge norms regarding gender and political power. Politicians from Kathleen Wynne (a lesbian becoming premier of Ontario) to Kamala Harris (the first woman and first racialized individual to be elected US vice president) to Thokozani Khupe (Zimbabwean politician and former deputy prime minister) and Yulia Tymoshenko (Ukrainian politician, co-leader of the Orange Revolution, and former prime minister) have faced widespread and intense online GBV-P. Further comparative research could determine when this experience is a "backlash" targeting the "first" individuals with particular identities to hold senior offices and when it continues to affect women and gender non-conforming politicians after "glass ceilings" have been broken.

Third, our comparative research reveals transnational dynamics to online GBV-P that warrant greater attention from researchers and policymakers. Studies identify transnational perpetrators, including members of misogynist and white supremacist online networks, as well as the leveraging of gender as part of hostile foreign political meddling campaigns. Diaspora communities can be vectors of transnational online abuse, and women politicians who belong to diaspora communities may face multiple and cross-cutting dynamics of online GBV-P. The social platforms that facilitate much online GBV-P are themselves transnational entities, meaning that women in politics globally face similar challenges. Meaningful effort to change platforms' designs and policies will also need to be transnational.

This comparative analysis reveals significant gaps in research on online GBV-P in Canada. We lack surveys of federal, provincial, or municipal politicians regarding the online abuse they face, including online GBV-P, which has been done more systematically in other countries (see, for example, Collignon and Rüdig 2021; Håkansson 2021), We lack any serious analysis of online GBV-P in languages other than English in Canada. Comparative study of English- and French-language online GBV-P, or across geographic regions or levels of government, may be illuminating. We also lack research on the sources or perpetrators of online abuse targeting politicians.

Further study of online GBV-P in Canada can build on and contribute to global comparative research. For instance, Canada is a prime country case for studying transnational patterns of online GBV-P. As a country with a high proportion of foreign-born residents, research on the patterns of abuse targeting diaspora politicians in Canada may be particularly illuminating. At the same time, research suggests that significant volumes of toxic online content disseminated among Canadians comes from American users, such as COVID-19 disinformation (Bridgman et al. 2021). More generally, Canada can serve as a helpful comparator to countries with different political culture and institutions with respect to women's participation in politics.

Implications for Action

The breadth of actors, mediums, types of harms, and jurisdictions involved in online GBV-P requires responses in four areas to prevent and mitigate harm.

First, legal measures need to be improved to respond to online GBV-P. In Canada, it includes using current legal tools more effectively (for example, laws on harassment, cyber-crime, defamation, and non-consensual distribution of intimate images) and enacting specific legislative reforms (see Khoo 2021). Proposed legal responses include regulation of social media platforms to require them to better prevent and mitigate harms and the creation of new transparency and accountability processes to ensure they do so, including establishing a centralized expert regulator (Canadian Commission on Democratic Expression 2022).

Second, social media companies must take on greater responsibility for reducing the extent and disproportionate harms of GBV-P on their platforms, including design improvements as well as updating and more reliably enforcing their own terms of service (Jankowicz et al. 2021; Tenove and Tworek 2020). Initiatives such as the United Nations Generation Equality Forum have spurred social media giants to improve user agency in the face of online gender-based violence. However, such solutions place the onus of dealing with online attacks on the targets and encourage them to bury the attacks they face through filters, blinders, and blocking functions (PEN America 2021). Social media companies must be held accountable, including providing greater transparency on their content moderation capacity, content-shaping algorithms, and ad-targeting system (Di Meco and Brechenmacher 2020).

Third, formal political institutions need to do more to tackle online GBV-P, including legislatures and electoral management bodies. Legislative actors are taking wide-ranging action, from the US Democratic Women's Caucus advocating reform on Facebook to Kyrgyz MPs proposing a bill on countering harassment and hate speech to the European Union's Digital Services Act and Digital Markets Act. Likewise, political parties should better support elected officials who face online abuse, particularly those facing intersecting obstacles to full participation in elected politics, and implement zero tolerance policies in their codes of conduct for members who engage in or condone online GBV-P.

Finally, civil society and community-based groups must continue to hold social media organizations to account, demand legislative responses, and address harmful stereotypes through constructive counter-speech, awareness raising, and advocacy (Bardall 2022). Online GBV-P is rooted in systemic inequalities and harmful social norms, and changing them ultimately requires a whole-of-society effort.

NOTES

1 A repository of many of these studies can be found at IFES 2020. Sections of this chapter draw on draft material developed in collaboration with the International Foundation for Electoral Studies and presented at the American Political Science Association (APSA), European Conference on Politics and Gender (ECPG), Canadian Political Science Association (CPSA), and Midwest Political Science Association (MPSA) conferences in 2019 (Bardall 2019).
2 Further details on research methods and findings can be found in Tenove and Tworek (2020) and Tenove et al. (2023). Special thanks to Trevor Deley, who developed our machine learning model, and to team members Jordan Buffie, Jaskiran Gakhal, Grace Lore, Sonya Manuel, Veronica Stolba, Maite Tabouda, and Erin Tolley. This research was supported by the Social Sciences and Humanities Research Council (SSHRC) and the Digital Ecosystem Research Challenge.
3 As an example of a method to address this problem, Wagner (2022) interviewed women who would be likely to run for office but have not, thereby accessing views of people who may have been pushed out of political life by online and offline barriers.
4 Just 7 per cent of tweets directed positive content at candidates. About 40 per cent were neutral, and 12 per cent had an unclear sentiment.
5 2SLGBTQQIA+ refers to two-spirit, lesbian, gay, bisexual, transgender, queer, questioning, intersex, androgynous, and asexual. "Two-spirit" is a term used by some Indigenous people to reflect the complex (and non-binary) nature of gender roles and identities in Indigenous communities.

REFERENCES

Al-Rawi, Ahmed, Wendy Hui Kyong Chun, and Salma Amer. 2022. "Vocal, Visible and Vulnerable: Female Politicians at the Intersection of Islamophobia, Sexism and Liberal Multiculturalism." *Feminist Media Studies* 22 (8): 1918–35. https://doi.org/10.1080/14680777.2021.1922487.

Amnesty International. 2018. *#ToxicTwitter: Violence and Abuse against Women Online*. Amnesty International. https://www.amnestyusa.org/wp-content/uploads/2018/03/Toxic-Twitter.pdf.

Bailey, Jane, and Carissima Mathen. 2019. "Technology-Facilitated Violence against Women & Girls: Assessing the Canadian Criminal Law Response." *The Canadian Bar Review* 97 (3): 664–96. https://cbr.cba.org/index.php/cbr/article/view/4562.

Banet-Weiser, Sarah. 2018. *Empowered: Popular Feminism and Popular Misogyny*. Durham, NC: Duke University Press.

Bardall, Gabrielle. 2013. "Gender-Specific Election Violence: The Role of Information and Communication Technologies." *Stability: International Journal of Security and Development* 2 (3): Article 60. http://doi.org/10.5334/sta.cs.

– 2019. "Defending Democracy in Digital Spaces: Ending Violence against Women in Politics Online." Presented at the *Electoral Integrity Project Workshop*. Pre–American Political Science Association (APSA) event, 28 August 2019, Washington DC.

– 2022. "Addressing Gender-Based Political Violence Online." In *Gender and Violence against Political Actors*, edited by Elin Bjarnegård and Pär Zetterberg. Philadelphia, PA: Temple University Press.

Bardall, Gabrielle, Elin Bjarnegård, and Jennifer M. Piscopo. 2020. "How Is Political Violence Gendered? Disentangling Motives, Forms, and Impacts." *Political Studies* 68 (4): 916–35. https://doi.org/10.1177/0032321719881812.

Biroli, Flávia. 2016. "Political Violence against Women in Brazil: Expressions and Definitions." *Revista Direito e Práxis* 7 (15): 557–89. https://www.redalyc.org/pdf/3509/350947688018.pdf.

Bradshaw, Samantha, and Amélie Henle. 2021. "The Gender Dimensions of Foreign Influence Operations." *International Journal of Communication* 15 (October): 4596–618. https://ijoc.org/index.php/ijoc/article/view/16332.

Bridgman, Aengus, Erik Merkley, Oleg Zhilin, Peter John Loewen, Taylor Owen, and Derek Ruths. 2021. "Infodemic Pathways: Evaluating the Role That Traditional and Social Media Play in Cross-National Information Transfer." *Frontiers in Political Science* 3. https://doi.org/10.3389/fpos.2021.648646.

Burke, Ashley. 2019. "Relentless Online Abuse of Female MPs Raises Concern for Safety of Staff." *CBC News*, 5 November 2019. https://www.cbc.ca/news/politics/mps-staff-online-hate-security-measures-1.5347221.

Canadian Commission on Democratic Expression. 2022. *How to Make Online Platforms More Transparent and Accountable to Canadian Users*. Ottawa: Public Policy Forum. https://ppforum.ca/articles/how-to-make-online-platforms-more-transparent-and-accountable-to-canadian-users/.

Chen, Gina Masullo. 2017. *Online Incivility and Public Debate: Nasty Talk*. Cham, CH: Palgrave Macmillan.

Citron, Danielle Keats, and Jonathon W. Penney. 2019. "When Law Frees Us to Speak." *Fordham Law Review* 87 (6): 2317–35. https://ir.lawnet.fordham.edu/flr/vol87/iss6/2.

Collignon, Sofia, and Wolfgang Rüdig. 2021. "Increasing the Cost of Female Representation? The Gendered Effects of Harassment, Abuse and Intimidation towards Parliamentary Candidates in the UK." *Journal of Elections, Public Opinion and Parties* 31 (4): 429–49. https://doi.org/10.1080/17457289.2021.1968413.

Cotter, Adam, and Laura Savage. 2019. "Gender-Based Violence and Unwanted Sexual Behaviour in Canada, 2018: Initial Findings from the Survey of Safety in Public and Private Spaces." *Juristat* 39 (1). Statistics Canada. Catalogue 85-002-X201900100017. https://www150.statcan.gc.ca/n1/en/catalogue/85-002-X201900100017.

Davidson, Thomas, Debasmita Bhattacharya, and Ingmar Weber. 2019. "Racial Bias in Hate Speech and Abusive Language Detection Datasets." In *Proceedings of the Third Workshop on Abusive Language Online*, 25–35. Florence, IT: Association for Computational Linguistics.

Dawson, Tyler. 2017. "Threats against Wynne Range from the Bizarre to the Serious, Documents Reveal." *Ottawa Citizen*, 21 June 2017. https://ottawacitizen.com/opinion/columnists/dawson-threats-against-wynne-range-from-the-bizarre-to-the-serious.

Di Meco, Lucina. 2019. *#SHEPERSISTED: Women, Politics & Power in the New Media World*. Washington, DC: The Wilson Center.

Di Meco, Lucina, and Saskia Brechenmacher. 2020. "Tackling Online Abuse and Disinformation Targeting Women in Politics." Carnegie Endowment for International Peace, 30 November 2020. https://carnegieendowment.org/2020/11/30/tackling-online-abuse-and-disinformation-targeting-women-in-politics-pub-83331.

Dunn, Suzie. 2020. *Technology-Facilitated Gender-Based Violence: An Overview*. Supporting a Safer Internet Paper No. 1. Waterloo, ON: Centre for International Governance Innovation. https://www.cigionline.org/publications/technology-facilitated-gender-based-violence-overview.

Gorrell, Genevieve, Mehmet E. Bakir, Ian Roberts, Mark A. Greenwood, and Kalina Bontcheva. 2020. "Which Politicians Receive Abuse? Four Factors Illuminated in the UK General Election 2019." *EPJ Data Science* 9 (1): 18. https://doi.org/10.1140/epjds/s13688-020-00236-9.

Håkansson, Sandra. 2021. "Do Women Pay a Higher Price for Power? Gender Bias in Political Violence in Sweden." *Journal of Politics* 83 (2): 515–31. https://doi.org/10.1086/709838.

Harmer, Emily, and Rosalynd Southern. 2021. "Digital Microaggressions and Everyday Othering: An Analysis of Tweets Sent to Women Members of Parliament in the UK." *Information, Communication & Society* 24 (14): 1998–2015. https://doi.org/10.1080/1369118X.2021.1962941.

Hodson, Jaigris, Chandell Gosse, George Veletsianos, and Shandell Houlden. 2018. "I Get By with a Little Help from My Friends: The Ecological Model and Support for Women Scholars Experiencing Online Harassment." *First Monday* 23 (8). https://doi.org/10.5210/fm.v23i8.9136.

IFES (International Foundation for Electoral Systems). 2019. *Violence against Women in Elections Online: A Social Media Analysis Tool.* Arlington, VA: International Foundation for Electoral Systems. https://www.ifes.org/publications/violence-against-women-elections-online-social-media-analysis-tool.
— 2020. *Violence against Women in Elections.* Repository of country case studies. International Foundation for Electoral Systems. https://web.archive.org/web/20210610083629/https://www.ifes.org/VAWE.
Inter-Parliamentary Union. 2016. *Sexism, Harassment and Violence against Women Parliamentarians.* Issues Brief, October 2016. https://www.ipu.org/resources/publications/reports/2016-10/sexism-harassment-and-violence-against-women-parliamentarians.
Jamieson, Kathleen Hall, Allyson Volinsky, Ilana Weitz, and Kate Kenski. 2017. "The Political Uses and Abuses of Civility and Incivility." In *The Oxford Handbook of Political Communication,* edited by Kate Kenski and Kathleen Hall Jamieson, 205–18. Oxford: Oxford University Press.
Jankowicz, Nina, Jillian Hunchak, Alexandra Pavliuc, Celia Davies, Shannon Pierson, and Zoë Kaufmann. 2021. *Malign Creativity: How Gender, Sex, and Lies are Weaponized against Women Online.* Washington, DC: The Wilson Center. https://www.wilsoncenter.org/publication/malign-creativity-how-gender-sex-and-lies-are-weaponized-against-women-online.
Khoo, Cynthia. 2021. *Deplatforming Misogyny: Report on Platform Liabilities for Technology-Facilitated Gender-Based Violence.* Toronto, ON: Women's Legal Education and Action Fund (LEAF).
McKay, Spencer, and Chris Tenove. 2021. "Disinformation as a Threat to Deliberative Democracy." *Political Research Quarterly* 74 (3): 703–17. https://doi.org/10.1177/1065912920938143.
Nadim, Marjan, and Audun Fladmoe. 2021. "Silencing Women? Gender and Online Harassment." *Social Science Computer Review* 39 (2): 245–58. https://doi.org/10.1177/0894439319865518.
NDI (National Democratic Union). 2019. *Tweets That Chill: Analyzing Online Violence against Women in Politics.* Washington, DC: National Democratic Institute. https://www.ndi.org/tweets-that-chill.
OHCHR (Office of the United Nations High Commissioner for Human Rights). 2018. *Report of the Special Rapporteur on Violence against Women, Its Causes and Consequences on Violence against Women in Politics.* A/73/301. Office of the United Nations High Commissioner for Human Rights. https://www.ohchr.org/en/documents/thematic-reports/a73301-violence-against-women-politics-note-secretary-general.
Okimoto, Tyler G., and Victoria L. Brescoll. 2010. "The Price of Power: Power Seeking and Backlash against Female Politicians." *Personality and Social Psychology Bulletin* 36 (7): 923–36. https://doi.org/10.1177/0146167210371949.
PEN America. 2021. *No Excuse for Abuse.* New York: PEN America. https://pen.org/report/no-excuse-for-abuse/.

Raney, Tracey, and Mackenzie Gregory. 2019. "Women Climate Leaders Face 'Green Rage' Attacks." *The Tyee*, 16 September 2019. https://thetyee.ca/Analysis/2019/09/16/Green-Rage-Against-Women/.

Reddi, Madhavi, Rachel Kuo, and Daniel Kreiss. 2023. "Identity Propaganda: Racial Narratives and Disinformation." *New Media & Society* 25 (8): 2201–18. https://doi.org/10.1177/14614448211029293.

Rheault, Ludovic, Erica Rayment, and Andreea Musulan. 2019. "Politicians in the Line of Fire: Incivility and the Treatment of Women on Social Media." *Research & Politics* 6 (1). https://doi.org/10.1177/2053168018816228.

Rossini, Patricia. 2022. "Beyond Incivility: Understanding Patterns of Uncivil and Intolerant Discourse in Online Political Talk." *Communication Research* 49 (3): 399–425. https://doi.org/10.1177/0093650220921314.

Sobieraj, Sarah. 2020. *Credible Threat: Attacks against Women Online and the Future of Democracy*. Oxford: Oxford University Press.

Sydnor, Emily. 2019. *Disrespectful Democracy: The Psychology of Political Incivility*. New York: Columbia University Press.

Tenove, Chris, and Heidi Tworek. 2020. *Trolled on the Campaign Trail: Online Incivility and Abuse in Canadian Politics*. Vancouver, BC: Centre for the Study of Democratic Institutions, University of British Columbia. https://democracy.ubc.ca/platforms/online-incivility-in-politics-in-canada/trolled-on-the-campaign-trail-online-incivility-and-abuse-in-canadian-politics/.

Tenove, Chris, Heidi Tworek, Grace Lore, Jordan Buffie, and Trevor Deley. 2023. "Damage Control: How Campaign Teams Interpret and Respond to Online Incivility." *Political Communication* 40 (3): 283–303. https://doi.org/10.1080/10584609.2022.2137743.

Theocharis, Yannis, Pablo Barberá, Zoltán Fazekas, and Sebastien Adrian Popa. 2020. "The Dynamics of Political Incivility on Twitter." *SAGE Open* 10 (2). https://doi.org/10.1177/2158244020919447.

Trynacity, Kim. 2018. "'A Wake-Up Call': Documents Detail Litany of Threats against Premier Rachel Notley." *CBC News*, 4 May 2018. https://www.cbc.ca/news/canada/edmonton/notley-premier-threats-security-1.4644989.

Wagner, Angelia. 2022. "Tolerating the Trolls? Gendered Perceptions of Online Harassment of Politicians in Canada." *Feminist Media Studies* 22 (1): 32–47. https://doi.org/10.1080/14680777.2020.1749691.

2 Digital Dangers: Theorizing Online Violence against Politicians

ANGELIA WAGNER AND TAYLER YOUNG

Introduction

Canadian politician Jenny Kwan is a regular target of online vitriol. As a racialized woman immigrant, she often receives abusive attacks from posters who wish "horrible things" to happen to her (Burke 2019). This online harassment is accompanied by offline violence. One time a man entered Kwan's constituency office and made violent sexist and racist threats against her, only leaving once she called the police (Smith 2021). Kwan's tires have also been slashed and her constituency office window shattered. Concerned about further violence to herself and her staff, Kwan installed a panic button with a direct line to the police three years before all members of Parliament (MPs) received them because of rising violence against politicians (Burke 2019). Kwan's experiences demonstrate not only how the line between online and offline attacks has become blurred (see Bardall and Tenove's chapter 1, this volume) but also how politicians who are racialized women in particular are being targeted by violence.

Kwan's case also illustrates how technology-facilitated violence against politicians is a growing concern around the world. Activists were the first to draw attention to how various actors use digital technologies to insult, harass, intimidate, and deter women politicians in particular (Atalanta 2018; Dhrodia 2017; Inter-Parliamentary Union 2016). Academic research has been slow to catch up, but recent studies have demonstrated that women of all social backgrounds face a challenging online environment (Harmer and Southern 2021; Rheault, Rayment, and Musulan 2019; Southern and Harmer 2019, 2021). Online gender-based violence in politics (GBV-P) ranges from rude comments that question women's ability to be good politicians to abusive messages that include threats of sexual violence and even death. In Canada, the two most threatened premiers in Alberta history are two women leaders: Rachel Notley of the New Democratic Party (NDP) and Alison Redford of the Progressive Conservatives (Trynacity 2017). One person even went so far as to try to pre-plan Notley's funeral. Online and offline death threats are not mere rhetoric. Worldwide, women have been assassinated for their political views and activities. British MP Jo Cox is the most famous example. Cox, a white heterosexual woman, was shot and killed by a purported fascist shortly before the country's Brexit referendum in 2016 (Aspden 2019). Lesser-known cases include Brazilian municipal politician Marielle Franco, a Black lesbian killed in 2018, likely for protesting against police brutality and advocating for the marginalized (Restrepo Sanin 2020). Consequently, many non-governmental organizations (NGOs) view online violence as part of a larger phenomenon of GBV-P (see Raney and Collier's introductory chapter, this volume).

While NGOs understand online violence as a form of political violence, scholars typically view it as part of a growing trend of incivility in political discourse. The traditional expectation is that people discuss politics in a respectful manner, usually without resorting to emotional displays, crude language, or personal insults. Debate is also conducted according to pre-determined rules, either set out by the institution or in popular manuals. While the norms of civil debate first arose in physical spaces like legislatures and pertained mainly to politicians, they are now expected in online spaces and from all participants, including citizens. Communication styles that violate these norms are labelled uncivil.

The exact nature of incivility in political communication remains up for debate, but most definitions start from a presumption of disrespectful behaviour. Brooks and Geer argue incivility "requires going an extra step" beyond criticism of an opponent to include "inflammatory comments that add little in the way of substance to the discussion" (2007, 5). Sydnor views incivility as "a continuum that ranges from the polite to insults to racial slurs and obscenities" (2019, 9). Mutz limits incivility to impoliteness, a discourse that violates the norms of interpersonal interaction, "the type of behaviour that would be considered impolite in face-to-face contexts" (2015, 6). Many scholars are concerned that incivility, and its rise within online spaces, is dangerous for democracy and leads to a decrease in political trust (Theocharis et al. 2020, 2) and an increase in polarization (Anderson et al. 2014, 382). However, the notion that incivility threatens democracy is debated. It might even elicit an interest in politics (Brooks and Geer 2007; Sydnor 2019).

Feminist scholars question the concept of civility and its connection to "particular normative conceptions of democratic politics" (Zerilli 2014, 107). What is considered civil deliberation is intrinsically linked to one's political access, status, and hierarchical position in society (Bickford 2011; Young 2000; Zerilli 2014). Until the twentieth century, political institutions in Western liberal democracies like Canada were the sole preserve of white, wealthy men. One consequence of this monopoly is that parliamentary procedures, including those regarding political debate, reflect the preferences of this social group (Collier and Raney 2018; Young 2000). For example, gender stereotypes presume men to be rational actors who should not easily succumb to emotion, hence the expectation that actors debate politics in a rational manner. Conventions regarding debate not only vary by gender but also across cultures and classes. Not all social groups engage in political debate in the same way. Critical scholars argue that members of powerful social groups typically label the actions and communication styles of historically marginalized and disenfranchised groups as uncivil to maintain the status quo and shield it from criticism (Bickford 2011; Zerilli 2014). In short, the norms of political debate in Canada are designed to reinforce the communicative power of white, wealthy men.

NGO and scholarly perspectives are useful for understanding online violence against politicians, but they have limited utility when it comes to exploring how this treatment can vary according to a politician's social background. The feminist digital media literature primarily focuses on the role of gender, while the political communication literature rarely does even that. Little attention is given to the role of class, race, sexuality, religion, and other social identities that can make online violence even more problematic for politicians from marginalized communities. Alongside Kuperberg (2018), we argue that an intersectional approach is necessary to fully comprehend the nature of online violence against politicians, the reasons why it occurs, and its implications for democracy. Intersectionality is a concept that emerged out of Black feminist thought and examines the interplay between different forms of discrimination based on gender, race/ethnicity, sexuality, and other factors (Crenshaw 1991).

Our chapter makes an important contribution to the literature on online political violence by offering an intersectional framework that scholars can use to empirically investigate comments made about and to politicians on social media forums such as Twitter (now known as X) and Facebook.[1] Focusing specifically on text-based messages, we conceptualize online comments directed at political actors as falling along a continuum from *tolerable* discourse featuring civil or uncivil language that criticizes or praises an actor at one end to *abusive* discourse designed to intimidate and expel an actor from the political sphere on the other, as shown in Figure 2.1. We include the concept of civility in our framework because of its widespread use in political communication,

Figure 2.1. Theoretical model of continuum of online discourse with or about a political actor

but we reiterate that perceptions of "civil" and "uncivil" language could vary by social group. The continuum accounts for the possibility that a single post could contain two or more types of discourses and thus falls between categories. Our framework, however, does not account for the role of virality. An uncivil but tolerable message retweeted thousands of times could do more harm to its target than a single abusive tweet. The intent of our framework is to capture the *range* of online textual discourse in which social media users engage as well as the motivations for, and consequences of, these communicative actions. The empirical challenges of this framework are reviewed later in the chapter. Complications aside, our chapter advances the field by offering a theoretical starting point to explore the complex nature of online political discourses. Only an intersectional approach can reveal the content, motivations, and consequences of online violence against diverse politicians.

The next section conceptualizes tolerable, delegitimizing, and abusive discourse, while the concluding section offers recommendations on mitigating online violence against politicians.

Theorizing Online Violence against Politicians

We agree with Kuperberg (2018) that an intersectional theory of online violence against politicians must account for the ways in which gender, race, sexuality, class, and other identities work with, and through, one another to shape the nature of online discourse. However, we argue that such a theory also requires making normative claims about what is tolerable, delegitimizing, and blatantly unacceptable discourse while being inclusive of different communicative styles.

Figure 2.1 is a visual representation of our theoretical model of online political discourse. At one end of the continuum is *tolerable* discourse, which is designed to communicate opinions about politics but can be "civil" or "uncivil" in tone, though without resorting to stereotypical language related to gender, race, sexuality, and other personal characteristics. Stereotypes are "widely held beliefs about the nature and behaviour of different groups and their individual members" (Wagner and Everitt 2019, 9). Examples of stereotypical language include "dumb blond" and "boys don't cry." At the other end of the continuum is *abusive* discourse, which relies upon a mixture of hateful, aggressive, violent, and stereotypical language to insult, intimidate, and expel an actor from the political sphere. Examples of abusive language include "just a piece of pig shit pond slime who should be fucking hung." Whether the language is stereotypical or abusive, the target does not need to be from the relevant social group: a poster might use homophobic language when talking about a heterosexual politician. At the mid-point is *delegitimizing* discourse, which resembles tolerable discourse in that it includes commentary about politics using either "civil" or "uncivil" language, but it is a subtler version of abusive discourse in that it openly questions an actor's competencies and political legitimacy. However, this type of discourse does not use hateful, aggressive, or violent language to do so, and its stereotypical language is less confrontational in tone.

We theorize each type of discourse in more depth in the following subsections, addressing the intersectional motivations, nature, and implications of each one and drawing upon Canadian and international examples to illustrate. The final subsection discusses the challenges of empirical research on online political violence.

Tolerable Discourse

Embedded within the political communication and GBV-P literatures is the assumption that political discourse should be "civil," regardless of whether the speaker or target is a politician, partisan, activist, or citizen. Actors engaged in political debate are expected to offer a series of logical arguments in a passionate, but not emotional, manner. Swear words, name-calling, and impolite or rude language should be avoided. This manner of speaking is strongly associated with white, upper-class men. Not socialized to these norms, women, racialized individuals, and working-class people often employ a different conversant style when discussing politics (Young 2000). In many cases, social groups resort to (perceived) impoliteness just to be heard: "If some citizens are more prone to shout, that may well be because those in power are not listening" (Zerilli 2014, 112). What is considered uncivil is often determined by the powerful "to stifle dissent and reinforce existing arrangements of power" (Sindorf 2014, 195). Communication norms are thus deeply classed, gendered, and raced. Our definition of tolerable online discourse is primarily centred on the explicit or implicit purpose of the communication and not on its civility. Regardless of speaker, online discussion should focus on politics, not personal attacks, and should avoid discriminatory or threatening language.

So-called uncivil language is tolerable when the poster's purpose is to critique the political ideas, decisions, and activities of elected representatives, candidates, and other actors. This expectation holds whether the critique is partisan-based or general in nature. Let us consider the phrase "give your head a shake." It is a common refrain in online discussion that could be classified as impolite but one that does not target a political actor based on social characteristics. Twitter talk about Alberta NDP leader Rachel Notley has long used this phrase:

> Dear Ms Notley, human capital is the lifeblood of this country and if you happen to think that dirty hydrocarbons are give your head a shake. (21 May 2018)

> Notley quit promising money Alberta doesn't have give your head a shake we don't have money. (29 March 2019)

These posters use a popular Canadian idiom to suggest Notley is not being sensible, but its use does not suggest that Notley should not be in politics *because she is a woman*, nor does it contain any inherently sexist sentiment. Because social media affords people from different social backgrounds an opportunity to participate more fully in political debates, we should expect to encounter varying styles of political communication in online spaces. It is undoubtedly uncomfortable for political actors to read impolite or rude tweets, but allowances need to be made to ensure everyone can communicate their thoughts on government, policy, and politics. The primary requirement of tolerable discourse is that it focuses on political issues and avoids stereotypical and abusive language.

Delegitimizing Discourse

Delegitimizing discourse is at the mid-point of our continuum because its language is more likely to be "uncivil" than abusive, and its motivations are rooted in questioning the legitimacy of certain political actors rather than trying to forcefully expel specific social groups from politics. Similar to news media discourses (Wagner, Trimble, and Sampert 2019), delegitimizing online commentary raises questions about the legitimacy, qualifications, experience, and ability of certain individuals to be political leaders (Harmer and Southern 2021; Southern and Harmer 2019). It sends the message that women and members of minority groups are not suitable to be elected representatives. Delegitimizing discourse can contain stereotypical language, but its tone is not explicitly hateful, aggressive, or violent.

Southern and Harmer (2019) highlight the dangers of delegitimizing discourses in their study of online interactions between British MPs and general citizens in June 2018. Overall, they found that online posters depicted women as political outsiders in four types of posts: (1) gendered and racist abuse, (2) silencing or dismissive posts, (3) disapproving posts, and (4) benevolent othering. We categorize the first approach as abusive discourse. The other three approaches fall within our category of delegitimizing discourse. Silencing or dismissive posts do focus on political matters, but they do so in such a way as to signal to some social groups that their views are neither welcome nor particularly insightful. Disapproving posts raise explicit questions about a politician's intelligence, qualifications, experiences, and thus suitability to be an elected representative. Finally, benevolent othering posts praise politicians but in ways that make it clear that they deviate from the white, male norm of political leadership. As with abusive discourses, delegitimizing discourses are designed to reinforce white, Christian, heterosexual men as the ideal politician.

While Southern and Harmer focused on women politicians, we can easily extend their analysis to politicians from other social groups. One example would be religious minorities. Jagmeet Singh is a Sikh who was elected in 2017 as leader of the federal NDP. During the leadership campaign, journalists talked at length about his turban, beard, and kirpan (religious dagger), which are physical manifestations of his religion. News coverage drew upon religious stereotypes to raise questions about Singh's suitability to lead a major political party and ability to appeal to voters in Quebec, which has banned public servants from wearing religious attire. Following Southern and Harmer's typology, we would expect online discussion to focus on Singh's race/ethnicity and religious attire as a way of trivializing him as a political leader. For example:

> @theJagmeetSingh what a joke this woke is. He wears a turban, but for money and power he can't bring himself to do the right thing and criticize Quebec on law 21. (21 September 2021)

As with gendered commentary, the purpose of delegitimizing discourses about politicians from religious minorities is to preserve historical social hierarchies, in this case the traditionally Christian political actor.

Abusive Discourse

Abusive discourse is on the other end of the online discourse continuum and is usually what is meant by online violence against politicians. It is one of many forms of GBV-P (Krook and Restrepo Sanin 2020). Abusive discourse uses (1) hateful, aggressive, and violent language, (2) extremely misogynistic, racist, homophobic, and other stereotypical language, or (3) both types of language to insult, degrade, and intimidate political actors. In its purist form, abusive discourse does not contain any discussion of political matters; it is only about personal attacks. Social media companies have policies that prohibit such hateful and violent conduct. The presence, nature, and intensity of abusive discourse will vary according to a politician's particular mix of social characteristics and level of public visibility (Rheault, Rayment, and Musulan 2019; Southern and Harmer 2019, 2021). Regardless of the speaker, the purpose of identity-based online violence is usually the same – to expel these individuals from the political sphere, reinforcing politics as the exclusive domain of the socially dominant group. In Canada, the exalted political subject is a white, Christian, heterosexual man from the middle to upper-middle classes. (Bardall and Tenove's chapter 1, this volume, takes a comparative look at the gendered motives, gendered forms, and gendered impacts of online violence against politicians in Canada and other countries.)

While political communication scholars examine "incivility" in general, feminist scholars are primarily interested in online violence that falls within the category of abusive discourse. Impolite language matters less than "e-bile," or the "extravagant invective, the sexualized threats of violence, and the recreational nastiness" that often occurs in online discussion about women (Jane 2014, 532). While our intent is to offer an intersectional theory of online violence against diverse politicians, Mantilla's (2013, 2015) theory of gendertrolling provides a useful starting point for understanding the motivations, nature, and implications of abusive discourse. General trolling is typically about disrupting online interactions and making mischief (Hardaker 2010; Golf-Papez and Veer 2017). But Mantilla argues that gendertrolling is "exponentially more vicious, virulent, aggressive, threatening, pervasive, and enduring" because its purpose is to reinforce a traditional gender hierarchy that positions men as political actors and women as domestic caregivers (2015, 11). Attacks are usually triggered by women simply conveying their opinions online and involve graphic gender-based insults, rape and death threats, and non-consensual circulation of intimate images, deepfakes, and deepnudes (see Lalonde's chapter 3, this volume, about image-based sexual violence against women politicians). Attacks can appear across social media platforms at a high rate of intensity and frequency over a long period of time and can involve many individuals coordinating their efforts (Mantilla 2013, 2015).

Gendertrolling can help explain how social media users target women politicians in an abusive fashion, but the concept is inadequate for theorizing the intersectional nature of online violence against a greater range of politicians. Variations in group stereotypes as well as the perceived threat different groups represent to the status quo mean online violence will reflect a politician's unique mix of characteristics (see Bardall and Tenove's chapter 1, this volume, for discussion of the Canadian context). We need to consider how gender, race/ethnicity, sexuality, class, and other factors work with, and through, one another to shape online violence. For example, race-based abusive discourse would draw upon language and imagery offensive to a specific racial/ethnic group. Lynching is a case in point. Social media users often evoke this white supremacist practice when attacking Black men politicians. Lynching was common in the United States, especially from the late nineteenth century to mid-twentieth century, and was designed to reinforce white racial superiority. Thousands of Black men were killed, but the larger intention was to control the Black population through fear and intimidation (Mowatt 2018). Lynching is rare today, but lynching effigies have taken its place. These symbolic acts became especially pronounced after the 2008 election of Barack Obama as president of the United States (Mowatt 2018). This example demonstrates the importance of an intersectional approach to exploring the complexities of online violence.

Politicians have also been harassed because of their sexuality. Sexuality-based abuse, typically aimed at those in the 2SLGBTQQIA+ community,[2] often describes the individual "as perverted and corrupt" and "whose nature represents a threat to the traditional, Christian values" that form the basis of society in Western liberal democracies (Vučenović 2019, 90). Political figures outside the heteronormative belief system transgress the "imposed parameters of normality" and face abuse centring on those deviations (91). Political actors within the community have spoken out about the discrimination they have faced online. Joanna Bernard, the first openly 2SLGBTQQIA+ person elected to the Nova Scotia legislature, reported receiving "rampant" homophobic abuse including death threats (McMillan 2016). Abuse also focused on her weight, confirming research findings regarding society's obsession with women's bodies, particularly those in the public realm (Trimble et al. 2013). The Bernard example demonstrates how a politician's physical appearance is often targeted in abusive discourse. For example, women politicians are often reduced to a single body part ("cunt"). Even when a politician's sexual orientation is not the target, online abuse often has a sexualized component.

Scholars need to consider the ways in which race/ethnicity work with, and through, gender, sexuality, and other identities to shape the nature of online violence against politicians. An intersectional analysis would reveal the complex character of the online environment for different types of politicians (see Al-Rawi, Chun, and Amer 2022). Such personal attacks might seem trivial on the surface but are really about larger issues. Disparaging a Muslim woman's hijab or a Sikh man's turban is not about critiquing their sartorial choices but about rejecting the presence of non-Christian individuals in politics. Physical appearance is an obvious signal of difference from the white heterosexist norms of Canadian politics and thus targeted as a form of rhetorical shorthand. This is not to say, however, that social media users are reluctant to express their rejections more directly. Nevertheless, when Twitter (now known as X) only allows 280 characters per tweet, these shortcuts allow a poster to express several sentiments within platform constraints.

Empirical Challenges of Categorizing Online Discourse

We have identified three types of online discourse to help theorize the nature and purpose of online political discourse and how they might vary according to the targeted actor's characteristics. But these categories are not mutually exclusive. Online posts rarely fit neatly into one category. For example, a tweet might critique a politician's policy stance and openly question their qualifications but use aggressive, hateful, or violent language to do so. This likelihood is why we have opted to conceptualize discourse as comprising a *continuum* rather than discrete categories. Depending upon the content, an online post could fall anywhere between being tolerable at one end to abusive at the other end. Another limitation of our theoretical framework relates to intensity. A high volume of tolerable and delegitimizing tweets, especially from a few sources, could feel abusive to the target. We have defined each type of online discourse to provide conceptual clarity, but how to code viral online communication remains an open question.

Another challenge of empirical research is distinguishing between tolerable, delegitimizing, and abusive language, especially in the eyes of those targeted. Language viewed as impolite by one group might be seen as abusive by another group. Differing perceptions of language is key to understanding the consequences of online violence. Attacks against transgender candidates illustrate this point. Posters use two strategies to signal their rejection of transgender candidates: misgendering and deadnaming. Misgendering references a person's former gender identity by using the wrong gender pronoun, while deadnaming involves using the person's former name without their consent. These acts are highly insulting because individuals usually change their name and pronouns when transitioning from one gender identity to another. A new name and pronoun are affirmations of their new identity. Trans activist Morgane Oger is often the target of misgendering, both during her unsuccessful 2017 bid for a seat in the British Columbia legislature and in the years since. For example:

> One either is born a girl and matured into a woman or one is born male and matured into a man. There is no other route. (5 May 2020)

> From one man to another, you're not a woman you're in need of counselling. (20 July 2016)

Where does misgendering fall on the continuum? Misgendering is clearly a personal attack against a transgender candidate based on their personal characteristics and cannot be categorized as tolerable discourse. Misgendering rejects transgender individuals as a social group and delegitimizes them as political actors, and as the above examples demonstrate, it uses stereotypical language to communicate this sentiment. Using the wrong gender pronoun is not violent in the way that rape or death threats are and therefore not explicitly abusive discourse. But categorizing misgendering as delegitimizing discourse ignores the emotional impact of the commentary on its target. If transgender individuals view misgendering as a form of semiotic violence, then it is both delegitimizing *and* abusive discourse. Scholars therefore need to place misgendering between these two points on the online discourse continuum.

Linguistic conundrums such as this one are why scholars must work with members of the relevant community to fully understand where communicative practices belong on the continuum. What linguistic practices do transgender individuals find transphobic? How do women define online sexual violence? What is the specific racist language that members of different racial/ethnic groups find abusive? Qualitative research is best positioned to answer these empirical questions. Scholars need to conduct interviews, focus groups, and language experiments with different types of political actors to establish their perceptions of online discourse in general and online violence in particular. This approach ensures the targets of online political discourses play an important role in shaping theoretical understandings and empirical investigations of online violence.

Implications for Action

Preventing online abuse and its associated harms is complicated. Some have demanded social media platforms play a larger role in removing problematic and abusive language. While placing a larger emphasis on social platforms is a logical step, it is not completely feasible. Few incentives exist to entice the social media industry to take robust action against online violence other than the value of social responsibility, which can compete with a corporation's goal to maximize profits. Facebook has shown strong resistance to tackling online hate, prompting the European Union to warn of regulations (Drozdiak 2020).

However, regulation of social media encounters issues. Algorithms and tools currently used by tech giants to detect abuse and hate speech are themselves problematic. Recent studies have shown that both human reviews and computer algorithms aimed at identifying hate speech might in fact amplify racial bias (Ghaffary 2019; Rubin, Blackwell, and Conley 2020). Others look to the legal system for change, but concerns around freedom of expression pose their own challenges.

Recommendation 1

Both legal and regulatory routes assume policymakers have a strong foundational knowledge about online violence to write effective legislation and regulations. That is far from the case. Continued debates regarding what constitutes abusive content, who should be the ultimate moderator, who are the primary victims, and what strategies could decrease the prevalence of online violence demonstrate that research on this topic is in its infancy. Extant research typically focuses on bullying directed at youths but rarely on online violence in particular. Existing data are limited and not easily obtainable, comprehensive, or consistent.

Our first recommendation to address online violence is to ramp up research capacity. The federal government can play an important role by generating national-level data on the various forms of online violence to assist with evidence-based policymaking. The Trudeau Liberals are focused on cyberbullying against young women and girls. They allocated $4 million over five years to prevent its occurrence as part of a $200 million action plan to address gender-based violence in Canada. The government also announced a three-year pilot program entitled Engage, Empower, Connect: Cyber-Empowerment for Girls and Young Women, which works "to provide girls with digital skills that help prevent online victimization" (Simpson 2019). This approach is problematic. It places the burden of prevention on the targets of online violence rather than on the perpetrators.

While (potential) victims of online violence should take steps to protect themselves, we argue that other actors need to help prevent or intervene to stop online violence. The federal government must fund projects aimed at understanding why online violence occurs, identifying who is most likely to face online violence, and developing effective prevention techniques directed at the perpetrators. By taking the lead in this research, the federal government can ensure a unified approach to the collection of data that enables easy comparisons, specific targets, and a focused approach in response efforts. Ottawa can also facilitate the growth of research in academia and civil society through priority funding and grants to achieve large-scale and appropriate research across the country. We also urge provincial and territorial governments to join this effort by fostering similar research in their own jurisdictions.

An intersectional analysis must be foundational to these research undertakings. A failure to disaggregate online violence based on factors other than gender and age hinder any understanding of society's diverse needs and experiences (Pittaway and Bartolomei 2018). Understanding that the axes of discrimination – such as racism, sexism, ableism, ageism, classism, and homophobia – are not separate or distinct from one another, but rather mutually reinforcing, is essential to produce a fuller understanding of who is most at risk of online abuse and how. As Crenshaw demonstrates, the experience of a Black woman is "greater than the sum of racism and sexism" (1989, 140). Researchers should also consider colonialism as a factor, especially when exploring online violence against Indigenous people. Future research that takes an intersectional approach will not only better identify the nature of online violence but also enable policymakers to recognize the unique barriers that individuals from diverse backgrounds face and to devise appropriate initiatives.

Recommendation 2

One of the barriers to adequately addressing online violence against politicians is the trivialization of this violence. Women and minorities in particular are told to ignore the trolls as online violence is the "cost of doing politics" (National Democratic Institute 2017). Individuals who take this advice employ coping mechanisms such as self-protection, resistance, acceptance, and self-blame (Veletsianos et al. 2018, 4697). These techniques are unfair and inadequate. They do not result in a positive outcome for a user's well-being (Veletsianos et al. 2018), with many victims of online violence reporting mental and/or emotional stress and fear for their physical safety (Duggan 2017; Inter-Parliamentary Union 2016). Placing the onus for prevention on the target instead of the perpetrator runs the risk of further suppressing already marginalized voices in the digital sphere.

Our second recommendation is for civil society to take a greater role in the prevention of online violence. As Jane argues, online activism and resistance by victims "need to be accompanied by the sorts of hard advocacy, political organization and collectivist approaches used by second-wave feminists in their campaigns" against violence (2016, 291). One collectivist approach is the development of awareness movements. NGOs and human rights activists can become the primary facilitators of these collaborative efforts. Social media itself can be used to raise awareness, recognize shared experiences, and build capacity to combat online violence. Just as violence transcends the online/offline binary, activism should also go beyond social platforms to offline venues or risk becoming invisible to the wider public (Schuster 2013). Awareness campaigns can educate the public about the forms of violence conducted online, the at-risk populations, and the far-reaching impacts on victims and bystanders. We know this approach can work. Previous research found sensitizing experiences motivated men to become allies and participate in anti-violence causes (Casey and Smith 2010). Raising awareness about the real harms that different types of individuals face is a crucial first step towards achieving equality in the digital sphere (Citron 2014).

Conclusions

Online violence against politicians is a global concern. It can make politics unattractive to potential candidates, thereby reducing the willingness of diverse individuals to seek office. Limited political representation reduces the responsiveness of public policy for women and marginalized communities. To combat this problem, scholars need to take an intersectional approach to understand the nature of online violence against politicians, the reasons why it occurs, and its implications for democracy. In this chapter, we offer an intersectional framework that conceptualizes online commentary directed at political figures as falling along a continuum from tolerable to abusive discourse. Tolerable discourse involves criticizing the policy ideas and actions of political actors without resorting to personal attacks or abusive language. Abusive discourse is the exact opposite, focusing on personal attacks and abusive language without any discussion of politics or policy. Its aim is to forcefully expel the actor from the political sphere. At the mid-point is delegitimizing discourse, which avoids abusive language but does raise explicit questions about the legitimacy of a political actor.

Conceptualizing online comments as falling along a continuum allows for a more nuanced exploration of online behaviour. By recasting "uncivil" discourse as tolerable under certain circumstances, we draw attention to how an insistence on "civil" discussion can be used against members of marginalized communities and reinforce existing asymmetrical power relations in politics. The complexity of online experiences is further captured through the addition of delegitimizing discourse at the mid-point of the continuum. While the language in this space is not explicitly violent, its motivations are rooted in a rejection of certain types of individuals as legitimate political actors. No government or NGO can act against this type of discourse, but scholars must monitor its impact on the political environment and the willingness of women and minorities to participate in politics (see Wagner 2022).

Abusive online discourse is where action must be taken. We recommend that Canadian governments ramp up research on the complexities of online violence and that civil society join efforts to raise public awareness about the problem. To increase the likelihood of success, we argue for an intersectional approach to program design and execution. An intersectional conceptualization of online violence against politicians recognizes that considering only a single aspect of a politician's social identity is limiting both theoretically and empirically. Our framework enables researchers to better comprehend where oppressions intersect.

NOTES

1 Abuse can occur on private messaging systems like WhatsApp or via the direct messaging function on public platforms like Twitter (now known as X), but the private nature of this communication limits its public influence. These comments only come to light when a politician publicly shares them. Research on private messages requires a theoretical framework attentive to their one-to-one nature and inability to go publicly viral on their own.
2 2SLGBTQQIA+ refers to those who identify as two-spirit, lesbian, gay, bisexual, transgender, queer, questioning, intersex, androgynous, and

asexual. "Two-spirit" is a term used by some Indigenous people to reflect the complex (and non-binary) nature of gender roles and identities in Indigenous communities.

REFERENCES

Al-Rawi, Ahmed, Wendy Hui Kyong Chun, and Salma Amer. 2022. "Vocal, Visible and Vulnerable: Female Politicians at the Intersection of Islamophobia, Sexism and Liberal Multiculturalism." *Feminist Media Studies* 22 (8): 1918–35. https://doi.org/10.1080/14680777.2021.1922487.

Anderson, Ashley A., Dominique Brossard, Dietram A. Scheufele, Michael A. Xenos, and Peter Ladwig. 2014. "The 'Nasty Effect': Online Incivility and Risk Perceptions of Emerging Technologies." *Journal of Computer-Mediated Communication* 19 (3): 373–87. https://doi.org/10.1111/jcc4.12009.

Aspden, Kester. 2019. "The Making of a Bedsit Nazi: Who Was the Man Who Killed Jo Cox?" *The Guardian*, 6 December 2019. https://www.theguardian.com/news/2019/dec/06/bedsit-nazi-man-killed-jo-cox-thomas-mair.

Atalanta. 2018. *(Anti)Social Media: The Benefits and Pitfalls of Digital for Female Politicians*. www.atalanta.co/s/AntiSocial_Media_Report-FINAL2-lowres.pdf.

Bickford, Susan. 2011. "Emotion Talk and Political Judgment." *Journal of Politics* 73 (4): 1025–37. https://doi.org/10.1017/S0022381611000740.

Brooks, Deborah Jordan, and John G. Geer. 2007. "Beyond Negativity: The Effects of Incivility on the Electorate." *American Journal of Political Science* 51 (1): 1–16. https://doi.org/10.1111/j.1540-5907.2007.00233.x.

Burke, Ashley. 2019. "Relentless Online Abuse of Female MPs Raises Concern for Safety of Staff." *CBC News*, 5 November 2019. https://www.cbc.ca/news/politics/mps-staff-online-hate-security-measures-1.5347221.

Casey, Erin, and Tyler Smith. 2010. "'How Can I Not?': Men's Pathways to Involvement in Anti-Violence against Women Work." *Violence Against Women* 16 (8): 953–73. https://doi.org/10.1177/1077801210376749.

Citron, Danielle Keats. 2014. *Hate Crimes in Cyberspace*. Cambridge, MA: Harvard University Press.

Collier, Cheryl N., and Tracey Raney. 2018. "Understanding Sexism and Sexual Harassment in Politics: A Comparison of Westminster Parliaments in Australia, the United Kingdom, and Canada." *Social Politics* 25 (3): 432–55. https://doi.org/10.1093/sp/jxy024.

Crenshaw, Kimberle. 1989. "Demarginalizing the Intersection of Race and Sex: A Black Feminist Critique of Antidiscrimination Doctrine, Feminist Theory and Antiracist Politics." *University of Chicago Legal Forum* 1989 (1): 139–67. https://scholarship.law.columbia.edu/cgi/viewcontent.cgi?article=4013&context=faculty_scholarship.

— 1991. "Mapping the Margins: Intersectionality, Identity Politics, and Violence against Women of Color." *Stanford Law Review* 43 (6): 1241–99. https://doi.org/10.2307/1229039.

Dhrodia, Azmina. 2017. "Unsocial Media: Tracking Twitter Abuse against Women MPs." *Medium.com*, 4 September 2017. https://medium.com/@AmnestyInsights/unsocial-media-tracking-twitter-abuse-against-women-mps-fc28aeca498a.

Drozdiak, Natalia. 2020. "EU Tech Chief Threatens Facebook's CEO with Regulation." *Bloomberg.com*, 18 May 2020. https://www.bloomberg.com/news/articles/2020-05-18/eu-tech-chief-threatens-facebook-s-zuckerberg-with-regulation.

Duggan, Maeve. 2017. *Online Harassment 2017*. Pew Research Center, 11 July 2017. https://www.pewresearch.org/internet/2017/07/11/online-harassment-2017/.

Ghaffary, Shirin. 2019. "The Algorithms That Detect Hate Speech Online Are Biased against Black People." *Vox*, 15 August 2019. https://www.vox.com/recode/2019/8/15/20806384/social-media-hate-speech-bias-black-african-american-facebook-twitter.

Golf-Papez, Maja, and Ekant Veer. 2017. "Don't Feed the Trolling: Rethinking How Online Trolling Is Being Defined and Combated." *Journal of Marketing Management* 33 (15/16): 1336–54. https://doi.org/10.1080/0267257X.2017.1383298.

Hardaker, Claire. 2010. "Trolling in Asynchronous Computer-Mediated Communication: From User Discussions to Academic Definitions." *Journal of Politeness Research: Language, Behavior, Culture* 6 (2): 215–42. https://doi.org/10.1515/jplr.2010.011.

Harmer, Emily, and Rosalynd Southern. 2021. "Digital Microaggressions and Everyday Othering: An Analysis of Tweets Sent to Women Members of Parliament in the UK." *Information, Communication and Society* 24 (14): 1998–2015. https://doi.org/10.1080/1369118X.2021.1962941.

Inter-Parliamentary Union. 2016. *Sexism, Harassment and Violence against Women Parliamentarians*. Issues Brief, October 2016. https://www.ipu.org/resources/publications/issue-briefs/2016-10/sexism-harassment-and-violence-against-women-parliamentarians.

Jane, Emma A. 2014. "'Your a Ugly, Whorish, Slut': Understanding E-Bile." *Feminist Media Studies* 14 (4): 531–46. https://doi.org/10.1080/14680777.2012.741073.

— 2016. "Online Misogyny and Feminist Digilantism." *Continuum: Journal of Media and Cultural Studies* 30 (3): 284–97. https://doi.org/10.1080/10304312.2016.1166560.

Krook, Mona Lena, and Juliana Restrepo Sanín. 2020. "The Cost of Doing Politics? Analyzing Violence and Harassment against Female Politicians." *Perspectives on Politics* 18 (3): 740–55. https://doi.org/10.1017/S1537592719001397.

Kuperberg, Rebecca. 2018. "Intersectional Violence against Women in Politics." *Politics and Gender* 14 (4): 685–90. https://doi.org/10.1017/S1743923X18000612.

Mantilla, Karla. 2013. "Gendertrolling: Misogyny Adapts to New Media." *Feminist Studies* 39 (2): 563–70. https://doi.org/10.1353/fem.2013.0039.

– 2015. *Gendertrolling: How Misogyny Went Viral*. Santa Barbara, CA: Praeger.

McMillan, Elizabeth. 2016. "MLAs Speak Out about Fat-Shaming, Death Threats and Homophobia." *CBC News*, 19 December 2016. https://www.cbc.ca/news/canada/nova-scotia/mla-joanne-bernard-sexism-harassment-fat-shaming-legislature-1.3900518.

Mowatt, Rasul A. 2018. "The Peculiar Heritage of Lynching in America." In *Heritage of Death: Landscapes of Emotion, Memory and Practice*, edited by Matthias Frihammar and Helaine Silverman, 178–92. New York: Routledge.

Mutz, Diana C. 2015. *In-Your-Face Politics: The Consequences of Uncivil Media*. Princeton, NJ: Princeton University Press.

National Democratic Institute. 2017. *#NotTheCost: Stopping Violence against Women in Politics*. Washington, DC: National Democratic Institute. https://www.ndi.org/sites/default/files/not-the-cost-program-guidance-final.pdf.

Pittaway, Eileen, and Linda Bartolomei. 2018. *From Rhetoric to Reality: Achieving Gender Equality for Refugee Women and Girls*. World Refugee Council Research Paper No. 3 – August 2018. Waterloo, ON: Centre for International Governance Innovation. https://www.cigionline.org/sites/default/files/documents/WRC%20Research%20Paper%20no.3_0.pdf.

Restrepo Sanín, Juliana. 2020. "Violence against Women in Politics: Latin America in an Era of Backlash." *Signs: Journal of Women in Culture and Society* 45 (2): 302–10. https://doi.org/10.1086/704954.

Rheault, Ludovic, Erica Rayment, and Andreea Musulan. 2019. "Politicians in the Line of Fire: Incivility and the Treatment of Women on Social Media." *Research and Politics* 6 (1): 1–7. https://doi.org/10.1177/2053168018816228.

Rubin, Jennifer D, Lindsay Blackwell, and Terri D. Conley. 2020. "Fragile Masculinity: Men, Gender, and Online Harassment." In *Proceedings of CHI '20: CHI Conference on Human Factors in Computing Systems*, 1–14. New York: Association for Computing Machinery. https://doi.org/10.1145/3313831.3376645.

Schuster, Julia. 2013. "Invisible Feminists? Social Media and Young Women's Political Participation." *Political Science* 65 (1): 8–24. https://doi.org/10.1177/0032318713486474.

Simpson, Meagan. 2019. "Actua Receives $600,000 to Launch Women and Girls Cyber-Empowerment Initiative." *BetaKit*, 28 August 2019. https://betakit.com/actua-receives-600000-to-launch-women-and-girls-cyber-empowerment-initiative/.

Sindorf, Shannon. 2014. "FCJ-162 Symbolic Violence in the Online Field: Calls for 'Civility' in Online Discussion." *Fibreculture Journal* 22 (April): 193–214. http://twentytwo.fibreculturejournal.org/fcj-162-symbolic-violence-in-the-online-field-calls-for-civility-in-online-discussion/.

Smith, Charlie. 2021. "B.C.'s Female Politicians Face Down Misogynistic, Hateful Bullies." *The Georgia Straight*, 3 March 2021. https://www.straight.com/news/bcs-female-politicians-face-down-misogynistic-hateful-bullies.

Southern, Rosalynd, and Emily Harmer. 2019. "Other Political Women: Online Misogyny, Racism and Ableism towards Women in Public Life." In *Online Othering: Exploring Digital Violence and Discrimination on the Web*, edited by Karen Lumsden and Emily Harmer, 197–210. Cham, CH: Palgrave Macmillan.

— 2021. "Twitter, Incivility and 'Everyday' Gendered Othering: An Analysis of Tweets Sent to UK Members of Parliament." *Social Science Computer Review* 39 (2): 259–75. https://doi.org/10.1177/0894439319865519.

Sydnor, Emily. 2019. *Disrespectful Democracy: The Psychology of Political Incivility*. New York: Columbia University Press.

Theocharis, Yannis, Pablo Barberá, Zoltán Fazekas, and Sebastian Adrian Popa. 2020. "The Dynamics of Political Incivility on Twitter." *SAGE Open* 10 (2). https://doi.org/10.1177/2158244020919447.

Trimble, Linda, Angelia Wagner, Shannon Sampert, Daisy Raphael, and Bailey Gerrits. 2013. "Is It Personal? Gendered Mediation in Newspaper Coverage of Canadian National Party Leadership Contests, 1975–2012." *International Journal of Press/Politics* 18 (4): 462–81. https://doi.org/10.1177/1940161213495455.

Trynacity, Kim. 2017. "Rachel Notley: Alberta's Most Threatened Premier." *CBC News*, 14 February 2017. https://www.cbc.ca/news/canada/edmonton/notley-threats-alberta-history-1.3982276.

Veletsianos, George, Shandell Houlden, Jaigris Hodson, and Chandell Gosse. 2018. "Women Scholars' Experiences with Online Harassment and Abuse: Self-Protection, Resistance, Acceptance, and Self-Blame." *New Media and Society* 20 (12): 4689–708. https://doi.org/10.1177/1461444818781324.

Vučenović, Nataša D. 2019. "Homophobia in Serbian Online Discourse: The Case of the 2016 Belgrade Pride Parade." *Philologist* 19 (19): 82–100. https://www.ceeol.com/search/article-detail?id=813611.

Wagner, Angelia. 2022. "Tolerating the Trolls? Gendered Perceptions of Online Harassment of Politicians in Canada." *Feminist Media Studies* 22 (1): 32–47. https://doi.org/10.1080/14680777.2020.1749691.

Wagner, Angelia, and Joanna Everitt. 2019. "Introduction: Gendered Identities and Political Communication." In *Gendered Mediation: Identity and Image Making in Canadian Politics*, edited by Angelia Wagner and Joanna Everitt, 3–23. Vancouver, BC: UBC Press.

Wagner, Angelia, Linda Trimble, and Shannon Sampert. 2019. "One Smart Politician: Gendered Mediation Discourses of Political Leadership in Canada." *Canadian Journal of Political Science* 52 (1): 141–62. https://doi.org/10.1017/S0008423918000471.

Young, Iris Marion. 2000. *Inclusion and Democracy*. Oxford: Oxford University Press.

Zerilli, Linda M.G. 2014. "Against Civility: A Feminist Perspective." In *Civility, Legality, and Justice in America*, edited by Austin Sarat, 107–31. Cambridge: Cambridge University Press.

3 Ringing an Early Alarm Bell: Image-Based Sexual Violence against Political Actors

DIANNE LALONDE

The #MeToo movement amplified the voices of advocates, researchers, and survivors, bringing awareness to the prevalence of sexual violence. Part of that awareness is recognizing the evolving ways sexual violence occurs as a result of technological advancements. One relatively new form of technology-facilitated violence is image-based sexual violence (IBSV). IBSV involves the non-consensual creation and/or distribution of intimate images and threats to distribute such images.[1] This chapter focuses on two forms of IBSV. First is the non-consensual distribution of intimate images (NCDII). Intimate images that are distributed without consent could have been sent privately, taken by another person consensually or by force, or gained through hacking. Second is non-consensual sexual deepfakes, which are artificially generated sexual imagery and videos. The ability to create non-consensual sexual deepfakes has increased dramatically since access to a computer or smartphone, an application, and images of an individual are often all that is needed. Each is a form of sexual violence primarily targeted at gender-oppressed individuals, including women. NCDII and non-consensual sexual deepfakes are comparatively less examined in the gender-based violence in politics (GBV-P) literature due to their emerging nature. Still, this violence continues to grow rapidly with political actors as targets. In 2021, Germany's Green Party leader, Annalena Baerbock, had fake images of her naked emerge online (Connolly 2021). In 2022, a series of Taiwanese women politicians, including legislator Kao Chia-yu and city councillor Huang Jie, were targeted with non-consensual sexual deepfakes (Pan 2022).

As the #MeToo movement shows, it is important to have the language and understanding of this violence in order to name and address it. Mona Lena Krook identifies the importance of naming GBV-P to make violence visible, highlight its structural nature, offer interpretative tools for survivors, and promote collective resistance (2020, 3). Accordingly, this chapter contributes to GBV-P work by naming and exploring IBSV at the cross-section of politics and gender. The ways in which IBSV occurs in politics remains under-acknowledged, with many scholars and activists concerned about deepfakes promoting political misinformation and disinformation as opposed to their most common use as sexual violence (Gosse and Burkell 2020). This chapter offers an invitation to the field to expand the scope of GBV-P to include and be responsive to IBSV. In doing so, the chapter aims as well to ring an early "alarm bell" to Canadian decision-makers and the public about the potential harms of this form of gender-based violence to Canada's democratic process and of the need to take IBSV seriously in efforts to combat GBV-P in the #MeToo era.

This chapter uses an intersectional anti-oppression lens to explore IBSV in politics. It starts by identifying why we need to ring an early "alarm bell" about IBSV and further defines the forms of IBSV, focusing on NCDII and non-consensual sexual deepfakes. Next, this chapter shares the gendered and intersectional targets and impacts of IBSV, including the personal and democratic costs. Finally, this chapter offers three implications for action on how we can respond to IBSV in Canada. Throughout, examples of IBSV against political actors are offered from the Canadian and international context.

Why We Need to Talk About IBSV in Canadian Politics Now

IBSV is an emerging form of violence with increasing rates; however, it has been trivialized and needs greater awareness as a form of violence. IBSV could deter individuals, especially those who identify as women or further marginalized group members, from participating in the political process out of fear or because intimate images already released have made it difficult for them to enter the political process. By recognizing and including IBSV in the continuum of GBV-P, we can minimize the harms experienced by individual targets as well as help to ensure a more inclusive democratic process where everyone can participate equally and fully without fear.

IBSV has developed from technological innovations that have made the non-consensual creation and distribution of intimate images easier, meaning that it is likely to become more prevalent in the public sphere. Relevant to NCDII, websites have emerged with the sole purpose of sharing this violent content to a broad audience. An NCDII website called AnonIB specifically targeted women at Canadian universities, including St. Francis Xavier University, Carleton University, and the University of Toronto (Hensley 2017). People would post on the website requesting and sharing images of women at the school. When non-consensual sexual images are shared, even prior to an individual entering politics, that individual's participation in politics can be negatively affected or ended. One example is that of former Nova Scotia Liberal candidate Robyn Ingram, who reports that she was dropped from the ticket due to boudoir photos she consensually shared online through her OnlyFans account (Ryan 2021). Further individuals, especially women, may be hindered from participating in political parties due to sexual images of them online, whether the images are consensually distributed or not and whether they are real or fake.

Likewise, non-consensual sexual deepfakes may play off of, and perpetuate, existing discriminatory practices that seek to exclude members of marginalized groups, such as 2SLGBTQQIA+ individuals, from being politically active.[2] As mentioned by Wagner and Young in chapter 2, this volume, Morgane Oger experienced cisnormative discrimination while running for provincial office when hateful flyers about her gender identity were printed and distributed in her Vancouver riding (see *Oger v. Whatcott*). In a similar way, non-consensual sexual deepfakes may be used against 2SLGBTQQIA+ candidates and politicians, including depicting them in intimate moments or claiming to "out" individuals. Such images and videos can impact voters, since "evidence suggests that many voters would prefer LGBT candidates whose sexual orientation is kept private or downplayed" (Everitt and Camp 2014, 246).

A barrier to addressing IBSV is the way it is trivialized in society. Trivialization occurs in multiple ways, including victim-blaming, labelling IBSV as a joke, and denying IBSV as a form of violence. An example can be seen in the case of Liberal member of Parliament (MP) William Amos. Various news and social media sources shared a non-consensual intimate image of Amos, with minimal censoring, which was taken during a hybrid parliamentary session when he was changing after a run (Tunney 2021). The trivialization of IBSV hinders it from being properly understood and reported, harms survivors, and contributes to a lack of recognition of the democratic consequences of IBSV. Discussing IBSV now and recognizing it as a form of violence, specifically GBV-P here, helps to challenge and dismantle such trivialization.

Forms of IBSV: A Focus on NCDII and Non-consensual Sexual Deepfakes

The two forms of IBSV discussed in this chapter are NCDII and non-consensual sexual deepfakes. NCDII refers to the sharing of intimate or sexual images that individuals do not consent to being shared. Such images can be exchanged in a variety of ways, including sending in a private chat, emailing to an employer or family member, sharing on social media, and/or posting on a website. Dedicated NCDII websites started to emerge around 2000 and continue to be popular (DeKeseredy and Schwartz 2016). Often when intimate images are posted, the individual is also doxed, as their private information (such as name, phone number, and address) is shared.

By comparison, non-consensual sexual deepfakes are artificially generated sexual images and videos. The main difference between deepfake images and videos is that videos are more difficult to create due to the necessity for good quality source material and sexual content that continuously match each other. Deepfakes use a form of artificial intelligence called deep learning (deepfakes are said to be the combination of deep learning and fake video), which was first developed in the 1950s and has recently experienced significant advancements. Deep learning can "grind through gigantic volumes of data, teaching itself how to detect and classify patterns or anomalies and make predictions and recommendations" (Tibbetts 2018, 5). To illustrate how deepfakes work, consider how to teach a machine to recognize a cat. Before deep learning, it would be necessary to tell the machine what features are characteristic of a cat (such as whiskers, paws, fur). With deep learning, the machine need only be shown some images of a cat, and it can extract from those images the features of a cat on its own. Researchers at the Université de Montréal introduced an even more advanced version of deep learning in 2014 called generative adversarial networks (GANs; Goodfellow et al. 2014). GANs work using two models: the discriminative model works to discern an image of a cat by what it is not (for example, a dog, mouse, rabbit), while the generative model works to create images for the discriminative model to test. In the context of deepfakes, GANs can be used to generate different images into a video and discern if the image's placement looks realistic. The two models operate to continually push the other to get better and better, resulting in more realistic deepfakes.

Some deepfakes are not sexual in nature, and typically those involve placing people into different comedy or action films. By comparison, sexual deepfakes consist of images and videos where an individual is artificially inserted into sexual content, usually without their consent. Often, the sexual content used is sourced from pornography. Adult performers describe the experience of having their videos used for non-consensual sexual deepfakes as "violating" and "eviscerating" (Alptraum 2020). Applications for creating non-consensual sexual deepfakes have been widely shared on the internet. The first popular application for non-consensual sexual deepfake images, DeepNude, emerged online in 2019.

While the original application was removed, many similar applications have emerged. Likewise, applications to make non-consensual sexual deepfake videos have spread widely after an original application was shared on Reddit in 2017. Non-consensual sexual deepfakes have proven to have an audience; one non-consensual sexual deepfake website launched in January 2021 amassed thirty-eight million hits in less than eight months (Cook 2021).

IBSV within the Continuum of GBV-P

IBSV can be used as a tool against political actors to harm them and their political careers. This chapter follows researchers and practitioners in defining those who may be subject to political violence as all those who are politically active, including activists, judges, and journalists (Krook 2020; Biroli 2018). Doing so recognizes the commonalities that individuals in these roles have, including that they operate publicly, disseminate political information, engage the public in political activities, and contribute through their work to democratic discourse. An intersectional analysis also highlights the necessity of recognizing political contributions beyond a formal politician role. Many racialized and oppressed individuals have been historically and currently denied politician roles or have opted not to engage in a state they view as an unjust colonial power. Instead, they have engaged in equally significant advocacy and journalistic endeavours. It should be noted, though, that individuals in these various political roles may be targeted or impacted in differing ways. For example, a journalist may lose their job at a paper, while a politician may lose their election or party membership.

This chapter considers IBSV as primarily, but not exclusively, a form of sexual violence within the continuum of GBV-P for two reasons. First, many survivors have either explicitly called IBSV sexual violence or likened it to further forms of sexual violence such as rape (Eaton and McGlynn 2020). For instance, one NCDII survivor stated: "How anyone can fail to see revenge porn as a sexual crime is beyond me" (Yorkshire Post 2016). Following the influential work on sexual violence by Liz Kelly, this chapter takes the stance that our consideration of where to place a form of violence on a continuum should be informed by survivors' own words and experiences (1988, 140).[3] Second, a commonality among forms of IBSV is that sexual imagery, whether it is real or fake, is being non-consensually displayed of the person, resulting in a violation of their sexual privacy and autonomy. An individual may consent to sharing their intimate images or to the creation and sharing of a sexual deepfake, and the ability to give consent is important to their sexual expression. When consent is not provided, the individual loses their sexual privacy (Citron 2019, 1874). Whether, when, and how to share sexual content is a personal decision, and that decision should be protected. Since IBSV denies sexual privacy, it is in line with further forms of sexual violence like harassment and assault, which also non-consensually and violently cross boundaries around bodies and intimate activities.

IBSV is also a form of semiotic violence within the continuum of GBV-P. Semiotic violence involves "the use of language and images to denigrate women in an attempt to deny their political rights" (Krook 2020, 67).[4] Semiotic violence further captures the intents and effects of IBSV because it aims to discredit individuals, often women, as political actors by sexually objectifying them. Many NCDII and non-consensual sexual deepfake websites feature comment sections rife with hypermasculine and sexually objectifying language (Henry and Flynn 2019). Sexual objectification is an act that reduces an individual into a physical object valued only for its appearance and use. Women disproportionately experience sexual objectification, especially Black, Indigenous, and racialized women (Razack 2016; Anderson et al. 2018; Sue et al. 2007). Krook identifies sexual objectification as "a potent tool for denigrating women and, particularly, for attacking women seeking a role in public life" (2020, 202). Sexual objectification can operate to undermine women's efforts to seek and maintain a political presence as it leads to diminished views regarding women's competence, morality, and humanity or personhood (Ward 2016; Loughnan et al. 2010). It has also been linked to greater tolerance of sexual violence towards women (Ward 2016; Seabrook, Ward, and Giaccardi 2019). As opposed to merely a process engaged in by others, objectification may become internalized as well. Self-objectification, including body surveillance and shame, has been linked to decreased political efficacy and engagement of women (Gothreau 2021).

Finally, in line with Wagner and Young's continuum of online discourse presented in chapter 2 of this book, IBSV is a form of abusive discourse. With IBSV, the violent act is meant to be shared. While there may be one primary distributor, distribution can become crowdsourced with many secondary distributors. In the context of politics, IBSV against political actors therefore becomes a part of online political discourse.

Gendered and Intersectional Targets and Impacts of IBSV

Who is targeted with IBSV and the impacts of IBSV differ for various groups in accordance with their privilege and marginalization in society. This section unpacks the gendered and intersectional targets and impacts of IBSV in the context of GBV-P.

Gendered and Intersectional Targets of IBSV

In Canada, NCDII was made a crime in 2015, and from when it was criminalized to 2022, there have been 13,421 police-reported incidents across Canada (Statistics Canada 2023). Since the onset of the COVID-19 pandemic, rates of NCDII have reportedly increased due to a greater use and reliance on online communication (De Rosa 2021). IBSV is a gendered crime; out of the 295 Canadian cases of NCDII reported to police in 2016, 92 per cent were reported by women (Aikenhead 2018, 122). Despite a lack of and need for a national survey in Canada that collects intersectional data on NCDII, we can learn from international surveys. A telephone survey by Data & Society of 3,002 American internet users aged fifteen and older found that Black internet users were more likely to have their images posted than white users (5 per cent versus 2 per cent; Lenhart, Ybarra, and Price-Feeney 2016, 6). The survey additionally found that internet users who identify as lesbian, gay, or bisexual were more likely than heterosexual internet users to have been threatened with NCDII (15 per cent versus 2 per cent) or to have experienced NCDII (7 per cent versus 5 per cent). A national survey in Australia of 4,274 participants found that individuals living with disabilities and Indigenous individuals were more likely to be targeted for NCDII (Henry, Powell, and Flynn 2017).

Although not yet widespread in Canadian politics, NCDII against public figures in Canada have occurred. Judge Lori Douglas in Manitoba had intimate photos of her posted online without her consent by her husband. Douglas was then subject to a disciplinary hearing during which the photos were shared with those at the hearing. After the hearing had gone on for four years without a result, Douglas retired, citing the trial and the victim-blaming she endured as the cause. She shared: "I was expendable to protect the view of what the judiciary should be. I was judged by a white male-dominated group of people who had a very particular take on how women should behave and what women should be about" (Giese 2016). Douglas's experience is similar to that of former representative Katie Hill in the United States, who also had her intimate photos posted online. It is purported that Hill's ex-partner leaked nude photos of Hill to conservative media (Finnegan and Pearce 2019). After the images were released more broadly by the media and amid wider controversy, Hill resigned, noting NCDII as the primary reason for her resignation. In her final speech in Congress, Hill decried the "misogynistic culture that gleefully consumed my naked pictures, capitalized on my sexuality, and enabled my abusive ex to continue that abuse, this time with the entire country watching" (Yashari 2019).

It is noteworthy that both Hill and Douglas had their intimate photos non-consensually shared by a partner. By comparison, former Canadian Conservative MP Tony Clement experienced the threat of NCDII as a result of him sharing sexually explicit images online to a person he thought was a woman, although it turned out to be someone soliciting the images for financial extortion (Tasker and Kapelos 2018). As more cases of NCDII are likely to emerge due to the proliferation of these technologies, it is essential to be attuned to gendered differences in perpetration and victimization and how that plays into broader systems of gender-based violence like intimate partner violence.

Similar to NCDII, non-consensual sexual deepfakes occur in a gendered manner. The first popular deepfake application, DeepNude, enabled users to upload a clothed woman who would then be "stripped" of her clothing, as the app would match the woman's face to a nude body. It only worked on women's bodies. New applications to produce sexual deepfake images include a version on popular messenger application Telegram, which also only works on women's bodies. Approximately 104,852 women internationally have had their images stripped and posted on Telegram as of the end of July 2020 (Ajder, Patrini, and Cavalli 2020). Non-consensual sexual deepfake videos have a similar history in focusing on women's bodies. The name for deepfakes comes from a Reddit user "deepfakes," who inserted celebrities into pornographic films starting with a popular non-consensual sexual deepfake of Gal Gadot, the actress from *Wonder Woman* (Turton and Justus 2018). A study of 14,678 deepfake videos in 2019 found that 96 per cent were pornographic, and of those, 99 per cent targeted women (Ajder et al. 2019).

While more research on rates of non-consensual sexual deepfakes experienced by individuals in politics remains to be done, one source of valuable information is the Sensity platform for deepfake tracing. Sensity scans the open and dark web in order to find deepfakes targeting public figures. It has a section specifically focused on politically active individuals. This chapter used the Sensity platform to track and assess deepfakes of the top two politically active men and women in the United States. In the absence of sufficient Canadian data, US-based data are illustrative of wider trends on the use of deepfakes and can allow us to project how this form of gender-based violence could disrupt the democratic process in Canada. Results are presented in Table 3.1.

As represented in Table 3.1, non-consensual sexual deepfakes target women in politics at extreme rates. In comparison, deepfakes of men in politics tend to insert men in different action and humour films.

Table 3.1. Percentage of sexual deepfakes of the top two US politically active men and women featured on the Sensity platform

Politically active individual by gender	General deepfakes	Sexual deepfakes	Total deepfakes	Percentage of sexual deepfakes (%)
Men				
Donald Trump	195	1	196	0.5
Arnold Schwarzenegger	96	0	96	0
Women				
Alexandria Ocasio-Cortez	4	42	46	91
Ivanka Trump	2	32	34	94

Note: Data was collected from the Sensity platform on 23 December 2020.

Gendered and Intersectional Impacts of IBSV

Gendered and intersectional impacts of IBSV capture how reactions to violence change based on the survivor's social locations, thus resulting in differing consequences for specific political actors (Bardall, Bjarnegård, and Piscopo 2020). There are many impacts of IBSV that are felt intensely and personally by survivors, including mental and physical health impacts (McGlynn et al. 2021). The impacts focused on here are those that relate more broadly to impacts when diverse political actors are targeted. This section starts by considering how IBSV has a gendered impact due to sexual double standards, which results in women being more likely to be blamed or discredited due to sexual imagery online. Next, it considers some general impacts of IBSV against political actors: silencing, distraction, and exclusion from political spaces. Finally, this section homes in specifically on impacts for individuals aspiring towards or currently in politician roles to capture differential impacts, depending on the political role.

When sexual images are released, women are impacted differently due to sexual double standards whereby women are disproportionately blamed and seen as sexually deviant after a non-consensual sexual image is shared (Mckinlay and Lavis 2020). Leading IBSV scholars Danielle Citron and Mary Anne Franks observed that "women would more likely suffer harm as a result of the posting of their naked images than their male counterparts. Gender stereotypes help explain why – women would be seen as immoral sluts for engaging in sexual activity, whereas men's sexual activity is generally a point of pride" (2014, 354).[5] Such a trend with IBSV is not unique but rather follows general sexual double standards where women are judged more harshly than men for comparable sexual behaviours (Zaikman and Mark 2014; Endendijk, van Baar, and Deković 2019). Due to the gendered and intersectional way in which women are impacted by sexual objectification and sexual double standards, they are also more likely to face consequences for sexual images and videos online.

Consistent with further forms of technology-facilitated violence, NCDII and non-consensual sexual deepfakes that target women and marginalized groups serve as another, emerging means to silence, exclude, and distract political actors. When individuals are silenced, their freedom of speech and democratic contribution is hindered. Bardall and Tenove's chapter 1 and Wagner and Young's chapter 2 in this book both share how violence in digital spaces like Twitter (now X) results in exclusion and silencing. Political actors are silenced as they fear engaging online due to the violence and hate they receive, which can result in closing their online accounts or limiting or altering their activity. IBSV also serves as a distraction from political work since political actors need to deal with this violence, including responding to it publicly, deleting or monitoring posts, and attempting to remove the content. As such, political actors who are targeted by IBSV have less time to do the work they want and need to do, including journalistic reporting, representing constituents, fundraising, drafting legislation, and holding rallies or events, diminishing their capacity to participate in the democratic process.

Although future research is needed on the topic, it is also possible that IBSV is targeted specifically at those who promote social justice issues like gender equality. Two examples are Anita Sarkeesian and Noelle Martin. Sarkeesian is a Canadian-American activist who explores women's representation in video games. A deepfake of her was uploaded to Pornhub, and users posted about how to share the video and ensure it did not get removed. Sarkeesian exclaimed that deepfakes are "used as a weapon to silence women, degrade women, show power over women, reducing us to sex objects" (Harwell 2018). Similarly, Martin found out while in university that non-consensual sexual deepfakes of her had been posted online. She shares that she spent years fighting to have the images removed. That struggle started a journey of activism to create legal responses to IBSV in her country, Australia, and globally. However, she points out: "You only seek to lose when you talk about something like this, because when you dare to speak about this kind of abuse, you expose yourself to more people seeing the very thing you don't want people to see" (Sherman 2021). Using video and images from Martin's public activism, more non-consensual sexual deepfakes of her have emerged.

For those who might aspire to a career in public office, IBSV may serve as another disincentive to consider this career path. Women already cite concerns about violence as a deterrent to entering politics. Consider a poll of 1,500 Canadian women between the ages of eighteen and thirty conducted by Abacus Data for Equal Voice in January 2022. The poll found that 73 per cent of young women were concerned about online harassment if they ran for office (Abacus Data 2022). Another survey conducted by Wagner (2022) found women, non-white individuals, and sexual minorities were most concerned about being attacked through social media. For those already in the role of a politician, IBSV can result in or contribute to the loss of their job, as cited by both Douglas and Hill. In her interview with survivors of NCDII, Samantha Bates (2012) interviewed Josephine (pseudonym), a former American politician, who had her intimate photos hacked. Despite the images not being shared, there were stories about alleged nude photos, and Josephine stepped down from her position, stating that the allegations were enough to ruin her reputation. All of these data point to the potential negative effects of IBSV for inclusive representation in Canada's political process.

When women and marginalized political actors are silenced or distracted, important stories, pieces of legislation, and advocacy efforts are hindered, resulting in a less democratic and less representative political system (Phillips 1995). IBSV against women and marginalized political actors makes a statement about who is and who is not welcome in politics. It serves to re-enforce traditional gender roles that deny women a right to be in political spaces. A joint letter by one hundred current and former women legislators from thirty countries called on Facebook to address gendered hate, including IBSV, on its platform, writing: "Make no mistake, these tactics, which are used on your platform for malicious intent, are meant to silence women, and ultimately undermine our democracies" (Di Meco and Wilfore 2021). When targeted at women and marginalized individuals, IBSV is not just an individual attack but also the re-enforcement of gender inequality and marginalization upon an entire group. It sends a message that is felt intimately by the targets and one that also invades their families, friends, colleagues, and communities.

Resistance and Strength of Survivors and Oppressed Groups

In addition to acknowledging the targets and impacts of IBSV, it is also critical to acknowledge the strength of survivors who share knowledge about this form of violence and lead advocacy efforts to end it. Similar to the #MeToo movement, IBSV has seen its own coming together of gender-oppressed individuals to support each other. Women on online platforms like TikTok have offered that, if someone looks like them and has a sexual image or video online, the person can claim it is the TikTok user as opposed to themself. This example is representative of ongoing solidarity among women and marginalized groups to care for each other in the face of systems of domination. Bardall and Tenove's chapter 1 in this book also shows how experiences of technology-facilitated violence can result in individuals becoming more resolute in their desire to engage politically, as well as prompting individuals to express solidarity with survivors. In addition to these individual efforts, broader changes and awareness are necessary to address IBSV.

Implications for Action

More generally as a form of sexual violence, IBSV will benefit from solutions geared to responding to sexual violence and serving survivors, including safe reporting mechanisms, bystander intervention training, and trauma-informed supports. Likewise, non-consensual sexual deepfakes will benefit from general responses to deepfakes (sexual or non-sexual). For instance, a report from the Standing Committee on Access to Information, Privacy and Ethics (2018) recommends legislation to regulate social media platforms, including removal of manipulated content like deepfakes. In addition to these more general responses, this chapter offers three implications for action specific to IBSV in politics.

1. Research IBSV in the Canadian Context

One of the barriers to more fully understanding IBSV is that national Canadian data on this issue are lacking. While there are national surveys in Australia and the United States, Canada has no equivalent research to help us discern the scale of the issue and those impacted (Henry, Powell, and Flynn 2017; Lenhart, Ybarra, and Price-Feeney 2016). There thus exists a necessity for quantitative, qualitative, and theoretical research on the gendered and intersectional nature of IBSV. In particular, a national survey that includes various questions about the intersecting oppressions individuals face would provide a clearer picture of this phenomenon in Canada. Specific to IBSV in politics, but also relevant to larger discussions of economic equity, is also the need to study the professional and democratic impacts of IBSV – a topic not typically included in existing research focused more on mental and physical health impacts. Questions should ask explicitly about the likelihood of running for politics and how that possibility was or could be impacted by IBSV.

2. Address Victim-Blaming and the Sexual Double Standards around Intimate Images

After former representative Katie Hill's intimate image was released, House Speaker Nancy Pelosi said: "It goes to show you, we should say to young candidates, and to kids in kindergarten really, be careful when transmitting photos" (Caygle and Ferris 2019). Likewise, the Canadian Centre for Child Protection campaign on NCDII, "Respect Yourself," held girls responsible for sending intimate photos with statements like the following:

> Do you think posting sexy poses of yourself online will get you attention? Reality check. Yeah! But is this the type of attention you want? **RESPECT YOURSELF**. (cited in Karaian 2014, 287)

Statements like those quoted above prop up a culture of victim-blaming, where the individual who is harmed is blamed for the violence they experienced. Similar to further forms of gender-based violence, women are disproportionately blamed for IBSV as well (Eaton and McGlynn 2020). To counter these narratives, organizations promoting political engagement need to challenge victim-blaming and sexual double standards. Advocates already doing this work include the US organization Run for Something, which, in response to Hill's NCDII, encouraged women to run regardless of intimate images. Amanda Litman (2019), co-founder of Run for Something, wrote: "You can run for office if you've been in sexual relationships or if you've taken private photos or sexted – and you wouldn't be alone ... Don't let anyone tell you it's not your turn or not your time." Likewise, Canadian organizations like Platform challenge victim-blaming as a result of sexual and gendered violence in Canadian politics.[6]

3. Build a National Initiative on IBSV

Thus far, Canada does not have a national initiative on IBSV that can coordinate awareness and prevention campaigns, in addition to supporting survivors. Building such an initiative is integral to sustained work on this form of violence. Canada could learn from the Revenge Porn Helpline in the United Kingdom, the Cyber Civil Rights Initiative in the United States (founded by IBSV survivor Holly Jacobs), and the Office of eSafety in Australia. These initiatives share information on IBSV, including how to request images be taken down and potential legal responses, in addition to providing front-line support to survivors through phone and chat services. A national initiative would signal that IBSV as a form of violence is not acceptable in Canada and could lead efforts to change behaviours that promote or trivialize IBSV.

Conclusion

This chapter contributes to the ongoing conversation about Canadian GBV-P by providing information about IBSV: what it is, who it targets, and how it impacts politics. IBSV remains a deeply concerning invasion of the autonomy, privacy, and equity of individuals in Canada that threatens the political participation of gender-oppressed and marginalized people. More and more Canadians are sharing intimate images as a form of sexual intimacy, and these images are being weaponized to produce harm. Likewise, intimate images are being falsely manufactured through non-consensual sexual deepfakes at increasing rates. Labelling IBSV as sexual violence and spreading awareness of it is a critical part of addressing GBV-P and supporting movements like #MeToo. While this chapter cautions that IBSV may harm political activity, it also recognizes the resilience and tenacity of survivors who continue to be politically active and without whom this chapter would not be possible. This chapter aims to support their work and promote the inclusion of more survivors in politics.

Supports

If you or someone you know has experienced IBSV, there are resources available. The British Columbia Society of Transition Houses offers information on technology safety and privacy, in addition to legal remedies for IBSV.[7] Please also reach out to your local sexual assault centre and culturally responsive organizations for support.

NOTES

1 Colloquially, IBSV is sometimes referred to as "revenge porn." However, the term "revenge porn" is inaccurate and offensive. Revenge implies that the person did something wrong that warrants or justifies violence and therefore places a problematic normative judgement on the survivor. The focus on revenge, furthermore, obscures the fact that sexual images are posted for a variety of motivations, including maintaining power and control over an individual or financial gain, not just or even primarily revenge (McGlynn et al. 2021). Likewise, the use of pornography to

describe IBSV serves to conflate consensual sex work with non-consensual sexual violence. As such, the use of pornography in this context stigmatizes sex work.
2 2SLGBTQQIA+ is an acronym for those who are two spirit, lesbian, gay, bisexual, transgender, queer, questioning, intersex, and asexual, with the inclusion of the plus sign acknowledging additional sexual orientations and gender identities.
3 It is important to note that survivors are not a monolithic group. What may be experienced by one survivor as a form of sexual violence may not be considered in the same way by another survivor. Likewise, there can be changes over time in whether something is considered a form of violence or what form it is considered to be.
4 Krook (2020) includes NCDII on page 204 and deepfakes on page 200 as forms of semiotic violence. She notes as well that forms of violence (for example, sexual, semiotic) overlap.
5 As Citron and Franks (2014) note, there are exceptions to this general observation, including instances where one's sexual orientation is oppressed.
6 Platform, on its website home page, defines itself as a "civic leadership platform for Black, Indigenous, and racialized young women and gender-diverse people." See the Platform website at https://www.theplatform.ca/.
7 The British Columbia Society of Transition Houses resources and information on technological safety and privacy can found at https://bcsth.ca/technology-safety-project-resources/.

REFERENCES

Abacus Data. 2022. *Women in Politics Study*. National Survey of 1,500 18–30 Year-Old Women in Canada. Conducted for Equal Voice. https://www.iknowpolitics.org/sites/default/files/equal-voice-jan-2022-tc-3.pdf.

Aikenhead, Moira. 2018. "Non-Consensual Disclosure of Intimate Images as a Crime of Gender-Based Violence." *Canadian Journal of Women and the Law* 30 (1): 117–43. https://doi.org/10.3138/cjwl.30.1.117.

Ajder, Henry, Giorgio Patrini, and Francesco Cavalli. 2020. *Automating Image Abuse: Deepfake Bots on Telegram*. Sensity. https://www.medianama.com/wp-content/uploads/Sensity-AutomatingImageAbuse.pdf.

Ajder, Henry, Giorgio Patrini, Francesco Cavalli, and Laurence Cullen. 2019. *The State of Deepfakes: Landscape, Threats, and Impact*. Sensity. https://regmedia.co.uk/2019/10/08/deepfake_report.pdf.

Alptraum, Lux. 2020. "Deepfake Porn Harms Adult Performers, Too." *Wired*, 15 January 2020. https://www.wired.com/story/deepfake-porn-harms-adult-performers-too/.

Anderson, Joel R., Elise Holland, Courtney Heldreth, and Scott P. Johnson. 2018. "Revisiting the Jezebel Stereotype: The Impact of Target Race on Sexual Objectification." *Psychology of Women Quarterly* 42 (4): 461–76. https://doi.org/10.1177/0361684318791543.

Bardall, Gabrielle, Elin Bjarnegård, and Jennifer M Piscopo. 2020. "How Is Political Violence Gendered? Disentangling Motives, Forms, and Impacts." *Political Studies* 68 (4): 916–35. https://doi.org/10.1177/0032321719881812.

Bates, Samantha. 2012. "'Stripped': An Analysis of Revenge Porn Victims' Lives after Victimization." Master's Thesis, Simon Fraser University.

Biroli, Flávia. 2018. "Violence against Women and Reactions to Gender Equality in Politics." *Politics & Gender* 14 (4): 681–5. https://doi.org/10.1017/S1743923X18000600.

Caygle, Heather, and Sarah Ferris. 2019. "Katie Hill's Downfall Highlights Stark Generational Divide among Democrats." *Politico*, 31 October 2019. https://www.politico.com/news/2019/10/31/katie-hill-resignation-splits-democrats-062082.

Citron, Danielle Keats. 2019. "Sexual Privacy." *The Yale Law Journal* 128 (7): 1870–1960. https://www.yalelawjournal.org/pdf/Citron_q8ew5jjf.pdf.

Citron, Danielle Keats, and Mary Anne Franks. 2014. "Criminalizing Revenge Porn." *Wake Forest Law Review* 49: 345–92. https://ssrn.com/abstract=2368946.

Connolly, Kate. 2021. "Suspected Russia-Led Cyber Campaign Targets Germany's Green Party Leader." *The Guardian*, 13 May 2021. https://www.theguardian.com/world/2021/may/13/suspected-russia-led-cyber-campaign-targets-germanys-green-party-leader.

Cook, Jesselyn. 2021. "A Powerful New Deepfake Tool Has Digitally Undressed Thousands of Women." *HuffPost*, 10 August 2021. https://www.huffpost.com/entry/deepfake-tool-nudify-women_n_6112d765e4b005ed49053822.

DeKeseredy, Walter S., and Martin D. Schwartz. 2016. "Thinking Sociologically about Image-Based Sexual Abuse: The Contribution of Male Peer Support Theory." *Sexualization, Media and Society* 2 (4). https://doi.org/10.1177/2374623816684692.

DeRosa, Katie. 2021. "As 'Revenge Porn' Spikes during Pandemic, B.C. Aims to Crack Down with Legislation." *Vancouver Sun*, 12 May 2021. https://vancouversun.com/news/local-news/as-revenge-porn-spikes-during-pandemic-b-c-aims-to-crack-down-with-legislation.

Di Meco, Lucina, and Kristina Wilfore. 2021. "Gendered Disinformation Is a National Security Problem." *Brookings*, 8 March 2021. https://www.brookings.edu/techstream/gendered-disinformation-is-a-national-security-problem/.

Eaton, Asia A., and Clare McGlynn. 2020. "The Psychology of Nonconsensual Porn: Understanding and Addressing a Growing Form of Sexual Violence." *Policy Insights from the Behavioral and Brain Sciences* 7 (2): 190–7. https://doi.org/10.1177/2372732220941534.

Endendijk, Joyce J., Anneloes L. van Baar, and Maja Deković. 2019. "He Is a Stud, She Is a Slut! A Meta-Analysis on the Continued Existence of Sexual Double Standards." *Personality and Social Psychology Review* 24 (2): 163–90. https://doi.org/10.1177/1088868319891310.

Everitt, Joanna Marie, and Michael Camp. 2014. "In Versus Out: LGBT Politicians in Canada." *Journal of Canadian Studies/Revue d'Études Canadiennes* 48 (1): 226–51. https://doi.org/10.3138/jcs.48.1.226.

Finnegan, Michael, and Matt Pearce. 2019. "GOP Enemies Wanted to Beat Katie Hill. Then They Got Her Nude Photos." *Los Angeles Times*, 31 October 2019. https://www.latimes.com/politics/story/2019-10-31/katie-hill-husband-revenge-porn-republicans.

Giese, Rachel. 2016. "Indecent Exposure." *Real Life*, 21 July 2016. https://reallifemag.com/indecent-exposure/.

Goodfellow, Ian J., Jean Pouget-Abadie, Mehdi Mirza, Bing Xu, David Warde-Farley, Sherjil Ozair, Aaron Courville, and Yoshua Bengio. 2014. "Generative Adversarial Networks." In *NIPS '14: Proceedings of the 27th International Conference on Neural Information Processing Systems – Volume 2*, edited by Z. Ghahramani, M. Welling, and C. Cortes, 2672–80. Cambridge, MA: MIT Press. https://dl.acm.org/doi/10.5555/2969033.2969125.

Gosse, Chandell, and Jacquelyn Burkell. 2020. "Politics and Porn: How News Media Characterizes Problems Presented by Deepfakes." *Critical Studies in Media Communication* 37 (5): 497–511. https://doi.org/10.1080/15295036.2020.1832697.

Gothreau, Claire M. 2021. "Sex Objects: How Self-Objectification Undermines Political Efficacy and Engagement." *Journal of Women, Politics & Policy* 42 (4): 275–96. https://doi.org/10.1080/1554477X.2021.1941630.

Harwell, Drew. 2018. "Fake-Porn Videos Are Being Weaponized to Harass and Humiliate Women." *The Washington Post*, 30 December 2018. https://www.washingtonpost.com/technology/2018/12/30/fake-porn-videos-are-being-weaponized-harass-humiliate-women-everybody-is-potential-target.

Henry, Nicola, and Asher Flynn. 2019. "Image-Based Sexual Abuse: Online Distribution Channels and Illicit Communities of Support." *Violence Against Women* 25 (16): 1932–55. https://doi.org/10.1177/1077801219863881.

Henry, Nicola, Anastasia Powell, and Asher Flynn. 2017. *Not Just 'Revenge Pornography': Australians' Experiences of Image-Based Abuse: A Summary Report*. Melbourne: RMIT University. https://researchmgt.monash.edu/ws/portalfiles/portal/214045352/revenge_porn_report_2017.pdf.

Hensley, Laura. 2017. "This Revenge Porn Site Targets Canadian University Students & No One Can Stop It." *Flare*, 4 July 2017. https://web.archive.org/web/20170915192634/http://www.flare.com/news/anonib-nude-photo-sharing-site/.

Karaian, Lara. 2014. "Policing 'Sexting': Responsibilization, Respectability and Sexual Subjectivity in Child Protection/Crime Prevention Responses to Teenagers' Digital Sexual Expression." *Theoretical Criminology* 18 (3): 282–99. https://doi.org/10.1177/1362480613504331.

Kelly, Liz. 1988. *Surviving Sexual Violence*. Cambridge: Polity Press.

Krook, Mona Lena. 2020. *Violence against Women in Politics*. New York: Oxford University Press.

Lenhart, Amanda, Michele Ybarra, and Myeshia Price-Feeney. 2016. *Nonconsensual Image Sharing: One in 25 Americans Has Been a Victim of 'Revenge Porn.'* New York: Data & Society Research Institute. https://datasociety.net/pubs/oh/Nonconsensual_Image_Sharing_2016.pdf.

Litman, Amanda. 2019. "A Fear of Revenge Porn Shouldn't Stop You from Running for Office." *MTV News*, 1 November 2019. http://www.mtv.com/news/3144642/katie-hill-revenge-porn-amanda-litman-run-for-something/.

Loughnan, Steve, Nick Haslam, Tess Murnane, Jeroen Vaes, Catherine Reynolds, and Caterina Suitner. 2010. "Objectification Leads to Depersonalization: The Denial of Mind and Moral Concern to Objectified Others." *European Journal of Social Psychology* 40 (5): 708–17. https://doi.org/10.1002/ejsp.755.

McGlynn, Clare, Kelly Johnson, Erika Rackley, Nicola Henry, Nicola Gavey, Asher Flynn, and Anastasia Powell. 2021. "'It's Torture for the Soul': The Harms of Image-Based Sexual Abuse." *Social & Legal Studies* 30 (4): 541–62. https://doi.org/10.1177/0964663920947791.

Mckinlay, Tahlee, and Tiffany Lavis. 2020. "Why Did She Send It in the First Place? Victim Blame in the Context of 'Revenge Porn.'" *Psychiatry, Psychology and Law* 27 (3): 386–96. https://doi.org/10.1080/13218719.2020.1734977.

Oger v. Whatcott (No. 7). 2019 BCHRT 58. https://www.canlii.org/en/bc/bchrt/doc/2019/2019bchrt58/2019bchrt58.html.

Pan, Jason. 2022. "Huang Jie Pans Court for Verdict in Deepfake Case." *Taipei Times*, 23 July 2022. https://www.taipeitimes.com/News/taiwan/archives/2022/07/23/2003782274.

Phillips, Anne. 1995. *The Politics of Presence*. Oxford: Clarendon Press.

Razack, Sherene H. 2016. "Sexualized Violence and Colonialism: Reflections on the Inquiry into Missing and Murdered Indigenous Women." *Canadian Journal of Women and the Law* 28 (2): i–iv. https://doi.org/10.3138/cjwl.28.2.i.

Ryan, Haley. 2021. "Former Dartmouth South Candidate Says Liberals Dropped Her over 'Boudoir' Photos." *CBC News*, 21 July 2021. https://

www.cbc.ca/news/canada/nova-scotia/former-dartmouth-south
-candidate-says-liberals-dropped-her-over-boudoir-photos-1.6112237.
Seabrook, Rita C., L. Monique Ward, and Soraya Giaccardi. 2019. "Less Than Human? Media Use, Objectification of Women, and Men's Acceptance of Sexual Aggression." *Psychology of Violence* 9 (5): 536–45. https://doi.org/10.1037/vio0000198.
Sherman, Justin. 2021. "'Completely Horrifying, Dehumanizing, Degrading': One Woman's Fight against Deepfake Porn." *CBS News*, 14 October 2021. https://www.cbsnews.com/news/deepfake-porn-woman-fights-online-abuse-cbsn-originals/.
Standing Committee on Access to Information, Privacy and Ethics. 2018. *Democracy under Threat: Risks and Solutions in the Era of Disinformation and Data Monopoly: Report of the Standing Committee on Access to Information, Privacy and Ethics*. House of Commons, Canada, 42nd Parliament, 1st Session, December 2018. https://www.ourcommons.ca/Content/Committee/421/ETHI/Reports/RP10242267/ethirp17/ethirp17-e.pdf.
Statistics Canada. 2023. "Table 35-10-0177-01. Incident-Based Crime Statistics, by Detailed Violations, Canada, Provinces, Territories, Census Metropolitan Areas and Canadian Forces Military Police." Statistics Canada. https://doi.org/10.25318/3510017701-eng.
Sue, Derald Wing, Jennifer Bucceri, Annie I. Lin, Kevin L. Nadal, and Gina C. Torino. 2007. "Racial Microaggressions and the Asian American Experience." *Cultural Diversity and Ethnic Minority Psychology* 13 (1): 72–81. https://doi.org/10.1037/1099-9809.13.1.72.
Tasker, John Paul, and Vassy Kapelos. 2018. "Conservative MP Tony Clement Resigns Commons Duties over Sexting Scandal." *CBC News*, 6 November 2018. https://www.cbc.ca/news/politics/tony-clement-sexting-1.4894889.
Tibbetts, John H. 2018. "The Frontiers of Artificial Intelligence." *Bioscience* 68 (1): 5–10. https://doi.org/10.1093/biosci/bix136.
Tunney, Catharine. 2021. "Government House Leader Calls for Investigation into Leaked Photo of Naked Liberal MP." *CBC News*, 15 April 2021. https://www.cbc.ca/news/politics/william-amos-liberal-mp-naked-parliament-1.5988649.
Turton, William, and Matthew Justus. 2018. "'Deepfake' Videos Like That Gal Gadot Porn Are Only Getting More Convincing – and More Dangerous." *Vice News*, 27 August 2018. https://www.vice.com/en/article/qvm97q/deepfake-videos-like-that-gal-gadot-porn-are-only-getting-more-convincing-and-more-dangerous.
Wagner, Angelia. 2022. "Tolerating the Trolls? Gendered Perceptions of Online Harassment of Politicians in Canada." *Feminist Media Studies* 22 (1): 32–47. https://doi.org/10.1080/14680777.2020.1749691.

Ward, L. Monique. 2016. "Media and Sexualization: State of Empirical Research, 1995–2015." *The Journal of Sex Research* 53 (4–5): 560–77. https://doi.org/10.1080/00224499.2016.1142496.

Yashari, Leora. 2019. "The Double Standard & Misogynist Culture That Chased Katie Hill Out of Congress." *Refinery29*, 1 November 2019. https://www.refinery29.com/en-ca/2019/11/8668889/the-double-standard-misogynist-culture-that-chased-katie-hill-out-of-congress.

Yorkshire Post, The. 2016. "'Revenge Porn' Is Not a Sexual Offence, Minister Tells Yorkshire Victim." *The Yorkshire Post*, 18 January 2016. https://www.yorkshirepost.co.uk/news/crime/revenge-porn-not-sexual-offence-minister-tells-yorkshire-victim-1805932.

Zaikman, Yuliana, and Michael J. Mark. 2014. "Ambivalent Sexism and the Sexual Double Standard." *Sex Roles* 71 (9–10): 333–44. https://doi.org/10.1007/s11199-014-0417-1.

PART TWO

Violence against Women in Politics Reporting in Canadian Mainstream Media

4 Psychological Violence, Media Effects, Counter-Speech, and Political Attitudes

MELANEE THOMAS AND SCOTT PRUYSERS

Introduction

Canadian workplaces are required by occupational health and safety guidelines to provide employees with a safe working environment free of harassment and abuse.[1] Despite this requirement, verbal harassment remains common, and women are more likely to experience verbal harassment than men (Hango and Moyser 2018). Still, many would consider it beyond the pale to be told "Fuck you!" as a result of their work. Consider, then, how violent that type of workplace harassment is when it is transposed into a public space and delivered in front of the target's children. This particularly egregious example happened to then federal minister of the environment, Catherine McKenna, in the fall of 2019 (Figure 4.1), although similar examples of violence and harassment directed at women in Canadian politics abound (see Rabson 2019; Glowacki and Foote 2019; Trynacity 2017, 2018; Crawley 2017; Burke 2019; Krook 2020).

Psychological violence is the most common form of gender-based violence in politics (GBV-P). It includes but is not limited to verbal harassment and abuse by members of the public, delivered in person, over email or the phone, and (increasingly) online via social media. The point of this violence is to attack women's place in politics and to stymie or prevent women from engaging in political work (Krook 2020). A 2016 study by the Inter-Parliamentary Union, for example, found that 82 per cent of women parliamentarians in their sample reported being subject to psychological violence. This figure includes 66 per cent who reported being subject to humiliating sexual or sexist remarks; 44 per cent who had been subject to threats of death, rape, beating, or abduction; and 42 per cent who had humiliating or sexually charged images of themselves spread through social media (Inter-Parliamentary Union 2016, 3).

Figure 4.1. Headline highlighting threats against Catherine McKenna

Politics

Threats, abuse move from online to real world, McKenna now requires security

Minister was confronted outside a movie theatre while walking with her children

Mia Rabson · The Canadian Press · Posted: Sep 07, 2019 11:34 AM ET | Last Updated: September 7, 2019

Though the study of GBV-P is relatively new (Krook 2020), it is commonly thought that witnessing psychological violence against women in politics directly and/or through news reports creates a chill for other women. Many expect that psychological violence against women in politics prevents other women from developing nascent political ambition and an interest in a political career. For example, former Australian prime minister Julia Gillard has explicitly stated that online harassment and fear it would translate into in-person attacks "is preventing women from standing up and serving in public life" (Hunt 2016). If left unmitigated, therefore, gender-based online harassment could translate into yet another barrier to women's participation in electoral politics as candidates (Wagner 2022). This violence works on two levels, either because some women choose not to run as candidates at all or because those women who do enter politics face a hostile working environment that does not exist for men. Psychological GBV-P may be common precisely because it is perceived to be effective at stopping women from doing political work. While limited, preliminary evidence shows that this violence is worse for Black women representatives, suggesting that GBV-P is exacerbated and amplified across other forms of systemic oppression beyond gender (Krook 2020).

This chapter builds on this research to ask how witnessing psychological GBV-P in news reports affects people as news consumers, outside of elected politics. We address two sets of research questions. First, how does learning about GBV-P affect how someone views *themself* in politics? Does exposure to media content that documents this violence suppress people's nascent political ambition, internal efficacy, and political interest? If consuming news media about GBV-P leads some, especially women, to (further) disengage from politics, they may not only be less likely to consider running for office but also less likely to make representational requests from their representatives and less willing to participate in democratic processes more generally. This reluctance, in turn, may have negative downstream consequences for the health and vibrancy of both representative and deliberative democracy. Second, how does witnessing GBV-P affect how people *evaluate* the objects of that violence? Is reading news about a violent attack against a politician associated with more negative evaluations of that politician's character and competence, especially if the victim is a woman? The fact that news reports about GBV-P may negatively affect voter perceptions of those representatives suggests that GBV-P creates additional perceptual barriers for women representatives beyond the already steep costs associated with it.

We answer these questions using an original survey experiment conducted with Canadian adults, where participants were randomly assigned to read a news story based on a report of the real-world attack on a federal politician in Canada. One experimental group read a news story in which the politician attacked was a woman; the other group read the same story, but the politician under attack was a man.[2] We also include a control condition in order to have a baseline understanding of political attitudes to compare against (that is, internal efficacy, political interest, and so on) for our first research question. Note, however, we do not utilize the control for our second research question since there is no politician to evaluate (this group did not read a news story). Instead, we compare the man and the woman politicians' conditions to explore whether being the victim of psychological violence penalizes women disproportionately. This set-up is a strict test because it examines the effects of exposure to a single instance of GBV-P. The reality, however, is that this violence is iterative and repeated, suggesting the effects we find from one single news story are likely to underestimate the full effects of GBV-P in practice, where there may be exposure to repeated, sometimes frequent, real-world instances.

The analysis reveals mixed, even unexpected, results. On the first question (internal attitudes), results show that exposure to media content documenting an instance of GBV-P against an elected official has no discernible effect on participants' ambition, interest, or efficacy. On the second question (perceptions of the victim), we find with remarkable consistency that the *man*, not the woman, victim is perceived as weaker on nearly every trait we consider. The unexpected results warrant replication and provide a variety of avenues for fruitful future research.

We begin by theorizing why events like those in the news story noted above constitute gender-based psychological violence in politics and why gendered mediation helps explain the reason we expect news reports about GBV-P might affect the political ambition and engagement of people who simply learn of it through the news, as well as why it might be expected to influence the perceptions of the elected official (that is, the victim). After outlining our data and experimental design, we present our results and then conclude with a brief discussion of the implications for action.

Defining Psychological GBV-P

While there are many forms of violence against women in politics, psychological GBV-P is the most common. It includes, but is not limited to, "death threats, rape threats, intimidation, threats against family members, verbal abuse" and can occur inside or outside political settings and be carried out "in person, by telephone, or via digital means" (Krook 2020, 139). The point is to negatively affect someone's "mental state or emotional" well-being by "degrading and demoralizing" them (139). Estimates suggest that over 80 per cent of women parliamentarians have experienced some form of psychological violence. Though lower numbers of women in politics report rape and death threats, these incidents increase when women parliamentarians are under the age of forty. The goal of these attacks is clear: "to frighten, degrade, and bully women to prevent them from continuing their political work" (140).

Examples in Canadian politics are commonplace. Following her party's unexpected election result in 2015, Rachel Notley quickly became one of, if not the most, threatened premiers in Canada. A particularly brutal attack involved pre-arranging her funeral (Trynacity 2018). Other examples include memes of Notley' face in the middle of a rifle's scope (CTV Calgary Staff 2016) and a variety of social media users commenting that someone should "kill her" or "just shoot her already" (Wagner 2022, 33). After the 2019 federal election, news coverage highlighted how strict several women members of Parliament (MPs) were about their office security in response to threats and also noted the toll those threats took on their staff (Burke 2019; see also Cloutier, chapter 9, this volume). Reporting on this GBV-P revealed a number of striking revelations. First, racialized women MPs and their staff, often also racialized women, appear to face a disproportionate amount of psychological abuse. Second, GBV-P is not limited to elected officials. Women involved in non-governmental organizations and political activism are also subject to similar abuse (Rabson 2019).[3] Third, a clear trajectory is evident: women elected to politics, or doing unelected political work, report that the psychological GBV-P starts, or is most clearly manifest, online and then shifts to in-person attacks. A growing body of evidence finds that online harassment and incivility, particularly on social media, is disproportionately directed at women in politics, especially racialized women (see Hunt, Evershed, and Liu 2016). Canada, of course, is no exception, especially in the case when women politicians are highly visible online (Rheault, Rayment, and Musulan 2019).

There are at least two grounds on which some may disagree being told "Fuck you!" constitutes psychological GBV-P. First, some may suggest that these kinds of verbal attacks are just part and parcel of doing politics. We argue that, because this incident occurred in a public setting when a woman politician was with her children, it appears that the motive behind the attack meets the definition of psychological violence outlined above, rather than just a regular cost of doing politics. Similarly, other aspects of the news report, including wishing terrible illnesses on politicians' children and threats of sexualized violence, are clearly best understood as incidents of psychological violence.[4]

Second, others may argue that gendered discrimination is a relic of the past and that these threats or attacks do not constitute gender-based political violence. Yet, denying that these attacks are gendered does not remove the gendered elements from them. Instead, the example is clear: McKenna is referred to as "Barbie," "bitch," and "cunt," all highly gendered terms. Sexualized violence and threats of sexualized violence are predominantly directed at women by men, both inside and outside of politics (Krook 2020; Cotter and Savage 2019). Denying the gendered aspects of this violence connects it closely to sexism, either by suggesting that women's gains are too large or too fast or that they are at the expense of men. Studies documenting psychological GBV-P specifically point to misogynists and anti-feminists as perpetrators (Krook 2020).

Mediated Violence, Mediated Attitudes?

It is well established that women's political ambition, internal efficacy, and interest are all significantly lower than that of comparable men (Gidengil et al. 2004; Thomas 2012). On the issue of ambition, for instance, evidence suggests men are twice as likely as women to have seriously considered running for political office (Fox and Lawless 2014). A variety of factors such as personality, socialization, gender norms, and persistent stereotypes have been identified as contributing to these gender gaps in political attitudes (Lawless and Fox 2005; Pruysers and Blais 2017; Gidengil, Giles, and Thomas 2008). We suspect that two additional factors – gendered mediation and media effects – also offer useful lenses to help explain why these gender gaps persist, since it is reasonable to expect that witnessing sexism and gender-based psychological violence in politics in the news might affect (women's) attitudes about politics such as political ambition, efficacy, and interest.

Gendered mediation refers to the process by which gender norms and roles are "(re)created and (re)enforced through the media's presentation of politics and politicians to the public" (Thomas et al. 2021, 389). The most obvious examples of this process are gendered coverage, where the volume, content, and tone of women politicians' news coverage are significantly different from men's.[5] Importantly, though, gendered mediation occurs when women and men in politics are covered the exact same way, precisely because politics is a masculinized activity. Sports, battle, and confrontation are all stereotypically associated with men and with politics; thus, when women politicians are covered in this same way, that coverage creates "subtle and insidious forms of gender bias" that cue women as atypical, less competent or appropriate, or otherwise not belonging in politics (Gidengil and Everitt 1999, 106).

Simply put, while some coverage of women in politics is explicitly gendered and sexist, other coverage that seems neutral precisely because it is exactly the same as men's coverage still has gendered consequences that are often (though not always) negative for women politicians (Trimble 2017). Reminding audiences that women are participating in a typically masculine activity, such as politics, conjures incongruence across stereotypes associated with being a "good woman" and a "good politician." This incongruence is perhaps one reason why women politicians are stereotyped much more negatively than are women in general *and* men in politics (Schneider and Bos 2014).

While most research on gendered mediation focuses on news and media content, we focus here on audience reaction to gendered mediation of political news. Audience reactions are the result of exposure to media and include "how people react to, digest, and perhaps even change their thinking and behaviour in response to the news" (Trimble 2017, 9). Reactions can be both intentional and not, fleeting or long-standing, and produce change or enforce the status quo (Potter 2012). And, because of masculine political norms, these audience effects may be clearly gendered, even when the news people are reacting to has no explicit or obvious gendered bias.

It is commonly assumed, though rarely tested, that gendered news coverage and gendered mediation are a barrier for women in politics because by (re)creating and (re)enforcing gendered norms, or creating dissonance between the idea of what it means to be a "woman" and a "politician," people in the audience may punish women politicians or infer that politics is not for them as women (Pruysers and Blais 2017). The effects generated by gendered mediation may lead women to disengage from politics in general, while men's political interest, efficacy, and ambition remain intact. This effect is consistent with evidence from outside the media and politics literature, which shows that exposure to "ambient" sexism can result in a decline of self-esteem, self-efficacy, and career aspiration in women (Bradley-Geist, Rivera, and Geringer 2015). The mechanism has been called the "bystander" effect: individuals can be negatively affected by sexism "despite not being targeted directly" (Haraldsson and Wängnerud 2019). Similarly, theories of gender-affinity and shared gender consciousness (Goodyear-Grant and Croskill 2011) also suggest that women might be affected by witnessing psychological violence against other women since they can empathize more strongly with the victim. Furthermore, research specifically on exposure to gender-based violence via films shows that audience reactions are gendered, with women being less and men being more accepting of intimate partner violence (Malamuth and Check 1981). Thus, it is plausible that indirect exposure to GBV-P via news media could have negative implications about how individuals, particularly women, view themselves in relation to political life. Consistent with the bystander effect, seeing other women treated in a violent fashion while engaging in politics is expected to dampen positive political attitudes such as ambition and political interest among women. This expectation holds if the reporting about GBV-P is neutral or seemingly analogous to attacks directed against politicians who are men (for example, gendered mediation) or if the news coverage is more negative in its presentation of women politicians as targets of GBV-P (for example, gender-biased coverage).

If gendered mediation and its corresponding media effects, especially with respect to content such as psychological GBV-P, are expected to influence internal political attitudes like political interest, it is likely that the same media content will also impact other attitudes such as candidate evaluations. There is a large literature on media effects regarding agenda setting, framing, priming, knowledge transmission, shaping of policy attitudes/preferences, and so on (see, for example, Weaver 2007; Meltzer et al. 2021; Druckman and Parkin 2005). Simply put, "citizens learn about politics and government from the news they watch on television and read in newspapers" (Gerber, Karlan, and Bergan 2009, 35). For example, voters learn about their representatives from the media. Given that the average voter does not personally interact with their elected officials, or even candidates during elections for that matter, their perceptions of these individuals are formed as a result of exposure to media coverage (Balmas and Sheafer 2010; Bos, van der Brug, and de Vreese 2011). As such, it is not surprising that there is good evidence documenting the way in which media content can shape trait perceptions of candidates (Eberl, Wagner, and Boomgaarden 2017). Evidence, for instance, explicitly shows that negative news coverage of a candidate's appearance – a key part of gendered mediation and gendered coverage – negatively affects how voters see them (Hayes, Lawless, and Baitinger 2014).

We suspect that being the victim of psychological violence will result in more negative candidate perceptions. This perception will be more salient for women politicians since it aligns with currently held stereotypes that view women as less well suited to hold political office (Streb et al. 2008; Chen et al. 2023). In addition, research suggests that women victims of assault and harassment are attributed more blame than men (Howard 1984; Bongiorno et al. 2020). As such, we expect the MP in the female politician condition to be rated systematically lower on trait perceptions compared to the MP in the male politician condition.

The preceding discussion creates a tension between GBV-P and gendered mediation and media effects. By definition, men in politics cannot experience violence the same way women do. This reality is analogous to other forms of sexism, misogyny, and sexualization. Some evidence suggests that men's political ambition falls to women's levels when they are presented with trivializing and sexualized news coverage of a man in politics, though, in reality, that coverage is almost exclusively reserved for women (Pruysers, Thomas, and Blais 2020). Thus, an additional problem of GBV-P is that women, non-binary, transgender, and gender non-conforming politicians are the exclusive targets, not men. Unlike sexualization, though, it is plausible that some men in politics may experience seemingly random members of the public shouting obscenities at them. The difference is that, for men in politics, this harassment may just be the cost of doing politics. But when directed at women, the goal of these attacks is "to frighten, degrade, and bully women to prevent them from continuing their political work" (Krook 2020, 140).

Given that psychological violence is the most common form of GBV-P (Krook 2020, 139), it follows that this form may also be the most widely reported in the media. Establishing whether, in fact, it is the case is beyond the scope of this chapter. Instead, our goal is to document some of the possible effects of news reports about these attacks on those consuming the news. Documentation will help determine how audience reaction to news about violence against women in politics affects women's subjective political self-evaluations or their evaluations of the subjects of those attacks. While we are not making a normative claim that the media should not report instances of psychological violence, we do expect exposure to have negative effects for many diverse representatives, including women, non-binary, transgender, and gender non-conforming politicians.

Data and Method

Our data are drawn from a survey experiment of 603 Canadians conducted in the fall of 2020. Data were collected by the research firm Leger using the online survey platform Decipher. Mean age of the participants in the study was 46.3 (SD = 17.3), with an age range of 18 to 88 years of age. Participants were evenly distributed among men (49.8 per cent) and women (49.9 per cent). Less than 1 per cent of participants identified as gender non-conforming or non-binary.[6] A majority of participants (72 per cent) identified as white or European. Participants completed a fifteen-minute survey about their media habits, demographics, and political attitudes.

Prior to receiving the politically oriented questions, participants were randomly assigned to one of three experimental conditions (two treatments and a control). In the experimental conditions, participants were asked to read a news story about a Canadian MP who was the victim of psychological violence (see appendix 1 for details). Adapted from a CBC story about Catherine McKenna (Rabson 2019), the article highlighted a verbal attack where a man approached the minister in public and yelled "Fuck you!" The article reports that the threats have escalated to the point that the minister, on occasion, needs a security detail and that the threats extend to her loved ones. The name and portfolio of the minister were altered from the original story in our treatment conditions so as not to cue partisanship, and the article was shortened to about 250 words to ensure participants remained attentive. In the first experimental condition (n = 200), the minister was named Stephanie Thompson, appointed to the Transport portfolio. In the second experimental condition (n = 201), we utilized the same treatment but altered the sex of the MP by changing their name (David rather than Stephanie) and gender pronouns. Participants in our control condition (n = 202) did not receive a news article and instead continued through the survey uninterrupted. Balance tests confirmed that random assignment worked as intended and that the conditions were equivalent in their make-up. Condition assignment does not predict factors such as income, education, gender, or age.[7]

To measure internal political attitudes, we drew upon a variety of measures, administered post-treatment, which were adapted from the broader political behaviour literature. To capture nascent political ambition, we asked participants to rate their interest in a political career on a scale ranging from 0 (no interest at all) to 10 (a great deal of interest) in response to the question, "In general, how interested are you in a career in politics?"[8] To capture political interest more generally, we relied on a similar question, "How interested are you in politics generally?" that asked participants to rate their political interest on the same 0 to 10 scale. To measure internal efficacy, we used a battery of seven items ("Sometimes politics and government seem so complicated that a person like me can't really understand what's going on"; "People like me don't have anything to say about what government does"; and the like). These seven items have a Cronbach's alpha of 0.71 and were analysed as a single item. All three outcomes (ambition, interest, efficacy) were rescaled to range from 0 to 1 to facilitate interpretation and comparison. Taken together, these three items allowed us to consider the extent to which exposure to media content that documents psychological violence affects attitudes about oneself in politics.

To assess attitudes about the target of psychological violence, we had respondents rate the (fictional) politician from the news story they had read on a series of traits. Rating was done on a 0 to 10 scale where "10" described the politician very well and "0" did not. The traits we assessed include intelligent, knowledgeable, ambitious, commands respect, inspiring, compassionate, moral, trustworthy, caring, and responsible. As the only difference between the two experimental conditions was the gender of the politician, this rating allowed us to compare across conditions (woman versus man) to consider whether women are systematically penalized for being the victim of psychological violence.

Results

Internal Political Attitudes

We begin by looking at the aggregate numbers by experimental condition. The question here is whether exposure to news content about psychological violence towards elected officials, regardless of the sex of the participant, affects political attitudes. Does, for instance, exposure to this kind of content – which shows elected officials being verbally attacked in public – dampen interest in a political career? Consider, for instance, a recent *Toronto Star* headline regarding the resignation of a prominent federal cabinet minister: "After all the threats and online abuse, no wonder Catherine McKenna is leaving politics" (Delacourt 2021). Figure 4.2 provides the mean score on each of our three attitudinal outcomes of interest (nascent ambition, political interest, and internal efficacy) by condition. Looking at the aggregate data by condition reveals no significant differences. Participants in the control condition (our baseline) did not express significantly higher interest, ambition, or efficacy compared to those exposed to the media treatments in which elected officials were verbally attacked. Mean political interest in the control condition was 0.57 (on a 0 to 1 scale). Interest in the treatment

Figure 4.2. Political attitudes by condition

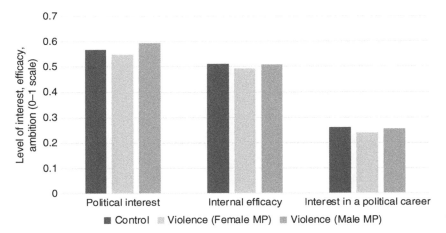

conditions is roughly equivalent, at 0.59 in the man politician condition and 0.55 in the woman politician condition.

This figure only tells us part of the story. While there may not be an identifiable pattern in the aggregate, it is entirely possible that there are meaningful differences when separating men and women. Since psychological violence, and toxicity and incivility more generally, are disproportionately targeted towards women, there is good reason to expect gender differences in the reaction to this kind of media content.[9] In particular, while there are no significant differences in the aggregate, we expect to see women's attitudes to be significantly dampened in the violence condition where the subject (victim) is also a woman. Figure 4.3 examines only women participants to explore this possibility further. Yet, as was the case in the aggregate, we see no significant differences across the various conditions. Mean political ambition, for example, is 0.18 in the control compared to 0.15 in the woman MP condition and 0.18 in the man MP condition. We find the same pattern with men (not shown): the media treatment had no observable effect on the political attitudes of participants.

On this first question, then, the answer is clear: exposure to our media treatments had no meaningful effect on how participants viewed themselves in politics. These null results are consistent across three different political attitudes (ambition, interest, and efficacy) as well as for both men and women. While we expected that media content documenting psychological

Figure 4.3. Political attitudes by condition (women only)

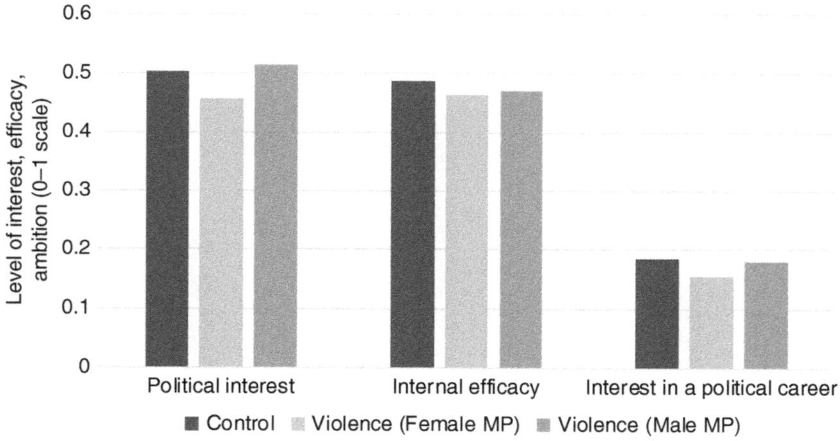

[Bar chart showing Level of interest, efficacy, ambition (0-1 scale) on y-axis for three categories: Political interest, Internal efficacy, Interest in a political career. Each category has three bars: Control, Violence (Female MP), Violence (Male MP). Political interest: ~0.50, ~0.46, ~0.51. Internal efficacy: ~0.48, ~0.46, ~0.47. Interest in a political career: ~0.18, ~0.15, ~0.17.]

violence against elected officials would dampen political attitudes, especially among women, this expectation isn't borne out by the data.

Perceptions of the Target

The next question we address is whether exposure to this content affects evaluations of the targets of psychological violence. In particular, are women politicians penalized more than men for being the subjects (that is, the victims) of psychological violence? Recall that to explore this question we had participants evaluate the MP in the news story they had been assigned to read. Participants made their evaluation on a 0 to 10 thermometer scale for ten different traits that are commonly used to assess candidates and politicians: intelligent, knowledgeable, ambitious, commands respect, inspiring, compassionate, moral, trustworthy, caring, and responsible. These traits are also gendered and congruent with some gender stereotypes of politicians (Schneider and Bos 2014). We were interested in whether the woman victim would be systematically rated lower than the man victim on these traits (see Table 4.1). Included is the mean and standard deviation (SD) for each trait by condition as well as the *p* value and effect size (Cohen's *d* with 95 per cent confidence interval [CI]) for each comparison.

In contrast to the previous results on internal political attitudes, here we find considerable gendered differences, though the results are not in the expected direction. For seven of the ten traits, the woman MP

Table 4.1. Perceptions of the victims of psychological violence

	Man MP mean (SD)	Woman MP mean (SD)	Cohen's d [95% CI]	p
Intelligent	5.85 (2.00)	6.51 (2.23)	0.31 [0.11, 0.51]	.002
Knowledgeable	5.62 (2.00)	6.31 (2.20)	0.33 [0.13, 0.52]	.001
Ambitious	5.63 (2.26)	6.19 (2.15)	0.25 [0.06, 0.45]	.012
Commands respect	5.39 (2.20)	6.26 (2.19)	0.40 [0.20, 0.59]	.000
Inspiring	5.18 (2.30)	5.85 (2.40)	0.28 [0.09, 0.48]	.005
Compassionate	5.58 (2.11)	5.96 (2.13)	0.18 [−0.02, 0.38]	.067
Moral	5.63 (2.14)	6.10 (2.32)	0.21 [0.01, 0.41]	.036
Trustworthy	5.30 (2.18)	5.92 (2.24)	0.28 [0.08, 0.48]	.005
Caring	5.58 (2.10)	5.97 (2.17)	0.18 [−0.01, 0.38]	.062
Responsible	5.87 (2.16)	6.29 (2.32)	0.19 [−0.01, 0.38]	.061

Note: Evaluations were made on 0 to 10 thermometer scale.

who was the victim of psychological violence was rated significantly *higher* than the man counterpart ($p < .05$). This is the case for the following traits: intelligent, knowledgeable, ambitious, commands respect, inspiring, moral, and trustworthy. Most of these are traits that are typically associated with *men* in politics, not women (Schneider and Bos 2014). The other three more feminine traits (compassionate, caring, and responsible) follow the same direction but do not reach conventional levels of significance, though it is worth noting that each is significant at the $p < .10$ level. Calculating the effect size for each comparison, using Cohen's *d*, reveals that, although the effects are consistent, they are relatively modest in size.

It is important to note that our design allows us to compare the man MP and the woman MP conditions and detect differences between them. It does not, however, allow us to isolate whether men in politics are penalized for being the victim of psychological violence or whether women, perhaps due to sympathy/empathy, are viewed more favourably for being attacked. Likewise, our design does not capture the possibility that voters have baseline preferences for candidates who are men over women (see Dassonneville, Quinlan, and McAllister 2021). While further research is needed, our results suggest that women are not heavily penalized systematically or disproportionately for being the subjects of psychological violence, at least with respect to voter evaluations. The penalty, perhaps, is being subjected to GBV-P in the first place. Future research is needed to untangle the precise direction of the effects identified here (perhaps longer vignettes with pre and post measures of candidate evaluations).

Discussion and Next Steps

We have good reason to expect that witnessing psychological GBV-P might suppress women's internal political attitudes. We also have good reason to believe that people may rate or evaluate the target of this psychological violence more poorly, especially if they are women. Yet, the evidence presented here is clear: reading about a woman politician being psychologically attacked in public in front of her children does not negatively affect women's internal political attitudes, such as their levels of political ambition, interest, and efficacy. Similarly, we find no compelling evidence showing that women politicians are disproportionately negatively evaluated as a result of news stories about the violence they experience.

How can we make sense of these unexpected and null findings? On the question of internal political attitudes, one possible explanation is that psychological violence is commonplace, even normalized, in contemporary democratic politics. As a result, additional exposure no longer has an impact on individuals' internal attitudes about politics. In other words, as a result of desensitization, exposure to this kind of media content really doesn't have an effect on political attitudes. Relatedly, another possibility is that one exposure to this kind of media content is simply not powerful enough to illicit a response. It is possible that sustained exposure over a longer period would yield results, particularly, perhaps, because that repeated exposure to such instances of violence is more consistent with reality. Another possibility is that this media effect simply maintains the status quo with respect to these political attitudes rather than sparking a change. All of these explanations are plausible and require further attention in future research.[10]

With respect to candidate evaluations, it is plausible that ideas surrounding masculinity and femininity inform how participants viewed these politicians under attack. Women may generate more sympathy as a stereotypical damsel in distress, while men may be punished simply because some think it is unmanly to be attacked in this manner. It is also possible that the politician's clear role as a caregiver in these treatments affects the evaluations. Both politicians in these treatments violate gender role congruity: the woman for being a politician and the man for being a victim. Women are generally stereotyped as being compassionate and caring as part of caring social roles that are stereotyped as feminine (see Ditonto, Hamilton, and Redlawsk 2014; Kahn 1996; Huddy and Terkildsen 1993). Given this stereotype, we find it striking that there are no statistically significant gender differences in ratings of the attacked politicians on being compassionate, caring, or responsible. This result may reflect a perceived violation of social roles on the part of women in politics and may be moderated or exacerbated by factors such as race and sexual orientation (see Schneider and Bos 2014, 2019; Thomas and Bittner 2017). Similarly, the male politician is rated especially low on "commands respect" and "inspiring." Future research could probe if this perception is part of a "masculinity" penalty associated with being attacked and if it is exacerbated by sexism and more traditional notions of masculinity.

Finally, one reason why these treatments may not have produced stronger results is that the treatment includes an example of counter-speech. Counter-speech helps address violent narratives about women in politics by presenting an alternative without censoring the violent speech itself (Krook 2020, 149). The article our experiment is based on includes counter-speech, and we retained it here. If the goal of psychological violence against women in politics is to keep them from doing their job (that is, politics), then the counter-speech makes it clear that women in politics say "I'm not going to let this stop me," which could be powerful indeed. Future research should address whether the effect of mediated psychological violence on individual political attitudes and candidate evaluations change when counter-speech is absent.

Implications for Action

In light of our findings, we propose the following recommendations:

1 All coverage of violence against women in politics should include counter-speech at a minimum, if not semiotic reversal. Unlike counter-speech, semiotic reversal openly challenges the violent and sexist language on the grounds of acceptability and demands those who use it take responsibility for their bad behaviour (Krook 2020, 211). Counter-speech and semiotic reversal can also be used by bystanders on social media and in person if the context is safe.
2 Attention should be drawn to the ubiquity of psychological GBV-P to raise awareness and build solidarity with the diverse representatives subjected to it. Relatedly, future research may also wish to consider the extent to which men are subjects of GBV-P as well as public perceptions of such instances of violence.
3 Evidence shows that some women committed to running for public office are not dissuaded by psychological violence (Wagner 2022). It is plausible, though, that awareness of psychological GBV-P creates a chill for potential candidates in the political pipeline. Those involved in candidate recruitment, including campaign schools for women candidates, should explicitly address this issue by offering

concrete advice and strategies for implementing counter-speech and semiotic reversal in campaigns.

APPENDIX 1: EXPERIMENTAL TREATMENT WORDING (FEMALE POLITICIAN CONDITION)

Stephanie Thompson Adds New Security Detail as Threats Move from Online to Real World[11]

Transport Minister Stephanie Thompson says she was recently walking outside a movie theatre when a car slowly pulled to a stop beside her. The driver rolled down his window and yelled "Fuck you!" and other insults at her as she tried to back away from his car.

Much has been written about the online abuse and threatening behaviour politicians and others in the public eye face every day. But Thompson says that abuse is going from anonymous online vitriol to terrifying in-person verbal assaults.

The incident at the movie theatre is just one of several times when someone in public began to yell at her. She has been called a traitor, an enemy, and a "piece of garbage." Her family's safety has been threatened more than once. Some people have wished she and her loved ones will get fatal diseases.

The threats have become real enough that Thompson sometimes now requires a security detail, a level of protection even cabinet ministers don't usually get.

"There are places, yes, that I have to have security now and I don't think that's a great situation," she said. "I'm someone who is trying to do my job, live my life, and talk and engage with people, and it makes it harder. I'm not going to let this stop me but I wish it would stop."

NOTES

1 For an example of a guideline on workplace safety, see Ministry of Labour (2016).
2 The control group did not read a news story.
3 The term "psychological violence" comes from Krook (2020).
4 These incidents, especially the one outside the movie theatre, may also constitute semiotic violence. Krook's (2020) definition of semiotic violence includes emphasizing the role incongruity between being a politician and being a woman. Given that Minister McKenna was with her children, it could

be argued that the incongruity rests between being a politician and a "good mother," as her children were party to the threats. Yet, semiotic violence requires that the goal of the attack is to identify group-based deficiencies. In this case, fear, disempowerment, and shame are obvious goals of the attack in question, making it better defined, in our view, as psychological violence.

5 In a large-scale meta-analysis that included more than 25,000 politicians and 750,000 media stories, Van der Pas and Aaldering (2020, 114) concluded that "women politicians receive more attention to their appearance and personal life, more negative viability coverage, and, to some extent, stereotypical issue and trait coverage."

6 Unfortunately, this small number of cases means that these participants are excluded from the analysis.

7 A priori power analyses were conducted using G*Power to estimate the sample size required for the study. Our parameters (two tailed tests, small effect [$d = .03$], alpha of .05, and power of .8) yielded a minimum required sample of 432 across the three conditions. Our sample of 603, therefore, has ample statistical power.

8 For a similar approach, see Pruysers, Thomas, and Blais (2020).

9 As Lawless (2009, 73) points out in a more general discussion of media sexism, women are likely to think to themselves: "Why would I ever want to endure that?"

10 A third explanation could be that participants did not pay close attention to the manipulation (that is, they did not read the content closely) and were therefore unaffected by the message. This possibility, however, is less of a concern, as we included a manipulation check question in the survey and asked participants to identify the primary content of the news story they were asked to read. This question was correctly answered by 90 per cent of respondents. As such, inattention to the manipulation is unlikely a concern here.

11 Two important notes regarding the treatments need to be made: First, to increase external validity, the article included the logo of a major Canadian newspaper. Second, it is important to note that the male politician condition was identical other than changing the gender of the MP, which required changing the name and gender pronouns used throughout. Otherwise, the content remained identical to the treatment shown here.

REFERENCES

Balmas, Meital, and Tamir Sheafer. 2010. "Candidate Image in Election Campaigns: Attribute Agenda Setting, Affective Priming, and Voting Intentions." *International Journal of Public Opinion Research* 22 (2): 204–29. https://doi.org/10.1093/ijpor/edq009.

Bongiorno, Renata, Chloe Langbroek, Paul G. Bain, Michelle Ting, and Michelle K. Ryan. 2020. "Why Women Are Blamed for Being Sexually Harassed: The Effects of Empathy for Female Victims and Male Perpetrators." *Psychology of Women Quarterly* 44 (1):11–27. https://doi.org/10.1177/0361684319868730.

Bos, Linda, Wouter van der Brug, and Claes de Vreese. 2011. "How the Media Shape Perceptions of Right-Wing Populist Leaders." *Political Communication* 28 (2): 182–206. https://doi.org/10.1080/10584609.2011.564605.

Bradley-Geist, Jill C., Ivy Rivera, and Susan D. Geringer. 2015. "The Collateral Damage of Ambient Sexism: Observing Sexism Impacts Bystander Self-Esteem and Career Aspirations." *Sex Roles* 73 (1–2): 29–42. https://doi.org/10.1007/s11199-015-0512-y.

Burke, Ashley. 2019. "Relentless Online Abuse of Female MPs Raises Concern for Safety of Staff." *CBC News*, 5 November 2019. https://www.cbc.ca/news/politics/mps-staff-online-hate-security-measures-1.5347221.

Chen, Philip, Melanee Thomas, Allison Harell, and Tania Gosselin. 2023. "Explicit Gender Stereotyping in Canadian Politics." *Canadian Journal of Political Science/Revue canadienne de science politique* 56 (1): 209–21. https://doi.org/10.1017/S0008423922000890.

Cotter, Adam, and Laura Savage. 2019. *Gender-Based Violence and Unwanted Sexual Behaviour in Canada 2018: Initial Findings from the Survey of Safety in Public and Private Spaces*. Catalogue no. 85-002-X. Ottawa, ON: Statistics Canada. https://www150.statcan.gc.ca/n1/pub/85-002-x/2019001/article/00017-eng.htm.

Crawley, Mike. 2017. "Premier Kathleen Wynne Bombarded on Social Media by Homophobic, Sexist Abuse." *CBC News*, 25 January 2017. https://www.cbc.ca/news/canada/toronto/kathleen-wynne-twitter-abuse-1.3949657.

CTV Calgary Staff. 2016. "Social Media Image of Notley Viewed through a Scope Draws Criticism." *CTV News*, 13 August 2016. https://calgary.ctvnews.ca/social-media-image-of-notley-viewed-through-a-scope-draws-criticism-1.3027998.

Dassonneville, Ruth, Stephen Quinlan, and Ian McAllister. 2021. "Female Leader Popularity and the Vote, 1996–2016: A Global Exploratory Analysis." *European Journal of Politics and Gender* 4 (3): 341–59. https://doi.org/10.1332/251510820X16073612895666.

Delacourt, Susan. 2021. "After All the Threats and Online Abuse, No Wonder Catherine McKenna Is Leaving Politics." *Toronto Star*, 28 June 2021. https://www.thestar.com/politics/political-opinion/2021/06/28/after-all-the-threats-and-online-abuse-no-wonder-catherine-mckenna-is-leaving-politics.html.

Ditonto, Tess M., Allison J. Hamilton, and David P. Redlawsk. 2014. "Gender Stereotypes, Information Search, and Voting Behavior in Political Campaigns." *Political Behavior* 36 (2): 335–58. https://doi.org/10.1007/s11109-013-9232-6.

Druckman, James N., and Michael Parkin. 2005. "The Impact of Media Bias: How Editorial Slant Affects Voters." *The Journal of Politics* 67 (4): 1030–49. https://doi.org/10.1111/j.1468-2508.2005.00349.x.

Eberl, Jakob-Moritz, Marcus Wagner, and Hajo G. Boomgaarden. 2017. "Are Perceptions of Candidate Traits Shaped by the Media? The Effects of Three Types of Media Bias." *International Journal of Press/Politics* 22 (1):111–32. https://doi.org/10.1177/1940161216674651.

Fox, Richard L., and Jennifer L. Lawless. 2014. "Uncovering the Origins of the Gender Gap in Political Ambition." *American Political Science Review* 108 (3): 499–519. https://doi.org/10.1017/S0003055414000227.

Gerber, Alan, Dean Karlan, and Daniel Bergan. 2009. "Does the Media Matter? A Field Experiment Measuring the Effect of Newspapers on Voting Behavior and Political Opinions." *American Economic Journal* 1 (2): 35–52. https://doi.org/10.1257/app.1.2.35.

Gidengil, Elizabeth, André Blais, Neil Nevitte, and Richard Nadeau. 2004. *Citizens*. Vancouver, BC: UBC Press.

Gidengil, Elisabeth, and Joanna Everitt. 1999. "Metaphors and Misrepresentation: Gendered Mediation in News Coverage of the 1993 Canadian Leaders' Debates." *Harvard International Journal of Press/Politics* 4 (1): 48–65. https://doi.org/10.1177/1081180X99004001005.

Gidengil, Elizabeth, Janine Giles, and Melanee Thomas. 2008. "The Gender Gap in Self-Perceived Understanding of Politics in Canada and the United States." *Politics & Gender* 4 (4): 535–61. https://doi.org/10.1017/S1743923X08000469.

Glowacki, Laura, and Andrew Foote. 2019. "Vulgar Slur Painted across MP Catherine McKenna's Office." *CBC News*, 24 October 2019. https://www.cbc.ca/news/canada/ottawa/catherine-mckenna-vandalism-office-1.5333420.

Goodyear-Grant, Elizabeth, and Julie Croskill. 2011. "Gender Affinity Effects in Vote Choice in Westminster Systems: Assessing 'Flexible' Voters in Canada." *Politics & Gender* 7 (2): 223–50. https://doi.org/10.1017/S1743923X11000079.

Hango, Darcy, and Melissa Moyser. 2018. *Insights in Canadian Society: Harassment in Canadian Workplaces*. Catalogue no. 75-006-X. Ottawa, ON: Statistics Canada. https://www150.statcan.gc.ca/n1/pub/75-006-x/2018001/article/54982-eng.htm.

Haraldsson, Amanda, and Lena Wängnerud. 2019. "The Effect of Media Sexism on Women's Political Ambition: Evidence from a Worldwide Study." *Feminist Media Studies* 19 (4): 525–41. https://doi.org/10.1080/14680777.2018.1468797.

Hayes, Danny, Jennifer L. Lawless, and Gail Baitinger. 2014. "Who Cares What They Wear? Gender, and the Influence of Candidate Appearance." *Social Science Quarterly* 95 (5): 1194–1212. https://doi.org/10.1111/ssqu.12113.

Howard, Judith A. 1984. "The 'Normal' Victim: The Effects of Gender Stereotypes on Reactions to Victims." *Social Psychology Quarterly* 47 (3): 270–81. https://doi.org/10.2307/3033824.

Huddy, Leonie, and Nayda Terkildsen. 1993. "The Consequences of Gender Stereotypes for Women Candidates at Different Levels and Types of Office." *Political Research Quarterly* 46 (3): 503–25. https://doi.org/10.1177/106591299304600304.

Hunt, Elle. 2016. "Julia Gillard Says Online Abuse Deters Women from Political Careers." *The Guardian*, 12 October 2016. https://www.theguardian.com/world/2016/oct/12/julia-gillard-says-online-abuse-deters-women-from-political-careers.

Hunt, Elle, Nick Evershed, and Ri Liu. 2016. "From Julia Gillard to Hillary Clinton: Online Abuse of Politicians around the World." *The Guardian*, 27 June 2016. https://www.theguardian.com/technology/datablog/ng-interactive/2016/jun/27/from-julia-gillard-to-hillary-clinton-online-abuse-of-politicians-around-the-world.

Inter-Parliamentary Union. 2016. *Sexism, Harassment and Violence against Women Parliamentarians*. Issues Brief, October 2016. https://www.ipu.org/resources/publications/reports/2016-10/sexism-harassment-and-violence-against-women-parliamentarians.

Kahn, Kim Fridkin. 1996. *The Political Consequences of Being a Woman*. New York: Columbia University Press.

Krook, Mona Lena. 2020. *Violence against Women in Politics*. Oxford: Oxford University Press.

Lawless, Jennifer L. 2009. "Sexism and Gender Bias in Election 2008: A More Complex Path for Women in Politics." *Politics & Gender* 5 (1): 70–80. https://doi.org/10.1017/S1743923X09000051.

Lawless, Jennifer L., and Richard L. Fox. 2005. *It Takes a Candidate: Why Women Don't Run for Office*. Cambridge: Cambridge University Press

Malamuth, Neil M., and James V.P. Check. 1981. "The Effects of Mass Media Exposure on Acceptance of Violence against Women: A Field Experiment." *Journal of Research in Personality* 15 (4): 436–46. https://doi.org/10.1016/0092-6566(81)90040-4.

Meltzer, Christine E., Jakob-Moritz Eberl, Nora Theorin, Tobias Heidenreich, Jesper Strömbäck, Hajo G. Boomgaarden, and Christian Schemer. 2021. "Media Effects on Policy Preferences toward Free Movement: Evidence from Five EU Member States." *Journal of Ethnic and Migration Studies* 47 (15): 3390–3408. https://doi.org/10.1080/1369183X.2020.1778454.

Ministry of Labour. 2016. *Health and Safety Guidelines: Workplace Violence and Harassment: Understanding the Law*. Toronto: Ontario Ministry of Labour. https://www.ontario.ca/page/understand-law-workplace-violence-and-harassment.

Potter, W. James. 2012. *Media Effects*. New York: SAGE Publications.
Pruysers, Scott, and Julie Blais. 2017. "Why Won't Lola Run? An Experiment Examining Stereotype Threat and Political Ambition." *Politics & Gender* 13 (2): 232–52. https://doi.org/10.1017/S1743923X16000544.
Pruysers, Scott, Melanee Thomas, and Julie Blais. 2020. "Mediated Ambition? Gender, News and the Desire to Seek Elected Office." *European Journal of Politics and Gender* 3 (1): 37–59. https://doi.org/10.1332/2515108 19X15701058119488.
Rabson, Mia. 2019. "Threats, Abuse Move from Online to Real World, McKenna Now Requires Security." *CBC News*, 7 September 2019. https://www.cbc.ca/news/politics/threats-abuse-move-from-online-to-real-world-mckenna-now-requires-security-1.5274766.
Rheault, Ludovic, Erica Rayment, and Andreea Musulan. 2019. "Politicians in the Line of Fire: Incivility and the Treatment of Women on Social Media." *Research & Politics* 6 (1). https://doi.org/10.1177/2053168018816228.
Schneider, Monica C., and Angela L. Bos. 2014. "Measuring Stereotypes of Female Politicians." *Political Psychology* 35 (2): 245–66. https://doi.org/10.1111/pops.12040.
– 2019. "The Application of Social Role Theory to the Study of Gender in Politics." *Political Psychology* 40 (S1): 173–213. https://doi.org/10.1111/pops.12573.
Streb, Matthew J., Barbara Burrell, Brian Frederick, and Michael A. Genovese. 2008. "Social Desirability Effects and Support for a Female American President." *Public Opinion Quarterly* 72 (1): 76–89. https://doi.org/10.1093/poq/nfm035.
Thomas, Melanee. 2012. "The Complexity Conundrum: Why Hasn't the Gender Gap in Subjective Political Competence Closed?" *Canadian Journal of Political Science* 45 (2): 337–58. https://doi.org/10.1017/S0008423912000352.
Thomas, Melanee, and Amanda Bittner, eds. 2017. *Mothers & Others: The Role of Parenthood in Politics*. Vancouver, BC: UBC Press.
Thomas, Melanee, Allison Harell, Sanne A.M. Rijkhoff, and Tania Gosselin. 2021. "Gendered News Coverage and Women as Heads of Government." *Political Communication* 38 (4): 388–406. https://doi.org/10.1080/10584609.2020.1784326.
Trimble, Linda. 2017. *Ms. Prime Minister: Gender, Media, and Leadership*. Toronto: University of Toronto Press.
Trynacity, Kim. 2017. "Rachel Notley: Alberta's Most Threatened Premier." *CBC News*, 14 February 2017. https://www.cbc.ca/news/canada/edmonton/notley-threats-alberta-history-1.3982276.
– 2018. "'A Wake-Up Call': Documents Detail Litany of Threats against Premier Rachel Notley." *CBC News*, 4 May 2018. https://www.cbc.ca/news/canada/edmonton/notley-premier-threats-security-1.4644989.

Van der Pas, Daphne Joanna, and Loes Aaldering. 2020. "Gender Differences in Political Media Coverage: A Meta-Analysis." *Journal of Communication* 70 (1): 114–43. https://doi.org/10.1093/joc/jqz046.

Wagner, Angelia. 2022. "Tolerating the Trolls? Gendered Perceptions of Online Harassment of Politicians in Canada." *Feminist Media Studies* 22 (1): 32–47. https://doi.org/10.1080/14680777.2020.1749691.

Weaver, David H. 2007. "Thoughts on Agenda Setting, Framing, and Priming." *Journal of Communication* 57 (1): 142–7. https://doi.org/10.1111/j.1460-2466.2006.00333.x.

5 Gender-Based Violence towards Political Women: Did Print News Coverage Shift after #MeToo?

ELIZABETH GOODYEAR-GRANT

Gender-based violence in politics (GBV-P) is a persistent impediment to equality in descriptive political representation. This chapter examines how violence against political women is portrayed in Canadian print news, focusing on whether coverage of abuse towards women politicians has changed since the #MeToo movement in 2017.

Abuse towards political women is rampant (Biroli 2016, 2018; Collier and Raney 2018b; Krook 2020, 2022), and major concerns arise that growing GBV-P will amplify women's exclusion from politics by deterring them from running, disrupting their nascent political ambition, or by causing women politicians to exit politics prematurely due to the mental toll of abuse or fear of physical violence, contributing to what Celis and Childs (2020) call the "poverty of representation." The increase in GBV-P is especially worrisome in the case of BIPOC[1] women's representation, for racialized and Indigenous women already face unique and burdensome challenges to candidacy and office (Brown 2014; Brown and Gershon 2021). Moreover, growing GBV-P is contributing to violence in politics generally, creating a more toxic political environment where women's subordination is reinforced and the acceptance of violence as a tool of political rivalry is growing. In this atmosphere, the public is encouraged to denigrate, dismiss, and/or undervalue women politicians and their work, perpetuating misogyny in politics. See Thomas and Pruysers's chapter 4, this volume, for an examination of the possible individual effects of exposure to GBV-P.

Respected actors in the information environment can play a powerful role in challenging harmful patterns. News media's mandate is to report and educate, so the chapter focuses on three questions. First, did coverage of violence towards political women increase after #MeToo? This chapter focuses on elected women politicians, but a broader focus would also include women journalists, activists, judges, and public health officers (Krook 2020). Second, has coverage become more likely to recognize violence towards political women as (a) a systemic problem rooted in misogyny and (b) an impediment to political equality? Third, was the GBV-P experienced uniquely by racialized and Indigenous women in politics represented in coverage?

This final question is an important one given criticisms about racial blind spots in the movement, including its very origin. As the introductory chapter in this volume points out, while the viral spread of #MeToo in 2017 is typically credited to actress Alyssa Milano, the #MeToo campaign was actually started ten years earlier by activist Tarana Burke to help racial minority women who had experienced sexual abuse (Garcia 2017). Burke was not credited in the 2017 viral tweets, and her work was largely unheralded in the ten years prior. This erasure is consistent with the neglect of race in scholarship and activism on gender-based violence and #MeToo specifically (Leung and Williams 2019; Onwuachi-Willig 2018), despite a Black woman having been the originator of the movement and despite racialized women being more vulnerable than white women to sexual harassment and less likely to be believed when they report (Onwuachi-Willig 2018, 107). Relevant questions for this chapter are, Has Canadian news coverage tended to replicate the erasure of racialized women's experiences, and if so, did that change post-#MeToo?

#MeToo's Effect on Understandings of Violence against Women in Politics

Women in politics have faced violence and abuse for a long time. Canada's first member of Parliament (MP) Agnes Macphail was heckled mercilessly. In one incident, a heckler at a rally shouted: "Don't you ever wish you were a man?" Macphail looked at him and said: "Yes, don't you?" (OurDigitalWorld n.d.). Former deputy prime minister and cabinet minister Sheila Copps was called "slut," "fishwife," and "bitch" by MP Bill Kempling inside the House of Commons, and none of these words were on the list of terms that were considered unparliamentary (CBC News 1991). Copps has also told of being sexually assaulted by a male politician while a provincial legislator in Ontario. More recently, the abuse continues and has moved into new venues, particularly online platforms. Former cabinet minister Catherine McKenna has been repeatedly assailed on and off social media, for example (Proudfoot 2019). As discussed by Cockram in chapter 11, this volume, Celina Caesar-Chavannes – former Liberal MP – points to the "barrage of social media abuse" (Evelyn 2018) as one of the reasons for her resignation, an issue discussed further in her 2021 book *Can You Hear Me Now?* Caesar-Chavannes has also detailed tense relations with Prime Minister Justin Trudeau, including incidents of him yelling at her (Stone 2019), which reminds us that GBV-P occurs inside the legislative workplace, not just on the campaign trail or Twitter (now X). MP Michelle Rempel has been a frequent target, particularly of online abuse, and in 2015 "won a court case against a Twitter stalker that threatened to rape her while she attended a campaign event in Winnipeg" (Collier and Raney 2019).

If GBV-P has been so consistent over time, why predict shifts in news coverage following #MeToo? #MeToo was an awakening in the broader public about gender-based harassment, particularly in the workplace. As Fileborn and Loney-Howes point out, the "flood of participation in #MeToo reaffirmed publicly just how widespread sexual assault and harassment actually are ... and, significantly, that these experiences are *routine* and *normalized*" (2019, 2; emphasis in the original). Workplace harassment and assault had become normalized, not only because of their frequency but also because they fit within patriarchal norms about who has power and autonomy, as well as with societal unease about changing gender roles. Violence against women is used to maintain patriarchal social structures and discourage women's equality (see Krook 2020). In other words, not only did #MeToo reveal the staggering volume of abuse towards women, but it also promoted a systemic understanding of the patriarchal and misogynistic foundations of the abuse and did so with the force of a viral, global social movement that was impossible to ignore.

The idea promoted by the movement that victim-survivors of workplace harassment and assault tend to know the offender is generally true (Fileborn and Loney-Howes 2019). However, women in politics also face abuse from strangers. Online platforms have created new opportunities for violence against political women, and relentless online harassment is common. In the United Kingdom, an unexpectedly high proportion of women MPs opted not to stand for re-election in 2019, and several of them explicitly said that abuse was one of the reasons (Oppenheim 2019). For racial minority women MPs, the abuse has been even worse (Kuperberg 2018). An Amnesty International study found that abusive behaviour towards UK MPs on Twitter (now X) targeted "Black, Asian, and Minority Ethnic (BAME) women MPs far more than their white colleagues. The 20 BAME MPs received almost half (41 per cent) of the abusive tweets, despite there being almost eight times as many white MPs in the study" (Amnesty International UK 2019). Initial reports from a Samara/Areto Labs collaboration analysing the toxicity of tweets in the 2021 Canadian federal election similarly show that women and racialized candidates receive disproportionate online hate (Samara Centre for Democracy 2022). The heightened abuse faced by minority women MPs has been acknowledged in the UK House of Commons by the deputy speaker in the context of the security review undertaken after the murder of MP Jo Cox by a right-wing extremist in 2016, a tragic example of the severest threat political women face from unknown abusers (Stone 2017).

That #MeToo revealed the remarkable volume of violence against women in the workplace and articulated its roots in patriarchy and misogyny leads to three hypotheses for the relationship of #MeToo to news coverage of GBV-P:

1 *Salience hypothesis*: Increased coverage of GBV-P occurred after #MeToo.
2 *Gender thematic hypothesis*: Increased use of a gender-focused thematic approach to coverage of GBV-P occurred after #MeToo.
3 *Intersectional hypothesis*: Coverage of racialized gender violence facing BIPOC women politicians did not increase after #MeToo.

First is the salience hypothesis. Measuring media attention can be done in various ways, including number of stories with mentions of abuse and violence towards women politicians as a group (rather than individual women politicians), number of mentions per story, and so on, comparing coverage before and after 15 October 2017 (when Milano's viral tweet went out). Not only would the growing visibility of the movement encourage greater attention to GBV-P, but the subject matter satisfies several criteria of newsworthiness, including conflict and elitism (Boukes, Jones, and Vliegenthart 2022; Cotter 2010).

Second is the gender thematic hypothesis. Media is predicted to pick up on the themes of patriarchy and misogyny framing the #MeToo analysis of workplace abuse, producing more thematic coverage of GBV-P acknowledging that gender-motivated abuse of women in patriarchal systems is intended to diminish, deter, devalue, and exclude them from political power. This thematic approach is captured in the analyses that follow in various ways. For example, the chapter examines whether post-#MeToo stories focus on women politicians as a group and whether abuse is identified as an impediment to women's representation.

On the other hand, maybe #MeToo was not sufficient to shift coverage in the way predicted by the second hypothesis. News media's gender biases are well documented (Goodyear-Grant 2013; Thomas, Harell, and Gosselin 2018; Trimble 2017), raising doubt about how quickly (if at all) news organizations could have shifted coverage to better recognize women's experience of GBV-P. News stories rely heavily on episodic framing, which may have discouraged adoption of #MeToo's thematic approach. Framing refers to the narrative or "peg" that weaves together components of a story and provides meaning to it (Gamson 1975). Episodic frames focus on incidents or discrete cases and often personalize coverage, while thematic frames focus on context, trends, or broader explanations (Iyengar 1991, 1996). The Frameworks Institute describes the difference using a camera metaphor, calling episodic framing a telephoto lens and thematic framing a wide-angle lens (Benjamin 2017).

Episodic framing is prevalent because it does not require specialized subject knowledge from journalists; episodically framed stories can be shorter; and episodic coverage is less vulnerable to accusations of bias because of the focus on events or "facts" rather than on interpretation (Iyengar 1996). Moreover, traditional media have faced financial pressures "as advertisers and consumers defect en masse to the Internet" (Baluja 2013). Media outlets have responded by cutting budgets; closing operations, particularly in small, local markets; and decreasing staff (Skelton 2018). All of these shifts diminish the capacity of news outlets to provide thematic coverage due to the stretching of resources and expertise. Simply put, there are structural, economic, and organizational deterrents to thematic news framing of GBV-P.

Third is the intersectional hypothesis. While #MeToo might have encouraged greater media attention to the gendered roots and implications of GBV-P, we cannot assume it included attention to the unique GBV-P experiences of BIPOC women politicians. In general, news coverage tends to sideline BIPOC women politicians (Tolley 2016; Van der Pas and Aaldering 2020), as has the #MeToo movement (Kuperberg 2018; Leung and Williams 2019). As Bowman Williams notes, "although women of color experience high rates of harassment and assault, the #MeToo movement has largely been left them on the margins in terms of (1) the online conversation, (2) the traditional social movement activity occurring offline, and (3) the consequential legal activity" (2021, 1798). The movement's blind spots could be replicated in news.

Data and Methods

This chapter analyses the three hypotheses using Canadian print news. Retrieved using the Canadian Major Dailies database, the articles come from a broad range of newspapers across the country:[2] two papers with a daily average circulation (print and digital) over 250K per day, six more with circulation of 100–249K, six with circulation 50–99K, and six with circulation under 50K. There is at least one newspaper from each province, although the one Quebec newspaper is the English-language *Montreal Gazette*. Two time periods are examined: news coverage prior to 15 October 2017 (the start of the viral spread of #MeToo) and news coverage 15 October 2017 to 17 November 2020. Stories were gathered by searching for coverage of women politicians that mentioned abuse or violence.[3] The focus was on collecting stories that mentioned women as a group in politics, rather than only specific women, which is consistent with the chapter's conceptual focus on whether #MeToo encouraged greater recognition of the systematic abuse against women as a category in politics (a thematic frame) as opposed to the individualized focus on specific women, events, and actions (an episodic frame). Stories that did mention women as a group still tended to centre specific events or people, and these tended overwhelmingly to be white women, as discussed below. The stories were manually coded using a simple coding scheme focused on stories' manifest features.

Results

Quantity and Prominence of Coverage

The search yielded 112 news stories from 2009 to 17 November 2020 that mentioned women as a group in politics in conjunction with GBV-P. Of the 112 stories, 38 were published in the eight years prior to 15 October 2017 (the earliest is from 2009), and 74 stories were published between 15 October 2017 and 17 November 2020. In other words, 65 per cent of the stories were written after #MeToo. Of the stories written after #MeToo, 23 per cent explicitly mention the movement, suggesting that journalists are not just paying greater attention to GBV-P but linking it explicitly with #MeToo.

Coverage of GBV-P is more prominent since #MeToo: 74 stories written in three years (approximately 25 per year) compared to 38 in eleven years (approximately 3 per year). Could there be other explanations for this shift, or is #MeToo the likely driver? Perhaps there were more women in politics after October 2017 than before, increasing awareness of the toxicity women as a group face in public life, independent of #MeToo. Women's proportion of federal legislative seats in 2017 had not changed much in nearly two decades and was still shy of the 30 per cent mark. This percentage has not changed much since 2017. Women's seat share grew about 5 percentage points from 22 per cent in 2008 to 27 per cent in 2015, prior to #MeToo, and only 2 percentage points in 2019. Provincially, legislatures have varied in terms of women's seat shares (Trimble, Arscott, and Tremblay 2013). Women currently represent 34 per cent of all provincial and territorial legislators, ranging from a low of 22 per cent in Nunavut to a high of 47 per cent in the Northwest Territories. There has been no general large-scale expansion of women's provincial/territorial seats from 2017 to 2020 that would trigger greater media attention to the unique experience of women in politics. That said, as women's numbers increase, particularly in visible positions, societal backlash against their growing power can occur, increasing GBV-P and thus its coverage in news. Indeed, "acts of violence against women in politics ... embody a form of backlash to women's greater inclusion in the political sphere, resisting the gains made possible by gender quotas and other mechanisms to empower women in decision-making" (Krook and Restrepo Sanin 2016, 137).

Another possibility is that a growing presence of women in visible, powerful positions has driven heightened attention to GBV-P in news media, not the #MeToo moment. Executive-level politicians receive more news coverage than backbenchers, which makes sense given their centrality (Bittner 2011). Or perhaps there has been an escalation of GBV-P on account of women's growing presence in executive positions, which could account for increased media attention and growing public awareness. Women executives have sometimes faced incredible abuse in office, and the articles analysed in this volume provide many examples. As pointed out in Wagner and Young's chapter 2, this volume, former Alberta premier Rachel Notley received the most threats of any Alberta premier throughout the province's history. Notley was the victim of "412 incidents of what is termed inappropriate contact and communication" in 2016 alone (Sampert 2019). Notley and former Alberta premier Alison Redford each had upwards of twenty incidents deemed more serious "medium threats," compared to three each for former premiers Ralph Klein and Jim Prentice (Sampert 2019). See Reist's chapter 6, this volume, for more discussion on GBV-P in Alberta politics, specifically the use of political cartoons to normalize GBV-P and centre "frontier masculinity." In terms of the timing of women's growing executive power in Canada, it does not seem to align as a direct cause of media attention to GBV-P post-#MeToo. The high point of women's executive office-holding occurred in 2014, when women held six of the thirteen provincial/territorial executive offices, establishing sex parity in premierships.[4] It has been downhill in women's numbers since then: as of November 2023 only two provinces were headed by women: Danielle Smith, premier of Alberta, and Caroline Cochrane, premier of the Northwest Territories. In the Northwest Territories, members of the twentieth assembly will vote for the next premier and cabinet ministers on 7 December 2023.

In terms of the prominence of GBV-P coverage, it can be assessed in several ways. One dimension would be how central the issue is to the story. Centrality was assessed by coding how many times abuse towards political women was mentioned in the story. On this point, there was no change in the post-#MeToo period compared to the pre-#MeToo period: 2.7 mentions per story on average in both periods.

Qualitative Patterns

What has the coding revealed about the patterns of coverage? The content analysis focused on whether there was a more group-based, systematic focus on GBV-P after #MeToo. The #MeToo movement provided a clear account of gender-based violence as a manifestation of misogyny and identified the violence as a tool of oppression and a symptom of women's subordinate location in social, economic, and political structures (Hillstrom 2019). What was different about #MeToo was its widespread reach and viral spread, encouraging ideas to trickle deeper into accounts of political life that do not typically incorporate women-centred analysis. The coding scheme contained questions about print coverage designed to reveal whether newsmakers had taken up the gender-focused analysis of abuse facing political women.

Recognition of Violence and Abuse

Figure 5.1 presents the result of some overall patterns comparing coverage before and after #MeToo. In both periods, there was recognition that violence and abuse generally face women in politics, as the first set of bars in the figure indicates. This result is owing in part to the search parameters used to retrieve articles, as the terms focused on women as a group versus individual women political actors. Over 80 per cent of stories within each period acknowledged that women in politics face abuse.

Recognition That the Violence Is Gender-Motivated

A much smaller proportion of the stories in each period explicitly identified gender as the basis of the abuse – 50 per cent in the period prior to #MeToo versus 47 per cent after #MeToo. Curiously, there is no uptick after #MeToo, as the second set of bars in Figure 5.1 reveals. Stories

Figure 5.1. Print media coverage of violence and abuse towards women in politics

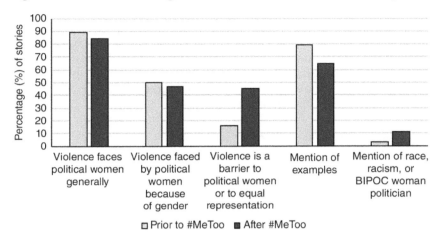

varied in terms of how they explicitly identified gender as the motivation for the violence. Some did so using terms such as "misogynistic" or "sexist" to describe the abuse, especially stories originating from Montreal papers or Montreal-connected writers, which sometimes link GBV-P to the 1989 École Polytechnique massacre (Hanes 2019). Other articles did too, even prior to #MeToo. For example, one article on abuse and threats towards former Ontario premier Kathleen Wynne interviewed a security consultant who had worked for several years on Alberta premiers' security details. The consultant had this to say about the abuse towards Wynne and other women politicians: "You have all the misogynists out there who … make threats just because a premier might be female. For some of them it doesn't matter whether they agree with her policies or not, it's just the fact that she's in a position of power that they feel traditionally belongs to a man" (Dawson 2017).

After #MeToo, various examples continue the theme, perhaps with even sharper language and deeper analysis of the gendered dimensions of violence against political women. For example, one story noted bluntly that "misogyny, verbal abuse, threats of sexual violence and body shaming … have become common tactics used to belittle and intimidate women in politics, not just in Canada, but worldwide" (Chronicle Herald 2020). Another article, citing an interview with MP Michelle Rempel, notes that "Ms. Rempel said the issue of sexual harassment should not be used for political gain between parties. She also said sexual harassment must be addressed by all parties, as well as people in other professions with dealings on Parliament Hill, including journalists, lobbyists, diplomats and public servants" (Curry and Stone 2018). These examples note a far-reaching and inclusive approach to the widespread culture of GBV-P, affecting not just politicians but staffers and journalists, and also advocating a non-partisan approach to dealing with the problem, which removes it from partisan politics and further underscores its systemic nature.

Recognition That Violence and Abuse Are Impediments to Women's Representation

Moving to the third set of bars in Figure 5.1, the coding scheme also asked whether stories explicitly portrayed GBV-P as a barrier to women's representation. A large shift occurred after #MeToo, with nearly half of the articles portraying GBV-P as a barrier versus only 16 per cent prior to #MeToo. This finding is consistent with accounts in the literature that GBV-P had been viewed historically as part of political life – the "cost of doing politics" (Krook 2020, 3). Violence against women was a "hidden problem" for so long because it has been viewed as "part of the game" of politics (3).

To give a sense of the expanded focus on GBV-P as a barrier for women's representation, a January 2018 article focuses on new rules on sexual harassment in federally regulated workplaces, which included Parliament Hill. Titled "The Hill's #MeToo Shameful, Inevitable," the article criticizes the fact that rules were not in place earlier to protect staffers and legislators, and goes on to say that "targeting sexual misconduct among our elected officials and those who work around and for them is especially imperative considering the longstanding problem of gender inequality in government" (Kingston Whig-Standard 2018). Canada had been the first Westminster parliament to adopt a member-to-member code of conduct on sexual harassment, though the code was flawed, as Collier and Raney (2018a, 2018b) have compellingly argued.

After #MeToo, some coverage explicitly traced the shift in how GBV-P was viewed. For example, one article had the headline "Sexual Harassment in Politics Is Finally Out of the Bottle" (Braid 2018). Another article linked workplace sexual harassment in politics to a candidate supply problem and diminished political ambition among women:

> Imagine always having to second guess whether or not you were actually good at your job because you didn't know if it was because your boss wanted to have sex with you. Imagine waking up every day thinking

of ways to thwart sexual advances from your colleagues. And then we wonder why more young women aren't choosing to run for public office. (Gee and Ifill 2018)

This kind of analysis existed in Canadian print news prior to #MeToo, though it was less common. Interestingly, in jurisdictions that had high-profile women executives prior to #MeToo, there seems to have been a fair bit of strong coverage on GBV-P and its effects on women's representation – for example, this observation from a *Calgary Herald* piece while Rachel Notley was premier:

> It's no wonder women struggle with the decision to run for office. It's a toxic environment where women are held to higher standards than their male colleagues ... The attacks women face don't only affect them, they affect their families and friends who hear these attacks. Sometimes, a woman's family becomes the focus of attack and she may choose not to run to protect her loved ones. (Tomney 2017)

Individualizing versus Group-Focused Coverage

Turning to the fourth set of bars in Figure 5.1, the coding scheme also recorded whether news stories mentioned incidents or discrete cases of GBV-P. This dimension was included in order to provide another angle on episodic versus thematic coverage of GBV-P. If very few particular incidents of abuse or individuals were mentioned – or none at all – we can assume the story focused on larger issues or tended towards more thematic coverage. If a story had a lot of mentions of incidents or individuals, we would assume a more episodic frame. Prior to #MeToo, nearly 80 per cent of stories that mention GBV-P included specific examples of abuse. After #MeToo, specific examples decreased to 65 per cent of stories. After #MeToo, perhaps the individual details have become less salient, and the themes of sexism, patriarchy, and misogyny more so – a landscape rather than a portrait, to return to the photography analogy.

Recognizing Violence and Abuse Are Intersectional

The fifth set of bars in Figure 5.1 plot whether stories mention the intersection of race and gender in producing unique forms of violence towards women in politics. The coding scheme adopted a liberal approach, coding affirmative for this category if the story explicitly mentioned race- and gender-based violence faced by BIPOC women politicians in general or if the story explicitly mentioned gender-motivated violence towards a specific BIPOC politician. Prior to #MeToo, only a single story recognized the intersectional violence,[5] a result the gendered mediation literature would call "symbolic annihilation" (Tuchman, Daniels, and Benet 1978). After #MeToo, mention of GBV-P towards BIPOC women grew modestly to 11 per cent of articles about women in politics.

On the whole, neither period has much focus on how race intersects with gender to produce unique forms of GBV-P. Looking at the coverage after #MeToo, many of the stories that incorporate race do so in a single sentence. For example, one article, which is 1,040 words in total, mentions that "NDP MP Jenny Kwan, after lengthy racist abuse, had panic buttons installed in her constituency office to protect her staff" (Renzetti 2019). Another pattern is the use of fairly indirect language around the lack of safety for BIPOC women in politics. For example, an article on supporting women in politics notes that increasing the number of women with "diverse backgrounds" in politics must be accompanied by "going a step further and working to ensure those spaces are safe for them and their families" (Gooch 2020b). The article implies that political spaces are not safe for BIPOC political women and their families, but it does not state this point very directly.

A fair number of the articles that mention race or racism in conjunction with violence against political women do not actually focus on Canada. After #MeToo, there are articles that mention the abusive experiences of US Vice President Kamala Harris, 2018 Democrat Georgia Governor candidate Stacey Abrams, and the first Muslim women elected to serve as members of the US Congress (Ilhan Omar and Rashida Tlaib). There are also stories that focus on racist and sexist abuse towards BIPOC MPs in the United Kingdom. In Canada, when specific examples are used or when they motivate a story that also focuses on women in general, the most common examples are Rachel Notley, Kathleen Wynne, and Catherine McKenna, followed next by stories on alleged or confirmed abusers, such as former Ontario PC leader Patrick Brown, former Liberal cabinet minister Kent Hehr, and Conservative MP Gerry Ritz. There is relatively little coverage of BIPOC women politicians in Canada, despite growth in their number, despite the tremendous abuse they face on account of gender and race, and despite the growing recognition in other countries that the issue requires attention. This finding may be another manifestation of the myth of Canadian ethnic and racial harmony, and of the harms of colour-blindness. As Thompson (2008, 534) states, "the dominant narrative of Canadian society and politics is one in which there are no major racial problems."

Of course, there are exceptions that point a way forward for news coverage of BIPOC women's experience of GBV-P. An article from Tiffany Gooch focuses on Black women, for example, and notes the particular types of hatred they face, as well as the "superhuman strength required to withstand constant racist and misogynistic attacks as they rise to power" (Gooch 2020a). Gooch is also clear that recruitment and election are not the end of the challenges for Black and racialized women generally, since "once elected, they should be respected, listened to and supported with an understanding of the pressures they are uniquely under, and the impact on their mental health and safety."

Conclusion

Turning back to the three hypotheses, there is evidence of a shift to more gender thematic coverage of GBV-P after #MeToo, with much more emphasis on revealing how violence towards women is an impediment to their equal representation as a group and less attention paid to specific acts of violence or specific victims/aggressors. Post-#MeToo, we see more attention to GBV-P as a systemic problem rather than a string of isolated incidents, highlighting the potential promise of the movement to raise awareness about these issues in national conversations. This observation speaks more broadly to the power of social movements such as #MeToo to mobilize political ideas and encourage or put pressure on institutions to adopt change. In this case, the movement has clearly enhanced the visibility of the issue of workplace abuse and harassment, causing newsmakers not only to connect these harms to coverage of political women but also to produce coverage that echoes the movement's key points about the structural, systemic origins of gender-based violence and its effects on women's equality in the workplace.

There has also been some expanded attention to race and its importance within coverage of GBV-P, although more needs to be done on this issue. The evidence for the intersectional hypothesis must be declared mixed. There was an increase post-#MeToo, but with only a single article prior to #MeToo, the bar was low. Indeed, it seems that news coverage of and inspired by #MeToo reproduces some of the movement's blind spots.

In terms of the salience hypothesis, #MeToo did seem to produce more coverage of GBV-P, and a sizeable plurality of post-#MeToo articles explicitly reference the movement. Within each period, however, the average number of mentions of GBV-P is identical, suggesting that articles are not devoting more space to the issue.

The grave threats faced by women politicians on account of gender- and race-motivated violence must be more accurately represented in news media and public conversations more generally. News media have a responsibility to do this representation and to acknowledge the trauma and challenges women politicians face, for they are agenda-setters in public discourse and can guide the way towards greater understanding of the harms of GBV-P for women and for democratic politics. GBV-P causes incredible psychological stress and hampers women's careers. It perpetuates the political exclusion of women. At its gravest, GBV-P can be fatal.

Implications for Action

The desire to identify solutions is matched by the difficulty of doing so given that culture in the form of patriarchal, misogynistic, and racist norms heavily drives news coverage. This culture permeates society and has been reproduced in journalist training and the news business, as well as in the ethos of Canadian politics. This reality does not mean that nothing can be done, but it certainly requires appropriate expectations about how quickly and dramatic change can be. Two immediate possibilities come out of the analyses in this chapter: better reporting standards guidelines and more educational efforts. For both of these forms of action, "affected representatives" (Celis and Childs 2020) from diverse groups of political women – racialized, Indigenous, and 2SLGBTQQIA+[6] women, for example – should be included in efforts to define reporting standards and education materials. The logic here is that their experiences of coverage of GBV-P are unique, and they should be included in action designed to address an issue that affects them.

1. Reporting Standards Guidelines

Many news outlets have very little in the way of specific guidelines about avoiding sexism and racism in reporting – if anything, they only have minimal rules about avoiding stereotypical language. For example, the *Globe and Mail*'s editorial guidelines have a single mention of sexism and racism, included in its photography policy, which states: "Avoid stereotyping by race, gender, age, religion, ethnicity, geography, sexual orientation, disability, physical appearance or social status" (Globe and Mail 2022, 17). This directive is inadequate. It assumes employees know how to avoid stereotyping; it does not define or give examples of stereotyping; it ignores the fact that stereotyping is not the only way in which reporting can be inequitable or biased.

In cases such as these, where guidelines are absent or minimal, where policy provides insufficient guidance, news outlets and professional organizations should develop principles and practices that would promote greater attention to and better reporting on GBV-P. This is what non-governmental and multilateral organizations have been urging. For example, the Organization of American States (OAS) in its 2017 report *Inter-American Model Law on the Prevention, Punishment and Eradication of Violence against Women in Political Life* recommends in article 27 that "the State will protect women from violence in the political life and in consequence will implement the necessary measures to guarantee that communication media ... develop suitable communication guidelines to contribute to the eradication of violence against women in the political life, avoid any expression that denigrates women on the basis of harmful gender stereotypes and highlight respect for the dignity of women; as well as condemn these actions, through their ethical codes" (OAS 2017, 32).

There are professional guidelines already existing in Canada that could provide a basis for expanded guidelines within news outlets. For example, the Canadian Association of Journalists (CAJ) has guidelines on diversity that "encourage our organizations to make room for the interests of all: minorities and majorities, those with power and those without it, holders of disparate and conflicting views" (CAJ 2011). This guideline supports the greater visibility of BIPOC women and their experience of GBV-P in the news. Another good example is *Reporting on Gender-Based Violence: A Guide for Journalists*, a report and set of recommendations written by Equal Press, a project of MOSAIC (Equal Press n.d.). This report has specific guidance on terminology, the psychological impact of gender-based violence on sources and on journalists, sensitive techniques for interviewing survivors of gender-based violence, sourcing, and much more. In terms of terminology, these guidelines direct journalists to avoid terms like "groped," for example, which is too soft or ambiguous to accurately convey unwanted touching/sexual assault. News outlets should adopt and actively enforce or incentivize adherence to expanded guidelines among their staff and ensure that these guidelines contain explicit information and standards for the reporting of intersectional identities and experiences.

2. Education

Related to guidelines for reporting GBV-P, the other possible solution is education of journalism students and current journalists regarding best practices in GBV-P reporting. It should include education on the effects of entrenched patterns of reporting, including some of those presented here, such as neglect of racialized women victims, focus on particular incidents or events, neglect of situating the larger context in terms of creating barriers to women's equal participation, and so on. This education can come in many forms: online modules provided by non-governmental organizations or one's media employer; reports; seminars at professional events; or YouTube videos. In journalism programs, courses could be adopted or revised to include more content instructing on GBV-P. Parallel toolkits and guidelines can be developed for women candidates and politicians that offer communications and professional strategies to support political women in confronting sexist behaviours from other politicians, news media, or the general public. This approach has been recommended by the Congress of Regional and Local Authorities of the Council of Europe in its 2020 report *Fighting Sexist Violence against Women in Politics at Local and Regional Level* (Congress and Council of Europe 2020). Similar to reporting standards guidelines, education and training efforts must also be designed to illuminate and sensitize newsmakers to how intersectionality affects experiences of GBV-P. The findings of this chapter strongly suggest that the first lesson should be about visibility and how prevailing cultural norms and news practices overlook and minimize the GBV-P experienced by BIPOC political women, in part an outcome of settler colonialism and white privilege that tends to focus on the experience of white women in analyses of discrimination and under-representation in politics.

NOTES

1 BIPOC refers to Black, Indigenous, and people of colour.
2 Articles retrieved came from the *Calgary Herald, Halifax Chronicle Herald, Daily News, Edmonton Journal, Financial Post, Globe and Mail, Charlottetown Guardian, Kingston Whig-Standard, Regina Leader Post, The Leader, Montreal Gazette, National Post, Ottawa Citizen, The Province, Saskatoon Star Phoenix, Sudbury Star, St. John's Telegram, Saint John Telegraph-Journal, Times-Colonist, Toronto Star, The Tri-Cities Now, Vancouver Sun, Windsor Star, Winnipeg Free Press.*
3 Search parameters were designed to collect stories across various terms for women as a group in politics, together with various terms indicating violence and abuse. The search was confined to Canadian news stories given the geographic focus of this analysis. Exact search parameters used were as follows: ((women/woman/female AND candidate(s)/politician(s)/leader(s)/ MP(s)) OR (woman/women in politics) AND (harass* OR violen* OR abus* OR slur OR attack* OR MeToo OR assault*).
4 Women premiers in 2014 were Christy Clark (BC), Allison Redford (AB), Eva Aariak (Nunavut), Kathleen Wynne (ON), Pauline Marois (QC), and Kathy Dunderdale (NL).

5 The data analyses have thus far focused only on disaggregating gender by race in terms of coding GBV-P, but future research must definitely include other disaggregated analyses (for example, by disability, trans status, and so on).
6 2SLGBTQQIA+ refers to those who identify as two-spirit, lesbian, gay, bisexual, transgender, queer, questioning, intersex, androgynous, and asexual. "Two-spirit" is a term used by some Indigenous people to reflect the complex (and non-binary) nature of gender roles and identities in Indigenous communities.

REFERENCES

Amnesty International UK. 2019. "Black and Asian Women MPs Abused More Online." Amnesty International UK. https://www.amnesty.org.uk/online-violence-women-mps.
Baluja, Tamara. 2013. "Canadian Media Guild Data Shows 10,000 Job Losses in Past Five Years." *J-Source*, 19 November 2013. https://j-source.ca/article/canadian-media-guild-data-shows-10000-job-losses-in-past-five-years/.
Benjamin, Diane. 2017. "Episodic vs. Thematic Stories: A FrameWorks Institute FrameByte." FrameWorks, 2 June 2017. https://www.frameworksinstitute.org/article/episodic-vs-thematic-stories/.
Biroli, Flávia. 2016. "Political Violence against Women in Brazil: Expressions and Definitions." *Revista Direito e Práxis* 7 (15): 557–89. https://www.redalyc.org/pdf/3509/350947688018.pdf.
– 2018. "Violence against Women and Reactions to Gender Equality in Politics." *Politics & Gender* 14 (4): 681–5. https://doi.org/10.1017/S1743923X18000600.
Bittner, Amanada. 2011. *Platform or Personality? The Role of Party Leaders in Elections*. New York: Oxford University Press.
Boukes, Mark, Natalie P. Jones, and Rens Vliegenthart. 2022. "Newsworthiness and Story Prominence: How the Presence of News Factors Relates to Upfront Position and Length of News Stories." *Journalism* 23 (1): 98–116. https://doi.org/10.1177/1464884919899313.
Bowman Williams, Jamillah. 2021. "Maximizing #MeToo: Intersectionality & the Movement." *Boston College Law Review* 62 (6): 1797–1864. https://doi.org/10.2139/ssrn.3620439.
Braid, Don. 2018. "Sexual Harassment in Politics is Finally Out of the Bottle." *Calgary Herald*, 25 January 2018, A.4. https://calgaryherald.com/news/politics/braid-sexual-harassment-in-politics-is-finally-is-out-of-the-bottle.
Brown, Nadia E. 2014. *Sisters in the Statehouse: Black Women and Legislative Decision Making*. New York: Oxford University Press.
Brown, Nadia E., and Sarah Allen Gershon. 2021. "Glass Half Full: Cautious Optimism and the Future of Black Women Political Elites in America." *Journal of Race, Ethnicity, and Politics* 6 (1): 3–15. https://doi.org/10.1017/REP.2020.44.

CAJ (Canadian Association of Journalists). 2011. *Ethics Guidelines*. Toronto, ON: CAJ. https://caj.ca/ethics/.

CBC News. 1991. "Sexism in the House of Commons." *CBC News*, 23 September 1991. CBC News Digital Archive. https://www.cbc.ca/player/play/2678274032.

Celis, Karen, and Sarah Childs. 2020. *Feminist Democratic Representation*. New York: Oxford University Press.

Chronicle Herald. 2020. "Hate Is Not Debate." *Chronicle Herald*, 13 August 2020, A.6.

Collier, Cheryl N., and Tracey Raney. 2018a. "Canada's Member-to-Member Code of Conduct on Sexual Harassment in the House of Commons: Progress or Regress?" *Canadian Journal of Political Science* 51 (4): 795–815. https://doi.org/10.1017/S000842391800032X.

– 2018b. "Understanding Sexism and Sexual Harassment in Politics: A Comparison of Westminster Parliaments in Australia, the United Kingdom, and Canada." *Social Politics: International Studies in Gender, State & Society* 25 (3): 432–55. https://doi.org/10.1093/sp/jxy024.

– 2019. "Another Barrier for Women in Politics: Violence." *The Conversation*, 5 May 2019. https://theconversation.com/another-barrier-for-women-in-politics-violence-113637.

Congress and Council of Europe. 2020. *Fighting Sexist Violence against Women in Politics at Local and Regional Level*. Statutory Forum. Report CG-FORUM(2020)02-04final, 7 December 2020. https://rm.coe.int/fighting-sexist-violence-against-women-in-politics-at-local-and-region/1680a061c3.

Cotter, Colleen. 2010. *News Talk: Investigating the Language of Journalism*. Cambridge: Cambridge University Press.

Curry, Bill, and Laura Stone. 2018. "MPs Warn of Harassment on Parliament Hill." *Globe and Mail*, 30 January 2018, A.4.

Dawson, Tyler. 2017. "Threats against Wynne Range from the Bizarre to the Serious, Documents Reveal." *Ottawa Citizen*, 21 June 2017, A.1. https://ottawacitizen.com/opinion/columnists/dawson-threats-against-wynne-range-from-the-bizarre-to-the-serious.

Equal Press. n.d. *Reporting on Gender-Based Violence: A Guide for Journalists*. A project of MOSAIC. https://web.archive.org/web/20220527215133if_/http://equalpress.ca/wp-content/uploads/2020/02/EP_Guidebook.pdf.

Evelyn, Charelle. 2018. "Stepping Back to Look Ahead: Why This Outspoken Parliamentary Secretary Volunteered to Be Demoted." *The Hill Times*, 12 September 2018. https://www.hilltimes.com/story/2018/09/12/stepping-back-look-ahead-celina-caesar-chavannes-explains-choice-drop-ps-job/226974/.

Fileborn, Bianca, and Rachel Loney-Howes, eds. 2019. *#MeToo and the Politics of Social Change*. Cham, CH: Palgrave Macmillan.

Gamson, William A. 1975. "Review of *Frame Analysis: An Essay on the Organization of Experience* by Erving Goffman." *Contemporary Sociology* 4 (6): 603–7. https://doi.org/10.2307/2064022.

Garcia, Sandra E. 2017. "The Woman Who Created #MeToo Long before Hashtags." *New York Times*, 20 October 2017. https://www.nytimes.com/2017/10/20/us/me-too-movement-tarana-burke.html.

Gee, Erin, and Erica Ifill. 2018. "Canada's 'Time's Up!' Reckoning Is Here." *Ottawa Citizen*, 25 January 2018. https://ottawacitizen.com/opinion/columnists/ifill-and-gee-canadas-times-up-reckoning-is-here.

Globe and Mail. 2022. *The Globe and Mail Editorial Code of Conduct*. https://www.theglobeandmail.com/files/editorial/EditorialCodeOfConduct.pdf.

Gooch, Tiffany. 2020a. "One Black Woman in Parliament Is Not Enough to Celebrate." *Toronto Star*, 1 November 2020, IN.7. https://www.thestar.com/opinion/contributors/one-black-woman-in-parliament-is-not-enough-to-celebrate/article_82b45f6d-084e-596d-80a3-db2c8ea61273.html.

– 2020b. "The Time to Support Women in Politics Is Now." *Toronto Star*, 16 August 2020, O.2. https://www.thestar.com/opinion/contributors/time-to-support-women-in-politics-is-now/article_36af0e75-9659-562b-ae8a-66a4bf0a36c9.html.

Goodyear-Grant, Elizabeth. 2013. *Gendered News: Media Coverage and Electoral Politics in Canada*. Vancouver, BC: UBC Press.

Hanes, Allison. 2019. "Women in Leadership Face a Perpetual Fight; Double Standards, Vitriol Persist 30 Years after Polytechnique." *Montreal Gazette*, 2 December 2019, A.1. https://montrealgazette.com/news/local-news/hanes-30-years-after-polytechnique-women-in-power-face-perpetual-fight.

Hillstrom, Laurie Collier. 2019. *The #MeToo Movement*. Santa Barbara, CA: ABC-Clio.

Iyengar, Shanto. 1991. *Is Anyone Responsible? How Television Frames Political Issues*. Chicago: University of Chicago Press.

– 1996. "Framing Responsibility for Political Issues." *The ANNALS of the American Academy of Political and Social Science* 546 (1): 59–70. https://doi.org/10.1177/0002716296546001006.

Kingston Whig-Standard. 2018. "The Hill's #MeToo Shameful, Inevitable." *Kingston Whig-Standard*, 6 January 2018, B.7.

Krook, Mona Lena. 2020. *Violence against Women in Politics*. New York: Oxford University Press.

– 2022. "Semiotic Violence against Women: Theorizing Harms against Female Politicians." *Signs* 47 (2): 371–97. https://doi.org/10.1086/716642.

Krook, Mona Lena, and Juliana Restrepo Sanin. 2016. "Gender and Political Violence in Latin America: Concepts, Debates, and Solutions." *Política y Gobierno* 23 (1): 125–57. http://www.politicaygobierno.cide.edu/index.php/pyg/article/view/737/592.

Kuperberg, Rebecca. 2018. "Intersectional Violence against Women in Politics." *Politics & Gender* 14 (4): 685–90. https://doi.org/10.1017/S1743923X18000612.

Leung, Rebecca, and Robert Williams. 2019. "#MeToo and Intersectionality: An Examination of the #MeToo Movement through the R. Kelly Scandal." *Journal of Communication Inquiry* 43 (4): 349–71. https://doi.org/10.1177/0196859919874138.

Onwuachi-Willig, Angela. 2018. "What About #UsToo: The Invisibility of Race in the #MeToo Movement." *Yale Law Journal Forum* 128. https://www.yalelawjournal.org/forum/what-about-ustoo.

Oppenheim, Maya. 2019. "General Election: Women MPs Standing Down over 'Horrific Abuse,' Campaigners Warn." *The Independent*, 31 October 2019. https://www.independent.co.uk/news/uk/politics/general-election-woman-mps-step-down-abuse-harassment-a9179906.html.

Organization of American States (OAS). 2017. *Inter-American Model Law on the Prevention, Punishment and Eradication of Violence against Women in Political Life*. Inter-American Commission on Women. Follow-up to Mechanism to the Belém do Pará Convention (MESECVI). Washington, DC: MESECVI. https://www.oas.org/en/mesecvi/docs/LeyModeloViolenciaPolitica-EN.pdf.

OurDigitalWorld. n.d. "Women's History in Ontario: Agnes Macphail, Member of Parliament." Ontario's Multicultural History. https://help.vitatoolkit.ca/472/exhibit/12.

Proudfoot, Shannon. 2019. "Why Would Anyone Hate Catherine McKenna?" *Maclean's*, 4 November 2019. https://www.macleans.ca/politics/ottawa/why-would-anyone-hate-catherine-mckenna/.

Renzetti, Elizabeth. 2019. "Let Your Daughters Grow Up to Be Politicians." *Globe and Mail*, 15 November 2019, O.2. https://www.theglobeandmail.com/opinion/article-let-your-daughters-grow-up-to-be-politicians/.

Samara Centre for Democracy. 2022. *SAMbot 2021 Federal Election Report*. Toronto, ON: Samara Centre for Democracy. www.samaracentre.ca/articles/sambot-2021-federal-election-snapshot.

Sampert, Shannon. 2019. "Misogyny, Violence Persist 30 Years On." *Winnipeg Free Press*, 5 December 2019. https://www.winnipegfreepress.com/opinion/analysis/2019/12/05/misogyny-violence-persist-30-years-on.

Skelton, Chad. 2018. "There Are Fewer Journalists in Canada than 15 Years Ago – But Not as Few as You Might Think." *J-Source*, 4 May 2018. https://j-source.ca/article/canadian-journalists-statistics/.

Stone, Jon. 2017. "Ethnic Minority Women MPs Most Targeted for Abuse and Attack, Parliamentary Authorities Say." *The Independent*, 21 March 2017. https://www.independent.co.uk/news/uk/politics/mps-abuse-attack-black-ethnic-minority-women-diane-abbott-jo-cox-murder-a7641916.html.

Stone, Laura. 2019. "Liberal MP Celina Caesar-Chavannes Says She Was Met with 'Hostility, Anger' in Private Trudeau Talks." *Globe and Mail*, 8 March 2019. https://www.theglobeandmail.com/canada/article-liberal-mp-celina-caesar-chavannes-says-she-was-met-with-hostility/.

Thomas, Melanee, Allison Harell, and Tania Gosselin. 2018. "Gender, Tone, and Content of Premiers' News Coverage: A Matched Comparison." In *Political Elites in Canada: Power and Influence in Instantaneous Times*, edited by Alex Marland, Thierry Giasson, and Andrea Lawlor, 89–108. Vancouver, BC: UBC Press.

Thompson, Debra. 2008. "Is Race Political?" *Canadian Journal of Political Science* 41 (3): 525–47. https://doi.org/10.1017/S0008423908080827.

Tolley, Erin. 2016. *Framed: Media and the Coverage of Race in Canadian Politics*. Vancouver, BC: UBC Press.

Tomney, Sue. 2017. "Stop the Attacks on Women; Misogyny Must Be Eliminated." *Calgary Herald*, 18 February 2017, A.11.

Trimble, Linda. 2017. *Ms. Prime Minister: Gender, Media, and Leadership*. Toronto, ON: University of Toronto Press.

Trimble, Linda, Jane Arscott, and Manon Tremblay. 2013. *Stalled: The Representation of Women in Canadian Governments*. Vancouver, BC: UBC Press.

Tuchman, Gaye, Arlene Kaplan Daniels, and James Benet, eds. 1978. *Hearth and Home: Images of Women in the Mass Media*. New York: Oxford University Press.

Van der Pas, Daphne Joanna, and Loes Aaldering. 2020. "Gender Differences in Political Media Coverage: A Meta-Analysis." *Journal of Communication* 70 (1): 114–43. https://doi.org/10.1093/joc/jqz046.

6 Gender-Based Violence, Humour, and Frontier Masculinity in Alberta Political Cartoons

RISSA REIST

Introduction

"I've been beating this drum for 10, 11 years. I will continue to beat it, I promise. But it's against the law to beat Rachel Notley."

Former Wildrose Party leader Brian Jean made these remarks in August 2016 during a town hall meeting in Fort McMurray, Alberta. According to a local newspaper, "much of the audience laughed, while other corners of the room gasped in shock." Jean would later go on to apologize for his words, referring to them as an "inappropriate attempt" at humour (McDermott 2016). These comments would come only weeks after an Alberta golf course used a picture of Alberta Premier Rachel Notley's face as a target during a local golf tournament. The president of the hosting organization, Ernest Bothi from the Brooks Big Country Oilmen's Association, later responded to the incident by saying: "My goal was just to make people laugh ... It was a thing of humour" (McIntosh 2016).

Following these events, an Alberta cartoonist published a cartoon where Brian Jean stood on a golf course angrily shouting: "Damn it! I thought she'd make an easier target!" At the same time, a man stands next to Jean and advises: "She's veering left again" (Mayes 2016c). The subsequent release of this cartoon emphasized the notion of violence towards women in politics as acceptable, normal, and even humorous. These events shed light on the importance of understanding the role that humour plays as a way of communicating violent discussions about who can and cannot participate in Canadian democracy.

Scholars of women's political representation have expressed concerns about the limited space given to women in politics who advocate for improvements to election laws and for parties to do more to recruit female candidates (Trimble, Arscott, and Tremblay 2013). With the gradual changing of women's roles, research has identified gender-based violence in politics (GBV-P) as a form of gendered backlash that dissuades women and other marginalized groups from engaging politically. In the case of Alberta, for instance, Postmedia found that former premiers Alison Redford and Rachel Notley received significantly more threats than did their male predecessors or successors (Gerein 2017). In 2018, the Canadian Broadcasting Corporation also found that Rachel Notley received eleven death threats during her first three years as premier (Trynacity 2018).

The events in Alberta are not isolated. Rather, they point to a greater need to understand how gendered discussions on violence and political leadership are constructed, especially through humour, which is rarely examined as a vehicle of violence.[1] How does hostile humour in political cartoons communicate socially and culturally resonant norms and assumptions about gender, violence, and politics? Through content and discourse analysis of a data set of 164 cartoons published in two leading Alberta newspapers, this chapter explores how hostile humour has been used as a tool to normalize violence in the political sphere. The findings of the chapter show that the use of hostile humour is not random or arbitrary. Rather, it is rooted in gendered intersectional ideals of frontier masculinity that reinforce long-standing views about politics. This type of humour positions politics as an aggressive white male pursuit and marks women as deviant to political life. Ultimately, hostile humour situates women as outsiders to politics and conveys discomfort with the idea of women exercising governmental power and authority.

Humour and Hostility

This chapter expands the concept of hostile humour to examine the ways that editorial cartoons published in Alberta newspapers convey hostile and gendered political meanings about former Alberta premiers Alison Redford, Rachel Notley, and Ed Stelmach. Hostile humour refers to humour targeted at an individual or group that results in them being "humiliated, insulted, embarrassed, or physically hurt" (Weinstein, Hodgins, and Ostvik-White 2011, 1044). It exists within a framework of GBV-P by working towards a more expansive definition of how violence functions in political discourse. Scholars, such as Krook (2020), note that research on political violence has primarily focused on physical violence. Hostile humour contributes to present conversations on gender, violence, and politics by accounting for the lesser spoken ways that violence is performed against women in politics. Humour, while often perceived as apolitical in nature, reflects commonly held beliefs and values circulated within a given community. As a result, studying the relationship between violence and gender in political humour reveals the extent to which violence acts as a normalized part of common discussions about women and democratic representation.

Hostility operates as an important element of political humour. For instance, Becker's (2012) study of satire in late-night comedy found that hostile humour dominated. Comedians consistently offered unflattering portrayals of politics, such as referring to the John McCain campaign as a bag of dog poop. As is the case for traditional news sources such as television and newspapers, political humour's use of aggressive metaphors casts politics, and especially elections, as a "battleground" (Gidengil and Everitt 1999). Scholars highlight that violence is often dismissed as "the cost of doing politics" (Krook and Restrepo Sanín 2020, 740). This chapter seeks to conceptualize how humour fits within broader discussions of GBV-P. Specifically, I focus on the concepts of hostile humour and frontier masculinity to help identify the intersectional ways that aggression communicated within political humour upholds the notion that politics is a male-dominated realm.

When considering the reception of hostile humour, research finds that this approach to joking is more likely to be appreciated by those who already possess feelings of aggression (Chan et al. 2016). Early work on hostile humour conducted by Byrne (1956) found that individuals who displayed hostile behaviour were more likely to enjoy cartoons that employed its use. Dworkin and Efran (1967) found that male undergraduate students who were previously disposed to criticism that caused them to become angry subsequently rated hostile humour as funnier than undergraduate students who had not previously had their moods altered. More contemporary research mirrors these findings. For instance, research conducted by Samson and Meyer (2010) determined that study participants were more likely to enjoy hostile humour if they themselves were aggressive.

Overall, hostile humour functions as a crucial element of political humour. However, hostile humour is more likely to be enjoyed by those already predisposed to feelings of aggression and anger. Hostile humour can also impact the attitudes and behaviours of individuals. Berkowitz (1970) found that women, when exposed to aggressive humour and then told to evaluate potential job candidates, were more aggressive towards the prospective applicants than those exposed to neutral types of humour. Additionally, the use of hostile humour by comedians can have more of an effect on political attitudes than humour deemed "friendlier" and more "playful" by the audience (Becker 2012,

806). What remains unknown is how hostile humour has been applied to the presence of women in political office.

Krook (2020) offers three levels at which the gendered dynamics of violence in politics operate: structural, cultural, and symbolic, wherein violence serves to uphold the public/private divide situating men as political beings and women as domesticated beings meant to occupy the space of the home. The research on how political humour treats women political actors mimics these assertions. Studies have found that the way in which women are made fun of in politics highlights their gendered differences through the use of overtly gendered stereotypes that frame women as political outsiders (Conners 2010; Edwards and McDonald 2010). Additionally, sexist beliefs that women are not funny and do not have the ability to speak about politics further delegitimizes women's capacity to act as political joke-makers (Wilkinson 2004).

Political cartoons are a crucial element of political communication due to their ability to communicate values about politics quickly and effectively. Political cartoons have been a consistent aspect of mainstream media coverage in Canada since the early 1900s. Like other sources of media, political cartoons draw on normalized assumptions and values, and serve as a cultural roadmap for understanding politics and identity. Like the media industry as a whole, the cartooning industry has generally been seen as a masculine space (Wilkinson 2004). Sue Dewar serves as Canada's first and only full-time female political cartoonist.

Political cartoons specifically highlight men's public roles and white women's caregiving activities (Reist and Trimble 2020). For instance, research on the representation of Canadian female political leaders Kim Campbell and Audrey McLaughlin in political cartoons found that "plus souvent que leurs homologues masculins les femmes sont montrées avec une faiblesse de caractère et n'ont pas le contrôle de la situation" (Tremblay and Bélanger 1997, 67).[2] Similarly, research on the representation of Hillary Clinton in political cartoons throughout different points of her political career highlight how feminine stereotypes were a vital part of how she was represented (Conners 2010). Meanwhile, editorial cartoons have cast other women, such as Indigenous women, as hyper-aggressive (Reist 2023). Humour becomes a site of GBV-P through its capacity to integrate thematic elements of structural, cultural, and symbolic violence into its content. This type of humour employs modes of aggression in order to "purposely alienate, hurt or manipulate others, mostly to defend oneself against threat" (Van den Broeck et al. 2012, 87). Questions that emerge from this existing literature include the following: Who is purposely harmed in humour? What values does hostile humour seek to defend?

Context

One cannot study humour or cartoons without understanding the culture from which they emerge. Hay demonstrates how humour is "culturally grounded" (2000, 738). Regarding political cartoons, Werner emphasizes that "every cartoon assumes an ideal viewer who has the relevant cultural memory" (2004, 1) to understand enough of the context to find it humorous. As such, the site of production greatly influences what can be communicated through humour and political cartoons, and what can be understood by audiences.

Alberta provides an important site for considering how GBV-P has been articulated in political humour due to the province, at the time of submission of this chapter, being the only Canadian province to have had three women premiers. The most recent Alberta woman premier is Danielle Smith, who assumed office in October 2022. At this point, Alberta is also the only province in Canada to have three different women premiers from three different political parties hold the position of premier long-term following a provincial election. Timing is also important. Within five years, Alberta has had two women as premier and, since 2012, has had three women opposition leaders, including Rachel Notley, following her defeat in the 2019 Alberta provincial election. This heightened presence of women in Alberta provincial politics within a relatively short period makes for an interesting and essential case study for considering how GBV-P is communicated in cartoons.

To provide a gendered assessment of Alberta political humour in political cartoons, an understanding of the culture in which humour and cartoons emerge needs to be considered. In this chapter, I offer an interpretation of gendered violence in Alberta through the lens of what I will be referring to as "frontier masculinity." Research on masculinity and identity in the Canadian context has identified numerous ways in which masculinities manifest themselves in Canada. However, this unique type of masculinity is one that is rooted in settler-colonial ideals of rugged individualism, white supremacy, dependence on natural resources, and misogyny. Collectively, these characteristics contribute to the violent nature of gendered joke-making in this province.

The concept of frontier masculinity can be used as an intersectional lens to capture the forms of masculinity evident in resource-reliant contexts, which valorize certain traits, behaviours, and attitudes (Miller 2004, 48). Frontier masculinity is rooted in ideals of the "frontier myth," which, according to Williams (2021, 61), involves an "expropriation of land, misogyny and white supremacy," along with the assumption that the land was empty before European contact. This assumption subsequently encourages the physical and cultural elimination of Indigenous peoples from their traditional lands. Frontier masculinity reflects intersectional notions of power by providing a framework for considering how the media appeal to preconceived notions of gender, race, and Indigeneity to determine who can and cannot successfully engage in political life.

Where does GBV-P fall within a framework of frontier masculinity? Here I propose three ways that frontier masculinity ensures the acceptance of GBV-P. First, under frontier masculinity, violence acts as a necessity for the continuation of the status quo. Violence exists as a "necessary sacrifice for the constitution of [a] dominant Albertan identity" (Montford 2013, 107). Frontier masculinity uses violence to construct the ideal image of a political individual as a rugged, aggressive white man. From an intersectional perspective, this appeal to the frontier myth maintains the continuation of what Williams refers to as "white men as institution" (2021, 43) by ensuring that white men exist as the architects of social order.

Second, violence, as enacted within a context of frontier masculinity, works as a form of cultural violence by placing marginalized people who challenge commonly accepted norms about their race, gender, sexuality, and so on "back in their place" (Krook 2020, 101). Frontier masculinity creates a definitive "other" within Alberta's cultural discourse. Women, Indigenous peoples, 2SLGBTQQIA+[3] individuals, and people who are not white constitute this "other." According to Wright (2001, 19), if these social divides are to be maintained, the frontier man must intervene in order to ensure that the "proper social order" is upheld. This process occurs by enacting violence that is seen as justified and hence encouraged. In doing so, just as land needs to be conquered, so too must these deviant individuals.

Finally, violence acts as a form of elimination. Elimination is multifaceted. It occurs through the elimination of Indigenous perspectives about colonization. Frontier masculinity then replaces these narratives with stories that centre the white male cowboy as the protagonist and ultimate hero in the establishment of settler-colonial society. Indigenous peoples are eliminated from these stories of origin, and if they are discussed, they are presented as villains that the frontier man must eliminate (Wright 2001). Following the establishment of such a society, frontier masculinity ensures that public spaces are synonymous with aggressive white male spaces and that women's presence is minimalized or erased completely (Carrington, McIntosh, and Scott 2010). Wright (2001) suggests that the repetition of public discourses upholding the supremacy of the rugged individualistic male hero positions this type of man as the sole contributor to economic growth and the only individual capable of possessing complete agency and autonomy. As a result, violence enacted through frontier masculinity ensures the erasure of groups who fail to meet the archetype of the aggressive white male. These groups include Indigenous peoples and particularly Indigenous women, who are targeted because of both their race and their gender, women, non-white people, and men who fail to live up to the ascribed norms of frontier masculinity.

As I will explain further in this chapter, the presence of frontier masculinity in Alberta helps inform our understanding of GBV-P in Canada by illustrating how gendered violence is normalized and reinforced through humour and rooted in culturally specific understandings of power, gender, and agency. This cultural rhetoric serves to justify the violence directed at women in politics, since they are constructed as not being able to perform properly within the white, masculine, and public realm of politics. As a result, rather than being an element of politics worth critiquing, violence is marked as a necessity for maintaining the political and cultural status quo.

Case Study

Humour is regularly used to normalize beliefs and values, yet little attention has been paid to humour's role in facilitating gendered and hostile representations of political leaders. How does one take a gendered approach to the study of hostile humour when examining Alberta politics? This chapter demonstrates that research must go beyond simply recognizing the joke expressed by a political cartoon. While I acknowledge that humour is multifaceted and complex, my focus is on the gendered meanings communicated by hostile humour. I created a gender-based framework for considering how hostility towards political leaders is articulated in political cartoons. The methodology draws on past research on gendered media framing, democratic representation, as well as research investigating the relationships between humour, hostility, and GBV-P (Shifman and Lemish 2010) to develop a framework for conducting content and discourse analysis of the cartoons. This framework allows me to identify and interpret the key aspects of hostile humour, which is further elaborated below. I propose two ways in which humour reinforces gendered hostility and gendered beliefs about political life. Briefly, these are (1) hostile humour themes, that is, jokes that position the premier as humiliated, insulted, embarrassed, or physically hurt; and (2) the way in which cartoonists direct violence at the premier, such as whether the violence came from a person or an event.

Political cartoons are essential to these discussions because of their ability to communicate important cultural meanings through visual and lexical framing techniques. This chapter carefully analyses political cartoons containing physical depictions of Alberta premiers Alison Redford, Rachel Notley, and Ed Stelmach published in Alberta's two highest circulating opinion-leading newspapers, the *Edmonton Journal* and the *Calgary Herald*, both of which are owned by Postmedia Network and play an important agenda-setting role in the province of Alberta. The corpus of cartoons was manually retrieved from the University of Alberta's microfiche copies of the two newspapers. The time period for this study was the first eighteen months in office. I did not consider repeat cartoons. A sample size of 164 cartoons was collected, of which 37 contained Alison Redford, 63 contained Rachel Notley, and 64 contained Ed Stelmach, representing all visual depictions of each of the three premiers over their first eighteen months in that office.

Findings

Hostile Humour Themes

Alberta cartoonists used hostile humour themes to mock and critique the leadership characteristics of Redford, Notley, and Stelmach. Of the three premiers studied, Alison Redford received the most hostile humour references, with ten cartoons or 27 per cent of cartoons about her depicting her featuring some form of hostile humour theme. In Rachel Notley's case, thirteen cartoons or 21 per cent of cartoons depicting her contained one of the forms of hostility. Male premier Ed Stelmach was the least likely to be the recipient of these references, with only ten cartoons or 16 per cent of all cartoons depicting him containing a reference to hostile humour.

The differences between Redford and Notley are likely a result of political context, with Redford being the only premier of the three studied to face an election campaign during her first eighteen months as premier. Political scientists note that elections are often used as opportunities to deploy violent metaphors (Gidengil and Everitt 1999) and game frames (Trimble and Sampert 2004), both of which highlight the aggressive nature of politics. Three of the cartoons published about the election contained a reference to violence. If this study had only accounted for non-election days, then seven cartoons containing Alison Redford, or 19 per cent of all cartoons about her, would have contained a hostile humour theme.

Crucially, of the four hostile humour themes identified by Weinstein, Hodgins, and Ostvik-White (2011, 1044), only one of the four themes, physical harm, was consistently found within the corpus of cartoons (see Table 6.1). Discourse analysis revealed that physical violence in the cartoons took two forms: the actual enactment of physical harm and the threat of bodily harm. As a result, I coded these as discrete categories. References to humiliation, insult, or embarrassment were rarely, if ever, overtly represented in any of the cartoons. This finding suggests that cartoonists are more likely to rely on explicit forms of violence that can be quickly visualized and understood.

Cartoonists provided multiple examples in which the bodies of the premiers became the targets of violence. In a cartoon entitled "Alison Redford's TV Address Details Alberta's Fiscal Woes," two people sit on a couch in front of a television as Redford is devoured by a killer whale (Larter 2013). Meanwhile, a cartoon by Malcolm Mayes showed Notley tied up and about to be pulled down a cliff by a man who represented the New Democratic Party (NDP) Leap Manifesto (Mayes 2016b). Incoming physical violence was the most often used hostile humour theme. In these cases, the premier's ignorance of the impending physical violence heightened the humorous nature of the cartoon. For instance, in a 2015 cartoon, Rachel Notley hangs a red blanket on a laundry line, remarking: "You see? ... This city girl knows a thing or two about getting farm chores done safely" (Mayes 2015a). In the cartoon, the premier remains unaware that a visibly angry bull representing Alberta farmers is about to charge in her direction. In another cartoon, Stelmach is featured standing with an open bucket under the back end of an elephant marked "oil sands," seemingly unaware of the consequences of such an action (Rodewalt 2008). Similarly, in a cartoon from the *Calgary Herald*, Alison Redford stands with a man representing an anonymous Progressive Conservative Party member. They gaze at a large elephant with the words "Alberta Deficit" written across the elephant's trunk. Redford says: "Gasp, it's huge! What does he eat?" The man next to her replies: "Premiers" (Larter 2012).

Direct references to humiliation, insult, or embarrassment were rarely present in the data collected. Discourse analysis, however, revealed harassment as an additional form of hostile humour, which was characterized by persistent behaviours that were presented as unwelcome by the premier but did not cause immediate or expected physical harm. While hostile humour has not typically included

Table 6.1. Hostile humour themes in representations of the premier

Hostile humour theme	Alison Redford (n = 37)		Rachel Notley (n = 63)		Ed Stelmach (n = 64)	
	N	%	N	%	N	%
Humiliated	0	0	1	2	0	0
Insulted	0	0	0	0	0	0
Embarrassed	0	0	0	0	0	0
Physically hurt	4	11	4	6	3	5
Physically hurt (incoming)	6	16	5	8	7	11
Harassed	0	0	3	5	0	0
Totals	10	27	13	21	10	16

harassment, and little research has considered the gendered nature of hostile humour in political cartoons, adding additional categories that are often gendered in nature provides a more nuanced understanding of how GBV-P subtly operates in Canadian democracy. Crucially, Rachel Notley was the only premier to be portrayed as the subject of harassment. References to harassment appeared in three of the cartoons, or 5 per cent of the total number of cartoons in which Notley is included. For example, harassment was depicted by showing Notley being taunted by crowds who shouted: "Lock her up! Lock her up!" (Mayes 2016a), which was a reference to chants that occurred at a political rally for Conservative Party of Canada leadership candidate Chris Alexander. Images like these become problematic insofar as humorous references to harassment contribute to what Krook notes as a tendency to "naturalize" violence, resulting in violence becoming trivialized and hidden (2020, 46).

Overall, cartoonists consistently subjected the premiers to one crucial form of hostile humour: physical violence. In particular, cartoonists emphasized the threat of physical harm. Only Notley was presented as the subject of harassment. This finding mirrors Alberta's political reality emulating the harassment received by Notley online. Additionally, the cartoons articulate these actions as humorous as opposed to societal problems rooted in broader concerns about women's democratic representation. The next section builds on this work. From here, I consider who the perpetrators of violence were against the three premiers studied. As discussed in the following section, the ways that cartoonists applied violence to the politicians in political cartoons reinforce gendered assumptions about agency, motivation, and power in the Alberta political context, which are rooted in broader intersectional themes of frontier masculinity.

Perpetrators of Violence against the Premiers

Focusing specifically on whom political cartoonists deem as acceptable perpetrators of violence, I found that Notley was most likely to be the recipient, or soon to be the recipient, of violence from Albertans or representations of Alberta voters. This finding can be seen in Table 6.2, where N represents the number of cartoons showing each premier as physically harmed or as about to be harmed. This focus encourages a clearer understanding of how cartoonists articulated the relationship between violence and political leadership. The table highlights that a significantly larger percentage of the depictions of violence against the two women premiers, and particularly Notley, result from a visible person or a representation of group interests.

Notley and Redford had their attackers present in the frame of the cartoons more often than not, highlighting the fact that cartoonists were more likely to see the actions of the two woman premiers as in need of direct retaliation and backlash from Albertans (see Table 6.2). Redford and Notley were chased by wolves and zombies, and characterized as about to be swallowed by large animals representing a form of the Alberta public. Thus, the direct targets of violence became the bodies of Redford and Notley.

Masculinity was also an important element of the violence enacted on the premiers. For instance, in a cartoon titled "Sales Tax Idea Catches Fire in Alberta," Redford was shown tied at the stake as a male farmer attempted to start the logs on fire (Mayes 2013). In response to the Notley government's farm safety legislation, Bill 6, a cartoon captioned "Yet Another Unfortunate Farm Accident" featured Notley with a pitchfork in her back while a male farmer stood behind her and simply said: "Oops" (Mayes 2015b). These findings illustrate the extent to which ideals of frontier masculinity have become entrenched in Alberta political humour. The images highlight the normality of showing the frontier man pushing back against a woman who challenges the status quo.

In these cartoons, men were more likely than women to be drawn as the unapologetic aggressors, enacting violence onto the body of a woman premier. They were also more likely to be shown as the exclusive representation of the Alberta public. The only woman drawn as the sole enactor of violence in the cartoons studied was former Wildrose Party leader Danielle Smith (now leader of the United Conservative Party and Alberta's premier), who directed violence at Alison Redford during the 2012 Alberta provincial election. Outside of this finding, the only women to be drawn as aggressors in the cartoons were women presented as part of a large group, such as the group shouting chants

Table 6.2. Perpetrators of physical violence directed at the premier

Perpetrator(s) of violence	Alison Redford (n = 10)		Rachel Notley (n = 9)		Ed Stelmach (n = 10)	
	N	%	N	%	N	%
Cartoons in which the perpetrator of physical violence is visible in the cartoon	9	90	9	100	2	20
Cartoons in which the visible perpetrator is represented by another person or representation of the interests of a group of people	5	50	6	78	2	20

of "lock her up" at Rachel Notley. In the cartoons depicting Notley and Redford, there were two cartoons each that featured anonymous individuals performing violence onto the premiers. In each of these four cases, this violence was performed by men. This finding reinforces ideals of frontier masculinity in that the cartoons emphasize the necessity for male violence in politics. In these cases, even when the leader is a woman, the audience is reminded of the importance of the aggressive male protagonist in shaping politics. The finding also shows that women in public life are held accountable to a public that is assumed to represent male interests disproportionately.

By contrast, when Ed Stelmach was harmed as a result of a human attacker, the attacker was almost always left out of the frame of the cartoon. Overall, Stelmach was cast as the "bumbling idiot" of the three premiers studied. Cartoonists defined Stelmach's antics by his ignorance and, in some cases, childlike innocence. They also highlighted the "nice guy" persona that he once embodied during his 2006 bid to become party leader (Harasymiw 2014). For example, a cartoon featured Stelmach dressed as the children's character Charlie Brown. In it, Stelmach stares at the reader as he walks through a field with a sign saying "Caution, minefield" in the background (Rodewalt 2007b). In these cases, frontier masculinity becomes an impetus for critiquing Stelmach for not being masculine enough.[4]

While these cartoons do question Stelmach's capacity to lead, they also emphasize that his actions do not have violent consequences as a result of collective anger from Albertans. In one cartoon, for example, Stelmach lies in a hospital bed wrapped in bandages while providing a statement. A reporter asks him: "And how would you say your relationship with the oilfield industry is now, Mr. Stelmach?" Stelmach responds: "Pretty good

I'd say. Nobody really got hurt" (Rodewalt 2007a). The oilfield industry itself is left out of the frame of the cartoon. Unlike in their depictions of Stelmach's female counterparts, cartoonists obscured the identities of the instigators of violence when it came to Stelmach. Although only one example, this cartoon is illustrative of how democratic norms in Canada rely upon the tacit acceptance of violence onto political bodies. It further highlights linkages between masculinity and violence in Canada's political discourse, with the encouragement of violence from an assumed white, cis-gendered, heterosexual male public.

That cartoonists did not visually or discursively criticize the men drawn in the cartoons for instigating the violence onto the female premiers is also of note. Instead, they depict men's (violent) resistance to women's leadership through the enactment of bodily harm as acceptable and necessary for Alberta to thrive. In this case, ideals of frontier masculinity were upheld through the recentring of the agency of the independent, violent male. In addition to reinforcing traditional gendered beliefs about leadership, frontier masculinity also serves to uphold the ideological status quo. This status quo can be seen with past government policy positions such as sales taxes or farm safety legislation being met with hyper-masculine aggression. Differences in political positions then become an opportunity for male violence. In this sense, male aggression is constructed as acceptable when directed at women who challenge Alberta's ideological norms, including challenging who can wield power in the highest echelons of public office. In these cases, violence directed towards these powerful women is deemed legitimate and even humorous. Frontier masculinity and hostile humour then work to limit both who can be represented in politics and what issues can be discussed in the political realm without the threat of male violence.

Conclusion

Political humour was consistently marked by the presence of hostile humour, with hostile humour tropes being present in just over one-fifth of all cartons in the dataset. The analysis finds that cartoonists were more likely to use overt forms of violence that could be made easily readable to audiences. This finding was illustrated in the numerous references to either enacted bodily harm or anticipated bodily harm in the cartoons studied. This chapter's findings are particularly concerning as they illustrate the centrality of violence as a key theme in political humour. There were also limited signs of public backlash to these images through the use of letters to the editor and op-ed pieces. Moreover, a vast number of the cartoons studied were then published on the Artizans website (https://www.artizans.com/), making them even more accessible for public consumption.

Cartoonists highlighted the centrality of frontier masculinity as both an important element of Alberta political humour as well as a justification for the violence directed at the two leaders. This highlighting occurred by constructing Rachel Notley and Alison Redford as deviant to the established social norms and practices of Alberta. Cartoonists also cast these women as submissive to an aggressive masculine public and passive to the violence that these men enacted upon them. By accentuating violence with humour and, in the cases of the women premiers, with violence from Albertans themselves, cartoonists further normalized hostility towards the premiers studied.

It is important to stress that the politicians studied were three white, cis individuals. In this chapter, I propose that frontier masculinity can be used as a platform for thinking about GBV-P within an intersectional context and in other jurisdictions and contexts. If the individuals studied had been, for example, Indigenous women, I would anticipate that they would receive a greater number of hostile humour references, and there would be a further push in the cartoons to highlight the agency and centrality of the aggressive white man. Examples such as Jody Wilson-Raybould and Mary Simon provide interesting opportunities to think about how intersectional violence operates through frontier masculinity in future research. The application of frontier masculinity when thinking about violence in an intersectional way can serve as an entry point for bringing into conversation questions of settler colonialism, gender, and race. This approach can be particularly helpful when thinking about the ways that humour uses violence as a form of backlash against individuals who have historically been considered outsiders to political life. Beyond the study of humour, frontier masculinity might also be applied as an intersectional lens when considering other phenomena where violence threatens the democratic process. The Freedom Convoy that saw thousands of protesters occupy multiple neighbourhoods in downtown Ottawa for weeks in early 2022 has been noted to exist in relation to issues of violence, settler colonialism, and reclamation of white masculine entitlement (Farokhi, Anderson, and Jiwani 2022; McLaren 2022). The relationship between masculinity, violence, and politics is one that requires further academic attention both inside and beyond Canada.

Violence in politics does not simply affect the individual targeted. It also provides a warning about the harsh and brutal consequences that come when women enter politics (Krook and Restrepo Sanín 2020). In the case of political cartoons, images of violence are often minimized by the false assertion that it is "just a joke" and should not be taken seriously. However, as political cartoons occupy a central platform for both reflecting and normalizing common assumptions about politics, gender, and violence, the jokes produced in these images are not simply "a thing of humour." Instead, they operate crucially as a mode of gender-based violence in politics.

Implications for Action

The chapter has revealed several concerns regarding how violence is directed at women premiers in Alberta by political cartoonists. In light of these concerns, I propose three recommendations for media producers.

1. When a cartoon, news article, or opinion piece reinforces the acceptance of violence towards individuals and groups, editorial control by news editors should be exercised, and editors should remove the piece from the newspaper.
2. Newspapers should create an internally defined process for recognizing articles, opinion pieces, and cartoons that perpetuate an acceptance of GBV-P. Key questions to consider include the following: (1) How is violence used in this piece? (2) Who is the intended audience for the cartoon? (3) What underlying assumptions are directly or indirectly communicated? (4) How might groups who already possess antagonistic views against the individual or group shown respond to the piece?
3. Newspapers should include editorial cartoons from a diverse group of cartoonists. The analysis found that three male cartoonists drew all of the 164 cartoons studied. Newspapers should encourage equal access and participation of groups, including women, Indigenous peoples, and those marginalized by race and sexuality, in the production of political humour.
4. Additional research is needed to explore the interrelationships between race, gender, violence, and politics in political cartoons in Canada and worldwide.

NOTES

1. For an exception, see Dufort, Roy, and Olivier (2020).
2. Translation (by the author): "more often than their male counterparts, women are shown to have weakness of character and no control of the situation."
3. 2SLGBTQQIA+ refers to those who identify as two-spirit, lesbian, gay, bisexual, transgender, queer, questioning, intersex, androgynous, and

asexual. "Two-spirit" is a term used by some Indigenous people to reflect the complex (and non-binary) nature of gender roles and identities in Indigenous communities.

4 Similarly, Stelmach's failure to adequately perform masculinity was highlighted in cartoons comparing him to his predecessor Ralph Klein. Images such as these highlighted the centrality of masculinity in politics while also presenting Stelmach as not masculine enough for the job.

REFERENCES

Becker, Amy B. 2012. "Mass Communication and Society Comedy Types and Political Campaigns: The Differential Influence of Other-Directed Hostile Humor and Self-Ridicule on Candidate Evaluations." *Mass Communication and Society* 15 (6): 791–812. https://doi.org/10.1080/15205436.2011.628431.

Berkowitz, Leonard. 1970. "Aggressive Humor as a Stimulus to Aggressive Responses." *Journal of Personality and Social Psychology* 16 (4): 710–17. https://doi.org/10.1037/H0030077.

Byrne, Donn. 1956. "The Relationship between Humor and the Expression of Hostility." *Journal of Abnormal and Social Psychology* 53 (1): 84–9. https://doi.org/10.1037/H0043918.

Carrington, Kerry, Alison McIntosh, and John Scott. 2010. "Globalization, Frontier Masculinities and Violence: Booze, Blokes and Brawls." *The British Journal of Criminology* 50 (3): 393–413. https://doi.org/10.1093/BJC/AZQ003.

Chan, Yu-Chen, Yi-Jun Liao, Cheng-Hao Tu, and Hsueh-Chih Chen. 2016. "Neural Correlates of Hostile Jokes: Cognitive and Motivational Processes in Humor Appreciation." *Frontiers in Human Neuroscience* 10 (October): 527–41. https://doi.org/10.3389/fnhum.2016.00527.

Conners, Joan L. 2010. "Barack versus Hillary: Race, Gender, and Political Cartoon Imagery of the 2008 Presidential Primaries." *American Behavioral Scientist* 54 (3): 298–312. https://doi.org/10.1177/0002764210381703.

Dufort, Julie, Martin Roy, and Lawrence Olivier, eds. 2020. *Humour et violence symbolique*. Quebec, QC: Presses de l'Université Laval.

Dworkin, Earl S., and Jay S. Efran. 1967. "The Angered: Their Susceptibility to Varieties of Humor." *Journal of Personality and Social Psychology* 6 (2): 233–6. https://doi.org/10.1037/h0024568.

Edwards, Janis L, and C. Austin McDonald. 2010. "Reading Hillary and Sarah: Contradictions of Feminism and Representation in 2008 Campaign Political Cartoons." *American Behavioral Scientist* 54 (3): 313–29. https://doi.org/10.1177/0002764210381704.

Farokhi, Zeinab, David Anderson, and Yasmin Jiwani. 2022. "A Twitter Investigation Reveals What the 'Freedom Convoy,' Islamophobes, Incels and Hindu Supremacists Have in Common." *The Conversation*, 15 February 2022. https://theconversation.com/a-twitter-investigation-reveals-what-the-freedom-convoy-islamophobes-incels-and-hindu-supremacists-have-in-common-177026.

Gerein, Keith. 2017. "Statistics Show Notley Has Been the Most Threatened Alberta Premier." *Edmonton Journal*, 14 February 2017. https://edmontonjournal.com/news/politics/statistics-show-notley-has-been-the-most-threatened-alberta-premier.

Gidengil, Elisabeth, and Joanna Everitt. 1999. "Metaphors and Misrepresentation: Gendered Mediation in News Coverage of the 1993 Canadian Leaders Debates." *Harvard International Journal of Press/Politics* 4 (1): 48–65. https://doi.org/10.1177/1081180X99004001005.

Harasymiw, Bohdan. 2014. "Alberta's Premier Ed Stelmach: The Anomalous Case of Leadership Selection and Removal in a Canadian Province." *American Review of Canadian Studies* 44 (2): 216–33. https://doi.org/10.1080/02722011.2014.914961.

Hay, Jennifer. 2000. "Functions of Humor in the Conversations of Men and Women." *Journal of Pragmatics* 32 (6): 709–42. https://doi.org/10.1016/S0378-2166(99)00069-7.

Krook, Mona Lena. 2020. *Violence against Women in Politics*. Oxford: Oxford University Press.

Krook, Mona Lena, and Juliana Restrepo Sanín. 2020. "The Cost of Doing Politics? Analyzing Violence and Harassment against Female Politicians." *Perspectives on Politics* 18 (3): 740–55. https://doi.org/10.1017/S1537592719001397.

Larter, John. 2012. "Alberta Deficit." *Calgary Herald*, 7 September 2012, A12.

– 2013. "Alison Redford's TV Address Details Alberta's Fiscal Woes." *Calgary Herald*, 25 January 2013, A12.

Mayes, Malcolm. 2013. "Sales Tax Idea Catches Fire in Alberta." *Edmonton Journal*, 13 February 2013, A20.

– 2015a. "Rachel Notley Waves Bill 6 Flag." *Edmonton Journal*, 2 December 2015, A12.

– 2015b. "Yet Another Unfortunate Farm Accident." *Edmonton Journal*, 3 December 2015, A10.

– 2016a. "Rachel Notley Faces 'Lock Her Up' Chants." *Calgary Herald*, 7 December 2016, A11.

– 2016b. "Rachel Notley Is Reluctantly Tied to Federal NDP Leap Manifesto." *Edmonton Journal*, 12 April 2016, A6.

– 2016c. "Ric McIvor and Brian Jean Target Rachel Notley on the Golf Course."*Artizans*, 21 June 2016. https://www.artizans.com/image/MAY3839/ric-mciver-and-brian-jean-target-rachel-notley-on-golf-course-color/.

McDermott, Vincent. 2016. "Brian Jean Apologizes for Joking about Beating Notley during Forum." *Edmonton Journal*, 31 August 2016. https://edmontonjournal.com/news/politics/wildrose-leader-brian-jean-apologizes-for-joking-about-beating-premier-notley-during-public-forum.

McIntosh, Emma. 2016. "Man behind Golf Course Target of Notley's Face Apologizes: 'It Was a Thing of Humour.'" *Calgary Herald*, 19 June 2016. https://calgaryherald.com/news/politics/notley-target-at-oilmen-association-golf-tournament-ignites-controversy.

McLaren, Peter. 2022. "Some Thoughts on Canada's 'Freedom Convoy' and the Settler Colonial State." *Educational Philosophy and Theory* 54 (7): 867–70. https://doi.org/10.1080/00131857.2022.2051478.

Miller, Gloria E. 2004. "Frontier Masculinity in the Oil Industry: The Experience of Women Engineers." *Gender, Work & Organization* 11 (1): 47–73. https://doi.org/10.1111/J.1468-0432.2004.00220.X.

Montford, Kelly Struthers. 2013. "The 'Present Referent': Nonhuman Animal Sacrifice and the Constitution of Dominant Albertan Identity." *PhaenEx* 8 (2): 105–34. https://doi.org/10.22329/P.V8I2.4089.

Reist, Rissa. 2023. "Gender, Morality and Violence in Anthropomorphic Metaphors Depicted in Canadian Political Humor." *Politics, Groups, and Identities* 11 (5): 1041–59. https://doi.org/10.1080/21565503.2022.2071304.

Reist, Wilissa, and Linda Trimble. 2020. "Gender and Political Cartoons." In *The International Encyclopedia of Gender, Media, and Communication*, edited by Karen Ross, Ingrid Bachmann, Valentina Cardo, Sujata Moorti, and Cosimo Marco Scarcelli., New York: John Wiley & Sons. https://doi.org/10.1002/9781119429128.iegmc207.

Rodewalt, Vance. 2007a. "Ed Stelmach's Relationship with Big Oil Is Battered." *Calgary Herald*, 26 October 2007, A24.

– 2007b. "Hapless Ed Stelmach Wanders into Minefield." *Calgary Herald*, 19 October 2007, A28.

– 2008. "Ed Stelmach Cleans Up after Oil Sands Elephant." *Calgary Herald*, 3 March 2008, A10.

Samson, Andrea Christiane, and Yonni Meyer. 2010. "Perception of Aggressive Humor in Relation to Gelotophobia, Gelotophilia and Katagelasticism." *Psychological Test and Assessment Modeling* 52 (2): 217–30. https://psycnet.apa.org/record/2010-17096-008.

Shifman, Limor, and Dafna Lemish. 2010. "Between Feminism and Fun(ny)mism: Analysing Gender in Popular Internet Humour." *Information, Communication & Society* 13 (6): 870–91. https://doi.org/10.1080/13691180903490560.

Tremblay, Manon, and Nathalie Bélanger. 1997. "Femmes chefs de partis politiques et caricatures éditoriales: L'élection fédérale canadienne de 1993." *Recherches féministes* 10 (1): 35–75. https://doi.org/10.7202/057910AR.

Trimble, Linda, Jane Arscott, and Manon Tremblay. 2013. *Stalled: The Representation of Women in Canadian Governments*. Vancouver, BC: UBC Press.

Trimble, Linda, and Shannon Sampert. 2004. "Who's in the Game? The Framing of the Canadian Election 2000 by *The Globe and Mail* and *The National Post*." *Canadian Journal of Political Science* 37 (1): 51–71. https://doi.org/10.1017/S0008423904040028.

Trynacity, Kim. 2018. "'A Wake-Up Call': Documents Detail Litany of Threats against Premier Rachel Notley." *CBC News*, 4 May 2018. http://www.cbc.ca/news/canada/edmonton/notley-premier-threats-security-1.4644989.

Van den Broeck, Anja, Tinne Vander Elst, Josje Dikkers, Annet De Lange, and Hans De Witte. 2012. "This Is Funny: On the Beneficial Role of Self-Enhancing and Affiliative Humour in Job Design." *Psicothema* 24 (1): 87–93. https://pubmed.ncbi.nlm.nih.gov/22269369/.

Weinstein, Netta, Holley S. Hodgins, and Elin Ostvik-White. 2011. "Humor as Aggression: Effects of Motivation on Hostility Expressed in Humor Appreciation." *Journal of Personality and Social Psychology* 100 (6): 1043–55. https://doi.org/10.1037/A0022495.

Werner, Walt. 2004. "On Political Cartoons and Social Studies Textbooks: Visual Analogies, Intertextuality, and Cultural Memory." *Canadian Social Studies* 38 (2): 1–10. https://files.eric.ed.gov/fulltext/EJ1073912.pdf.

Wilkinson, Signe. 2004. "Where the Girls Aren't." *Nieman Reports* 58 (4): 30–21. https://niemanreports.org/articles/where-the-girls-arent/.

Williams, Kimberly A. 2021. *Stampede: Misogyny, White Supremacy and Settler Colonialism*. Halifax, NS: Fernwood Publishing.

Wright, Will. 2001. *The Wild West: The Mythical Cowboy and Social Theory*. London: Sage.

PART THREE

Experiences of Violence against Women in Politics

7 Blurred Lines: Boundaries and Consequences for Indigenous Women in Politics in the Era of #MeToo

REBECCA MAJOR AND CYNTHIA NIIOO-BINEH-SEH-KWE STIRBYS

Introduction

In recent years, Indigenous women started speaking about the varied ways they experience violence inside and outside their communities. As professionals, whether in the classroom or other organizational settings, Indigenous women must put in extra labour to address colonial stereotypes and biases, and correct misnomers. As such, the common thread of Indigenous feminism is the colonial experience. When Indigenous women share their experiences, their words are often not given weight and seemingly do not count, especially when discussing the effects of colonialism. The mainstream #MeToo movement was intended, in part, to provide a forum so women could *stand up and speak out* about their traumas. This foundational difference may be why Indigenous women didn't participate in the #MeToo movement and instead choose to tell their stories in their own time. The two Indigenous authors of this chapter – Dr. Rebecca Major, a Métis and Mi'kmaq woman, and Dr. Cynthia Niioo-bineh-seh-kwe Stirbys, Saulteaux-Cree (Treaty 4) – both with experience in Indigenous bureaucracy and politics, hope to demonstrate these nuanced differences in a time when Indigenous women are looking to return to a power place. This power position is distinct from the non-Indigenous female experience.

While some research has considered the way in which formal political institutions have addressed violence against women in Canadian politics (see Collier and Raney 2018), institutional forms of feminist inquiry could also provide support in areas less researched: violence against women in non-formal political arenas, particularly from an Indigenous perspective (Collier and Raney 2018). The institutionalization of Indigenous women's roles in the Canadian context created a situation where a person's very existence is a political act; from birth, the existence, and actions of Indigenous life, especially for a woman, is a statistical existence. Within Indigenous communities and space, there is no separation of political space from community space per se, since many aspects of Indigenous community life contribute to governance and, by extension, political space. The Canadian government used institutions and policy to entrench marginalization; the Crown directly targeted female status and identity through federal government policy, making them subservient to their male counterparts. This institutional targeting of women through the colonial state directly affected the Indigenous female experience and the power positions they held. There is no pan-Indigenous experience, but there are common experiences that Indigenous women face that are different from non-Indigenous peoples' experiences generally. The relationships disconnect shows the way in which the problem of colonial influences over gender roles remains. When exploring gender-based violence in politics (GBV-P) as part of the intersectional layers, the embeddedness of colonization must be understood within the intersectionality of Indigenous women in politics.

Indigenous Feminism

There is tremendous depth to Indigenous feminism. As illustrated by Sarah Nickel and Amanda Fehr in their recent anthology *In Good Relation: History, Gender, and Kinship in Indigenous Feminism*, Indigenous feminism isn't straightforward (Nickel and Fehr 2020). This complexity is because Indigenous culture is neither unison nor static. The diversity of culture impacts the diversity of lens in Indigenous feminism. Nickel and Fehr further discuss how, for women, feminism is a journey because colonization upended Indigenous women's roles, and Indigenous feminism can be a journey of decolonization. Even with diversity, there are similar threads in Indigenous feminism because of the colonial experience (Huhndorf and Suzack 2010). This point is critical to establish at the beginning of this discussion because it grounds the violence that Indigenous women face in political spaces. Additionally, political space is also important to understand and is explored further in the discussion.

Intersectionality between Indigenous feminism and mainstream feminism exists in challenging institutional barriers. Women's barriers are compounded by race for Indigenous women since they are situated in two "subordinate groups" and need to account for the structural barriers of colonization (Kuokkanen 2017). As explained by Huhndorf and Suzack, "for Indigenous women, the marginalization of their issues is compounded by the fact that a critical component of colonialism through the Americas involved the imposition of Western gender roles and patriarchal social structures" (2010, 2). Colonization affected women by institutionalizing patriarchy in general, but it also changed relationships within communities and reshaped how women interacted with men and with one another. Men also experienced disruption of community relationships through colonization. There is a two-fold space issue: one space where Indigenous women don't generally belong in non-Indigenous spaces and a second space in which Indigenous men believe Indigenous women don't belong due to the impacts of colonial patriarchy.

When colonization affects communities, the political institutions and the people occupying that space are also affected. Along with the institutionalized targeting of Indigenous women, the Western patriarchy that empowers men resulted in targeted violence towards women from both outside and inside the community. Juliana Restrepo Sanín (2018) critically examines the experiences of women in politics who encounter violence. She differentiates between "political harassment" and "political violence," and discusses why this way of understanding is problematic, since the violence that women experience is more of a continuum with related acts:

> In most cases, victims of VAW [violence against women] suffer from multiple types of abuse simultaneously, including economic control, psychological or physical violence, harassment, persecution, coercion, and stalking. These behaviours are not mutually exclusive, and they are not experienced as separate occurrences but instead as deeply linked ... [H]arassment and abuse – even when they do not culminate in physical harm – constitute part of the same phenomenon and thus should be conceptualized as such. (Restrepo Sanín 2018, 679)

Mona Krook's argument that "understanding sexual harassment as a systemic, cultural problem that is not merely confined to the aberrant acts of particular individuals" resonates with the intersectionality of Indigenous female experiences (2018, 66). Colonialism compounds Indigenous women's marginalization over time, affecting Indigenous and female identities. For Indigenous women who work in non-Indigenous bureaucratic spaces or engage in modern-day politics, lived experience tells the story of voracious attacks on their credibility because they are occupying space where colonial institutions worked to create barriers to prevent them from entering. Various attacks are occurring, all with the same goal: to demonstrate that the Indigenous woman doesn't truly belong in that space.

Historical Colonial Trauma

Before settler patriarchal norms infiltrated Indigenous communities, Indigenous governance models were built on an egalitarian foundation (Chataway 1994, 6). This governance model (unlike democracy) meant that all community members had a role to play, including women. Indigenous society's goal was always one of "peaceful unity"; Indigenous society could not function well without Indigenous women's important roles in the family and political life (Chataway 1994). The imposition of a colonial social and political fabric created the space for violence specific to Indigenous women and for her to "know her place" within colonial society. Colonialists used law, education, and religion to change Indigenous people's governance and political systems and to eradicate their distinctive gender roles. First, the 1876 Indian Act was enacted; according to this legislation, an "Indian" was deemed a male, and Indigenous women were relegated to non-person status (much like European women were considered non-persons). Second, the traditional system of appointing chiefs through the Council of Elders was replaced with a "modern, electoral-style [colonial] government system" (RCAP 1996, 124). Hence, the imposed Indian Act system only required "a political voice [from] the elected chiefs" and silenced the voices of women, Elders, and youth (124). These imposed gender roles, reinforced through policy, created space for violence towards Indigenous women in every sphere, including the political realm.

With the politicization of Indigenous identity and the regulation of life through policy, a person's very existence was used as a weapon to destroy a culture. For example, attendance at Indian residential school (IRS) was formally mandated under the authority of the 1920 amendment to the Indian Act, although these institutions existed well before that time. All Indigenous children (some as young as three years old, although the official age was seven) were then expected to attend (Annett 2016). Because of their patriarchal nature, IRSs implemented a "military-style hierarchy" and a colonial "contact zone" to establish ongoing relations and conditions to which children had to conform (Annett 2016, 66; Stirbys 2016, 21). Indigenous children did not have much of a chance to learn about loving and respectful relations; without reprieve from the psychological pressures of IRS, for survival's sake, many children came to adopt the "imperialistic nature of the European colonizers, transforming their own psychology into that of the oppressor" (Stirbys 2016, 16). This internalized expectation of silence and compliance carried forward into aspects of community relationships and behaviour. The oppressive regime and the traumatic experiences that have been the legacy of residential schools continue in the fourth and fifth generation descendants' lives (Stirbys 2016).

The rearing of children in a Western ideology where women are considered inferior to men is one of the most significant factors behind the treatment of Indigenous women today (Miller 1996). This ideology ran counter to the Indigenous world view in which females were not only respected but revered for the role they played in nation-building efforts (RCAP 1996). Through the boys' and girls' social conditioning at IRS, it did not take long for either gender to lose sight of female students' potential as leaders and decision-makers (Miller 1996). This intergenerational experience entrenched the marginalization of Indigenous women within patriarchal colonialism, which did not support their female leadership.

Paternalistic influences infiltrated Indigenous communities before Confederation in Canada and have had long-standing effects on those communities. Thus, the intergenerational nature of patriarchal violence that is now seen in the behaviours of Indigenous women challenges what most people think they know about GBV-P. The full realm of ongoing violence against Indigenous women cannot be captured through the lens of GBV-P alone. It is only through an intersectional lens that captures gender, race, historical trauma, and economic and social exclusion that a fulsome picture of what Indigenous women must endure in the community and political spheres can be seen.

Violence Directed by Women

Violence against women was not tolerated in traditional Indigenous societies, but at IRS, the nuns abused with impunity. Looking back in Canada's history, the nuns or women supervisors of IRS were often in charge of disciplining the children. Nuns groomed young Indigenous girls to carry out similar violence against other female students. For instance, when one female student could not stand being isolated from her brother, she tried to sneak over to his dormitory but was caught. Consequently, the other girls were told to give her the "gauntlet treatment," whereby the girl students were lined up and instructed by the nuns to use heavy belts and sticks to beat the young girl as she ran down the line (Annett 2016, 69). It became a regular practice for female students to beat other more vulnerable female students. This behaviour taught by the IRS shaped how Indigenous females treat each other, behaviour that is the result of cultural interference. While the traditional lens of GBV-P would see the intersectionality of violence targeting Indigenous women because of layers of race and gender, the depth of this violence must also include the internalized violence that created weaponry to mimic the oppressor.

Due to the Truth and Reconciliation Commission (TRC) gatherings across Canada, it is now more commonly known that children attending IRS were physically and sexually abused by staff (TRC 2015). However, in 2014 the Aboriginal Healing Foundation released a report documenting the many ways in which Indigenous children experienced abuse from both staff and students. While the abuse was "instigated by staff treatment," bullying and physical violence occurred when the older kids dominated the younger ones (Bombay 2014, 56). Bullying included anything from ridiculing and belittling to shaming students and occurred daily. This abuse was meant to "keep the victim under their control and silence" (56). Bullies would threaten physical violence if younger boys or girls did not perform sexual favours. Due to the segregation of boys and girls at the schools, the abuse took the form of "male-to-male or female-to-female child sexual abuse" (56). Thus, physical and/or sexual harm became normalized in Indigenous communities.

In recent years, "female violence against females" in Indigenous communities has been a primary concern of female residential school survivors and descendants of residential school survivors (Stirbys 2016, 63). Their goal was/is to release the *sickness* they habitually learned through the church-run residential schools over generations. Thus, "violence that has historically been dictated and directed towards Indigenous women (learned behaviour), created by men, and viewed as acceptable and appropriate has been brought on by paternalistic influences of colonialism" (63).

Understanding the uptake of patriarchal violence by Indigenous women cannot be seen from a single standpoint. It must be viewed through an intersectional lens that considers the intersecting social identities of Indigenous women and provides a more in-depth analysis of their everyday lived realities. These identities and the environments in which Indigenous women work and live can create discrimination and privilege; be a source of empowerment and oppression, advantage and disadvantage; and provide a view often experienced in colonial endeavours.

Violence Directed by Men

When talking about the effects of colonization on Indigenous political spaces and Indigenous women, the conversation cannot neglect the relationships within the community and with male counterparts because the political and familial spaces are too closely connected. When thinking of political space in an Indigenous context, it is important to understand that political space is more than where "politics take place" in the non-Indigenous sense. Political space is where there is the exercise of governance, which includes nation-building actions in the community. In Indigenous traditional culture, every community member had a role to play in societal governance structures: men, women, Elders, and youth. Through colonization, Indigenous women's authoritative and revered societal roles changed due to patriarchy, creating power issues between men and women. With the implementation of policy devices like the Indian Act, men within Indigenous communities internalized the patriarchal system. The government's actions furthered the internalization of patriarchal gender roles through assimilation policy instruments such as the IRS system (Huhndorf and Suzack 2010). The imperialist's implementation was purposeful, positioning men in both settler and Indigenous societies in power positions above the power that Indigenous women held.

This significant power shift through the assimilation and colonization process targeted Indigenous women's traditional roles, including decision-making power. It reflected a Eurocentric society where women were property under British colonial law, a new concept for Indigenous communities. Notably, coverture, where a woman became her husband's property in marriage, exemplified women's legal status in the British Empire (Stretton and Kesselring 2013). This British law contextualized women's marginalization generally. For Indigenous women, the colonial experience removed them from previous positions of importance while positioning men as the (new) authority. Madeline Rose Knickerbocker (2020) points out that there is much evidence showing the significant roles Indigenous women played as leaders in Stó:lō communities historically, positions they were then excluded from through colonization, leading to men overlooking Indigenous women's voices and agency.

Effects of historical policies that disempowered Indigenous women are visible today through the violence directed towards Indigenous women identified in the National Inquiry into Missing and Murdered Indigenous Women and Girls (MMIWG; 2019).[1] As noted by Huhndorf and Suzack, "although Indigenous women do not share a single culture, they do have a common colonial history, and the imposition of patriarchy has transformed Indigenous societies by diminishing Indigenous women's power, status, and material circumstances" (2010, 3). This common colonial history extends to shared experiences of violence. As noted by Restrepo Sanín, there is a spectrum of harassment and violence, which is part of the same problem, and the acts are related. This pattern is also true of the violence experienced by men who have internalized gender colonial power (2018, 677). With respect to violence directed at Indigenous women in political spaces by Indigenous men specifically, various targeted attacks towards an Indigenous woman are meant to compound her eventual exiting of political space – a space where traditionally Indigenous women held the final decision. The National Inquiry into MMIWG's final report explains that at the root of all violence directed towards Indigenous women and girls is the perpetuation of Eurocentric beliefs through colonial policies.

The government disempowered and marginalized Indigenous women through race and gender by institutionalizing patriarchy through colonization. This marginalization exacerbated how Indigenous men internalized the beliefs and contributed to the violence Indigenous women experience(d). Rauna Kuokkanen argues that dismantling patriarchal social relations requires an analysis of the "scope and nature of gendered violence and forms of intragroup oppression in Indigenous communities" (2017, 120). To change this hierarchical relationship, matriarchal culture must be returned to inform decolonization and men's role in the process. Externalizing men's responsibility in women's marginalization is problematic because it positions men as victims only, rather than acknowledging their role. Although when Indigenous men engage in the colonial paradigm against Indigenous women, it is recognized that Indigenous men were also harmed through colonial policies enacted against Indigenous peoples. However, Indigenous men's victimhood cannot excuse their behaviour towards Indigenous women (120). In acknowledging Indigenous men's role in Indigenous women's marginalization, we can collectively address needed change within Indigenous communities.

#MeToo – In the Community

The connection between family violence and political violence in Indigenous communities is closely enmeshed. Community space is political and explored in the discussion of the "political arena." It must be understood that what happens in communities today started with the church and state, and was by design. The church and state were in partnership to run IRSs as a means of carrying out the assimilation policies intended "to eliminate Indigenous Peoples' rights and Treaties, eliminate Indigenous governments, and cause Indigenous peoples 'to cease to exist as distinct legal, social, cultural, religious, and racial entities in Canada'" (TRC 2015, 1). Duncan Campbell Scott, former deputy superintendent in the Department of Indian Affairs, framed Indigenous peoples in Canada as an "Indian problem" in the House of Commons. He explained that Indigenous peoples must be absorbed into settler society (Scott 1920) – meaning that the destruction of Indigenous communities would translate into a loss of all cultural distinction.

One can see how the legacy of IRSs and government/church interference goes way beyond the loss of parenting skills and kinship ties. Indigenous communities continue to be affected by "Canadian policy ... undermining internal control and cooperation" and reflect the changing value system and decision-making protocols in which community members are not equally and respectfully considered (Chataway 1994, 287). As Chataway states in her thesis, this lack of consideration occurs due to the "parallel, yet unequal, systems of government ... a traditional and an elected system," whereby only a small portion of Indigenous leaders in the latter system are recognized by the Canadian federal government (29). These same leaders are granted decision-making authority over the administration of band resources. Many Indigenous communities are working to return to their social norms despite government interference.

Unfortunately, the leadership comprises mostly men who take up the "assimilationist" agenda, which contrarily does not stand up for women's and children's rights (Chataway 1994, 23). Women's roles have also changed, whereby the traditional roles of knowledge keepers, nurturers, and nation-builders are put to the wayside when the main goal is to control others. For example, given historical policies that seep into the chief electoral process in the present day, community members are still coping with learned maladaptive behaviours from both the conditions and the consequences of IRSs. Physical, sexual, and emotional abuse remain a primary concern for many Indigenous peoples (Stirbys 2016). Former IRS attendees may not realize that they began their legacy of *family violence* by bringing the abuse they experienced as children into their families and communities.

The research of Warhaft, Palys, and Boyce showed that, in one community, upwards of "eighty percent of people had been sexually abused ... whether it be in residential school or in [their] own homes" (1999, 171). The severity of the problem for this community was shown through statistics gathered (175). As Baskin states, family violence takes an intersectional lens (gender, race, class), including the "ethic of domination" (2003, 217). The Indigenous definition of family violence links to wider society and multiple systems, and is expressed as

> a multi-faceted problem which encompasses physical, sexual, psychological, and economic violations of women and which is integrally linked to the social/economic/political structures, values and policies that silence women in our society, support gender-based discrimination and maintain women's inequality. (Warhaft, Palys, and Boyce 1999, 175)

As a result of deeply ingrained social conditioning, abuse, and trauma on many levels, Indigenous leadership behaves more like that of colonial authorities, including former IRS staff or the "okakwatakihiwew" (one who torments and/or tortures; Stirbys 2016, 115). Indigenous communities must now be wary of perpetrators of violent acts from both inside and outside the community.

Family Incest and Violence

Part of the violence in communities is violence in the family, which connects to colonization. According to Sarah Deer, rape was once rare in Indigenous communities. "Rape is more than a metaphor for colonization – it is part and parcel of colonization," she said, citing the high rates of violence Indigenous women experience (2009, 150). With the diminishment of women's status through colonization, internalized gendered violence affects family life. Historically, there were strong taboos regarding violence against women in various Indigenous communities (National Inquiry into MMIWG 2019, 167). But with colonization, it became unacceptable to speak of violence, especially family violence, as highlighted below. Although speaking about violence is now frowned upon, women are talking about their experiences despite the backlash many face.

A topic virtually absent when examining family violence is the issue of incest. In his opening remarks to the Assembly of First Nations (AFN) Annual General Assembly, delivered in July 2017, National Chief Perry Bellegarde included the word "incest." Referring to the "lateral violence" as a result of the IRS system and colonialism, to the "physical, sexual and emotional abuse," the "incest," he stated: "These are ugly words. But we cannot be afraid to speak to them. We cannot be afraid to listen when someone says them" (AFN 2017). This statement illustrates that space is required for conversations to happen, for people to feel safe and to know they aren't alone. Given the National Chief's comments and the lack of discussion about incest, this issue continues to be a taboo topic, something we aren't allowed to discuss. Lawrence states that violence isn't surprising, given that leadership generally reinforced Indigenous women's marginalization (2003, 5). The silence on the issue of incest is an extension of the "She No Speaks" woman described by Martin-Hill (2003, 157).

While violence towards Indigenous women takes various forms, it often begins in childhood and is connected to intergenerational trauma. The MMIWG National Inquiry final report discusses childhood sexual abuse in families and communities, but you will not find the word "incest" (National Inquiry into MMIWG 2019, 310). Talking about family violence and how it connects to family and community, observations were made by those who participated in the national inquiry about how their identities, particularly intersectional identities, played a role in the abuse they experienced. The identity piece is crucial: it is the general underlying cause of violence against Indigenous women, since violence directly results from colonization and stereotypes around gender. The stigmatization of the abuse Indigenous women face makes family violence and targeted assaults challenging to address. It is challenging when you must live in a community with traumatized Indigenous people. Still, another level of difficulty is added when abusers are found within the family, which becomes compounded when living in smaller communities without support.

Political Arena

Indigenous and Western concepts of what constitutes political space are very different. For example, blends of community and traditional Western politics in Northern Saskatchewan involve various activities, including voting, attending meetings, and volunteering (Beatty et al. 2013, 6). Notably, the concept of political space outside of Indigenous communities is generally limited to public office and employment based on the public sphere. Political acts for Indigenous peoples, however, take place during decision-making, whether in public or private spaces. Indigenous women face violence in multiple forms and spaces, according to the spectrum of interrelated acts that Restrepo Sanín (2018) illustrates. Problematic as it is that women experience violence, there is the conditioning of "She No Speaks." She No Speaks is the silent woman, obedient to male authority – a colonial construct that contributes to the silencing of abused women's experiences (Martin-Hill 2003, 107). So, while women venture back into the decision-making space after being pushed aside through colonization, there is resistance to their re-emergence in the form of violence that is not very different from what we see in the GBV-P literature (Krook 2017). Following GBV-P's theoretical notions, when Indigenous women experience violence in a political space, the expectation is silence; consequently, when a misogynistic act takes place and a woman pushes back, she is negatively labelled (81).

In political spaces, when men become the oppressors of women, they are empowered through colonization. According to Rauna Kuokkanen, "internalization and adoption of colonial policies and patriarchal attitudes designed to regulate and discriminate against Indigenous women have resulted in a general reluctance and refusal by Indigenous leaders and communities to deal with gendered violence" (2017, 121). The findings of the MMIWG National Inquiry showed that the violence expressed is systemic and comes in many forms, as identified on Restrepo Sanín's (2018) spectrum. The marginalization and victimization may be economic, social, political, misogynistic, physical, or sexual (National Inquiry into MMIWG 2019, 56). What makes the outcomes even worse is that, while many Indigenous women are taking back their power to lead organizations, they do it in such a way that they take up patriarchal notions of violence whereby they actively continue to marginalize and control women as part of maintaining the (political) status quo (Stirbys 2016).

While efforts "to impede women's political participation" in the Western world are not new because a woman's place has been traditionally seen to be in the "private sphere" of home and family, Indigenous nations did not organize the roles of women in that way (Krook 2017, 7 4). Traditionally, Indigenous men were often seen and heard in the public sphere insofar as Indigenous women directed them on what to say on behalf of their nation. However, as we see today, just as non-Indigenous women experience violence in politics, Indigenous women are not sheltered from acts of violence in the political space. This directed violence comes from both men and women, and is both overt and covert. Indigenous women are beginning to speak up in various spaces about their experiences and to shed light on violence towards women in political spaces. When Indigenous women come forward, it is often about speaking their truth and not being attached to any movement.

Bureaucratic Arena

The majority Liberal government of Prime Minister Justin Trudeau came to power in 2015 on the platform of rebuilding respectful relations with Indigenous peoples based on a nation-to-nation premise. Just before the 2015 election, the TRC held its final event in Ottawa in June. The TRC mandate was to create a historical record of the residential school system as part of the "truth telling and reconciliation process" and "a profound commitment to establishing new relationships embedded in mutual recognition and respect that will forge a brighter future" (TRC 2015, 339). For Indigenous women, the idea of advancing a nation-to-nation relationship was on track to advance Indigenous women's rights and privileges. Still, in real time, there has been no substantive change while Trudeau has been in charge.

On 15 December 2015, Prime Minister Trudeau reiterated the government of Canada's commitment to implement the 94 Calls to Action issued in the final report of the TRC (Trudeau 2015). Within the TRC Calls to Action, there is a call for justice and addressing the violence that disproportionately affects Indigenous women (Government of Canada 2023, Call 41). Violence targeting Indigenous women aligns with the typology of violence identified in the GBV-P literature (Krook 2020). Another Call to Action demands that all levels of government "provide education to public servants on the history of Aboriginal peoples, including the history and legacy of residential schools," which will require training in "intercultural competency, conflict resolution, human rights, and anti-racism" (Government of Canada 2023, Call 57). This type of training intends to make safe spaces for Indigenous peoples, which would impact the spaces Indigenous women occupy or should occupy. Universities and governments alike are finding ways to implement the Calls to Action. Concurrently, millions of dollars *to implement reconciliation recommendations* are being given to any organization, government department, or non-governmental agency that receives government transfers, including pan-Canadian health organizations and Indigenous organizations.

One way to demonstrate reconciliation is to hire Indigenous people and, more specifically, Indigenous women.[2] However, even when Indigenous women are hired in these spaces, they are often given lower ranking positions without any authority or decision-making power on recommendations or policies affecting their communities. Furthermore, Indigenous women are supervised by non-Indigenous staff, who often have less experience and credentials than they do, especially regarding intergenerational trauma, historical injustices, Indigenous social determinants of health, and politics (Stirbys in conversation with Indigenous women between January 2021–22). A way to correct these historical injustices is to move beyond tokenistic positions when hiring Indigenous women and provide opportunities for employment in decision-making positions where real power is exercised.

As chapter 9 by Cloutier in this volume suggests, those with lower ranking employment circumstances are often more vulnerable to abuse within the workplace. From an Indigenous perspective, Indigenous women often experience aggression from non-Indigenous supervisors due to "differing worldviews" (Stirbys 2008). It is not uncommon for Indigenous women to experience microaggressions. The comments from their often less experienced or less educated supervisors can be subtle or overt, happening so regularly that negative stereotypes about Indigenous peoples are reinforced. Microaggressions and gaslighting directed towards Indigenous women are tactics used to denigrate them, to make them feel lesser than others, and are attempts to silence them from using their voices to advocate for Indigenous people's rights. Gaslighting is a tactic used against Indigenous peoples when non-Indigenous leadership tires of hearing about ways to level the field and address ongoing injustices and harms including the "pattern of disproportionate imprisonment and victimization of Aboriginal people" (TRC 2015, 164). As Krook (2020) highlights, gaslighting is a form of psychological manipulation utilized to cause a person to doubt their lived experience. Krook also states that gaslighting, in the context of cultural violence, uses cultural tropes to support/rationalize the action directed at the recipient of the aggression. This type of psychological violence is one of the forms of violence experienced by Indigenous women when they engage in traditionally defined political spaces in Canada.

Despite the violence against Indigenous women by Indigenous men and women, professional Indigenous women will advocate for improving the quality of life for all Indigenous peoples now and for the next seven generations. Indigenous women clearly understand that the political will of the dominant non-Indigenous society is not strong enough to act. For competitive reasons, Indigenous women can also experience microaggressions, gaslighting, or lateral violence by other Indigenous women in the workplace who want to gain an element of control over their peers for reasons that sometimes the *oppressed become the oppressors* (Freire 2005). The paradox, however, is that non-Indigenous organizations receive millions of dollars "to do" reconciliation. Still, the onus for achieving it is on Indigenous peoples and, more specifically, Indigenous women. They are expected to educate non-Indigenous staff and leadership on what righting the injustices looks like while trying to fight the injustices happening to them in the bureaucratic space.

Closing Remarks

Today, Indigenous women use social media platforms, among other conventional reporting methods, to shine a light on the violence they experience. When exploring violence against women, Restrepo Sanín's (2018) interpretation of interrelated acts speaks to the Indigenous experience. As reported in the National Inquiry into MMIWG (2019) final report, colonialism, racism, and genocidal notions in Canada lie at the root of violence against Indigenous women. Additionally, Canada failed to implement the protections of international treaties and instruments. The final report also showed that, after the Forensic Document Review Project concluded the review of over 135,000 documents, evidence confirmed that police services (including the Royal Canadian Mounted Police [RCMP]) showed an "indifference" (234) towards the deaths and disappearances of Indigenous women and girls, and at the same time failed to properly conduct investigations and keep factual statistics and data as it relates to protecting Indigenous women against colonial harms or violence that includes death.

The colonial state reinforced the colonialist mindset through policies and institutions, such as the Indian Act and IRSs. These institutional mechanisms enforced patriarchy – a concept that contributes to intersectional marginalization for Indigenous women, first by gender and then by race. These colonial norms of patriarchy were enforced to the point of internalization, which led to abuse in communities (including political spaces) and families. As more Indigenous women speak up, safe spaces and support systems develop informally. Safe space creation is essential in restoring Indigenous women's roles, "reclaiming power and place" in communities, and returning communities to balance, where men and women can take up their separate but equally valued roles and violence, in any form, is not tolerated, as before settlement (National Inquiry into MMIWG 2019, 2). Balance means that Indigenous women support others just like them. Indigenous men must show their support by standing behind and beside Indigenous women. These elements are all part of the reclamation of traditional Indigenous knowledge systems, including Indigenous women taking back their authority as knowledge keepers, leaders, and nation-builders. Indigenous women's roles are truly the protective factors required to keep Indigenous women safe from colonial structures designed to prevent them from taking their rightful seat at the decision-making table. While Indigenous women work to regain their rightful space, it is essential to remember that democratic spaces developed through colonization have institutional barriers to ensure Indigenous women will not succeed.

Implications for Action

Naming the violence in GBV-P is central to Krook's work, and it is paramount to understanding violence from an Indigenous female perspective (2020, 256). While there are commonalities between GBV-P and violence experienced by Indigenous women, the colonial experience is a unique position for Indigenous women to be coming from. As such, the uniqueness is why the TRC and the MMIWG Inquiry final reports are so pivotal to understanding these concepts. The following recommendations support Indigenous women's autonomy and sovereignty within private and public spaces, and address inclusivity and access to culture, health, security, and justice (National Inquiry into MMIWG 2019). When a society works together to eradicate violence towards Indigenous women, these efforts will, in turn, eradicate violence in political spaces, because all space is political for Indigenous women.

Therefore, the prevention of GBV-P for Indigenous women is directly tied to the implementation of the TRC's 94 Calls to Action and the recommendations made in the MMIWG Inquiry final report.

1 Centring Relationships to End Violence
   - Implement the 94 Calls to Action, specifically Articles 45–47, which aim to develop a Royal Proclamation and Covenant of Reconciliation to affirm a nation-to-nation relationship that supports Indigenous women's traditional decision-making roles.
   - End the genocide through a permanent commitment by the Crown and all Canadian governments and organizations to do so, which requires addressing the cultural, health, security, and justice needs of Indigenous women, girls, and 2SLGBTQQIA+[3] people explored within the MMIWG Inquiry's final report.
     i Culture: change laws or policies that deny Indigenous identity and contribute to loss of cultural knowing.
     ii Health: develop cross-jurisdictional access to services, including on university campuses, which provide cultural services to meet the distinct needs of Indigenous women.
     iii Security: end colonial policies that violate social, economic, and political rights to increase security and safety.
     iv Justice: incorporate Indigenous concepts of justice into law. Make unlawful RCMP male officers and others accountable for the violence inflicted upon Indigenous women and girls (including 2SLGBTQQIA+ people).

2 Emphasizing Accountability through Human Rights Tools
   - Implement anti-racist policy in all institutions, including but not limited to municipal offices, universities, and public governments, to ensure people who abuse human rights (through bias/stereotyping, ignoring needs, withholding services) are made accountable.

3 Recognizing Indigenous Power and Place
   - Support Indigenous women to take up leadership roles where they hold decision-making authority.

4 Eliminating Colonization as Gendered Oppression
   - Create support networks at the community level whereby abuse, including familial abuse (that is, incest), can be safely discussed.
   - Fund these initiatives and efforts to make them more accessible.

NOTES

1 MMIWG is not the focal point of this chapter since there was a formal national inquiry, and an action plan has also been developed. In this chapter, the authors bring attention to how Indigenous women who are seen as elevating themselves in society are still being abused and violated in covert and insidious ways. One incident alone may not be seen as discriminatory, but when experienced daily, the abuse compounds into trauma-inducing stressors. The authors are not looking to take the space of those for whom the MMIWG inquiry was held. The inquiry and its findings explain the history of how Indigenous women were violated through colonization.
2 According to Arriagada (2016, 15), Aboriginal women were more likely to have a university degree than Aboriginal men: 12 per cent compared to 7 per cent.
3 2SLGBTQQIA+ refers to those who identify as two-spirit, lesbian, gay, bisexual, transgender, queer, questioning, intersex, androgynous, and asexual. "Two-spirit" is a term used by some Indigenous people to reflect the complex (and non-binary) nature of gender roles and identities in Indigenous communities.

REFERENCES

AFN (Assembly of First Nations). 2017. "Assembly of First Nations National Chief Perry Bellegarde – Opening Remarks to the AFN Annual General Assembly." *AFN News*, 25 July 2017. https://www.afn.ca/assembly-first-nations-national-chief-perry-bellegarde-opening-remarks-afn-annual-general-assembly/.

Annett, Kevin Daniel. 2016. *Murder by Decree: The Crime of Genocide in Canada. A Counter Report to the "Truth and Reconciliation Commission."* Toronto, ON: International Tribunal for the Disappeared of Canada.

Arriagada, Paula. 2016. *First Nations, Métis and Inuit Women*. Women in Canada: A Gender-based Statistical Report. Statistics Canada. Catalogue no. 89-503-X. https://www150.statcan.gc.ca/pub/89-503-x/2015001/article/14313-eng.pdf.

Baskin, Cyndy. 2003. "From Victims to Leaders: Activism against Violence towards Women." In *Strong Women Stories: Native Vision and Community Survival*, edited by Kim Anderson and Bonita Lawrence, 213–27. Toronto, ON: Sumach Press.

Beatty, Bonita, Kelton Doraty, Meritt Kocdag, Sara Waldbillig, Dana Carriere, Loleen Berdahl, and Greg Poelzer. 2013. *Northern Voices: A Look Inside Political Attitudes and Behaviours in Northern Saskatchewan: Northern Aboriginal Political Culture Study*. Saskatoon, SK: International Centre for Northern Governance and Development, University of Saskatchewan.

Bombay, Amy, with Kim Matheson and Hymie Anisman. 2014. *Origins of Lateral Violence in Aboriginal Communities: A Preliminary Study of Student-*

to-Student Abuse in Residential Schools. Ottawa, ON: The Aboriginal Healing Foundation. https://www.ahf.ca/files/lateral-violence-english.pdf.

Chataway, Cynthia Joyce. 1994. "Imposed Democracy: Political Alienation and Perception of Justice in an Aboriginal Community." PhD diss., Harvard University.

Collier, Cheryl N., and Tracey Raney. 2018. "Understanding Sexism and Sexual Harassment in Politics: A Comparison of Westminster Parliaments in Australia, the United Kingdom, and Canada." *Social Politics* 25 (3): 432–55. https://doi.org/10.1093/sp/jxy024.

Deer, Sarah. 2009. "Decolonizing Rape Law: A Native Feminist Synthesis of Safety and Sovereignty." *Wicazo Sa Review* 24 (2): 149–67. https://doi.org/10.1353/wic.0.0037.

Freire, Paulo. 2005. *Pedagogy of the Oppressed*. 30th anniv. ed. Translated by Myra Bergman Ramos. New York: Continuum.

Government of Canada. 2023. "Delivering on Truth and Reconciliation Calls to Action." https://www.rcaanc-cirnac.gc.ca/eng/1524494530110/1557511412801.

Huhndorf, Shari M., and Cheryl Suzack. 2010. "Indigenous Feminism: Theorizing the Issues." In *Indigenous Women and Feminism: Politics, Activism, Culture*, edited by Cheryl Suzack, Shari M. Huhndorf, Jeanne Perreault, and Jean Barman, 1–17. Vancouver, BC: UBC Press

Knickerbocker, Madeline Rose. 2020. "Making Matriarchs at Coqualeetza: Stó:lō Women's Politics and History across Generations." In *In Good Relation: History, Gender, and Kinship in Indigenous Feminisms*, edited by Sarah Nickel and Amanda Fehr, 25–47. Winnipeg: University of Manitoba Press.

Krook, Mona Lena. 2017. "Violence against Women in Politics." *Journal of Democracy* 28 (1): 74–88. https://doi.org/10.1353/jod.2017.0007.

– 2018. "Westminster Too: On Sexual Harassment in British Politics." *Political Quarterly* 89 (1): 65–72. https://doi.org/10.1111/1467-923X.12458.

– 2020. *Violence against Women in Politics*. New York: Oxford University Press.

Kuokkanen, Rauna. 2017. "Politics of Gendered Violence in Indigenous Communities." In *Making Space for Indigenous Feminism*, 2nd ed., edited by Joyce Greene, 103–211. Halifax, NS: Fernwood Publishing.

Lawrence, Bonita. 2003. "Gender, Race, and the Regulation of Native Identity in Canada and the United States: An Overview." *Hypatia* 18 (2): 3–31. https://doi.org/10.1111/j.1527-2001.2003.tb00799.x.

Martin-Hill, Dawn. 2003. "She No Speaks and Other Colonial Constructs of the 'Traditional Woman.'" In *Strong Women Stories: Native Women and Community Survival*, edited by Kim Anderson and Bonita Lawrence, 106–120. Toronto, ON: Sumach Press

Miller, James Roger. 1996. *Shingwauk's Vision: A History of Native Residential Schools*. Toronto, ON: University of Toronto Press.

National Inquiry into Missing and Murdered Indigenous Women and Girls (MMIWG). 2019. *Reclaiming Power and Place: The Final Report of the National*

Inquiry into Missing and Murdered Indigenous Women and Girls. Volume 1B. Gatineau, QC: National Inquiry into Missing and Murdered Indigenous Women and Girls. https://www.mmiwg-ffada.ca/final-report/.

Nickel, Sarah, and Amanda Fehr, eds. 2020. *In Good Relation: History, Gender, and Kinship in Indigenous Feminisms.* Winnipeg: University of Manitoba Press.

RCAP (Royal Commission on Aboriginal Peoples). 1996. "Governance." In *Restructuring the Relationship*, 105–419. Vol. 2 of *Report of the Royal Commission on Aboriginal Peoples.* Ottawa, ON: Royal Commission on Aboriginal Peoples. https://publications.gc.ca/collections/collection_2016/bcp-pco/Z1-1991-1-2-1-eng.pdf.

Restrepo Sanín, Juliana. 2018. "The Law and Violence against Women in Politics." *Politics & Gender* 14 (4): 676–80. https://doi.org/10.1017/S1743923X18000594.

Scott, Duncan Campbell. 1920. "Evidence of D.C. Scott to the Special Committee of the House of Commons Examining the Indian Act Amendments of 1920." National Archives of Canada, Record Group 10, vol. 6810, file 470-2-3, vol. 7, 55 (L-3) and 63 (N-3).

Stirbys, Cynthia D. 2008. "Gender-Based Analysis and Differing Worldviews." *Canadian Woman's Studies* 26 (3, 4): 138–45. https://cws.journals.yorku.ca/index.php/cws/article/view/22123/20777.

– 2016. "Potentializing Wellness through the Stories of Female Survivors and Descendants of Indian Residential School Survivors: A Grounded Theory Study." PhD diss., University of Ottawa. https://ruor.uottawa.ca/handle/10393/34264.

Stretton, Tim, and Krista J. Kesselring. 2013. "Introduction: Coverture and Continuity." In *Married Women and the Law: Coverture in England and the Common Law World*, edited by Tim Stretton and Krista J. Kesselring, 3–23. Montreal and Kingston: McGill-Queen's University Press.

TRC (Truth and Reconciliation Commission of Canada). 2015. "Appendix 1: The Mandate of the Truth and Reconciliation Commission: Schedule N of the Indian Residential Schools Settlement Agreement." In *Honoring the Truth, Reconciling for the Future: Summary of the Final Report of the Truth and Reconciliation Commission of Canada*, 339–50. Ottawa, ON: Truth and Reconciliation Commission of Canada. https://publications.gc.ca/site/eng/9.800288/publication.html.

Trudeau, Justin. 2015, 15 December. "Statement by Prime Minister on Release of the Final Report of the Truth and Reconciliation Commission." https://pm.gc.ca/en/news/statements/2015/12/15/statement-prime-minister-release-final-report-truth-and-reconciliation.

Warhaft, E. Barry, Ted Palys, and Wilma Boyce. 1999. "'This Is How We Did It': One Canadian First Nation Community's Efforts to Achieve Aboriginal Justice." *Australian and New Zealand Journal of Criminology* 32 (2): 168–81. https://doi.org/10.1177/000486589903200206.

8 Who Calls Foul? Gender-Based Violence on the Municipal Campaign Trail

KATE GRAHAM

"How would you describe the actions of a London city councillor – featured on the front of the *London Free Press* today – forcing her seven-year-old son to sit through nine hours of a city council meeting?! That would be abusive if you did that to an adult! I would suggest that verges on child abuse or neglect, even if the kid did have an iPad" (Oudman 2016).

It was March 2016. These words filled the radio waves in London and Southwestern Ontario as media personality Andy Oudman spouted off about the leading story of the day: that London City Councillor Virginia Ridley had taken her son with her to a budget meeting.

Ridley was elected to London City Council in October 2014. Before entering politics, the thirty-one-year-old mother of two had spent her career in social services. She pursued a bachelor of arts in social development studies and a diploma in child and youth work. She worked at the London Children's Aid Society as a child and youth worker. As a first-time candidate, Ridley successfully challenged a ten-year incumbent – no small feat.

Two years into her first term, Ridley and her colleagues faced a contentious budget process. When a special added Saturday budget meeting was called, Ridley found herself without childcare for her son. She opted to bring him to City Hall with her for the day and pre-arranged appropriate activities, space, and supports for him.

An image of her son was then featured on the front page of the 6 March 2016 *London Free Press*, referring to him as a hero for sitting through the meeting. Radio host Oudman (2016) took the opportunity to ridicule Ridley on air:

> "You mean to tell me that a duly elected city councillor could not get a babysitter?!"

He referenced a likeness to "people who leave their dogs in the basement for hours." He invited callers to weigh in. A few came to Ridley's defence, but most did not. His vitriol continued:

> "If a teacher put a kid in a corner, there would be hell to pay!"
> "That's the same as locking her kid in the car!"
> "Imagine if Children's Aid found out?!"

This verbal abuse was not an isolated conversation on Oudman's show, but it did spark reaction. There were calls for Oudman to apologize. Some of Ridley's council colleagues began to boycott Oudman by refusing to appear on his show. In a prepared statement, Bell Media (the owner of radio CJBK) indicated that management had discussed the station's on-air code of conduct with Oudman (Duhatschek 2018).

Almost two years later – as the #MeToo movement was picking up steam in Canada and internationally – a moment of reckoning arrived (Duhatschek 2018). In a February 2018 "open letter to the people of London," several high-profile women community leaders, as well as five male members of council listed as allies, called for action:

> Most if not all women have felt the impact of misogyny and inequity in their lives. However, the #metoo, #timesup, #shinethelight, and #nomore campaigns have shifted the landscape. Women are at a pivotal point in the history of the women's movement where we are rising collectively to demand equality. Over the recent months we have seen survivors of abuse, sexual harassment, and sexism come forward in a way never seen before. With strength and conviction we speak our truth and know we are believed. Our stories inspire others to find their voice and call out abusive and sexist behaviour.
>
> As women leaders in the community, we have experienced harassment and verbal abuse by Andy Oudman on his CJBK radio show. Some of us have experienced this for years. We have spoken to senior management at Bell Media only to have our complaints addressed as isolated incidents. This response is particularly inappropriate given the acknowledgement by Bell Media of addressing similar problems with Mr. Oudman in the past. The failure by Bell Media to address Mr. Oudman's pattern of harassing and verbally abusive behaviour towards women has forced us to refuse to appear on his show. Women in London and across the world have a right to live their lives free from violence, abuse and harassment. Until Bell Media takes appropriate action to ensure women are treated with respect during its 3:00 to 6:00 p.m. timeslot on CJBK, we will continue to utilize other news forums to share our editorial content and views. (Stacey 2018a)

The letter gathered attention and support, shared by local media and through social media platforms, and culminated in Oudman apologizing on air (Stacey 2018b). In May 2018, Oudman and Bell Media parted ways.

For Ridley, this incident was not the last she would hear of the "child abuse" comment nor was Oudman's departure from talk radio the end of his impact on her political brand and fortunes. This narrative had already been constructed and, as detailed in the case study that follows, it would find its way into her re-election campaign and ultimately contribute to her political defeat.

This volume examines the impact of gender-based violence in politics (GBV-P), asking important and needed questions about how the phenomena manifests itself in Canada and the broader ramifications on the political participation, engagement, representation, and empowerment of women.

This chapter tackles a specific part of this enquiry: political campaigns and municipal politics. How does GBV-P shape the contemporary environment and experience of women on the campaign trail? Do municipal politics provide a more welcoming space for diverse candidates, as is often assumed? Are the empowerment and reckoning that have become characteristic of the #MeToo movement finding their way into political campaigns in Canada – at the local level, and beyond? Who holds the perpetrators of gender-based violence on the campaign trail to account? This chapter examines these questions, first through a review of relevant literature and contemporary research and then through a case study of Virginia Ridley's 2018 re-election campaign. This case was chosen because it provides rich territory through which to examine critical questions about campaign dynamics in the digital age and the practical challenges of addressing GBV-P on the campaign trail, particularly the accountability mechanisms. It also sheds light on an especially problematic angle through which GBV-P can take hold: attacking the identities of mothers. Through deep, qualitative investigation, important insights emerge about the gaps that remain in order to meaningfully respond to incidences of GBV-P and some of the failings of current electoral processes to anticipate and address the barriers faced by women in the digital age. The chapter closes with recommendations for policy approaches aimed to prevent and address gender-based violence faced by women on the campaign trail – in municipal politics and beyond.

Gender-Based Violence and Political Campaigns

Women remain under-represented at all levels of Canadian politics. Although some progress is being made, at the current rate it will take another five decades to achieve gender parity in electoral politics (Trimble, Arscott, and Tremblay 2013, 290). Scholars have been examining the reasons for this persistent under-representation since the 1970s. Trimble, Arscott, and Tremblay characterize the state of knowledge in Canada as unfolding through three periods of research (based on a similar examination in the American literature): examinations of the descriptive representation of women in various political arenas (1970s and 1980s); examinations of the substantive representation of women (starting in the 1980s), importantly including a field of work related to barriers experienced at each stage of the political lifecycle including eligibility, recruitment, selection, and election as well as once holding political office; and, most recently (2000s onwards), examinations of whether the participation of women in political life has translated into action towards gender equity, framed in a critique of the gender-binary nature of most of the literature and with needed attention to intersectional dynamics (Trimble, Arscott, and Tremblay 2013). The authors conclude, as others have, that descriptive representation is a "necessary but insufficient condition for substantive representation" (9) and that ultimately the participation of women in politics is "emblematic" as a broader marker of gender equality in Canada's democracy and society (11). In simpler terms: when women are not elected, it both reflects and perpetuates systemic gender inequality in Canada.

Political campaigns are, of course, an important part of this story. It is now generally accepted that women candidates, when they run, are just as likely to win as men. In other words, the under-representation of women in politics is not a product of electoral outcomes but rather of a shortage of women running as candidates during political campaigns. The tendency of political parties to run women as "sacrificial lambs" (Thomas and Bodet 2013) in less competitive ridings compounds this effect.

There is some debate about whether the campaign experience itself still puts women at a disadvantage. The conventional argument holds that voters maintain gender stereotypes that make it more difficult for women to meet expectations. These gendered perceptions can translate into all manner of struggles, including sexist media coverage (more negative, focused on family or appearance, and so on), difficulty being taken seriously or perceived as being "qualified" for office, and greater challenges in various activities such as fundraising, which contribute towards electoral success. Others have argued that, in the United States at least, this argument reflects an outdated understanding of the contemporary electoral environment and that the declining "novelty" of women in politics combined with the much stronger force of partisan polarization has had the combined effect of "significantly levelling the electoral playing field" (Hayes and Lawless 2016, 7). Hayes and Lawless draw on an analysis of 1,500 candidates during campaign periods in the United States (including an analysis of more than 400,000 campaign ads, 10,000 local newspaper stories, and a detailed voter survey) and conclude that, while women still encounter sexist behaviour during campaigns, systemic gender bias in political campaigns has largely disappeared (8).

Other observers disagree. Collignon and Rüdig's (2020) survey of 1,495 political candidates (57 per cent identifying as women) in 2017–18 in Britain found that young and leading women candidates were significantly more likely to experience abuse and harassment on the campaign trail. The most frequent forums of these experiences among women were on social media (34 per cent), through email (28 per cent), and being approached (15 per cent) or threatened (12 per cent). Small but still concerning numbers also reported property damage (5 per cent), physical contact (5 per cent), and sexual assault (3 per cent). Collignon and Rüdig conclude that these experiences have a major emotional effect on the victims and can deter both the candidates who endure the experience as well as other potential candidates – or, in their words, the effect of these experiences is that individuals are "deterred from becoming active in politics or are effectively pushed into abandoning their political career before it has really started" (428). The intimidation of political candidates, both active and potential, poses both a challenge towards achieving gender parity in political representation and a broader threat to the health of a democracy.

To what extent is the campaign experience a barrier for women's political engagement in Canada? The gender gap in voter turnout disappeared in Canada around the 1980s, and recent studies find that race now trumps gender in Canada for impact on vote choice (Goodyear-Grant and Tolley 2019). There is evidence that the visibility gap for women candidates in Canada has closed, even in leadership contests (Goodyear-Grant 2013; Wagner et al. 2017; Trimble 2007). A study of online harassment of men and women candidates found discernible differences only among the highest profile candidates; for most candidates seeking elected office, the frequency of incidences of attack and harassment among women and men was largely the same (Rheault, Rayment, and Musulan 2019). However, it would be erroneous to conclude that the campaign trail has become a "level playing field" for women candidates. This chapter explores important differences in the campaign experience for women, not just in the frequency of GBV-P but importantly in the severity and nature of the aggressions.

A central contribution of this edited volume is the application for the first time of the GBV-P concept within a Canadian context. As articulated by Raney and Collier in the introductory chapter to this volume, GBV-P encompasses acts designed to discourage or restrict political engagement on the basis of gender. Violence is understood to be "gender-based" rather than "woman-based" to ensure all dimensions of gender expression are considered, with an explicitly intersectional lens.

This concept is an important advancement, as it forces the eye beyond the institutional arrangements and political dynamics of the campaign trail towards the experiences of those who stand as candidates – and to those who might one day stand as candidates. The GBV-P framework calls for greater reflection on features of campaigns that discourage or prevent the political participation of those who have not yet formally entered the political arena.

In Canada, much work has been done to address gender inequities on the campaign trail. Often these efforts have focused on the institutional arrangements that can disadvantage women. The national Standing Committee on the Status of Women produced a report in 2019 based on a series of witness testimonies, briefings from national organizations, and written submissions (Standing Committee on the Status of Women 2019). The report includes a section on "Women Running for Elected Office," which focuses mostly on institutional barriers such as nomination processes and campaign finance regimes. There are several campaign schools for women,[1] across all levels of government, to support women with system navigation and the building of competencies in the mechanics of a political campaign. All of these supports can benefit women when they step forward to run as candidates, but they do not remedy the more complex (and less visible) problem of campaign experiences that fundamentally project a message that politics is not a place for women – thus limiting the participation of potential future candidates and perpetuating the chronic under-representation of women in politics.

The case presented in this chapter presents one such example, where a gendered misinformation campaign – defined as an active effort to spread knowledge that is factually incorrect (Hochschild and Einstein 2015) – shaped one women candidate's experience (and ultimately, her political defeat) with no avenues for recourse available within the relatively short time frame of a political campaign. Instead, pursuing justice is left as a burden for the victim after the fact, seeking court action at a cost of significant time and money. Perhaps more importantly, the high-profile nature of the attack led to widespread sharing of a message that discourages the participation of women – in this case, by projecting an incompatibility between motherhood and political participation – with the true cost remaining unknown. This examination sheds needed light on several lingering inequities in the contemporary political campaign experience for women in Canada.

This case is one that is well known to people in London, Ontario, as it received significant local media attention; and it is well known to this author.[2] The details of the case presented in the section to follow are drawn from personal correspondences with the plaintiff's representative as well as from publicly available sources, including case law and local media reports (radio and print) and the plaintiff Statement of Claim (Ontario Superior Court of Justice 2020; LeBel 2021).

Case Study: Virginia Ridley's 2018 Re-election Campaign

Ontario municipalities held elections on 22 October 2018. For the City of London, it was a notable moment: the first municipal election in Canada using ranked choice voting ("ranked ballots"), celebrated as a long-fought victory towards equality in political representation and a more civil campaign discourse. At least, that was the idea.

Ward 10 is a mostly suburban residential area in the southwest part of London. For more than a decade, the ward was represented by Councillor Paul Van Meerbergen, a conservative known locally as "Mr. No" for voting against most motions raised at council, including final votes on the budget nearly every year during his time in office. In the ward, he remained popular, increasing his vote share during each subsequent election. In 2010, he was re-elected with nearly 80 per cent of the vote.

This situation changed in 2014. The 2010–14 council term was marked by controversy and chaos, culminating in the resignation of Mayor Joe Fontana after being investigated by the RCMP and then charged and convicted for paying personal expenses for his son's wedding from his office account while serving as a federal member of Parliament years before. This highly public saga unfolded alongside a more contemporary, local scandal around illegal governance and decision-making practices at London City Council. The "Fontana 8" (named for a voting bloc representing a majority of London's fifteen-member city council who supported Mayor Fontana) were found to be in violation of the open meeting requirements under the Ontario Municipal Act for meeting privately in the backroom at Billy T's, a local tap and grill, just before a final budget vote in February 2013. This incident was the second time this group was investigated for similar reasons, after initially being reported for a meeting at the Harmony Grand Buffet Restaurant in February 2012. The "backroom Billy T's" story dominated media headlines up to and after the investigation findings were released in October 2013 – sparking a sustained period of political division, media scrutiny, and public backlash for council, which continued up until the mayor's ultimate resignation in June 2014. Perhaps not surprisingly, the October 2014 election represented the largest turnover in London City Council history: the election of a new mayor and eleven new councillors. Every member of the Fontana 8 who sought re-election lost – including Paul Van Meerbergen in Ward 10.

Ward 10 elected thirty-one-year-old Virginia Ridley. As an engaged community member and accomplished social services professional, the mother of two ran an energetic campaign that led to victory over Van Meerbergen and one other contender (also white and male) in the race. She quickly developed a reputation at City Hall for being hard-working, well-prepared, and a highly capable advocate on behalf of her constituents. She communicated frequently with her constituents, including regular meeting opportunities and newsletters, and hosted an unusual "360 review" where people could provide her with feedback on her performance as a councillor. Despite being a relatively new political actor, she was directly elected by her peers province-wide to serve on the board of the Ontario Good Roads Association (OGRA). By most measures, it seemed she had served her constituents well as their councillor when she offered for a second term heading into the 2018 election.

The dynamics of this election campaign, however, were quite different. The introduction of ranked ballots was the obvious institutional change, but there was also an underlying sense of lingering anger from the political faction (and the community who supported them) over the 2014 defeats. Paul Van Meerbergen opted to run again in Ward 10 and was not the only former Fontana 8 member to do so. The overriding election narrative was mostly framed around the 2014–18 council's decision to build a rapid transit system in London (the largest city in Canada without one, by a fairly wide margin). Although staff reports urging a move towards higher order transit dated back more than a decade, they were not met with political support until the 2014–18 council term, where new, progressive-leaning councillors held the majority of votes. The rapid transit debate was fierce, driven by an opposition campaign including lawn signs ("Don't let council throw London under the bus!") and a 1000-person public meeting held at the city's largest concert venue and arena. In many ways, the 2018 election became – on the surface, at least – a referendum about rapid transit, with some of the most visible supporters being incumbent first-term councillors facing political challengers from the past. Ward 10 was one such example.

Despite being an election reflecting reforms expressly aimed towards increasing diversity on council and improving the civility of the campaign, this new approach did not translate into the campaign experience for Virginia Ridley. On 2 October 2018 – just three weeks before election day – Ridley became aware of a new Facebook page called "The Truth about Virginia Ridley." The page linked to a website (virginiaridley.ca), which she neither knew about nor owned the domain. As a ".ca" domain, the site was registered with the Canadian Internet Registration Authority (CIRA) and was hosted by GoDaddy Inc. but was set up to be anonymous. Both the Facebook page and website presented an attack campaign against Ridley, with the headline "Why Voting for Virginia Ridley Is a Mistake." The site included the reference to "child abuse" for taking her son with her to a council budget meeting and inferring that her decision-making was impaired as a result. The site stated:

> When dealing with taxpayer dollars, any distraction that could impact decisions on the application of taxpayer dollars is unacceptable, but it is moreover irresponsible ... Ridley was given due notice of the Saturday budget meeting, hence alternate arrangements could have been made – no excuses. The City of London is a business, not a boutique nursery.

The site went on to describe Ridley as "a colossal spendthrift, greedy, irresponsible and simply unacceptable candidate for Ward 10." A similar website was set up about another first-term female councillor, Maureen Cassidy, who was also seeking re-election.

Ridley suspected that both websites were created by Amir Farahi, a partner in a local public affairs company called Blackridge Strategy. He was a leading proponent in the anti–rapid transit movement, was working on the campaigns of several conservative-leaning candidates in the election (including those running against Ridley and Cassidy), and had used similar language in public posts and blogs to what was on the websites. Ridley found a link online for website account holders to retrieve their lost passwords with a cell phone number. She tried her own number, and it did not work. She tried Farahi's cell phone number and received confirmation that a message had been sent to that number to reset the password. Ridley, through a lawyer, contacted Farahi to request an apology, who offered no response. The websites received much local media attention and sparked public outrage about the sexist nature of the content. For Ridley (and Cassidy), this issue became the majority of their local media mentions from the point of the websites' publication through to the election.

On the 22 October 2018 election night, Ridley lost her seat with 36.7 per cent of the vote. Van Meerbergen garnered 53.1 per cent of the vote for a first ballot victory. Several of the "Blackridge councillors" (those who hired Farahi and Blackridge Strategy to provide services to their campaigns, including Van Meerbergen) were elected to council.

Three days after the election, Farahi reached out to CTV News and invited them to interview him about the websites. In a teary interview, he claimed he was being framed. He referred to the websites as "one of the nastiest things [he'd] ever seen in an election" and stated that someone had stolen his identity in order to publish the sites in connection with his name and firm.

For Ridley, the attack campaign impacted her credibility and reputation even after the election. In discussions with her former colleagues in the child and youth field, it was clear that the words "child abuse" coming up in a background search for Ridley by an employer would pose a significant challenge as part of the recruitment process.

In April 2019, Ridley and Cassidy (who won her seat back on council) brought an application against GoDaddy, Facebook, CIRA, and others to determine who was behind the sites containing attack content about them. A Norwich Order was granted, and the information revealed that the sites were indeed created, registered, and paid for by Amir Farahi. Blackridge issued two statements in response, this time defending the contents of the websites by referring to them as "factual." They also admitted that they had "binding, contractual campaign service agreements" with Van Meerbergen.

On 12 June 2019, Van Meerbergen's campaign manager Barry Phillips came to Ridley's home without notice. He indicated that he was behind the website and the Facebook page. The next day, Van Meerbergen made a public statement that Phillips was behind the sites but without his knowledge. Ridley brought forward a second Norwich Order, this time against Blackridge Strategy, to determine who was responsible for the content. Blackridge produced documents showing that Van Meerbergen was personally invoiced, including itemized expenses "Attack ads against Virginia Ridley" and "Anonymous website." Van Meerbergen's public response was that the invoices produced were fake.

In August 2020, the Ontario Provincial Police Anti-Rackets Branch charged Barry Phillips (as well as Randy Warden, the leading opponent of Maureen Cassidy who also hired Blackridge Strategy to provide services to his campaign) with failing to identify themselves on election advertising.

The efforts to hold those behind the websites to account continues. In January 2021, twenty-seven months after the election, news broke that Ridley had filed a lawsuit against Blackridge Strategy, Farahi, Van Meerbergen, and others for damages. The claim asks for $375,000 in damages, including covering the out-of-pocket legal expenses. As of the date of writing this chapter, the ultimate outcome of this process remains unknown.

Who Calls Foul?

Municipal politics is sometimes thought to be a more accessible place for women to hold elected office. Observers have often pointed to the absence of political parties (in most but not all Canadian municipalities), lower campaign costs, and generally being "closer to home" with less demanding time and travel costs as reasons why holding local office may be more conducive to women. Urban politics scholars would argue that this notion is rooted in assumptions that discount the importance of municipal government, understanding orders of government in Canada as a hierarchy with the local level at the bottom, and have challenged this notion. Mayoral contests in Canada's twenty-eight largest cities, for example, require candidates to seek and secure more direct votes than any federal or provincial elected official in the country (Graham 2018). In an examination of the representation of women across levels of government in Canada over more than three decades, Tolley (2011) finds instead that the electoral presence of women is roughly the same across orders of government.

This case study adds another challenge to assumptions that local government is more hospitable to women than provincial/state or federal/national levels. Should the gendered attack against Ridley have occurred within a federal or provincial riding campaign, Ridley may have had more – and more immediate – avenues for recourse. Party-affiliated political candidates are often subject to some form of harassment policy and can have their nomination status revoked if they are found to breach ethical conduct. Vote choice is also influenced by more factors – including the information shortcut of the party brand, leader perceptions, and more – so the electoral outcomes may be less sensitive to candidate name recognition and personal brands, which are paramount in local campaigns. There may also be broader democratic implications; municipal politics can be a "stepping stone" or part of a "political pipeline" for candidates who later seek or hold provincial or federal office. Whether the attacks on Ridley limited her ability to be a candidate for other levels of government remains unknown but is an important consequence of GBV-P at the local level.

Beyond the municipal implications, this case also raises critical questions within the GBV-P literature about gender-based barriers on the contemporary campaign trail and the responsiveness of accountability measures. The #MeToo movement has empowered women to speak up about their experiences, and much is being learned about the kinds of reckoning that can hold the perpetrators of gender-based violence to account. But when these attacks come as part of political campaigns in Canada – and particularly in a digital age, when attacks can easily be made under a veil of anonymity – what are the appropriate and effective mechanisms for holding people to account? Election outcomes are sensitive to many variables – the candidates, the issues, the electoral district, the overarching issues and narratives – and are ill-equipped to be understood as the "adjudication" process for specific incidences. In the case described in this chapter, many of the pertinent details were not widely known before the election. The processes established within a jurisdiction or through legal avenues are slow, arduous, and expensive. As illustrated in the Ridley case, all expressions of accountability thus far have relied on Ridley (and Cassidy) taking significant personal time and expense to pursue justice. In other words, the mechanisms place the onus on the victims to pursue action and on a timeline that has almost no political relevance. Perhaps even more importantly, research on misinformation campaigns during elections emphasizes the troubling effect of promulgating problematic gender stereotypes about women, gender diverse, and other under-represented groups (Bauer 2015; Stabile et al. 2019).

This case raises two larger questions for the GBV-P literature with respect to accountability. First, who exactly should be responsible for holding the perpetrators of GBV-P during political campaigns to account, and how? Municipalities are familiar with mechanisms of enforcement in the built and natural environment. If Ridley's neighbour had an unkept front lawn, a simple phone call would trigger a visit from a by-law enforcement officer and, if a property standards violation were found, the homeowner would be required to address the issue within a set time frame or face financial penalties. But what about the digital environment? Or instances of gender-based harassment in a municipal campaign? Or if a website describing you as a child abuser is posted at the eleventh hour before a decision is made about whether you can keep your job? Good luck! Like most municipalities, the City of London has a process for campaign violations including a compliance audit committee. Another city councillor made an application for a compliance audit in July 2019 (nine months after the election), and Van Meerbergen simply denied knowledge of the websites. Even when campaign violations are determined, the penalties rarely have a politically material impact such as removing an elected official from office.

The narrative used against Ridley was established years earlier by radio host Andy Oudman in March 2016. Complaints were made and no action was taken. Two years later (February 2018), the letter from a group of high-profile women community leaders and co-signed by male city councillors made public their collective refusal to appear on Oudman's show. Oudman was held to account by his employer, parting ways in May 2018, but as Ridley's case demonstrates, this reckoning does not address the totality of the damage done, including to her professional reputation. The complaints, the letter, and Oudman's departure were all highly publicized moments in the London community that were covered in local media and received much attention online through social media. Even so, it was not enough to deter others from using the most problematic part of Oudman's attack on Ridley for personal and political purposes. In this case, the accountability mechanisms of Oudman's employer were not sufficient to address the damages.

Are civil actions in courts the most appropriate place for campaign violations to be adjudicated? Is it a fair expectation of victims to pursue this path? As a white, heterosexual, able-bodied woman, Ridley benefits from privilege, and others who endure a similar campaign experience may not have the same capacity to pursue legal action. It will be years after the election before the legal proceedings conclude, and regardless of the damages awarded, they will not address the political cost paid by Ridley in terms of her own opportunities for political engagement.

The second larger question this case poses is, how do we fully assess and understand the magnitude of the impact for acts of GBV-P on the campaign trail? If GBV-P is defined as including "harmful actions that are directed at an individual because of their gender, gender expression, gender identity, or perceived gender and are designed to discourage or restrict them from being active in informal ... or formal ... political spaces" (see Raney and Collier's introduction, this volume), incidences that occur on political campaigns are particularly problematic because of their high-profile nature. Ridley's Statement of Claim acknowledges the broader implications:

> This kind of offensive attack casts a chill on decent members of the community – and particularly women – who will be less inclined to participate in politics for fear of attacks which cannot be defended or confronted because the attacker is cloaked in invisibility ...
>
> As a result of the Defendants' expressions, Virginia was harmed. She failed to win re-election, despite being a popular incumbent, and it harmed her professional credibility. She was no longer able to fall back upon her education and work experience after politics and has instead pursued work in a different field. She has had to, professionally, start over.

> The Defendants' expressions sent a chill amongst women and discourage women from running as candidates in future elections. Hiding behind a cloak of anonymity made defending against the false expressions more difficult and insidious for Virginia. It provided an unfair advantage to the Defendants' dissemination of hate and vitriol. (Ontario Superior Court of Justice 2020)

How many women were discouraged from seeking political office by seeing Ridley targeted in this way? How many mothers saw Ridley's son on the front page of the newspaper or heard her parenting decisions critiqued in a public arena and thought to themselves, why would I risk putting myself or my family through that? How many people who harbour a belief that motherhood and politics are seemingly incompatible felt legitimized in those views through this public discourse? The impacts of these attacks on Ridley are significant but relatively easy to identify; the impacts on women candidates or prospective candidates, on a community, or on the health of a local democracy are not. The ability to fully understand and articulate the magnitude of impact for acts of GBV-P on campaigns is necessary in order to determine what accountability mechanisms might be most appropriate. Broader implications for the democratic process should also be considered, including how and whether gendered misinformation campaigns cast a chill on women who otherwise might have considered running for public office. If indeed misinformation campaigns like the one documented here suppress women's interest in politics, they could pose another barrier to women's political representation in legislatures around the world.

In sum, this case illuminates that central and unresolved questions about accountability represent an inequity for women within contemporary political campaigns. Existing avenues place the burden of justice on the victim – and they unfold in timelines that are politically irrelevant. Moreover, the nature of GBV-P within highly politicized arenas such as political campaigns is especially problematic as it can discourage the political participation of women. Gendered misinformation can also serve to further entrench problematic gender stereotypes. As noted at the outset of this chapter, the chronic under-representation of women in politics has long been a product of fewer women being willing to stand for elected office – and incidences of GBV-P on the campaign trial represent part of why that remains true today.

Ridley's Statement of Claim states the following:

> The Defendants targeted Virginia because she was a woman. Despite there being multiple other candidates that could have been targeted, the Defendants ... chose to attack only women candidates ... The Defendants,

in accusing Virginia of child abuse, chose a particularly gendered line of attack that disproportionately harms and damages women. A man in a similar position would not have been accused of child abuse. As a result of this differential treatment, and the infringement on her human rights, Virginia suffered injury to dignity, feelings and self-respect. (Ontario Superior Court of Justice 2020)

And Van Meerbergen continues to occupy the Ward 10 seat at London City Council.

Implications for Action

Addressing GBV-P requires appropriate mechanisms to hold perpetrators to account. The practical difficulty of actually doing so should not be underestimated. Appropriate accountability mechanisms may differ depending on the context and type of aggression. With respect to addressing accountability for GBV-P on the campaign trail, the following would mark steps in the right direction:

1. Those who administer elections, and the governance bodies who oversee them, should routinely examine their processes for addressing unethical, discriminatory, and/or acts of gender-based violence within the campaign period. In particular, contemporaneous actions designed with political consequences in mind may have greater efficiency. These could include immediate investigations, efforts to heighten public awareness of violations (for example, a direct mailing to voters within the riding), and financial penalties to the campaign and/or individual (perhaps to pay for the direct mailing or otherwise), or actions up to withdrawal of the candidate to stand for office. The complaints mechanism should be publicly funded to remove the financial barrier of candidates paying for legal counsel. Given that technology can make assigning responsibility more difficult (such as the website in this case) and time consuming, consideration should be given to other levers that may deter others from such actions – such as direct communication with all donors to a candidate's campaign, for example, carrying the threat of weakening a political base of support should a violation be determined.
2. Allyship matters. The letter from high-profile community leaders and elected officials, both women and men, with a public statement about not appearing on a radio show until action was taken, led to action in this case. The onus to call out and address acts of GBV-P cannot rest with victims at a moment of great personal strain and difficulty, and who may reasonably have varied capacities to

respond. This arrangement compounds inequities among political candidates. Organized and resourced groups who can call out GBV-P incidences and mobilize people to apply public and other forms of pressure play an essential role in lessening the burden that already rests with victims. Institutionalized forms of allyship may also increase the efficacy of allyship efforts. For example, a political party or local council could adopt a policy committing all of its members to not agree to speak with media personalities and/or outlets providing platforms for sexist or misogynistic commentary.
3 Further research is needed on the implications of GBV-P at the local level. There continue to be many assumptions about everything from the campaign experience to the role of elected officials in municipal politics rooted in perspectives that discount and devalue the importance of local politics. This problem extends into assumptions about whether local politics is more supportive of female candidates, which, as this chapter and other observers have pointed out, is not always true. The inclusion of local politics and the experiences of women in local politics in more research on GBV-P is needed.
4 Finally, political candidates should be encouraged (including internally within themselves!) to seek out any and all supports they need during and after what can be a gruelling and thankless experience. Even in the best of times, political campaigns are enormously taxing (physically, emotionally, financially, and otherwise) on the individuals who are brave enough to put their names on a ballot. Many people will be affected by incidences of GBV-P that occur on the campaign trail, but the weight of these experiences is borne largely and uniquely by the candidate themselves – particularly when the attacks are of a personal nature or involve one's family. There is pressure during campaigns for the candidate to be something of a superhero, forging on at full steam no matter the circumstance as a way of conveying strength and motivating the team. We must stop expecting this behaviour from our candidates, our leaders, and ourselves. Demanding space for self-care and accessing support is not a sign of weakness; rather, it is a strength – done both in service to self as well as to the women who will follow.

NOTES

1 For an excellent summary, see Thomas (2019).
2 This author has personal connections to this case. Kate Graham worked at London City Hall from 2006–17, including as the director of Community & Economic Innovation from 2014–18. Graham left her role to run in a

provincial election in 2017–18 and knows a number of the political actors referenced in the case personally, including Virginia Ridley and Maureen Cassidy. Finally, in 2019 the author married a member of the London City Council who was one of the five male allies who signed the letter referenced at the beginning of the chapter.

REFERENCES

Bauer, Nichole M. 2015. "Emotional, Sensitive and Unfit for Office? Gender Stereotype Activation and Support Female Candidates." *Political Psychology* 36 (6): 691–708. https://doi.org/10.1111/pops.12186.

Collignon, Sofia, and Wolfgang Rüdig. 2020. "Harassment and Intimidation of Parliamentary Candidates in the United Kingdom." *The Political Quarterly* 91 (2): 422–9. https://doi.org/10.1111/1467-923X.12855.

Duhatschek, Paula. 2018. "14 London Councillors and Leaders to Boycott *The Live Drive with Andy Oudman*." *CBC News*, 8 February 2018. https://www.cbc.ca/news/canada/london/14-london-councillors-and-leaders-to-boycott-the-live-drive-with-andy-oudman-1.4527143.

Goodyear-Grant, Elizabeth. 2013. *Gendered News: Media Coverage and Electoral Politics in Canada*. Vancouver, BC: UBC Press.

Goodyear-Grant, Elizabeth, and Erin Tolley. 2019. "Voting for One's Own: Racial Group Identification and Candidate Preferences." *Politics, Groups and Identities* 7 (1): 131–47. https://doi.org/10.1080/21565503.2017.1338970.

Graham, Kate. 2018. "Leading Canada's Cities: A Study of Urban Mayors." PhD diss., University of Western Ontario. *Electronic Thesis and Dissertation Repository*, 5745.https://ir.lib.uwo.ca/etd/5745.

Hayes, Danny, and Jennifer L. Lawless. 2016. *Women on the Run: Gender, Media and Political Campaigns in a Polarized Era*. New York: Cambridge University Press.

Hochschild, Jennifer L., and Katherine Levine Einstein. 2015. *Do Facts Matter? Information and Misinformation in American Politics*. Norman, OK: University of Oklahoma Press.

LeBel, Jacquelyn. 2021. "Former London, Ont., Councillor Virginia Ridley Launches Lawsuit over Websites Scandal." *Global News*, 8 January 2021. https://globalnews.ca/news/7564028/virginia-ridley-blackridge-strategy-lawsuit-defamation/.

Ontario Superior Court of Justice. 2020. "Statement of Claim by Plaintiff Virginia Ridley." 30 September 2020.

Oudman, Andy. 2016. *The Live Drive with Andy Oudman*. Newstalk, 1290 CJBK Radio, 8 March, 2016. London, ON: Bell Media.

Rheault, Ludovic, Erica Rayment, and Andreea Musulan. 2019. "Politicians in the Line of Fire: Incivility and the Treatment of Women on Social Media." *Research and Politics* 6 (1). https://doi.org/10.1177/2053168018816228.

Stabile, Bonnie, Aubrey Grant, Hemant Purohit, and Kelsey Harris. 2019. "Sex, Lies and Stereotypes: Gendered Implications of Fake News for Women in Politics." *Public Integrity* 21 (5): 491–502. https://doi.org/10.1080/10999922.2019.1626695.

Stacey, Megan. 2018a. "An Open Letter to the People of London." Twitter [now X], 8 February 2018. https://twitter.com/meganestacey/status/961816050906972160.

– 2018b. "Radio Host Sorry for Anti-Women Vitriol." *London Free Press*, 9 February 2018. https://lfpress.com/2018/02/08/radio-host-sorry-for-anti-women-vitriol.

Standing Committee on the Status of Women. 2019. *Elect Her: A Roadmap for Improving the Representation of Women in Canadian Politics: Report of the Standing Committee on the Status of Women*. House of Commons, Canada, 42nd Parliament, 1st Session, April 2019. https://www.ourcommons.ca/Content/Committee/421/FEWO/Reports/RP10366034/feworp14/feworp14-e.pdf.

Thomas, Melanee. 2019. "Barriers to Women's Political Participation in Canada." *University of New Brunswick Law Journal* 64 (2013): 218–33. https://journals.lib.unb.ca/index.php/unblj/article/view/29130.

Thomas, Melanee, and Marc André Bodet. 2013. "Sacrificial Lambs, Women Candidates and District Competitiveness in Canada." *Electoral Studies* 32 (1): 153–66. https://doi.org/10.1016/j.electstud.2012.12.001.

Tolley, Erin. 2011. "Do Women 'Do Better' in Municipal Politics? Electoral Representation across Three Levels of Government." *Canadian Journal of Political Science* 44 (3): 573–94. https://doi.org/10.1017/S0008423911000503.

Trimble, Linda. 2007. "Gender, Political Leadership and Media Visibility: *Globe and Mail* Coverage of Conservative Party of Canada Leadership Contests." *Canadian Journal of Political Science* 40 (4): 969–93. https://doi.org/10.1017/S0008423907071120.

Trimble, Linda, Jane Arscott, and Manon Tremblay, eds. 2013. *Stalled: The Representation of Women in Canadian Governments*. Vancouver, BC: UBC Press.

Wagner, Angelina, Linda Trimble, Shannon Sampert, and Bailey Gerrits. 2017. "Gender, Competitiveness and Candidate Visibility in Newspaper Coverage of Canadian Party Leadership Contests." *The International Journal of Press/Politics* 22 (4): 471–89. https://doi.org/10.1177/1940161217723150.

9 The Dark Side of Working in Politics: A Study of MP Staff in Canada

MEAGAN CLOUTIER

Introduction

Staff members are often the first to handle abuse from constituents. There are many highly publicized reports of staff members being the first to encounter harassment directed towards politicians. One story explains how some messages that member of Parliament (MP) Jenny Kwan receives make staff want to shield her from the "violently grotesque" content (Smith 2021). Around 50,000 messages were sent to MP Iqra Khalid's office following her private member's motion condemning Islamophobia, systemic racism, and religious discrimination, with many messages being hateful and threatening the safety of Khalid, her family, and her staff (Parry 2017). Journalists reported that MPs' assistants are the "first line of defence, reporting racist comments to social media platforms, answering angry phone calls and dealing with outraged visitors," during which staffers sometimes feel intimidated and worried about their own safety (Burke 2019). Staffers are often the first to see and manage harassment against MPs, through either interacting directly with constituents or reading emails, letters, social media posts, or answering phone calls.

The goal of this chapter is to understand the challenges that MPs' staffers experience while working for an MP, including the gendered nature of harassment at work, and to evaluate existing policies in place to prevent and address harassment in MPs' offices. Using original data collected from a survey of MPs' staff in November 2018, this chapter also investigates the magnitude and frequency of harassment cases within these offices. This research is the first of its kind to explore gender-based harassment of political staff in the Canadian context.

The results of the survey are illuminating. Despite being crucial actors who help elected representatives do their work, staff are overlooked in the literature and in the administration of Parliament. Both instead focus almost entirely on MPs. As staff, women are more likely to hold administrative roles, while men are more likely to hold policy roles with more "impressive" titles (Cloutier 2019). Women staff are harassed more often than men by both the public and MPs. The chapter concludes by discussing recommendations for improving the safety and well-being of MPs' employees, including implementing training for how to manage constituent and online harassment.

Staff Harassment in Context

Staff members are crucial to the everyday functioning of representative democracy, yet they are overlooked in the literature and in the administration of Parliament in favour of MPs. MPs recognize that staffers are essential components in their work.[1] Staff usually identify and solve most constituent issues more effectively than MPs (Docherty 1997). Research shows that men staffers tend to be in policy positions whereas women tend to be in front-facing administrative positions (Cloutier 2019). These roles provide fertile ground for harassment since women staffers are undervalued and are more public-facing compared to men staffers (Cloutier 2019).

This chapter explores staffers' experiences of harassment: a form of gender-based violence in politics (GBV-P; Krook 2020). According to Bill C-65, harassment is "any action, conduct, or comment, including of a sexual nature, that can reasonably be expected to cause offence, humiliation or other physical or psychological injury or illness to an employee, including any prescribed action, conduct or comment" (Parliament of Canada 2018, 1). While politicians themselves are the main targets of harassment, their staff often manage and address the harassment and abuse politicians receive. As such, staffers are potentially exposed to much more violence than is often reported in the media. As the introduction to this volume points out, workplace harassment affects workers emotionally, physically, psychologically, and economically. Employees who experience harassment may be less effective at their job and can experience mental health issues like depression. Harassment can also have serious negative effects with respect to career choice and advancement (Houle et al. 2011). While no workplace is immune to harassment, Verge emphasizes that having sexism and sexual harassment occur in Parliament (and, by extension, MPs' offices) signals that "women's rights to fully and equally participate in political life is severely infringed" (2022, 94). As more women are present among staff than among elected representatives, it is imperative that conversations about GBV-P include political staff.

Political staffers are often victims of harassment, and many of their stories go untold due to their unique workplace environment. These offices are managed by MPs themselves, which presents another challenge for staff: MPs can also be harassers (Canadian Press 2019). Men accused of harassment in Canadian politics range from government ministers and backbenchers, to political party leaders, to *Maclean's* "most collegial parliamentarian" (Ward 2010; Aiello and McGregor 2018; Tunney 2018; Connolly 2018; Leeder 2018; Bryden and Ditchburn 2014; CBC News 2014). While harassment can and does happen to men,[2] it occurs far more often to women, both in society and on Parliament Hill (Foote and Goodman-Delahunty 2005; McLaughlin, Uggen, and Blackstone 2017). Due to the public personas of MPs and the support of political party resources, staffers often find coming forward about their experiences difficult, though victims' voices have been amplified by the rise of the #MeToo movement (Zubi 2017).

The 2014 House of Commons Policy on Preventing and Addressing Harassment was the policy guiding MPs and staff on issues of harassment in the workplace (House of Commons 2014). However, the 2014 policy contained many pitfalls, including unclear examples of what counts as harassment and problematic reporting procedures (Raney and Collier 2022). An updated 2021 policy – Members of the House of Commons Workplace Harassment and Violence Prevention Program (House of Commons 2021) – applies to all MPs as employers as well as to staff, paid and unpaid interns, and volunteers employed by MPs. This policy provides definitions and examples of what constitutes abuse of authority, harassment, and sexual harassment. It also includes updated definitions of a workplace since MPs' activities exist beyond Parliament Hill and local constituency offices. The policy applies to any situation in parliamentary settings and "any location where work-related activities are performed, including the locations of business travel, conferences, training activities and Member-sponsored social events" (6). However, this definition is unclear about whether the policy applies on the campaign trail and to social events like going out for dinner with an MP.

The 2021 policy does outline preventative measures for harassment, including the training programs available; the reporting protocols, conflict resolution solutions, roles and responsibilities of political party whips, the Chief Human Resources Officer, MPs, and their employees; and the rights of complainants and respondents. The policy states that new MPs and employees must receive training on harassment and violence in the workplace within three months after starting their position and again every three years. The updated policy clarifies issues of previous policies, such as reporting procedures requiring staff to file complaints with their MP first, which is an issue if the MP was the harasser (House of Commons 2021).

An area that is problematically omitted from the policy is harassment that is experienced between staffers and constituents, as well as online harassment (Krook 2020). The policy still denotes that any complainant who files a harassment claim "that is found to be frivolous, vexatious or made in bad faith may be subject to corrective or disciplinary action" (House of Commons 2021, 10). As Raney and Collier observe, this provision propagates "a harmful myth that victims (mostly women) are prone to falsely report sexual misconduct, reducing their willingness to report a claim out of fear of not being believed" (2022, 392).

Data and Methods

To document who harasses MPs' staff and to what extent, this chapter uses a mixed methods approach by surveying MP employees, gathering both qualitative and quantitative data simultaneously. The survey contained both closed-ended and open-ended questions and was available in English and French. Relying solely on statistics would not illustrate the varying and complex experiences of MPs' staffers, so open-ended questions provided rich new insights into their work, which has not yet been systematically studied.

Surveying current political staffers is challenging because of their potential hesitation to draw unwanted attention to themselves, the MP, or the MP's party, especially in a survey with questions that are sensitive in nature. Using the MPs' associated email accounts, a total of 1,038 email invitations were successfully sent in November 2018, one year after the #MeToo movement began.[3] The survey was open to responses until December 2018. The response rate was 17.7 per cent; 220 surveys were started, and 184 were completed.[4] This response rate is comparable to US research on congressional staff, and surveys on parliamentary staff in Canada report similar complete responses (Hertel-Fernandez, Mildenberger, and Stokes 2019; Snagovsky and Kerby 2019; Samara Centre for Democracy 2018). Due to the relatively small sample size and the high turnover of employees, generalization of all MPs' staffers is not appropriate based on these data. However, this survey provides a good starting point to understand some of the challenges of working for an MP and common issues that have occurred across Canada in MP offices, regardless of partisan affiliation or geography. The survey also collected demographic information, including employees' gender, age, and education, as well as the employee's and MP's political party. Research shows that race is a key component of GBV-P, and a serious limitation to these data is not asking for staff race, ethnicity, ability, and sexuality, limiting the ability to conduct intersectional analysis of GBV-P for political staffers. Future research must seriously consider how diversity shapes the experiences of political staffers working for an MP (Krook 2020).

To understand the frequency and magnitude of harassment incidents that the staff members experience, the survey featured a section about harassment, referencing definitions, reporting protocols, and training procedures from 2014 House of Commons Policy on Preventing and Addressing Harassment (House of Commons 2014).[5] One goal of the survey was to gather descriptive statistics about the frequency and magnitude of harassment cases. However, after analysing the question "What do you dislike about your job?," which was presented before the harassment section in the survey, many respondents pre-emptively explained their experiences of harassment and abuse at work in an open-text format. The qualitative results presented are verbatim quotations, allowing respondents to describe in their own words what they dislike about their job (Curry, Nembhard, and Bradley 2009). When appropriate, these quotations are supported by descriptive statistics to emphasize that certain issues are common across MP staff who participated in the survey.[6]

Results

Respondents were first asked whether they knew what constitutes harassment in the workplace. A large majority (83 per cent) stated they knew what counts as workplace harassment. They were then shown the 2014 House of Commons Policy on Preventing and Addressing Harassment's definition of harassment and asked if they had experienced harassment in the workplace in the past year.[7] Almost one-quarter (23 per cent) of respondents reported that they had experienced harassment at work. As shown in Table 9.1, the gender gap in harassment is almost 38 per cent: of the respondents who reported harassment at work, 69 per cent were women and 31 per cent were men.[8] Interestingly, when provided with the statutory definition, 8 per cent of respondents were not sure if they had experienced harassment, suggesting that some MP staff are still unclear about what counts as inappropriate behaviour at work. This finding raises questions about the educational value of existing harassment training programs, a topic discussed in Cockram's chapter 11 in this volume.

Respondents were then asked to select all possible options concerning who was involved in the harassment.[9] Respondents identified constituents (47 per cent) as the main perpetrators of the harassment, followed by co-workers (33 per cent), and the MP they work for (14 per cent).

Table 9.1. The gender gap in harassment

	N	Women (%)	Men (%)	Gender gap (%)
Women	84			
Men	57			
Experienced Harassment	32	69	31	38
Perpetrator				
Co-Worker	14	64	36	28
MP Employer	6	50	50	
Constituent	18	78	22	56
Frequency of Harassment				
Frequently	14	64	29	35
Occasionally	9	67	33	34
Rarely	5	80	20	60
Witnessed Harassment	24	63	38	25
Perpetrator				
Co-Worker	17	59	41	18
MP Employer	5	40	60	−20
Constituent	12	75	25	50
Completed Online Training Program	45	49	51	−2

Only one respondent selected another MP, and two respondents provided other answers, including Canadians from other ridings and union representatives.

The results reveal gendered patterns. Women (78 per cent) were more likely to say they experienced harassment from constituents compared to men (22 per cent), for a difference of 56 per cent.[10] Women (64 per cent) were more likely to say they experienced harassment from co-workers compared to men (36 per cent), for a difference of 28 per cent.[11] Both women and men were equal in their experiences of harassment from their MP employer. When asked how often harassment occurs at work, a plurality – or almost half – of respondents stated that harassment occurs frequently (46 per cent). This percentage is higher than the average workplace in Canada.[12] Women (64 per cent) were more likely to say that the harassment occurs frequently compared to men (29 per cent), for a difference of 35 per cent.

Respondents were also asked if they have witnessed harassment in the workplace in the past year, and 19 per cent of respondents indicated they had. Of those, women (63 per cent) were more likely than men (38 per cent) to report witnessing harassment, for a difference of 25 per cent.[13] Again, respondents were asked to select all possible options of who was involved in the harassment. Co-workers (43 per cent) and constituents (35 per cent) were the most common sources, followed by the MP the employee works for (13 per cent).[14] Women (75 per cent) were more likely than men (25 per cent) to witness constituents as being involved in the harassment, for a difference of 50 per cent.[15] However, some of the open-ended questions provide more clarity in how constituents treat the MPs' staff. One man respondent wrote: "It has happened where the constituent has become [aggressive] and harassed my co-worker. They can also be quite rude, particularly because my co-worker is a woman." As these results show, addressing harassment is an ongoing issue for MPs' staff, especially for women.[16]

Before the harassment section in the survey, respondents were asked an open-ended question about what they disliked about their job. One-quarter of respondents openly discussed issues of harassment in this section: 29 per cent of women respondents and 21 per cent of men respondents.[17] Twenty women respondents discussed their negative experiences dealing with angry constituents, and most of the candid comments about constituent harassment come from women staff members. For example, one woman respondent wrote:

> People are assholes, and that includes the public. The amount of misogynistic and bigoted commentary by the public opposed to thoughtful critical responses is abhorrent and disgusting. The fact that Members' offices and Members are not able to call out this behaviour or identify constituents in that capacity further enables that behaviour.

Other women observed that "constituents tend to forget that we are humans with feelings, so being a stranger's personal punching bag isn't fun" and that constituents act inappropriately with staff members, being "angry, rude, and sexist." One woman wrote: "The aggression, people typically reach out to the gov't when they have no other choice meaning they're aggressive, political talk tends to be very emotional for people." One man provided one possible explanation as to why constituents may be angry towards staff members: "People turn to their MP as a last resort and are often agitated/hostile." Another man wrote that staff members need to have "a thick skin" when working for an MP.

One woman wrote that she disliked "being yelled at by the general populous [sic] who think that I personally have somehow formed the current policies." She continued by saying that people tell her directly that she should "be ashamed for working for the government," thinking that she is a personal government representative. Others reported they did not "like being blamed for the decision that the government makes" and that there was a general "lack of respect about the work the staff does for [a] constituent." Another woman respondent wrote how "it can be frustrating to be the forward face of the office for a Member who is not as involved in the community as they should be." These reports suggest that, while MPs may be representing constituents in Ottawa, their staff members are bearing the brunt of constituents' anger.

Staff members react to harassment in several ways that appear structured by gender. Approximately 30 per cent of respondents ignored harassment when they experienced it, including all men who said they experienced harassment at work. By contrast, women directly discussed the harassment with their MPs or co-workers, outside of filing a formal complaint. This response could include talking to the person harassing them directly (21 per cent), talking to a co-worker (16 per cent), talking with their MP (19 per cent), or seeking assistance from a third party (8 per cent). Two women contacted the police. Only two respondents filed a formal harassment complaint. This finding suggests that women staff who are harassed are more likely to turn to a "whisper-network" among women, at least on Parliament Hill, rather than access more formal channels.[18] Even though women are more likely to be targeted than men (Uggen and Blackstone 2004), the societal expectation that men cannot be or feel harassed has made it a taboo subject for them, which may explain why men always appear to try to ignore the harassment first rather than seek a different remedy.

Comments from the survey show that MP staffers who experience harassment are clearly anxious about reporting it or have experienced reprisals upon their reporting. One woman said she planned to address her co-worker who was harassing her, but she "chickened out." One man wrote: "I was always taught if you have a problem with someone you should address it with them. I attempted this and the following few months were bad. I felt like my job was at risk every day and now I just ignore it because short of going to a newspaper (and still losing my job) there's nothing you can do. Even our resources [in the office] work to protect the members." These responses comport with research on sexual harassment in the workplace that shows that most victims quit their jobs because there are few mechanisms to meaningfully improve their work environment (McLaughlin, Uggen, and Blackstone 2017). News stories have reported that victims of sexual harassment on Parliament Hill chose to quit their job rather than report the abuse or continue their work alongside their harasser (Zubi 2017). It is plausible that many employees who experience harassment within these offices choose to leave their position instead of reporting the incident.

These responses to the harassment that MP staff report experiencing are not adequate, even though there is training and policy in place. The survey asked directly about the 2014 policy's training on harassment in the workplace, which the study found to be another responsibility that is not adequately managed. This training included a one-hour video for MPs and their employees.[19] Only 33 per cent of survey respondents indicated they had completed the training. Of the 61 per cent of respondents who had not completed the training, 83 per cent were full-time employees. This result indicates that simply listing harassment training as a government priority is insufficient because there is no guarantee most staff will take the training. As Cockram (chapter 11, this volume) argues, MPs, the House, and political parties must take additional measures to address and prevent harassment and violence, and infrequent anti-harassment training can only be so useful in combating GBV-P. Future research should assess whether the new 2021 policy provisions, which require all new MPs and employees to receive training within three months after they start their position, helps remedy this issue.

Discussion

The results of the survey gave several interesting insights about the working conditions of MPs' staff in Canada and the GBV-P they face from constituents, other staff, and even MPs. The high rate of staffers' harassment is particularly noteworthy.[20] Staffers often rationalize the anger and aggression they receive from constituents. As one man who responded put it, "people turn to their MP as a last resort." This rationalization does not explain, however, why women staff are clearly more likely to be targets of this aggression than men. This gendered pattern suggests that at least some generalizations about sexism and GBV-P generated about women politicians may also extend to women working in unelected political positions.

In the 2021 policy, the workplace is defined as any place where the employee is engaged in work for the MP (House of Commons 2021, 6). However, it is not clear whether partisan events, which may not be encompassed under working for the MP, fit within this definition, even if MPs require their staff to attend those events. Some social gatherings, such as going for drinks with the MPs or co-workers after a work function, may not be covered by the policy. Many of the publicly reported cases of harassment occur in these grey areas. For example, a young staffer working for Conservative MP Rick Dykstra experienced improper behaviour during an informal post-budget party at a tavern and proceeded to file a police report against Dykstra. The Dykstra event occurred before the 2014 policy was in place, but after the policy was implemented, former prime minister Stephen Harper still allowed

Dykstra to run as a candidate in the following election. Both were aware of the policy report filed against Dykstra (Maher 2018). This lack of action from party leadership suggests that, even after a well-known incident, vetted candidates with a history of sexual harassment allegations are still welcome to run for federal office. What is perhaps most striking is the connection that can be drawn across men's reactions to harassment. Between the public reports about cases such as Dykstra's and the staff survey, the default response men have to harassment in politics is to ignore it, whether the target is themselves or a colleague.

The event with Dykstra shows how informal – but work-related – social events, as well as the diverse duties assigned to MPs' staffers, can further complicate instances of harassment. The workplace of MPs' staffers extends beyond the office. One respondent wrote that MPs' work "goes well beyond a normal workday [sic]" and that staffers often "work evenings and every single weekend." One respondent wrote that they "don't enjoy the weekend events that we are often forced to go to," and another noted how social events can be stressful to attend. Attending events is often a job expectation. Social events are an example of a grey area in politics, where the parliamentary workplace extends beyond the House of Commons and MPs' constituency offices. Social events can be more conducive for situations to arise where staff experience violence and harassment, as these settings often do not feel like they are a professional part of the workplace. The current policy is inadequate, for it does not cover the after-work events that are part of the culture of working in politics.

When cases of harassment occur within MPs' offices, the 2021 policy has complainants report to the MP or the designated recipient, which is now the Chief Human Resources Officer, based in the House of Commons' Board of Internal Economy. While there is improvement in the policy's reporting procedures, there can be hesitation in reporting harassment against other office members. Since MPs have few employees, employees may be hesitant to report harassment as it may alter the overall working dynamic and could leave other employees feeling resentful (Eberhard, Moser, and McFadden 1999). This problem raises the main issue of fear of reprisal from victims, "especially when they speak out against high-power perpetrators" or those who can directly "impose penalties" (Hershcovis 2018). A key barrier in reporting harassment is that reporters fear the situation turning into a case of credibility (Foote and Goodman-Delahunty 2005). Regardless of gender, people may view reporting an incident of harassment to their employer as a sign of weakness or of being unable to fend for themselves. Thomas and Pruysers show in chapter 4 of this volume that, when psychological violence occurs, the man politician is perceived as weaker than the woman politician. Toxic masculinity structures the idea that harassment should not happen to men, leading men political staffers to ignore the harassment, with the stigma being that harassment does not happen to men (Eberhardt, Moser, and McFadden 1999).

Implications for Action

From the survey of MPs' staff members, I find that almost one in four employees working for an MP in Canada experiences harassment at work. Approximately 69 per cent of those who reported experiencing harassment were women, with a large amount of the harassment coming from constituents. The findings also may not fully capture the extent of the harassment or abuse that occurs to politicians and their staff. Krook and Restrepo Sanín (2020) argue that silence on the amount of harassment and abuse politicians receive might be the result of staffers protecting their boss from abusive correspondence. Future research should investigate the emotional and psychological impacts that staffers experience when managing this form of harassment and abuse. In an ideal world, MP staff would not have to deal with harassment at work, but as a reality of the workplace, it is imperative that staff are supported and provided all necessary tools to address and prevent this harassment.

1 Include clear descriptions and examples of what counts as online and social media harassment, and how to manage and address these interactions.
2 Include anti-harassment training for dealing with harassment from constituents. This is one clear area where further training protocols and resources to support staff to manage hostility from constituents would be useful, especially since approximately half the cases of harassment reported in the survey saw constituents as the perpetrators.
3 Make grey areas less grey: clarify job expectations and roles for staffers, including explicitly stating what is considered part of the workplace, especially around social events, partisan events, and on the campaign trail.

Acknowledgment

This chapter draws on my master's research supported by the Social Sciences and Humanities Research Council. I wish to thank my supervisor Melanee Thomas for her amazing guidance and support.

APPENDIX

The thirty-question survey asks staff about their career path, typical work week, their political ambition, their experiences with workplace harassment, and demographic information. This chapter draws on thirteen distinct questions from the survey – questions 1–3, 19–24, and 26–29 – with questions 21 and 22 having follow-up questions, for a total of nineteen questions. Questions 4–18, 25, and 30 of the survey are not relevant for this chapter. (Note that the questions below have been renumbered Q1–Q13.)

This survey data is part of a larger research project for my doctoral dissertation. Please contact me for additional questions about the full questionnaire and information about the larger research project on political staffers.

Q1: How long have you worked in your current position? (N = 167)
    a) Less than 6 months
    b) Between 6 months and 1 year
    c) 1–2 years
    d) 2–4 years
    e) More than 4 years

Q2: Which party does the Member of Parliament you work for belong to? Information collected from this survey will only be reported in the aggregate and separate from other identifying information. (N = 167)
    a) Bloc Québécois
    b) Conservative Party of Canada
    c) Green Party of Canada
    d) Liberal Party of Canada
    e) New Democratic Party of Canada
    f) Québec Debout
    g) Independent Candidate
    h) Prefer not to say

Q3: Which party do you belong to? (N = 166)
    a) Bloc Québécois
    b) Conservative Party of Canada
    c) Green Party of Canada
    d) Liberal Party of Canada
    e) New Democratic Party of Canada
    f) Québec Debout

g) I am not a member of a political party
h) Prefer not to say

Q4: What do you dislike about your job? (Open answer) (N = 128)

Over the past few years, there have been reports in the news of harassment in constituency offices. This part of the survey will ask you about your thoughts and experiences with harassment in the workplace. Please answer the following statement on a scale of strongly disagree to strongly agree.

Q5: I am not sure what counts as harassment in the workplace. (N = 147)

1 Strongly Disagree	2 Disagree	3 Neither Agree nor Disagree	4 Agree	5 Strongly Agree

The current [2014] House of Commons Policy on Preventing and Addressing Harassment defines harassment as "any improper behaviour by a person that is directed at someone else, that is offensive and which that person knew or ought reasonably to have known would be unwelcome. It comprises any objectionable conduct, comment or display made either on a one-time or a continuous basis that demeans, belittles or causes personal humiliation or embarrassment to an employee." Based on this definition, please answer the following questions.

Q6: Have you experienced harassment in the workplace? Please note that this survey is anonymous and you will not be able to be identified. You may skip any and all questions you do not wish to respond to. If you need support services, please go to http://www.crisisservicescanada.ca/en for a list of national, provincial, and territorial hotlines and crisis centres. (N = 149)
   a) Yes
   b) No
   c) Not Sure

Q6a: (If yes) Who was involved in the harassment? Select all that apply. Please note that this survey is anonymous and you will not be able to be identified. You may skip any and all questions you do not wish to respond to. If you need support services, please go

to http://www.crisisservicescanada.ca/en for a list of national, provincial, and territorial hotlines and crisis centres. (N = 35)
    a) Co-worker
    b) Member of Parliament I work for
    c) Another Member of Parliament
    d) Constituent
    e) Other (Please specify)

Q6b: (If yes) How often does harassment occur? (N = 35)
    a) Very frequently
    b) Frequently
    c) Occasionally
    d) Rarely
    e) Very rarely

Q6c: (If yes) How did you deal with the situation? Select all that apply. (N = 34)
    a) Talked to the person directly
    b) Talked to a co-worker
    c) Talked to the Member of Parliament
    d) Filed a formal harassment complaint
    e) Used the harassment prevention program
    f) Sought assistance from a third party
    g) Ignored it
    h) Other (Please specify)

Q6d: (If filed a complaint or used the harassment prevention program) Please describe the process of filing a complaint or using the harassment prevention program. Did you find it effective? (Open answer) (N = 1)

Q7: In the past year, have you witnessed harassment in the workplace? (N = 149)
    a) Yes
    b) No
    c) Not Sure

Q7a: (If yes) Who was involved? Select all that apply. (N = 27)
    a) Co-worker
    b) The Member of Parliament I work for
    c) Another Member of Parliament
    d) Constituent
    e) Other (Please Specify)

Q7b: (If yes) How did you handle the situation? (N = 27)
  a) Talked to the person directly
  b) Talked to a co-worker
  c) Talked to the Member of Parliament
  d) Filed a formal harassment complaint
  e) Used the harassment prevention program
  f) Sought assistance from a third party
  g) Ignored it
  h) Other (Please specify)

Q8: I have completed the online training program for preventing and addressing harassment. (N = 147)
  a) Yes
  b) No
  c) Not Sure

Please answer the following statement on a scale of strongly disagree to strongly agree.

Q9: The government is doing enough to address harassment in politics. (N = 145)

1	2	3	4	5
Strongly Disagree	Disagree	Neither Agree nor Disagree	Agree	Strongly Agree

Q10: Do you work … ? (N = 145)
  a) Full-time (32 hours or more a week)
  b) Part-time (Less than 32 hours a week)

Q11: To which gender identity do you most identify? (N = 145)
  a) Male
  b) Female
  c) Prefer not to disclose
  d) You do not have an option that applies to me. I identify as
      _____ (Open).

Q12: What is your age? (N = 144)
  a) 18–24 years old
  b) 25–34 years old
  c) 35–44 years old

d) 45–54 years old
  e) 55–64 years old
  f) 65–74 years old
  g) 75 years or older

Q13: What is the highest degree or level of school you have completed? (If currently enrolled, please indicate the highest degree received.) (N = 145)
  a) No schooling completed
  b) Some high school, no diploma
  c) High school graduate, diploma or the equivalent (e.g., GED)
  d) Some university or college, no degree
  e) Trade/technical/vocational training
  f) Associate's degree
  g) Bachelor's degree
  h) Master's degree
  i) Professional degree
  j) Doctorate degree

NOTES

1 The term "political staff" can include MP staff, ministerial staff, political party staff, and caucus staff. However, the focus of this chapter is MP staff.
2 For example, Christine Moore was accused of sexual misconduct while sitting as a New Democratic Party MP.
3 The survey was sent out in Qualtrics. MPs have many email addresses assigned to their office. To reach as many staff as possible, surveys were sent to all possible emails associated with the MP.
4 Staffers may be reluctant to disclose their experiences of harassment using their work email addresses, especially if their MP has access to it.
5 See the appendix in this chapter for the questionnaire.
6 Statistics are analysed using STATA.
7 See the appendix in this chapter for the policy's 2014 definition and the exact wording and response count per question.
8 This result is statistically significant, $p = 0.10$. Men (M = 1.81, SD = 0.39) and Women (M = 1.71, SD = 0.45); (t = 1.32[129], $p = 0.10$).
9 Many respondents selected multiple perpetrators. A suggestion for future work is to use an open-ended question to allow for respondents to describe their own experiences.
10 Men (M = 0.40, SD = 0.52) and Women (M = 0.64, SD = 0.490); (t = −1.24[30], $p = 0.11$).

11 Men (M = 0.50, SD = 0.53) and Women (M = 0.41, SD = 0.50); (t = 0.47[30], p = 0.30).
12 Hango and Moyser (2018, 1) report that "19% of women and 13% of men reported that they had experienced harassment in their workplace in the past year."
13 Men (M = 1.89, SD = 0.45) and Women (M = 1.93, SD = 0.53); (t = –0.39[139], p = 0.35).
14 This question's wording is unclear regarding who exactly the perpetrator was, as employees may have witnessed MPs being harassed.
15 Men (M = 0.375, SD = 0.52) and Women (M = 0.60, SD = 0.51); (t = –0.39[139], p = 0.35).
16 Future research should further investigate the gendered nature of dealing with harassment from constituents.
17 This question was open-ended and qualitatively coded. There were 53 responses from men and 11 discussed harassment, or 21 per cent of responses. There were 70 responses from women, and 20 discussed harassment, or 29 per cent of responses. This result is a difference of 8 per cent.
18 See the speech that Michelle Rempel (Calgary Nose Hill, CPC) made on 29 January 2018 to the House of Commons in response to Bill C-65 (Rempel 2018).
19 See Cockram's chapter 11 in this volume for a detailed investigation of the anti-harassment training protocols.
20 My study echoes the Samara Centre for Democracy's 2018 report "Elephant on the Hill," with similar results concerning the extent of harassment towards staffers, and staffers who experienced harassment often did not report it.

REFERENCES

Aiello, Rachel, and Glen McGregor. 2018. "Patrick Brown Denies Sexual Misconduct Allegations from Two Women, Resigns as Ontario PC Leader." *CTV News*, 24 January 2018. https://www.ctvnews.ca/politics/patrick-brown-denies-sexual-misconduct-allegations-from-two-women-resigns-as-ontario-pc-leader-1.3774686.
Bryden, Joan, and Jennifer Ditchburn. 2014. "Scott Andrews Accused of Groping, Grinding Pelvis against Complainant." *CBC News*, 26 November 2014. https://www.cbc.ca/news/canada/newfoundland-labrador/scott-andrews-accused-of-groping-grinding-pelvis-against-complainant-1.2850457.
Burke, Ashley. 2019. "Relentless Online Abuse of Female MPs Raises Concern for Safety of Staff." *CBC News*, 5 November 2019. https://www.cbc.ca/news/politics/mps-staff-online-hate-security-measures-1.5347221.
Canadian Press. 2019. "Ex-Liberal MP Darshan Kang Apologizes but Defends Conduct after Probe Found He Harassed Staffer." *Global News*, 6 May 2019.

https://globalnews.ca/news/5245231/darshan-kang-sexual-harassment-complaint/.

CBC News. 2014. "Liberal MPs Scott Andrews, Massimo Pacetti Suspended from Caucus amid Harassment Allegations." *CBC News*, 5 November 2014. https://www.cbc.ca/news/politics/liberal-mps-scott-andrews-massimo-pacetti-suspended-from-caucus-amid-harassment-allegations-1.2824396.

Cloutier, Meagan. 2019. "Women in the Office: MP Staff in Canada." MA Thesis, University of Calgary.

Connolly, Amanda. 2018. "Kent Hehr Resigns from Liberal Cabinet over Sexual Harassment Allegations." *Global News*, 25 January 2018. https://globalnews.ca/news/3986503/kent-hehr-sexual-harassment-allegations/.

Curry, Leslie A., Ingrid M. Nembhard, and Elizabeth H. Bradley. 2009. "Qualitative and Mixed Methods Provide Unique Contributions to Outcomes Research." *Circulation* 119 (10): 1442–52. https://doi.org/10.1161/CIRCULATIONAHA.107.742775.

Docherty, David C. 1997. *Mr. Smith Goes to Ottawa: Life in the House of Commons*. Vancouver, BC: UBC Press.

Eberhardt, Bruce J., Steven B. Moser, and David McFadden. 1999. "Sexual Harassment in Small Government Units: An Investigation of Policies and Attitudes." *Public Personnel Management* 28 (3): 351–64. https://doi.org/10.1177/009102609902800303.

Foote, William E., and Jane Goodman-Delahunty. 2005. *Evaluating Sexual Harassment: Psychological, Social, and Legal Considerations in Forensic Examinations*. Washington, DC: American Psychological Association.

Hango, Darcy, and Melissa Moyser. 2018. "Harassment in Canadian Workplaces." Statistics Canada. Catalogue no. 75-006-X. Ottawa, ON: Statistics Canada. https://www150.statcan.gc.ca/pub/75-006-x/2018001/article/54982-eng.pdf.

Hershcovis, Sandy. 2018. "Brief to the Standing Committee on HUMA – Bill C-65." https://www.ourcommons.ca/Content/Committee/421/HUMA/Brief/BR9708263/br-external/HershcovisSandy-e.pdf.

Hertel-Fernandez, Alexander, Matto Mildenberger, and Leah C. Stokes. 2019. "Legislative Staff and Representation in Congress." *American Political Science Review* 113 (1): 1–18. https://doi.org/10.1017/S0003055418000606.

Houle, Jason N., Jeremy Staff, Jeylan T. Mortimer, Christopher Uggen, and Amy Blackstone. 2011. "The Impact of Sexual Harassment on Depressive Symptoms during the Early Occupational Career." *Society and Mental Health* 1 (2): 89–105. https://doi.org/10.1177/2156869311416827.

House of Commons, Canada. 2014. *House of Commons Policy on Preventing and Addressing Harassment*. Approved by the Board of Internal Economy. Ottawa, ON: House of Commons, Canada.

– 2021. *Members of the House of Commons Workplace Harassment and Violence Prevention Policy*. Approved by the Board of Internal Economy. Ottawa, ON:

House of Commons, Canada. https://www.ourcommons.ca/Content/Boie/pdf/policy_preventing_harassment-e.pdf.

Krook, Mona Lena. 2020. *Violence against Women in Politics*. London: Oxford University Press.

Krook, Mona Lena, and Juliana Restrepo Sanín. 2020. "The Cost of Doing Politics? Analyzing Violence and Harassment against Female Politicians." *Perspectives on Politics* 18 (3): 740–55. https://doi.org/10.1017/S1537592719001397.

Leeder, Jessica. 2018. "Nova Scotia PC Leader Jamie Baillie Resigns after Harassment Investigation." *The Globe and Mail*, 24 January 2018. https://www.theglobeandmail.com/news/politics/nova-scotia-pc-leader-jamie-baillie-resigns-after-harassment-investigation/article37717772/.

Maher, Stephen. 2018. "Inside the Explosive Conservative Party Fight over Rick Dykstra." *Maclean's*, 2 February 2018. https://www.macleans.ca/politics/ottawa/inside-the-explosive-conservative-party-fight-over-rick-dykstra/.

McLaughlin, Heather, Christopher Uggen, and Amy Blackstone. 2017. "The Economic and Career Effects of Sexual Harassment on Working Women." *Gender and Society* 31 (3): 333–58. https://doi.org/10.1177/0891243217704631.

Parliament of Canada. 2018. Bill C-65: An Act to Amend the Canada Labour Code (Harassment and Violence), the Parliamentary Employment and Staff Relations Act and the Budget Implementation Act, 2017, No. 1. S.C. 2018, c. 22. https://www.parl.ca/Content/Bills/421/Government/C-65/C-65_4/C-65_4.PDF.

Parry, Tom. 2017. "Police Offer Extra Protection to MP Iqra Khalid Following Threatening Messages." *CBC News*, 17 February 2017. https://www.cbc.ca/news/politics/khalid-police-protection-messages-islamophobia-1.3989476.

Raney, Tracey, and Cheryl N. Collier. 2022. "Privilege and Gendered Violence in the Canadian and British House of Commons: A Feminist Institutionalist Analysis." *Parliamentary Affairs* 75 (2): 382–99. https://doi.org/10.1093/pa/gsaa069.

Rempel, Michelle. 2018, 29 January. "Speech to the House of Commons by Hon. Michelle Rempel (Calgary Nose Hill, CPC)." In *House of Commons Debates*, vol. 148, no. 252, 42nd Parliament, 1st Session (Hansard 252). http://www.ourcommons.ca/DocumentViewer/en/42-1/house/sitting-252/hansard#9929271.

Samara Centre for Democracy. 2018, 4 December. "The Elephant on the Hill." https://www.samaracentre.ca/articles/the-elephant-on-the-hill.

Smith, Charlie. 2021. "B.C.'s Female Politicians Face Down Misogynistic, Hateful Bullies." *The Georgia Straight*, 3 March 2021. https://www.straight.com/news/bcs-female-politicians-face-down-misogynistic-hateful-bullies.

Snagovsky, Feodor, and Matthew Kerby. 2019. "Political Staff and the Gendered Division of Political Labour in Canada." *Parliamentary Affairs* 72 (3): 616–37. https://doi.org/10.1093/pa/gsy032.

Tunney, Catharine. 2018. "MP Erin Weir Expelled from NDP Caucus after Harassment Investigation." *CBC News*, 3 May 2018. https://www.cbc.ca/news/politics/erin-weir-caucus-ndp-1.4646224.

Uggen, Christopher, and Amy Blackstone. 2004. "Sexual Harassment as a Gendered Expression of Power." *American Sociological Review* 69 (1): 64–92. https://doi.org/10.1177/000312240406900105.

Verge, Tània. 2022. "Too Few, Too Little: Parliaments' Response to Sexism and Sexual Harassment." *Parliamentary Affairs* 75 (1): 94–112. https://doi.org/10.1093/pa/gsaa052.

Ward, Claire. 2010. "Most Collegial: Peter Stoffer." *Maclean's*, 2 June 2010. https://www.macleans.ca/news/canada/most-collegial-peter-stoffer-2010/.

Zubi, Beisan. 2017. "Here's Why I Never Reported Sexual Harassment When Working in Parliament." *Vice News*, 13 March 2017. https://news.vice.com/en_ca/article/nedpzq/heres-why-i-never-reported-sexual-harassment-while-working-on-parliament-hill.

PART FOUR

Assessing "Solutions" to Violence against Women in Politics in Canada

10 Just Bad Apples? Political Accountability and Canadian MPs Accused of Gender-Based Violence

BAILEY GERRITS

Introduction

After #MeToo, previously silenced claims about federal Canadian politicians engaging in gender-based violence (GBV) were made public.[1] A party leader. A cabinet minister. Current and former backbenchers spanning the political spectrum. It appeared to be a turning point. In this chapter, I analyse whether #MeToo did in fact serve as a flashpoint for greater political accountability on GBV in Canadian federal politics. This chapter examines eleven cases of federal politicians accused of GBV that were made public three years prior to and three years after #MeToo. Rather than institutions or political parties acknowledging and addressing gender-based violence in politics (GBV-P) as a systemic problem, I find that most often accountability on GBV-P took the form of punishments imposed upon "bad apple" individuals both before and after #MeToo. In the absence of strong accountability mechanisms inside legislatures and political parties to address the systemic causes of GBV-P, this problem is likely to continue to negatively affect Canada's democracy.

GBV-P and Political Accountability

Three interrelated arguments together explain why GBV-P is prevalent in Canadian politics and why politicians causing harm seem to avoid accountability. First, their authority arises from the sexist, racist, and colonial norms embedded within Canada's Westminster-style system of governance (Cossette and Craig 2019; Dalton 2019). These norms contribute processes that silence victims (Dalton 2019; Hopke 2019; Collier and Raney 2018b), concealing GBV-P from public view. Second, the authority given to elected officials enables them to wield significant power over others (Cossette and Craig 2019). Third, since more men hold these powerful positions, they are afforded more opportunities to abuse that power than are women.

This chapter evaluates how specific cases of GBV-P have been addressed by decision-makers in Canadian federal politics before and after the 2017 #MeToo wave, with a focus on political accountability. Political accountability is a cornerstone of democratic systems, and accountability for GBV-P requires three components: answerability (providing an account of harm); transparency (releasing timely and reliable information); and enforceability (taking action to redress the problem; Bradshaw, Linneker, and Overton 2016, 39). Accountability is compatible with several GBV responses from restorative to criminal.[2] While addressing individual motivating factors and holding individuals who perpetrate GBV-P accountable are important pieces of the puzzle (Bardall, Bjarnegård, and Piscopo 2020, 917; Berthet and Kantola 2021, 9), the GBV-P literature convincingly suggests that institutions and norms (Bardall, Bjarnegård, and Piscopo 2020, 918; Collier and Raney 2018b; Dalton 2019; Krook 2018) – legislatures, political parties, and societal attitudes towards GBV – must be addressed too. Changing institutions and norms is difficult, especially as political institutions often fail to hold themselves accountable (Hopke 2019). At the same time, focusing on "bad apples" alone is not sufficient to change a systemic problem (Dalton 2019).

Accountability mechanisms that specifically deal with some forms of GBV-P are relatively new in Canada (see Collier and Raney, chapter 13, this volume). The 2015 Code of Conduct for Members of the House of Commons: Sexual Harassment, for example, addresses non-criminal forms of sexual harassment between members, while the 2014 staffing policy applies to House of Commons staff (Collier and Raney 2018a). The Board of Internal Economy – which is the governing body of the House of Commons – is in charge of enforcing relevant policies. These policies focus largely on individuals. Measures to address GBV-P more broadly by the House, including anti-harassment training (see Cloutier, chapter 9 and Cockram, chapter 11 in this volume), are limited.

In addition to the formal rules of the House, political accountability for politicians who engage in GBV-P can also come in other forms, including through an individual, via political parties, and during elections. Individuals who cause harm could take personal responsibility by apologizing for the harm they have caused; they could admit to their behaviour publicly and face self-imposed or other-imposed consequences (Tadros and Edwards 2020, 7). Political parties also have a role to play in holding their members who engage in GBV-P accountable.

Parties can discipline members publicly or privately when they engage in GBV-P, including by denying them coveted committee appointments or not allowing a candidate to run under the party banner in future elections. When these "punishments" occur behind closed doors, it arguably limits how accountable parties are to the public. Political parties, themselves, may need to account for party norms or lack of individual member accountability that contribute to GBV-P. Political parties can self-impose changes, face consequences from the public or their members, or from changes to the governing legislation of political parties, the Canada Election Act.

Elections could provide another means to hold elected officials and parties accountable (Cossette and Craig 2019). However, existing research shows that elections may not always produce this outcome, as voters are less likely to hold politicians accountable when there is incomplete information or partisan bias (Vivyan, Wagner, and Tarlov 2012). Voters are also less likely to penalize sexual misconduct compared to financial crimes (Cossette and Craig 2019, 17). At the same time, a more recent study suggests that American voters are less likely to support a candidate facing credible sexual harassment allegations (Stark and Collignon 2022). Elections are one of the few avenues through which voters can hold elected officials and parties contributing to GBV-P accountable. However, voters have a lot to consider, leading to the question: would electoral accountability be evenly applied (Dalton 2019)?

The institutions and actors contributing to GBV-P are also products of a Canadian society that maintains systems of oppression, racism, colonialism, sexism, and the like, which buttress GBV. Society needs to answer for the harm caused by these systems, ensure transparency of information about GBV, and enforce change, just as political institutions and individuals need to face accountability. Beyond voters, societal accountability includes the media, civil society, educational systems, and so on. Society can be a source of accountability (for example, voting out politicians engaging in GBV-P or reporting on cases and the political responses), just as a collective accounting for the prevalence of GBV-P is necessary. Societal accountability is harder to measure and achieve. While societal accountability is outside the scope of this chapter, it is important to recognize that GBV-P requires both attention to the institutional and individual remedies within the political system itself and, importantly, remedies to broader facilitative systems of oppression. Since #MeToo called attention to structures, institutions, and individuals that cause harm, these broader forms of accountability could be more possible after #MeToo. I assess this possibility below.

Methods

This chapter takes a qualitative case study approach to evaluate how instances of GBV in Canadian federal politics were handled both before and after #MeToo. I examine eleven cases of recent GBV-P that meet two criteria: (1) the claim of GBV was first publicized between 15 October 2014 and 15 October 2020; and (2) the person accused of GBV was a member of Parliament (MP), either at the time of the incident or at the time the incident was made public. Cases were selected both before and after #MeToo in order to assess how and whether this global movement and heightened media interest in workplace sexual harassment (see Goodyear-Grant's chapter 5, this volume) improved the holding of politicians who commit GBV-P accountable for their actions. The analysis includes only cases where allegations of gender-based harassment or physical/sexual violence were made public and reported by the media, and excludes one-off gendered or sexist comments.[3] Three politicians accused of GBV before #MeToo and eight afterwards meet these criteria. More non-public cases occurred during this time frame, as documented in anonymous surveys conducted by the House of Commons (2020) and the Samara Centre for Democracy (2018). Accountability in these non-public cases is not assessed here.

I analysed the eleven cases in three steps. First, I collected primary documents and news stories to identify the GBV claims, how and when the accusations were made public, and the responses of the accused, political parties, House of Commons, and voters. Second, I constructed a narrative of each case. The fallibility of the news media and the subjectivity of GBV make it impossible to write a definitive account. However, my aim is to analyse the publicly known forms of accountability, both before and after #MeToo. Third, I identified themes across the cases. This case study comparison generates insights through descriptive inference.

The Cases

The eleven cases span the major federal parties, revealing that GBV-P is a multi-partisan problem. MPs from the Liberal Party of Canada (Liberal), Conservative Party of Canada (Conservative), New Democratic Party (NDP), and Bloc Québécois (Bloc) all faced accusations. A case's inclusion does not mean the claims are true. The descriptions of chronologically organized cases provide the particulars to understand the conditions, opportunities, and failures of accountability.

Politicians Publicly Accused before #MeToo

Scott Andrews, a former Liberal MP, was accused of following a woman NDP MP home in March 2014, forcing himself into her place, pushing her against the wall, groping her, and grinding against her (Canadian Press 2015). That same month, Massimo Pacetti, a former Liberal MP, was accused of having sex with another woman NDP MP without her "explicit consent" (Smith 2014). Pacetti's accuser told Liberal leader Justin Trudeau about her experience and about her colleague's experience with Andrews. CBC publicized the accusations in November 2014. Trudeau suspended the men from the Liberal caucus shortly afterwards, although both men maintained their innocence (CBC News 2015). After an internal party investigation concluded that both incidents occurred and that there were likely more victims, Trudeau permanently removed both men from the Liberal caucus in March 2015. Andrews complained about the process's fairness but said he "learned a lot about ... how [his] jovial Newfoundland friendliness can be perceived" (Canadian Press 2015). Andrews ran for re-election in 2015 as an independent and came in second to the Liberal candidate. Pacetti did not seek re-election.

In 2017 Darshan Kang, a former Liberal MP, was accused of sexually harassing two staffers. The incidents included unwanted touching and kissing, harassing comments, attempting to enter one woman's hotel room, and attempting to bribe one woman (Carbert 2017). One staffer made a harassment complaint in August 2017 while still working in Kang's office. The news media reported the complaint that month. Kang resigned from the Liberal caucus to "focus on clearing his name" (Carbert 2017). The House hired an independent investigator to review the staffer's claims, following the 2014 staffing policy.[4] In March 2018, the investigator found the claims to be "partially substantiated," disputing the attempted bribe accusation (Potkins 2018). Kang appealed the findings but lost his appeal in August 2018. The Board of Internal Economy directed Kang to take and pay for an individual awareness training program in October 2018 (Naumetz 2018). Kang apologized for his behaviour in May 2019 in the House. He did not seek re-election in 2019.

Politicians Publicly Accused after #MeToo

Kent Hehr, the former minister of sport and persons with disabilities and Liberal MP, was accused of saying unwanted and sexually suggestive comments to a former staffer about tweets she posted on 24 January 2018 (Connolly 2018). The next day, Hehr tweeted he was resigning from cabinet "pending the outcome of the investigation." On

27 January 2018, another woman accused Hehr of groping her (Zimonjic 2018). Prime Minister Trudeau commissioned Rubin Thomlinson LLP to conduct an investigation as the incidents took place before Hehr was an MP. On 6 June 2018, the investigation concluded that Hehr's comments made the staffer feel uncomfortable and that the touch was unintentional. Hehr publicly apologized, saying he did not remember saying anything inappropriate (Zimonjic 2018). Hehr remained a Liberal but did not return to cabinet. In 2019, Hehr lost re-election as a Liberal in his Calgary Centre riding.

Rick Dykstra, a former Conservative MP, was reported to the police for sexually assaulting a Conservative staffer in 2014, but she did not press charges. The Conservative leadership was aware of the report but permitted Dykstra to run in 2015. He lost the election and became the president of the Conservative Party of Ontario. In January 2018, the report was made public; Dykstra denied the allegations and resigned as president. The federal Conservatives hired lawyer Carol Nielsen to investigate the party process. Nielsen's six recommendations, later accepted by the party, focused on individuals[5] and creating stronger party protocols[6] (Smith 2019).

Erin Weir, a former NDP MP, was accused in a group email by NDP MP Christine Moore of making other women feel uncomfortable (Tunney 2018). The news media reported the accusations on 1 February 2018 (Gilmore 2018). The leader of the NDP, Jagmeet Singh, initiated an independent third-party investigation that asked complainants to come forward (Tunney 2018). In May 2018, the report concluded that there was at least one credible harassment complaint and three credible sexual harassment complaints against Weir. Weir responded through the news media, social media, and his blog, claiming the accusations were politically motivated, calling the investigation "deeply flawed," and apologizing for not understanding social cues. Singh expelled Weir from caucus and did not allow Weir to appeal the decision or to run as an NDP candidate in 2019.

Peter Stoffer, a retired NDP MP, was accused in the *National Post* on 9 February 2018 of groping and kissing three women while he was an MP in the 2000s. Stoffer denied wrongdoing but apologized for the unintended effects of his behaviour. NDP leader Jagmeet Singh said the allegations were "deeply" disturbing, but the party did not investigate further (Ferreira 2018).

The only woman in the time frame, Christine Moore, a former NDP MP, was accused on 8 May 2018 of abusing her power to sleep with a member of the public, Glen Kirkland. Moore denied the accusations, claiming it was a consensual relationship, and directed her lawyer to send a cease-and-desist letter to Kirkland. NDP leader Singh suspended Moore from caucus duties and commissioned an independent inquiry; Kirkland declined to participate. The investigation concluded that Moore did not abuse her power and did not sexually harass Kirkland, and Singh reinstated Moore on 19 July 2018 (Harris 2018). Moore did not seek re-election in 2019.

Tony Clement, a former Conservative MP, admitted to sharing sexually explicit images and having inappropriate conversations with young women on social media. This behaviour came to light when Clement announced on 6 November 2018 that a recipient of the images was trying to extort him. Clement resigned from the Conservative shadow cabinet and national security committees. Days later, multiple young women said Clement inappropriately communicated with them on social media and shared sexually explicit images. Clement apologized again. The Conservatives asked Clement to resign, and he did (Gerster 2018).

Marwan Tabbara, a former independent MP and former Liberal MP, faced two separate public GBV accusations in 2020 (Burke and Everson 2020). The police claim that Tabbara criminally harassed a woman on 9 April 2020, broke into a house, and assaulted a man and woman in the house (Bueckert 2020). The arrests were made public on 5 June 2020 (Burke and Everson 2020). Tabbara left the Liberal caucus. The prime minister claimed he learned about the arrest from the media (Canadian Press 2020). On 19 June 2020, sexual harassment allegations were made public by an anonymous source, worried about being "blacklisted within Liberal circles," that Tabbara inappropriately touched a former staffer and made sexual comments to her when he was running as a Liberal candidate in 2015 (Burke and Everson 2020). The Liberal leadership knew about the sexual harassment claims before the 2019 election, said they found the claims credible after investigating them, but allowed Tabbara to run for and win re-election in 2019. Tabbara did not run in the 2021 election.

Finally, Yves-François Blanchet, the current Bloc Québécois leader, was accused of pulling down a woman's skirt, non-consensually kissing her, physically preventing her from leaving the room, and masturbating in front of her in a Montreal bar in 1999. An anonymous Facebook page, Hyènes en jupons, posted the accusation in July 2020, joining a wave of accusations against Québécois celebrities (Kappler 2020). Blanchet denied the claims, asked "real victims" to report to the police, denounced politically motivated allegations, and threatened to sue the Facebook page's editors (CBC News 2020). He stepped back from the threat after the Facebook post was deleted. All thirty-one members of the Bloc caucus co-signed a letter supporting Blanchet. Blanchet ran in the 2021 election as Bloc leader and won.

Discussion

From these eleven cases, what accountability patterns emerge? Did #MeToo change the conditions for accountability? Table 10.1 summarizes the accountability actions taken for each case. Four patterns emerge. First, accountability consistently focuses on the individual, even after #MeToo. Second, results below show that political parties are not particularly good arbiters of individual accountability and themselves need to be held accountable. Third, public accusations of GBV-P are negatively associated with running in or winning the next election, both before and after #MeToo. Fourth, the increase in public cases of reported GBV-P after #MeToo is a step towards increased accountability, even if it narrowly focused on individuals.

Table 10.1 reveals that the most common form of accountability across the time frame analysed was focused on holding individuals responsible for their actions. As a result of media attention, some individuals were investigated, although all findings were kept private. Some individuals resigned, some lost re-elections, and some were cleared after investigations. Even in cases where people and institutions beyond the individual were directly implicated, the focus was on the individual. The cases of Dykstra and Tabbara are instructive. Even though both parties indicated that they would investigate internally, no one was publicly held accountable for the party's role in allowing these two men to run. The Conservatives implemented some of Nielsen's recommendations, including revising their harassment policy and running a training program (Canadian Press 2019). As this process remained shrouded in secrecy, it is unclear if MPs, candidates, and staffers had to take the programming. None of the recommendations made anyone in the party answerable for not providing transparent information about claims against the candidate or allowing the candidate to run. In these two cases, the leaders of the parties (both prime ministers at the time) knew about the allegations and allowed the men to run for the party. Yet, neither of the leaders nor their parties faced any public consequences. Dykstra and Tabbara may have caused the discrete harms, but it was the parties that endorsed these men.

Indeed, results suggest that political parties are not the best accountability arbiters in dealing with GBV-P. Parties are not motivated to penalize incumbent candidates if allegations are only known internally. That the Conservatives and the Liberals fielded Dykstra and Tabbara,

Table 10.1. Type of accountability pursued

Politician	Individual	Party	House	Electoral
Pre-#MeToo				
Scott Andrews (Liberal)	Denial of responsibility. Accepted report findings.	Removed from Liberal caucus.	Created new staffing policy (2014) and MP-to-MP Code of Conduct (2015).*	Ran and lost.
Massimo Pacetti (Liberal)	Denial of responsibility.	Removed from Liberal caucus.		Did not run again.
Darshan Kang (Liberal)	Denial. Later apology. Resigned.**	None.	Requested to publicly apologize.	Did not run again.
Post-#MeToo				
Kent Hehr (Liberal)	Initial denial. Resigned cabinet position.** Apologized.	None.	None.	Ran and lost.
Rick Dykstra (Conservative)	Denial. Resigned as president of Ontario Progressive Conservatives.**	Hired third party to investigate the party process. Party claimed to implement recommendations, but no public transparency on its response.	None.	N/A
Erin Weir (NDP)	Denial. Later apology. Disputed the investigation.	None.	None.	Did not run again.
Peter Stoffer (NDP)	Denial and apology.	None.	None.	N/A
Christine Moore (NDP)	Denial. Threatened to sue accuser.	None.	None.	Did not run again.
Tony Clement (Conservative)	Admitted his actions were wrong. Apologized. Resigned and quit politics.**	None.	None.	Did not run again.
Marwan Tabbara (Liberal)	Resigned as a Liberal. Remained an independent MP.**	Claimed to be investigating claims and/or party process, but no public transparency on the process.	None.	Did not run again.
Yves-François Blanchet (Bloc Québécois)	Denial. Threatened to sue Facebook page editors. Asked "real victims" to report to police.	None.	None.	Re-elected.

* The Andrews and Pacetti cases highlighted a gap in the tools available to the House of Commons. By creating the two policies, the House engaged in a form of accountability by trying to create tools to address future harm. These policies did not get applied to the discipline of either Andrews or Pacetti.
** In some cases, it is unclear whether the party exerted private pressure on the MP to resign. Even if a party intervenes by "requesting" that an MP resign, the secrecy surrounding such actions signals a problematic lack of willingness to be publicly seen as addressing GBV in a systemic way, rather than a problem of one individual actor who has "voluntarily" chosen to resign.

respectively, after credible accusations of GBV (which were kept secret from the public) were known about within the party, is troubling. Since House processes do not apply to incidents that occurred before an MP took up federal office or to all forms of GBV (or to cases not reported to them; Collier and Raney 2018a), parties may be the only relevant authority to investigate. Weir, for example, was not subject to a House investigation, as no one reported the allegations to the House authorities. Instead, the NDP investigated on its own. While the NDP released parts of the report, parties are generally not obligated to investigate or share the outcome of the investigation. The lack of transparency in how political parties address instances of GBV within their ranks is problematic, as their membership and the Canadian public are unable to determine how/whether the accused is being sufficiently held accountable or if additional steps to change party norms or policies need to be taken.

The cases of Moore and Blanchet are further instructive of the problem of leaving accountability in cases of GBV-P to political parties. Both politicians threatened to sue their accusers. Moore's accuser said that the libel threat influenced his decision to not participate in the NDP's investigation (Harris 2018). The NDP welcomed Moore back into caucus after the investigation, and the Bloc vehemently defended their leader without investigating the allegations against Blanchet. It is possible that Moore and Blanchet were wrongly accused. It is also possible that the threat of legal action undermined the possibility for accountability. In both cases, the parties were unwilling to publicly consider the tension created by the threat of legal action by a politician.

In the case of Kang, the relatively new House rules did kick in. While the allegations against him became public only two months prior to #MeToo in August 2017, the House hired an independent investigator to review the staffer's claims just as the movement was in full swing. As a result of the investigation, Kang was required to apologize and take an individual awareness training program. In no other case were the House's anti-harassment rules used to hold politicians accused of GBV-P accountable, at least publicly.

Electoral accountability is also limited in the cases under review here, either before or after #MeToo. Politicians who were publicly accused of GBV were unlikely to run in the next election, meaning that the opportunity for the electorate to hold these politicians accountable for their actions was not provided. In the three cases before #MeToo, two men did not seek re-election. After #MeToo, four of the six politicians who could have run after the allegations were made public – Clement, Moore, Weir, and Tabbara – did not seek re-election. The remaining two – Dykstra and Stoffer – were not involved in federal politics at the time the allegations were made public and have not attempted re-election. A lot could influence a politician's decision to not run (including internal party pressures), but the public nature of these particular accusations likely factored into their decisions. Moore, the one case where the investigation concluded the claims were unsubstantiated, did not reference the allegations in her decision to leave politics but did make earlier comments about how difficult the public accusations were for her and her family (Paas-Lang 2019; Berthiaume 2018). Not running for re-election, though, negates the possibility of voters holding a politician accountable. Not running could be read as evading electoral accountability or as a form of self-imposed accountability. It is unsatisfactory as it does not address the conditions that facilitate GBV-P in the first place.

Two of the three politicians who did attempt re-election lost. Before #MeToo, Andrews lost as an independent to the challenging Liberal in 2015. After #MeToo, Hehr lost as the Liberal candidate in 2019. However, public allegations alone in these cases likely did not cause the negative electoral outcomes. Hehr, for example, lost in the 2019 election in which the Liberals lost all their Prairie seats (Platt 2019). There is also an intermediary factor influencing both voters and the decision not to run for re-election. Andrews and several of the MPs who returned to the private sector after the public GBV claims were first kicked out by their party. Canadian voters tend to favour politicians tied to parties (Blais et al. 2003), even as other research suggests that the benefits of incumbency are tied to the individual, not the party (Kendall and Rekkas 2012). In the case of Andrews, voters may have penalized him and/or opted to support the Liberal Party. These cases suggest that public allegations of GBV post-#MeToo did make it more difficult for a politician accused of GBV-P to regain power. More research on electoral accountability on GBV-P in the Canadian context is needed.

Blanchet, the current leader of the Bloc, is the only politician who remained a member of his party and won re-election after the public allegation of sexual violence. The 2021 federal election included little reference to the allegations made public the summer prior. One of the few references to the allegations came in a column in *Maclean's*, noting that Blanchet "skated through this election without ever having to respond" to the allegations (Ling 2021). There are several potential explanations. Party leaders who hold the confidence of their party may be shielded from the negative consequences of allegations. Bloc party officials vehemently supported Blanchet after the Facebook post went live. The wave of #MeToo allegations in Quebec included more vociferous discussions of "mob justice," perhaps leading to a more sympathetic response to Blanchet's proclamation of innocence.

Based on these case studies, #MeToo appears to have been a catalyst for the public airing of abuse by Canadian federal politicians. While some may have tried to hold politicians accountable before October 2017, the groundswell of public airing of GBV-P after #MeToo can be understood as a form of accountability. Individual accountability starts with the accused accounting for their actions (Tadros and Edwards 2020). Public pressure can make it harder for claims to be ignored. In this sense, we can view #MeToo as a form of collective action that created conditions for increased accountability for powerful men who cause harm. Even so, given the lack of formal accountability in cases of GBV-P in Canada, it is highly likely that, even in the #MeToo era, the number of reported cases is much higher than what is publicly known. The MP-to-MP Code of Conduct includes confidentiality provisions that prevent survivors from disclosing anything about their case, as do policies for the Senate (see Raney's chapter 12, this volume) and staffing (see Cloutier's chapter 9, this volume). Survivors themselves might not want to report for many valid reasons, including distrust of the process or fear of reprisal and reputational damage. While #MeToo created additional opportunities for accountability, it was not a panacea.

Conclusion

In this chapter, I identify eleven cases of GBV-P in Canada's federal politics that occurred shortly before and after #MeToo. All of these cases were publicized in the media. Presumably, the #MeToo movement might have resulted in increased accountability mechanisms to deal with GBV in Canadian politics. However, my results showed that, even after #MeToo, the House of Commons and political parties did not seem more likely to take swift, serious, and consistent action to address this problem than they were prior to 2017. In some cases, political parties controlled handling cases of GBV-P, and their internal mechanisms did not always result in full, transparent accountability in these cases. Many of these processes occurred behind doors, away from the public eye.

Irrespective of #MeToo, accountability for GBV-P in Canada continues to focus on accused individuals, rather than on the structures, rules, norms, and practices embedded inside political institutions and parties themselves. The lack of institutional responsibility has potentially negative consequences for Canadian democracy. As Restrepo Sanín argues, GBV-P arises from unequal gender power relations and is embedded inside (white) male-dominated political institutions/organizations (Restrepo Sanín 2022; see also Dalton 2019; Collier and Raney 2018a, 2018b). Without serious attempts to reform, address, and deal with GBV at a deeper institutional and cultural level, political accountability on this issue is not likely to be achieved. Despite the promise of #MeToo, GBV in Canadian federal politics continues to be treated largely as a "bad apple" problem, with insufficient institutional accountability to deal with this issue.

Implications for Action

1. The Canada Election Act could require parties to disclose knowledge of credible GBV allegations. Obligatory disclosure (with the permission of the complainants) might discourage the accused from running, or, if they do run, the electorate may be less likely to elect such a representative. Parties could also not support candidates who have credible claims of GBV against them. Careful attention would be needed to assess the credibility of claims to avoid people advancing specious accusations.
2. Additional federal money could provide expanded prevention programming for all politicians, focusing around shifting norms. Existing training first offered in 2019 only focuses on workplace harassment and does not include other forms of GBV (House of Commons 2020).
3. Additional research about GBV and candidate vetting processes would provide additional insights and opportunities to improve accountability.
4. Future research may want to consider whether federal political parties, individuals, media, and other interested parties respond differently to accusations against racialized men. Including the most recent GBV allegations against one Conservative and two Liberal candidates, four of the fourteen cases accuse men of colour. While this pool is small, the proportion of racialized men accused exceeds their representation in the House. The relationship between public accusations, accountability, and racialization warrants additional research.

NOTES

1. This study benefited from the excellent research assistance of Danielle Hermann. Thank you!
2. Justice mechanisms for responding to GBV vary from criminal sanctions to civil remedies to restorative meetings aimed at repairing relationships/community. There are debates about the relationship between GBV

accountability and justice mechanisms that are outside the scope of this chapter. The literatures on carceral feminism and feminist critiques of restorative justice provide two different entry points.

3 Excluding comments does not minimize their harm. I have also excluded the resurfaced claims that Prime Minister Justin Trudeau groped a reporter at a festival in 2000 because these allegations were first publicized outside the time frame.

4 The House of Commons process did not investigate the claims made by the former member of the Legislative Assembly (MLA) of Alberta staffer. The federal Liberals investigated past claims of abuse against Kent Hehr in 2018, but did not investigate past claims against Kang.

5 Recommendations concerning individuals included strengthening candidate vetting, requiring candidates to disclose issues after nomination, more extensive police checks, and additional candidate training on harassment and equality (Lim 2019).

6 Recommendations concerning party protocols included complaint procedure, a code of conduct for candidates, a harassment policy for candidates, and a reporting policy outside the campaign (Lim 2019).

REFERENCES

Bardall, Gabrielle, Elin Bjarnegård, and Jennifer M Piscopo. 2020. "How Is Political Violence Gendered? Disentangling Motives, Forms, and Impacts." *Political Studies* 68 (4): 916–35. https://doi.org/10.1177/0032321719881812.

Berthet, Valentine, and Johanna Kantola. 2021. "Gender, Violence, and Political Institutions: Struggles over Sexual Harassment in the European Parliament." *Social Politics: International Studies in Gender, State & Society* 28 (1): 143–67. https://doi.org/10.1093/sp/jxaa015.

Berthiaume, Lee. 2018. "NDP MP Moore Says Family Hit Hard by Allegations of Impropriety." *CTV News*, 14 May 2018. https://www.ctvnews.ca/politics/ndp-mp-moore-says-family-hit-hard-by-allegations-of-impropriety-1.3929294.

Blais, André, Elisabeth Gidengil, Agnieszka Dobrzynska, Neil Nevitte, and Richard Adeau. 2003. "Does the Local Candidate Matter? Candidate Effects in the Canadian Election of 2000." *Canadian Journal of Political Science/Revue canadienne de science politique* 36 (3): 657–64. https://doi.org/10.1017/S0008423903778810.

Bradshaw, Sarah, with Brian Linneker and Lisa Overton. 2016. *Gender and Social Accountability: Ensuring Women's Inclusion in Citizen-Led Accountability Programming Relating to Extractive Industries*. Research Backgrounder. Washington, DC: Oxfam America. https://www.oxfamamerica.org/explore/research-publications/gender-and-social-accountability/.

Bueckert, Kate. 2020. "Guelph Police Admit Error with Media Officers about MP Tabbara's Arrest." *CBC News*, 12 August 2020. https://www.cbc.ca

/news/canada/kitchener-waterloo/marwan-tabbara-arrest-foi-name-not-released-guelph-police-1.5683235.
Burke, Ashley, and Kristin Everson. 2020. "Liberals Allowed MP Marwan Tabbara to Run in 2019 despite Sexual Harassment Investigation." *CBC News*, 19 June 2020. https://www.cbc.ca/news/politics/mp-marwan-tabbara-past-liberal-party-misconduct-investigation-1.5617740.
Canadian Press. 2015. "MP Scott Andrews Accepts Findings of Misconduct Review, Says Process Frustrating." *Maclean's*, 19 March 2015. https://www.macleans.ca/politics/ottawa/mp-scott-andrews-accepts-findings-of-misconduct-review-says-process-frustrating/.
– 2019. "Conservatives Still Working on Candidate Harassment Policy Promised This Year." *CP24*, 6 September 2019. https://www.cp24.com/news/conservatives-still-working-on-candidate-harassment-policy-promised-this-year-1.4581559.
– 2020. "Trudeau Says Rule Requiring House of Commons Be Informed of MP Arrests Was Not Followed in Case of Marwan Tabbara." *The Globe and Mail*, 19 June 2020. https://www.theglobeandmail.com/politics/article-trudeau-says-rule-requiring-house-of-commons-be-informed-of-mp-arrests/.
Carbert, Michelle. 2017. "Liberal MP Darshan Kang Resigns from Caucus amid Sexual-Harassment Allegations." *The Globe and Mail*, 31 August 2017. https://www.theglobeandmail.com/news/politics/liberal-mp-darshan-kang-resigns-from-caucus-amid-sexual-harassment-allegations/article36140289/.
CBC News. 2015. "Massimo Pacetti, Scott Andrews Out of Liberal Caucus for Good, Sources Say." *CBC News*, 18 March 2015. https://www.cbc.ca/news/politics/massimo-pacetti-scott-andrews-out-of-liberal-caucus-for-good-sources-say-1.2999426.
– 2020. "Blanchet Denies Sexual Misconduct Allegations as Bloc Caucus Stands behind Leader." *CBC News*, 19 July 2020. https://www.cbc.ca/news/politics/bloc-quebecois-leader-sexual-misconduct-allegations-1.5655309.
Collier, Cheryl N., and Tracey Raney. 2018a. "Canada's Member-to-Member Code of Conduct on Sexual Harassment in the House of Commons: Progress or Regress?" *Canadian Journal of Political Science* 51 (4): 795–815. https://doi.org/10.1017/S000842391800032X.
– 2018b. "Understanding Sexism and Sexual Harassment in Politics: A Comparison of Westminster Parliaments in Australia, the United Kingdom, and Canada." *Social Politics: International Studies in Gender, State & Society* 25 (3): 432–55. https://doi.org/10.1093/sp/jxy024.
Connolly, Amanda. 2018. "Kent Hehr Resigns from Liberal Cabinet over Sexual Harassment Allegations." *Global News*, 25 January 2018. https://globalnews.ca/news/3986503/kent-hehr-sexual-harassment-allegations/.

Cossette, Paulina S., and Stephen C. Craig. 2019. *Politicians Behaving Badly: Men, Women, and the Politics of Sexual Harassment*. New York: Routledge.

Dalton, Emma. 2019. "A Feminist Critical Discourse Analysis of Sexual Harassment in the Japanese Political and Media Worlds." *Women's Studies International Forum* 77 (November–December): 102276. https://doi.org/10.1016/j.wsif.2019.102276.

Ferreira, Victor. 2018. "Former NDP MP Peter Stoffer Apologizes after Three Women Accuse Him of Inappropriate Behaviour on Parliament Hill." *National Post*, 9 February 2018. https://nationalpost.com/news/politics/former-ndp-mp-peter-stoffer-apologizes-after-three-women-accuse-him-of-inappropriate-behaviour-on-parliament-hill.

Gerster, Jane. 2018. "'Inappropriate' but Not Illegal: Why Women Tony Clement Followed Online Are Going Public." *Global News*, 9 November 2018. https://globalnews.ca/news/4646287/tony-clement-instagram-women/.

Gilmore, Rachel. 2018. "NDP MP Erin Weir Accused of Harassment." *iPolitics*, 1 February 2018. https://ipolitics.ca/2018/02/01/ndp-mp-erin-weir-accused-harassment/.

Harris, Kathleen. 2018. "Moore Cleared of Sexual Misconduct Claims." *CBC News*, 19 July 2018. https://www.cbc.ca/news/politics/ndp-christine-moore-investigation-1.4753168.

Hopke, Christina C. 2019. "Is Congress Holding Itself to Account: Addressing Congress's Sexual Harassment Problem and the Congressional Accountability Act of 1995 Reform Act." *Notre Dame Law Review* 94 (5): 2159–88. https://scholarship.law.nd.edu/ndlr/vol94/iss5/11/.

House of Commons, Canada. 2020. *Annual Report on the House of Commons Policy on Preventing and Addressing Harassment 2019–2020*. https://www.ourcommons.ca/Content/Misc/2019-2020-PreventionReport-e.pdf.

Kappler, Maija. 2020. "A Me Too Reckoning Is On in Quebec, but the Rest of Canada Has Barely Noticed." *HuffPost Canada*, 19 July 2020. https://www.huffpost.com/archive/ca/entry/quebec-me-too-music-sexual-assault_ca_5f0dc75bc5b6df6cc0b1ae9b.

Kendall, Chad, and Marie Rekkas. 2012. "Incumbency Advantages in the Canadian Parliament." *Canadian Journal of Economics/Revue canadienne d'économique* 45 (4): 1560–85. https://doi.org/10.1111/j.1540-5982.2012.01739.x.

Krook, Mona Lena. 2018. "Westminster Too: On Sexual Harassment in British Politics." *The Political Quarterly* 89 (1): 65–72. https://doi.org/10.1111/1467-923X.12458.

Lim, Jolson. 2019. "Conservatives Lacked Protocols to Probe Dykstra Allegations: Report." *iPolitics*, 3 May 2019. https://ipolitics.ca/2019/05/03/conservatives-lacked-protocols-to-probe-dykstra-allegations-report/.

Ling, Justin. 2021. "Federal Election 2021: The Men on the Campaign Trail." *Maclean's*, 17 September 2021. https://www.macleans.ca/opinion/federal-election-2021-the-men-on-the-campaign-trail/.

Naumetz, Tim. 2018. "MP Ordered to Take Sexual-Harassment-Awareness Training." *iPolitics*, 6 October 2018. https://ipolitics.ca/2018/10/06/mp-ordered-to-take-sexual-harassment-awareness-training/.

Paas-Lang, Christian. 2019. "NDP MP Christine Moore Decides Not to Seek Re-Election This Fall." *Toronto Star*, 7 June 2019. https://www.thestar.com/news/canada/ndp-mp-christine-moore-decides-not-to-seek-re-election-this-fall/article_41eaa6cd-57a5-56d7-aec7-910e1e074b3e.html.

Platt, Brian. 2019. "With Liberals Wiped Out in Alberta and Sask., Trudeau Promises to Do 'a Lot More' to Rebuild Western Support." *National Post*, 23 October 2019. https://nationalpost.com/news/politics/election-2019/with-liberals-wiped-out-in-alberta-and-sask-trudeau-promises-to-do-a-lot-more-to-rebuild-western-support.

Potkins, Meghan. 2018. "Calgary MP Darshan Kang Loses Appeal of Harassment Probe." *Calgary Herald*, 21 August 2018. https://calgaryherald.com/news/politics/calgary-mp-loses-appeal-of-house-of-commons-harassment-investigation.

Restrepo Sanín, Juliana. 2022. "Criminalizing Violence against Women in Politics: Innovation, Diffusion, and Transformation." *Politics & Gender* 18 (1): 1–32. https://doi.org/10.1017/S1743923X20000173.

Samara Centre for Democracy. 2018. "The Elephant on the Hill." https://www.samaracentre.ca/articles/the-elephant-on-the-hill.

Smith, Joanna. 2014. "NDP MP Details Harassment Allegations: 'It Was Sex without Explicit Consent.'" *Toronto Star*, 25 November 2014. https://www.thestar.com/news/canada/2014/11/25/ndp_mp_details_harassment_allegations_it_was_sex_without_explicit_consent.html.

— 2019. "After Sexual Harassment Problem of the Past, Conservatives Work to Raise Party Standards." *Canada's National Observer*, 7 September 2019. https://www.nationalobserver.com/2019/09/07/news/after-sexual-harassment-problem-past-conservatives-work-raise-party-standards.

Stark, Stephanie, and Sofía Collignon. 2022. "Sexual Predators in the Contest for Public Office: How the American Electorate Responds to News of Allegations of Candidates Committing Sexual Assault and Harassment." *Political Studies Review* 20 (3): 329–52. https://doi.org/10.1177/1478929921995333.

Tadros, Mariz, and Jenny Edwards. 2020. "Collective Struggles against Sexual Harassment: What We Have Learnt about Pathways to Accountability and Their Outcomes." *Institute of Development Studies* 51 (2): 1–19. https://doi.org/10.19088/1968-2020.127.

Tunney, Catharine. 2018. "Saskatchewan MP Erin Weir Expelled from NDP Caucus after Harassment Investigation." *CBC News*, 3 May 2018. https://www.cbc.ca/news/politics/erin-weir-caucus-ndp-1.4646224.

Vivyan, Nick, Markus Wagner, and Jessica Tarlov. 2012. "Representative Misconduct, Voter Perceptions and Accountability: Evidence from the 2009 House of Commons Expenses Scandal." *Electoral Studies* 31 (4): 750–63. https://doi.org/10.1016/j.electstud.2012.06.010.

Zimonjic, Peter. 2018. "Hehr Won't Return to Cabinet, but Remains in Liberal Caucus after Harassment Investigation." *CBC News*, 6 June 2018. https://www.cbc.ca/news/politics/hehr-harassment-report-liberal-1.4694165.

11 Can MP Anti-harassment Training Combat Gender-Based Violence in the House of Commons? A Comparative Analysis of Canada and the United Kingdom

LOUISE COCKRAM

This chapter focuses on the anti-harassment training for members of Parliament (MPs), which is overseen by the Canadian and UK Houses of Commons. In response to instances of gender-based violence in politics (GBV-P),[1] the Canadian House of Commons adopted the House of Commons Policy on Preventing and Addressing Harassment in Canada in 2014 (now referred to as the Workplace Harassment and Violence Prevention Policy) and the MP-to-MP Code of Conduct in 2015. Similarly, in 2018 the UK House of Commons implemented the Independent Complaints and Grievances Scheme (ICGS) to combat sexual harassment and prevent workplace bullying. The Workplace Harassment and Violence Prevention Policy/Code of Conduct in Canada and the ICGS in the United Kingdom represent a widespread change to the behavioural standards for MPs and staff in both legislatures. The anti-harassment training aims to familiarize MPs with these new behavioural standards and rules. Through the cases from Canada and the United Kingdom, I hope to demonstrate how anti-harassment training plays out in two Westminster legislatures. While Canada is an instructive case on its own, comparing two legislatures demonstrates the importance of parliamentary party leadership. The parliamentary party leadership influences their members' attendance at anti-harassment training sessions.

Although anti-harassment training is common in corporate environments (Roehling and Huang 2018), it is relatively new to the Houses of Commons in Canada and the United Kingdom. Other legislatures, such as the United States Congress and the European Parliament, have launched anti-harassment training, with mixed results. For instance, some members of the European Parliament see the training as "just ticking boxes" rather than a measure that addresses structural gender imbalances within the institution itself (Berthet and Kantola 2021, 162).

230   Louise Cockram

Drawing from scholarship on parliamentary training and orientation (Neesham 2016; Fox and Korris 2012; Rosenblatt 2006), news articles, interviews with House staff, and documents from the Houses of Commons, I argue that the anti-harassment training offered by the Houses of Commons in Canada and the United Kingdom is a necessary, yet insufficient, measure to address what Collier and Raney (2018b) describe as entrenched patterns of sexism and harassment within the Canadian and UK Houses of Commons. The anti-harassment training is a good first step to familiarize MPs with the Workplace Harassment and Violence Prevention Policy and the Code of Conduct in Canada and the ICGS in the United Kingdom. However, the House, political parties, and MPs themselves must take additional measures to combat GBV-P, such as those suggested by Gerrits (chapter 10) and Cloutier (chapter 9) in this volume.

The questions that drive this chapter are the following: What forms of training do the Houses of Commons in Canada and the United Kingdom provide to familiarize MPs with the Workplace Harassment and Violence Prevention Policy/Code of Conduct in Canada and the ICGS in the United Kingdom? Is this training effective in inculcating MPs into the rules and standards of behaviour outlined in the Canadian Workplace Harassment and Violence Prevention Policy/Code of Conduct and the UK ICGS? Does this training address GBV-P? How can the training be improved?

The chapter sets out to describe the nature of MP orientation/training in Canada and the United Kingdom. It then briefly outlines the context of GBV-P in the Canadian and UK Houses of Commons, followed by a description of the training that the House of Commons provides to MPs in Canada and the United Kingdom to familiarize MPs with the rules and standards of behaviour in relation to GBV-P. The chapter ends with three implications for action to improve the House of Commons training to address GBV-P in both Canada and the United Kingdom.

MP Orientation/Training

Along with anti-harassment training, the Canadian and UK Houses of Commons provide a general orientation for newly elected MPs.[2] Through this orientation, MPs learn parliamentary procedure and the administrative rules surrounding office budgets and hiring staff. These orientation sessions provide MPs with a great deal of information in a brief time period. Indeed, rookie MPs often describe the transition from candidate to elected member as a "trial by fire."[3] The House argues that this tight timeline is necessary since there is a limited window to capture the attention of MPs before they get swept away by their parties.[4] Further, while attendance at the orientation is high among MPs in Canada, it is not the case in the United Kingdom, where the sessions are generally ill-attended (Fox and Korris 2012, 567). In theory, the Houses of Commons in Canada and the United Kingdom could combat the problem of information overload and scheduling through offering additional orientation sessions throughout the MPs' first term in office. However, when the Houses of Commons in both countries have organized these sessions in the past, they have been ill-attended (567),[5] perhaps because MPs' schedules become busier as they take on further responsibilities in the House and gradually feel more comfortable with the role.

As well, the conflicting definitions of the role of an MP (Searing 1994; Loat and MacMillan 2014) mean that much of the orientation on the substantive aspects of the role (that is, whether MPs plan to devote their time to constituency versus legislative work) is left for MPs to figure out through instructions from their party or informally through other MPs. Newly elected MPs often fumble in their role, learning through ad-hoc advice from fellow MPs and trial and error in addition to their partisan training. Through some of my research on the orientation of newly elected MPs, I have found that MPs either learn their role from the party, drawing on past career/legislative experience, or socialization in the House by learning on the job or copying the behaviour of colleagues (Rosenblatt 2006, 25; Norton 2019). Through these other forms of orientation, MPs absorb the norms of the House. While some of these norms might be innocuous (for example, the propensity of Canadian MPs to applaud speeches in the House), other informal norms, such as a highly masculinized or aggressive culture, can help perpetuate sexist attitudes and beliefs that give rise to gender-based violence (Collier and Raney 2018a, 2018b). If the House orientation is insufficient or absent, MPs often rely on absorbing informal norms they learn through fellow politicians. Despite the best efforts of the House in both Canada and the United Kingdom to improve the orientation for new MPs following each election, MPs claim that the House provides little guidance on the role.

The Canadian and UK Houses of Commons are reluctant to be prescriptive about the role of an MP during the new members' orientation and often leave guidance to each political party. Conversely, the rules surrounding harassment and violence are codified, and it is within the remit of the Houses of Commons to be prescriptive about how MPs should behave in accordance with these institutional rules and behavioural standards. In other words, the clear rules in the Workplace

Harassment and Violence Prevention Policy/Code of Conduct in Canada and the ICGS in the United Kingdom empower the Houses to provide greater guidance to MPs on how they should adhere to these new rules and standards of behaviour.

GBV-P in the Houses of Commons

While GBV-P comprises a wide array of violent acts and threats, this chapter focuses on MP-to-MP and MP-to-staff violence and harassment as defined by each of the Houses. The focus of this chapter is on anti-harassment training for MPs, but it is necessary to include a brief discussion of members' staff as they are referenced in the anti-harassment orientation in both countries. Further, since staffers, especially women and racialized people, are likely to be targets of violence and harassment, I reference them in my analysis (see also Cloutier, chapter 9, this volume).

Canada

The extent of GBV-P in the Canadian House of Commons became public knowledge when in 2015 two NDP MPs accused two Liberal MPs, Massimo Pacetti and Scott Andrews, of sexual misconduct (see Gerrits's chapter 10, this volume, for detailed accounts of these events). There are myriad other instances of sexual misconduct or harassment that have been publicly reported between MPs or between MPs and parliamentary staff, many of which are discussed in this book. An important theme that emerges from this book is that gender-based violence in Canada and elsewhere is not limited to any one political party: Liberal MP Kent Hehr was forced to apologize after making unwanted sexual comments to women staff in an elevator; NDP MP Erin Weir was ejected from his party after being accused of sexual misconduct; and one former staffer reported that she was continually harassed both online and in person by a male Conservative MP (Beaumont 2018).

Along with GBV-P, racialized MPs are also subject to race-based harassment. Often this race-based harassment is compounded with GBV-P to target racialized women in particular. Former MP Celina Caesar-Chavannes has described experiencing racism during her time in office, such as repeatedly being asked for security credentials by Parliament Hill security staff (Krishnan 2021) and having a fellow MP threaten to touch her hair, a common form of harassment against Black women (Caesar-Chavannes 2021, 189).

To combat instances of sexual harassment and misconduct, the Board of Internal Economy introduced the House of Commons Policy on Preventing and Addressing Harassment in Canada in 2014. Following the passage of Bill C-65, the Board of Internal Economy revised the policy in January 2021, and it is now referred to as the Workplace Harassment and Violence Prevention Policy. The Workplace Harassment and Violence Prevention Policy requires staff and MPs to take the training within three months after they start their position and then again every three years (House of Commons 2021).

In 2015, the Procedure and House Affairs Committee introduced the MP Code of Conduct. The Code of Conduct was passed as an amendment in the standing orders and is restricted to behaviour between MPs, whereas the Workplace Harassment and Violence Prevention Policy applies to MPs, House of Commons staff, and members' staff. Section 67 of the Code of Conduct mandates the Chief Human Resources Officer of the House to "undertake educational activities for Members on the content of this Code and on matters related to the prevention of sexual harassment." Section 68 further mandates the Chief Human Resources Officer to provide MPs with a briefing on the contents of the code at the beginning of each Parliament (House of Commons 2023). The provisions in section 68 of the Code of Conduct and the provisions in the Workplace Harassment and Violence Prevention Policy mean that, for subsequent elections, anti-harassment training will be folded into the orientation for new members following each federal election. The content and delivery of the educational activities mandated for MPs will be discussed later in the chapter.

United Kingdom

Harassment in the British House of Commons was widely reported in the media following accusations made against multiple MPs, including high-profile Liberal Democrat Chris Rennard in 2013 (Krook 2018, 65). Later instances of sexual misconduct by members of all three major parties, along with the prominence of the #MeToo movement, led to widespread attention to sexual harassment at Westminster, referred to by the British media as the "Pestminster" scandal. GBV-P in British politics became so widespread that women staffers in the United Kingdom warned each other of "problem" MPs through a WhatsApp group (65). Race-based harassment is also prevalent in British politics. Much like the experience of Celina Caesar-Chavannes in Canada, racialized MPs in the United Kingdom have been subject to greater scrutiny from the

House security and have also reported receiving racist comments from their MP colleagues (Walker 2020).

Following allegations into sexual misconduct, along with added media pressure (Kelly 2021), the British House began to address issues of harassment and bullying shortly after the 2017 #MeToo wave. It also commissioned two independent reports, the first by Dame Laura Cox, which explored harassment against members' staff by MPs (Cox 2018). Through interviewing staff in the House of Commons, the Cox report uncovered a culture of harassment between MPs and their staff. The second report, headed by Gemma White, came to similar conclusions about the widespread nature of harassment in the UK House of Commons (White 2019). The findings from the Cox and White reports precipitated the confidential hotline for staff and MPs, facilitated by the Speaker. The hotline received more calls than anticipated, revealing the extent of the harassment in Parliament. The ICGS was launched in 2018 and is comprised of a Behaviour Code, the Bullying and Harassment Policy, as well as the Sexual Misconduct Policy. In the next two sections of this chapter, I examine the contents of MPs' training in both countries in more detail.

Training on Canada's Member-to-Member Code of Conduct and the House of Commons Policy on Preventing and Addressing Harassment

The anti-harassment training for MPs and staff in Canada began with an online seminar in 2016, but since 2018, it has consisted of a mix of in-person and online training (Rana 2018). The purpose of the training is to inform MPs and staff about their roles and responsibilities in the Workplace Harassment and Violence Prevention Policy/Code of Conduct, along with reporting/dispute mechanisms for those who experience harassment.

The online training seminar is asynchronous and takes about an hour to complete. It begins with an introduction to the harassment rules discussed above, which is voiced by a narrator. The rest of the online seminar consists of scenarios intended to demonstrate the scope of both the Workplace Harassment and Violence Prevention Policy and the Code of Conduct. Three actors – two men and a woman – enact these scenarios. The scenarios focus on both appropriate behaviour between MPs and between MPs and staff, and are interspersed with clarification from the narrator on how the scenarios relate to the Workplace Harassment and Violence Prevention Policy/Code of Conduct, as well as with multiple-choice questions to test the knowledge of the viewer. For example, in one scenario, a woman staffer expresses discomfort about the behaviour of her boss who is a male MP. The behaviour includes compliments from the MP about her appearance and unwanted invitations to lunch to discuss workplace matters. In another scenario, a male MP berates a male staff member for being reluctant to help organize the MP's anniversary party over a weekend, even though this task is not within the operational requirements of the office. The MP threatens the employee with non-renewal of their contract. These scenarios are filmed in Centre Block, which, according to the House, is to provide MPs with a familiar context so they could "see themselves" in the training. By contrast, if the scenarios took place in a generic office environment, the MPs might not be able to relate to it, given the unique architecture of the parliamentary workplace.[6] Again, the anti-harassment training seems to be much more prescriptive about how MPs should behave, relative to the general orientation it offers for new members.

Unfortunately, the House does not publicly track how many MPs have completed the online training or whether those who have completed the training managed to get the multiple-choice questions correct.[7] Throughout the training, the narrator and scenario actors emphasize early resolution between a complainant and respondent. Further, the training encourages the MPs to consider their practices as an employer. However, although the online seminar implies the gendered nature of harassment (for example, through the scenario with the woman staffer who feels uncomfortable about compliments and lunch invitations from her boss), it does not explicitly define or discuss GBV-P specifically, nor does it address race-based violence and harassment.

Originally, the online seminar was the sole source of training provided by the House, and the parties were reluctant for the House to provide in-person training. According to a House staff person, the parties changed their stance on in-person training following the #MeToo movement and encouraged the House to organize in-person training sessions.[8] MPs' schedules are quickly captured by their party following the election, and so the intervention from the parties was crucial in ensuring that the in-person training took place. The three main parties, the Liberal Party, Conservative Party, and the New Democratic Party, all mandate their members to participate in the training. As of June 2018, 95 per cent of MPs from the 42nd Parliament had participated in the training (Evelyn 2018; see also House of Commons 2020).

The in-person training is similar to the online seminar in that it is a mix of information and reflection. It takes place over the course of two hours in smaller groups (around twenty) of MPs from the same party. In one of the exercises, the facilitator asks all MPs to stand up. The facilitator then reads out a series of statements that progressively become more offensive. MPs are asked to sit down when they are offended. Similar to the online training session, the MPs are presented with a series of scenarios that they have to discuss in smaller groups and then present their findings to the whole session. The workbook provided to MPs during the sessions has space for MPs to write their reflections on what they have learned and develop an action plan to strengthen a healthy workplace culture based on the policy and code of conduct.

The training described above is consistent with research on adult learning, which shows that adults learn more effectively by working through scenarios rather than by just being presented with rules. Indeed, Neesham notes that parliamentarians can feel patronized when they are presented with firm rules and that MPs adapt better to ethical regimes when they are given the space and opportunity to discuss and reflect on what constitutes ethical and unethical conduct (2016, 65). In this respect, the Canadian anti-harassment training, both online and in person, is successful since it provides MPs with the opportunity to reflect on the rules in the Workplace Harassment and Violence Prevention Policy/MP Code of Conduct.

The House also has separate anti-harassment sessions for both administrative and partisan staff who work in the House of Commons (in addition to the online seminar, which is available to both MPs and staff). GBV-P in the House is not confined to MPs and sometimes happens between staff as well. The online training session is especially helpful to send to constituency staff as there are logistical challenges in providing in-person orientation to offices across a country as large as Canada.[9]

Valuing Everyone Orientation in the United Kingdom

Following the White and Cox reports on harassment of staff within the UK House of Commons, along with the adoption of the ICGS in 2018, the House administration introduced a training program called Valuing Everyone. The delivery report for the ICGS recommended that twenty- to thirty-minute segments be incorporated into the orientation for new MPs and that sessions of three hours be organized for the rest of the parliamentary community (Independent Complaints and Grievance Policy Program Team 2018, 15–16). The Valuing Everyone training is mandatory for staff within the House administration and members of the Lords, though it is still voluntary for MPs and their staff (Stanley 2021). Through an access to information request, a *Vice News* investigation in August 2020 found that 140 MPs, including Prime Minister Boris Johnson, as well as senior members of the cabinet, had not attended the Valuing Everyone training (Wilkinson 2020a). While some MPs had legitimate reasons for not attending the Valuing Everyone training (one was on maternity leave at the time the training was offered), others were resistant to attending the sessions. Of this latter group, some MPs claimed that their positive track record as an employer exempted them from the training, while others questioned the utility of the training itself. Conservative MP Ben Bradley (2020) wrote of the Valuing Everyone training: "I don't doubt that there are more than a small number of MPs who are a nightmare to work for and who can behave inappropriately. I'm just not convinced that two hours of training will have made the blindest bit of difference, despite the huge cost. In truth, if you asked the staffers in this building, they could tell you who those bad bosses and managers are in seconds – it's not a secret – and you could deal with the actual problem rather than just 'being seen to do something.'"

According to a February 2021 review of the ICGS, 89 per cent of UK MPs had attended the training as of February of that year (Stanley 2021), slightly less than the 95 per cent who attended in Canada. Further, in Canada there was a faster uptake in the number of MPs who attended the anti-harassment training, whereas it took a longer time for the UK House and the parties to persuade UK MPs to undergo the Valuing Everyone sessions. This difference is consistent with findings that there is a lower uptake from UK MPs during new MP orientation sessions (Fox and Korris 2012, 567). In Canada, Prime Minister Justin Trudeau led by example by being one of the first to take the anti-harassment training from the Canadian House of Commons. By contrast, former prime minister Boris Johnson was late in attending the Valuing Everyone training (he did not attend until late August 2020, five days after the *Vice News* investigation was published), and during House debates he has referred to concerns from women MPs about the GBV-P they face from constituents as "humbug" (Mason and Perraudin 2019).

Johnson subsequently launched an inquiry into harassment directed towards women MPs (Johnson 2021), which suggests he started to take the problem of GBV-P more seriously before his exit as prime minister in 2022. Nevertheless, it would have been beneficial for Johnson to act as a role model for his parliamentary party during the initial implementation of the Valuing Everyone training and attend through his own initiative rather than being shamed into attending by the media. The fact that there was a lower uptake for the training among MPs in the United Kingdom compared to Canada illustrates the need for partisan buy-in for MPs to attend the orientation. In Canada, the Liberal, Conservative, and New Democratic parties all make it mandatory for MPs in their caucuses to attend the anti-harassment orientation, which is a partial explanation as to why there is higher attendance in Canada versus the United Kingdom. Previous research confirms that role models are an effective way to instil MPs with ethical rules and behaviour, and can help create a culture of ethics beyond the orientation (Neesham 2016, 69). In the case of anti-harassment orientation, Trudeau acted as an ethical role model by attending the training early, thereby conferring importance onto anti-harassment efforts in the House. By contrast, Johnson's lack of attendance signalled to MPs that anti-harassment training was not important. Johnson's successor as prime minister, Rishi Sunak, appears to have attended the Valuing Everyone training (Wilkinson 2020b). Liz Truss has actually not taken the training.

Similar to what was done in the Canadian House of Commons, the Valuing Everyone training was incorporated into the training for newly elected MPs following the December 2019 general election. The content of the Valuing Everyone training has not been made public, but according to White, the training is of high quality, and the scenarios that participants are encouraged to reflect on are similar to the instances of workplace bullying that she found in her original report (White 2019). The White report has further recommended that the Independent Parliamentary Standards Authority (IPSA)[10] withhold employment allowances to MPs who have not undergone the Valuing Everyone training. This measure would prevent MPs from hiring staff until they have completed anti-harassment training. Such a measure has not yet been implemented but would go a long way in encouraging UK MPs to attend the training. In the absence of encouragement from the party leadership, financial penalties are the next best thing to motivate MPs to attend the Valuing Everyone training.

Discussion and Conclusion

The Canadian and UK Houses of Commons both provide anti-harassment training to MPs. In Canada, this training covers the Code of Conduct and the Workplace Violence and Harassment Prevention Policy, and in the United Kingdom the training covers the rules in the ICGS. In both countries, efforts to curb sexual harassment were spurred by the #MeToo movement. Both the Canadian and British Houses of Commons have provisions to provide anti-harassment training to MPs in their respective codes of conduct for MPs. These training programs are important elements in the efforts of both Houses to prevent gender-based violence from happening in the first place.

With regards to the delivery of the training, MPs in the United Kingdom were initially more resistant to attending anti-harassment training than MPs in Canada, since, unlike the MPs in Canada, UK MPs are not mandated to attend the training. This difference is likely due to the lack of encouragement from their party's leadership. Due to the pervasiveness of party discipline and reluctance of the House to be prescriptive about what representatives should do, MPs are more likely to take direction from their political parties in both Canada and the United Kingdom. Despite the flaws of the Code of Conduct and the Workplace Harassment and Violence Prevention Policy identified by Collier and Raney (2018a), political parties in Canada seem to be doing a better job than their UK counterparts at encouraging their members to attend the training. Of course, there are complex logistical challenges in providing training of any kind to MPs in the United Kingdom, given that there are almost twice as many members as there are in Canada. However, the fact remains that encouragement and support from political parties appears to be a key motivator in persuading MPs to attend orientation. To this end, future research on the topic of GBV-P in legislative orientations should explore the efforts of political parties to provide their members with encouragement to make learning about harassment rules a high priority for all their members, along with the content and delivery of anti-harassment training within the parties. There are benefits to party training in that MPs seem especially likely to participate in programs offered by their own parties, given the MPs' familiarity with their party and the advice that parties provide to new MPs. At the same time, the benefit of the House training is that it is consistent and, by nature, non-partisan, meaning that all MPs receive the same information. If the training were provided solely by party caucuses, MPs would not be guaranteed to receive standard information on how to address GBV-P in the political sphere. If left up to the parties exclusively, a new party leader with no or a weak commitment to tackling GBV-P could decide that their members do not have to take the training at all. Further, GBV-P and racist harassment can take place within an MP's own party. For instance, much of the racism and sexism that Celina Caesar-Chavannes faced, including being shouted at and tokenized, came from within her own party (Caesar-Chavannes 2021). In these circumstances, anti-harassment training provided by the party could exacerbate existing problems of racist and gendered harassment.

The anti-harassment training in Canada and the Valuing Everyone training in the United Kingdom is now incorporated into the orientation for newly elected MPs. Therefore, in order to assess the effectiveness of anti-harassment training, it is helpful to address concerns about the orientation for newly elected MPs as a whole. These concerns include the influence of parties on whether MPs attend the orientation, as well as the effective delivery of information to new MPs, some of whom have been elected for the first-time and face other employment/human resources challenges (for example, setting up the administrative infrastructure of their office, familiarizing themselves with parliamentary procedure). Further, since some MPs either do not attend the orientation at all or find the orientation and their early experiences in the House to be overwhelming, it is possible that new MPs who attend future sessions of the anti-harassment training might miss this vital information even if it is not their intention.

Regarding the content, the focus on bullying and early resolution in the online training in Canada, rather than naming GBV-P and racism as particular problems, means that MPs are not encouraged to explore the source and ramifications of violence against women and racialized people in politics. These are difficult conversations for MPs to have, especially since MPs are under considerable time pressures (Jowhari 2018) and may be reluctant to spend part of their day engaging in fraught debates about gender and race. However, naming and discussing GBV-P, along with racism, in these sessions is vital in beginning to understand and take steps to mitigate GBV-P in the House.

Without structured orientation, new MPs resort to learning on the job or copying the behaviour of colleagues (Rosenblatt 2006). Through informal socialization, MPs absorb the institutional culture of the House – the good, the benign, and the bad – which means that orientations need to be proactive, take place early in an MP's career, and must be supported by the political parties. While training can educate MPs about the rules and procedures, it is unrealistic to expect that it can on its own challenge the male "logic of appropriateness" embedded within most political institutions (Collier and Raney 2018b, 433). As Neesham argues, conveying the rules outlined in the codes of conduct is a necessary but insufficient condition to instil MPs with ethical behaviour (2016, 65). Therefore, a broader culture change is required in addition to conveying rules through the anti-harassment training. Given the limitations of orientation, as MPs are busy and distracted, other measures must happen in tandem to reinforce the preventative measures to end GBV-P offered in MPs' orientations. The prevalence of GBV-P within the Canadian and UK Houses of Commons means that MPs cannot be left to rely on informal norms alone for information on how to address this problem. At the same time, orientation should not be the only effort that the House makes to prevent GBV-P, and broader measures are necessary to improve the state of politics for women and racialized people. As a recent case suggests, MPs still commit GBV-P despite receiving anti-harassment training. Former Canadian MP Raj Saini was dropped as a Liberal candidate during the 2021 election following revelations in the media that at least four separate women staff members had accused him of making unwanted advances and inappropriate comments. Saini was elected in 2015 and would have presumably received in-person anti-harassment training through the Canadian House of Commons prior to these accusations (Paas-Lang and Burke 2021).

There is a precedent in the United Kingdom for overhauling the behaviour of MPs and the institutional culture of the House. Following a widespread expenses scandal in 2009, the UK House of Commons created the IPSA to regulate the spending of MPs. Despite complaints about the IPSA (Fox and Korris 2012, 564),[11] it has broadly stopped MPs from claiming frivolous expenses. A similar culture change could happen to mitigate GBV-P and racist harassment. The solutions posed by Gerrits (chapter 10) and Cloutier (chapter 9) in this volume are valuable steps to take beyond anti-harassment training. For instance, Gerrits's solution to tighten accountability for politicians accused of harassment would signal to MPs that GBV-P is unacceptable. Cloutier's suggestions to improve the rules against the harassment of parliamentary staff by constituents and MPs themselves is another measure that could help to improve the culture of the House.

Implications for Action

1 The House of Commons in Canada and the United Kingdom should make anti-harassment training mandatory for MPs. Financial misconduct is very different from the problem of GBV-P. However, the threat of withholding expenses, while extreme, is a powerful tool to encourage MPs to attend the training. To this end, the IPSA should follow the recommendation in the White report to impose financial penalties on UK MPs who do not attend the Valuing Everyone training. There is no equivalent to the IPSA in Canada, and there is higher attendance at the anti-harassment training among Canadian MPs, but the Canadian House of Commons should impose a similar financial penalty for MPs for non-attendance.
2 The anti-harassment orientation in Canada and the Valuing Everyone orientation in the United Kingdom should name and focus on GBV-P and racist violence and harassment as particular problems.

3 The House orientation to combat harassment needs to have the support of all the political parties. As the evidence in this chapter suggests, MPs in the United Kingdom need more persuasion from their party leadership to attend anti-harassment training.

NOTES

1 GBV-P has been documented at length throughout this volume.
2 Orientation refers to the program that MPs receive from the House to familiarize them with their new role as a parliamentarian at the beginning of their career, whereas training refers to the process of learning a specific set of rules or processes (for example, anti-harassment training).
3 Author interview with MP in Canada, February 2019.
4 Author interview with House staff in the United Kingdom, September 2019.
5 Also mentioned in author interview with House staff in Canada, September 2018.
6 Author interview with House staff in Canada, June 2019.
7 Author interview with House staff in Canada, June 2019.
8 Author interview with House staff in Canada, June 2019.
9 Author interview with House staff in Canada, June 2019.
10 IPSA is an independent body that regulates the spending of MPs.
11 Also mentioned in author interview with a UK MP, September 2019.

REFERENCES

Beaumont, Hillary. 2018. "Parliament Hill's Weak Anti-Harassment Policies and Toxic Culture Are Threatening Women." *Vice News*, 14 March 2018. https://www.vice.com/en/article/evmy4a/parliament-hills-weak-anti-harassment-policies-and-toxic-culture-are-failing-women.

Berthet, Valentine, and Johanna Kantola. 2021. "Gender, Violence, and Political Institutions: Struggles over Sexual Harassment in the European Parliament." *Social Politics: International Studies in Gender, State & Society* 28 (1): 143–67. https://doi.org/10.1093/sp/jxaa015.

Bradley, Ben. 2020. "I Will Not Be Undertaking Unconscious Bias Training – and Call on My Colleagues to Take the Same Stand." *Conservative Home*, 15 September 2020. https://conservativehome.com/2020/09/15/ben-bradley-i-will-not-be-undertaking-unconscious-bias-training-and-call-on-my-colleagues-to-take-the-same-stand/.

Caesar-Chavannes, Celina. 2021. *Can You Hear Me Now? How I Found My Voice and Learned to Live with Passion and Purpose*. Toronto, ON: Penguin Random House Canada.

Collier, Cheryl N., and Tracey Raney. 2018a. "Canada's Member-to-Member Code of Conduct on Sexual Harassment in the House of Commons: Progress or Regress?" *Canadian Journal of Political Science* 51 (4): 795–815. https://doi.org/10.1017/S000842391800032X.
— 2018b. "Understanding Sexism and Sexual Harassment in Politics: A Comparison of Westminster Parliaments in Australia, the United Kingdom, and Canada." *Social Politics: International Studies in Gender, State & Society* 25 (3): 432–55. https://doi.org/10.1093/sp/jxy024.
Cox, Laura. 2018. *The Bullying and Harassment of House of Commons Staff*. Independent Inquiry Report. London: Parliament, UK. https://www.parliament.uk/globalassets/documents/Conduct-in-Parliament/dame-laura-cox-independent-inquiry-report.pdf.
Evelyn, Charelle. 2018. "More Than 95 Per Cent of MPs Finish Anti-Harassment Training, All Senators to Start in Fall." *The Hill Times*, 20 June 2018, News Section, 6.
Fox, Ruth, and Matt Korris. 2012. "A Fresh Start? The Orientation and Induction of New MPs at Westminster Following the 2010 General Election." *Parliamentary Affairs* 65 (3): 559–75. https://doi.org/10.1093/pa/gss014.
House of Commons, Canada. 2020. *Annual Report on the House of Commons Policy on Preventing and Addressing Harassment 2019–2020*. Ottawa, ON: House of Commons, Canada. https://www.ourcommons.ca/Content/Misc/2019-2020-PreventionReport-e.pdf.
— 2021. *Members of the House of Commons Workplace Harassment and Violence Prevention Policy*. Approved by the Board of Internal Economy. Ottawa, ON: House of Commons, Canada. https://www.ourcommons.ca/Content/Boie/pdf/policy_preventing_harassment-e.pdf.
— 2023. "Appendix II: Code of Conduct for Members of the House of Commons: Sexual Harassment between Members." In *Standing Orders of the House of Commons (consolidated version as of 18 September 2023)*, 187–216. Ottawa, ON: House of Commons, Canada. https://www.ourcommons.ca/About/StandingOrders/Appa2-e.html.
Independent Complaints and Grievance Policy Program Team. 2018. *Independent Complaints and Grievance Scheme Delivery Report*. London: UK Parliament. https://www.parliament.uk/globalassets/documents/news/2018/1-ICGP-Delivery-Report.pdf.
Johnson, John. 2021. "Boris Johnson Has Ordered a Review into Tackling 'Rancid' Sexist Abuse of Female MPs." *Politics Home*, 4 February 2021. https://www.politicshome.com/news/article/boris-johnson-has-ordered-a-review-into-tackling-rancid-sexist-abuse-of-female-mps.
Jowhari, Majid. 2018. "What It's Like to Be a Rookie MP in a Workplace That Fetishizes Exhaustion." *The Hill Times*, 3 October 2018, Opinion Section, 19.
Kelly, Richard. 2021. *Independent Complaints and Grievances Scheme*. House of Commons Library Briefing Paper, No. 08369, 27 April 2021. London: UK

Parliament. https://researchbriefings.files.parliament.uk/documents/CBP-8369/CBP-8369.pdf.

Krishnan, Manisha. 2021. "'Fake as Fuck': Ex-Politician Details Racism in Ottawa and Her Blowout with Trudeau." *Vice News*, 5 February 2021. https://www.vice.com/en/article/dy8edm/celina-caeasar-chavannes-justin-trudeau-fake.

Krook, Mona Lena. 2018. "Westminster Too: On Harassment in British Politics." *The Political Quarterly* 89 (1): 65–72. https://doi.org/10.1111/1467-923X.12458.

Loat, Allison, and Michael MacMillan. 2014. *Tragedy in the Commons: Former Members of Parliament Speak Out about Canada's Failing Democracy*. Toronto, ON: Random House.

Mason, Rowena, and Frances Perraudin. 2019. "Boris Johnson Refuses to Apologise for Language about Jo Cox." *The Guardian*, 26 September 2019. https://www.theguardian.com/politics/2019/sep/26/boris-johnson-refuses-to-apologise-for-language-about-jo-cox.

Neesham, Cristina. 2016. "The Value of Ethics Education for Parliamentarians." In *Parliamentarians' Professional Development: The Need for Reform*, edited by Collen Lewis and Ken Coghill, 59–79. Cham, CH: Springer.

Norton, Phillip. 2019. "Power behind the Scenes: The Importance of Informal Space in Legislatures." *Parliamentary Affairs* 72 (2): 245–66. https://doi.org/10.1093/pa/gsy018.

Paas-Lang, Christian, and Ashley Burke. 2021. "Embattled Liberal Candidate Raj Saini Ends Bid for Re-election." *CBC News*, 4 September 2021. https://www.cbc.ca/news/politics/raj-saini-ends-campaign-1.6165229.

Rana, Abbas. 2018. "House Spending $50,000 on In-Person Sexual Harassment Training for MPs, PM, Cabinet Ministers, Opposition Party Leaders; All Caucuses Say It's 'Mandatory.'" *The Hill Times*, 30 January 2018, News Section, 6.

Roehling, Mark, and Jason Huang. 2018. "Sexual Harassment Training Effectiveness: An Interdisciplinary Review and Call for Research." *Journal of Organizational Behavior* 39 (2): 134–50. https://doi.org/10.1002/job.2257.

Rosenblatt, Gemma. 2006. *A Year in the Life: From Member of Public to Member of Parliament*. London: Hansard Society.

Searing, Donald D. 1994. *Westminster's World: Understanding Political Roles*. Cambridge, MA: Harvard University Press.

Stanley, Alison. 2021, 22 February. *Independent Complaints and Grievances Scheme: Independent 18-Month Review*. https://www.parliament.uk/contentassets/e3ed0297d92a400bb249c887a30aa59b/icgs-18-month-review_final.pdf.

Walker, Peter. 2020. "Most BME MPs Have Experienced Racism in Parliament, Study Finds." *The Guardian*, 17 February 2020. https://www.theguardian.com/politics/2020/feb/17/black-minority-ethnic-mps-racism-in-parliament-study.

White, Gemma. 2019. *Bullying and Harassment of MPs' Parliamentary Staff*. Independent Inquiry Report. London: Parliament, UK. https://www.parliament.uk/globalassets/documents/conduct-in-parliament/gwqc-inquiry-report-11-july-2019_.pdf.

Wilkinson, Sophie. 2020a. "140 MPs – Including Boris Johnson – Failed to Attend Anti-Sexual Harassment Training." *Vice News*, 26 August 2020. https://www.vice.com/en/article/xg8kew/141-tory-mps-including-boris-johnson-missed-anti-sexual-harassment-training.

– 2020b. "72 Conservative MPs Have Still Not Attended Anti-Sexual Harassment Training." *Vice News*, 2 October 2020. https://www.vice.com/en/article/3az3kb/uk-mps-not-attended-anti-bullying-harassment-training.

12 Fixing the Upper House: A Gender and Intersectional Analysis of the Canadian Senate's 2021 Harassment and Violence Prevention Policy

TRACEY RANEY

Introduction

The #MeToo and #TimesUp movements that emerged in fall 2017 demonstrated the prevalence of violence in workplaces around the world.[1] Canada's Parliament is no exception: politicians and staffers (most of whom are women) have since spoken publicly about the rampant nature of sexual harassment on Parliament Hill.[2] Violence and harassment inside legislatures pose unique threats to democracies. Those who work inside political workplaces (for example, politicians, staffers, administrative employees, interns, and journalists) are, in varying ways, engaged in work that supports the functioning of the legislative process. This work includes conducting research; proposing, passing, or making public policies; and more generally, representing the interests of the people. Violence that occurs within political workplaces thus constitutes a threat not only to those who are individually targeted but also to the democratic process itself.

In this chapter, I examine how the Senate of Canada has sought to address the problems of harassment and violence inside its workplace. Canada's Senate is an interesting case study on gender-based violence in politics (GBV-P) for a number of reasons. Although still predominantly white, the Senate is on the verge of gender parity; it also has the highest percentage of women in any federal or provincial legislature in Canadian history.[3] This milestone is cause for celebration among gender equality advocates, but it may be perceived by others as a threat to the Senate's male-dominated history, resulting in antipathy towards, or potential hostility against, non-white, women "space invaders" within the institution (Puwar 2004). As legislatures like Canada's Senate become more diverse, transparent and effective rules that prevent and prohibit abusive behaviour against those who have been traditionally excluded from legislatures are urgently needed.

Analysis of the Senate's Harassment and Violence Prevention Policy 247

In this volume, chapters by Cloutier (chapter 9), Gerrits (chapter 10), and Collier and Raney (chapter 13) evaluate how gender-based violence has been addressed by legislative bodies with elected members, including the House of Commons and the provincial/territorial legislatures. This chapter constitutes an initial foray into how an unelected, appointed chamber is tackling this problem and builds on research on violence against women in politics in elected legislatures in other countries (Krook 2018a, 2018b; Restrepo Sanín 2022). Studies on elected chambers are useful, yet likely insufficient, to explain harassment and violence in unelected chambers, which have arguably different – and potentially starker – power dynamics. Due to their appointed positions, senators hold considerable entrenched power within Canada's Parliament.[4] Compared to members of Parliament (MPs) in the House of Commons, most senators are also less bound by formal partisan ties, with the vast majority sitting as independents.[5] In the absence of periodic elections (or parties) to hold senators accountable for their actions, the Senate's own internal rules governing members' behaviours must strive to meet the highest possible ethical standards in order for it to be democratically accountable to the Canadian public. This chapter seeks to attend to some of these institution-specific dynamics. It also contributes to the broader literature on women's political representation, showing how newly adopted legislative rules on harassment and violence can be hampered by pre-existing institutional rules, norms, and practices impeding women's abilities to participate fully in the political process (Chappell 2006; Collier and Raney 2018a, 2018b; Lowndes 2020; Verge 2022).

For its own part, the Senate of Canada adopted a new policy, the Senate Harassment and Violence Prevention Policy, in March 2021. The main goal of this chapter is to analyse this policy by answering two central research questions: What are the policy's main strengths and weaknesses? Can this policy be expected to sufficiently prevent these behaviours from occurring in the future? To answer these questions, I begin with an overview of the case of Senator Don Meredith, which reveals how the Senate's existing ethics rules failed to protect those who work there from persistent abusive behaviour. In the #MeToo era, a new policy was clearly needed to prevent and address harassment and violence in Canada's upper house. Next, I provide an overview of some of the new policy's strengths. Following Bacchi's ([1999] 2008) "what's the problem?" approach, I then identify a number of gaps in how the "problem" is represented in the 2021 policy. An important shortcoming is its insufficient attention to the underlying causes of violence from a gender and intersectional perspective.

I then evaluate which institutional actors the new policy is likely to empower (and disempower) and find that it gives those who have held the most power inside the Senate historically – senators – significant authority over harassment and violence cases, at the expense of victim/survivors.[6] Senators' powers include oversight over most sanctioning decisions, the ability to keep the identities of perpetrators secret, and the retainment of their freedom of speech during parliamentary proceedings, with few limitations. On the basis of these deficiencies, I argue that the Senate's new harassment and violence policy will not be sufficient to address these issues in the institution. Without amendments, additional rule changes, and broader diversity-sensitizing reforms, these problems are likely to remain within the upper house, weakening its democratic potential to sufficiently represent and be held accountable to the Canadian public.

Data in the chapter are drawn from discourse analysis of related texts, including committee reports, meeting notes and transcripts, floor debates, and media reports. Qualitative, semi-structured interviews with a small number (N = 12) of key institutional actors involved in drafting the new policy were also conducted. To analyse these texts, I draw from feminist intersectional policy research and feminist institutionalist theories, both of which seek to uncover and critically examine gender (and other) power relations in institutional policies and rules (Hankivsky and Cormier 2011; Chappell 2006; Chappell and Waylen 2013; Waylen 2014). Throughout, my analysis is centred on the actors who have the least amount of power and are often treated as invisible within political institutions: women, people who are racialized minorities, and 2SLGBTQQIA+[7] staffers. The chapter concludes with recommendations on how the upper house can better fix these problems.

Institutional Context: Weak Ethics Rules and the Need for a New Policy

The need for a new Senate harassment policy became evident in 2015 when the *Toronto Star* reported that Senator Don Meredith had allegedly engaged in an inappropriate relationship with a teenager (Donovan 2015).[8] This scandal came shortly after an expense scandal involving several senators made national headlines, putting the unethical conduct of these unelected (and well-paid) politicians into the public eye (CBC News 2016). After looking into an unusually high volume of staff turnover in Senator Meredith's office, the Speaker of the Senate subsequently initiated a confidential "workplace assessment" of the senator's office. This secret investigation was followed by a 2015 inquiry overseen by the independent Senate Ethics Officer (SEO), which concluded that Senator Meredith had breached the Senate's Ethics and Conflict of Interest Code for Senators in his alleged sexual misconduct with a teenager. The senator has denied all allegations against him.

Upon receiving the SEO's first report in 2017, the Standing Committee on Ethics and Conflict of Interest for Senators recommended to the Senate that Meredith be expelled. However, before a vote could be held, the senator resigned from his seat, allowing him to keep his honourable title and collect a pension for life. After his resignation, the committee requested that the SEO launch a second inquiry into the former senator's behaviours against Senate employees. This second inquiry – made public in 2019 – concluded that Meredith had contributed to a "poisoned work environment" with behaviour that was belittling, demeaning, and humiliating, and that he had sexually harassed and acted in a retaliatory manner against several Senate employees.[9] Meredith's victim/survivors reported to the media that, over the course of these multiple Senate investigations, they had been asked to recount their abuses and consequently experienced re-traumatization over a five-year period (Raney 2021). While some of the delays were due to unavoidable events (such as the retirement of the first SEO), others were the result of some senators who refused to participate in the SEO's inquiry process, citing parliamentary privilege as a rationale. In June 2020, the Senate issued a rare, formal "public statement of regret" to some of Meredith's victim/survivors.[10] Following an independent evaluator's report into the matter, in October 2020 the Senate announced that nine employees would be provided financial compensation of $500,000 in total (Lum 2020). In October 2022, Meredith was charged with three counts of sexual assault and one count of criminal harassment in relation to events that occurred at the time he was a senator.

It is important to note that these events occurred despite the existence of several Senate ethics rules that presumably applied to harassment, bullying, and other violent behaviour. They include the Ethics Code discussed above, which contains two "general behaviour" provisions added in 2014 that require senators to "uphold the highest standards of dignity inherent to the position" and to "refrain from acting in a way that could reflect adversely on … the institution itself" (sections 7.1. and 7.2). More specifically, the Senate also had a 2009 stand-alone policy (updated from 1993) that supposedly covered harassment, sexual harassment, and abuses of authority. The events surrounding former senator Meredith thus demonstrate that, even with legislative ethics rules in place, harassment and violence can occur and that a new approach was needed to address these issues in the institution.

The realization that additional action was needed to curb violence and harassment in the Senate was further cemented by the #MeToo movement in fall 2017, which arguably created a "window of opportunity" for institutional actors to press for stronger anti-harassment measures. These events were the catalyst for the creation of a new Senate subcommittee in December 2017, the Subcommittee on Human Resources (HRRH), established by the Standing Committee on Internal Economy, Budgets, and Administration (CIBA). The subcommittee was tasked with reviewing the Senate's 2009 anti-harassment policy and examining existing workplace conditions to address harassment in the Senate.

In February 2019, CIBA tabled its report, *Modernizing the Senate's Anti-Harassment Policy: Together Let's Protect Our Healthy Worklife* (Senate of Canada 2019). It included twenty-eight recommendations to be given to the Senate Administration in order for it to prepare "a new, rather than a revised, anti-harassment policy."[11] The report explicitly references #MeToo and #TimesUp as reasons to act, noting how these movements have "prompted people to speak more openly about harassment" (iii). The subcommittee further identified the need to align the Senate's policies with Bill C-65, a federal law passed in 2018 that updated and strengthened existing legislation imposing certain duties on employers in relation to workplace harassment and violence inside all federally regulated workplaces (Government of Canada 2020). On 6 February 2020, CIBA presented its Policy on Prevention and Resolution of Harassment in the Senate Workplace (Senate of Canada 2020).[12] This report included a new anti-harassment policy for the Senate. However, after Senator Marilou McPhedran moved an amendment to send the policy to the Human Rights Committee for a human rights analysis, the report died on the Order Paper when Parliament was prorogued, leaving the future of a new Senate anti-harassment policy uncertain.

After Parliament returned in August 2020, CIBA tabled a new harassment and violence policy in February 2021, the Senate Harassment and Violence Prevention Policy (Senate of Canada 2021). This updated version more closely aligns with the regulations of Bill C-65 mentioned above. The Senate's new policy applies to all senators, Senate employees, those employed by senators, and to students, interns, and volunteers. After a technical motion was passed to repeal the existing 2009 policy, the new policy came into force in March 2021.

A Few Steps Forward: The Senate's 2021 Harassment and Violence Policy

From the vantage point of victim/survivors, the Senate's new policy offers some improvements over the existing 2009 anti-harassment policy. To start, it covers a wider array of conduct that includes all non-criminal, harassing, and violent behaviour, defined as "any action, conduct or comment, including of a sexual nature, that can reasonably be expected to cause offence, humiliation or other physical or psychological injury or illness to an employee, including any prescribed action, conduct or comment" (Senate of Canada 2021, 2). This definition aligns with the regulations of Bill C-65. While the previous policy only allowed for an individual who was harassed to file a formal complaint, the 2021 policy permits either an individual who was the object of harassment and violence or a witness to provide notice of an occurrence.

The 2021 policy further introduces a new, impartial third party (ITP) that will receive complaints and negotiate a resolution between the parties involved. If both the complainant and the respondent agree, the ITP oversees a conciliation phase. If both parties do not agree to conciliation, the ITP selects from a list of investigators drafted jointly by the CIBA subcommittee and the Policy Health and Safety Committee. In accordance with Bill C-65, all investigators must have previous training and experience in handling cases related to violence and harassment.[13] These provisions add an element of independence to the Senate's rules. By contrast, the 2009 policy gave authority to government and opposition whips to appoint an impartial and experienced person or to strike a review panel consisting of themselves (or their nominees), with a third member selected by the first two members in order to investigate complaints (Senate of Canada 2009, 12).[14]

To support the policy's implementation, the Senate also updated its Ethics and Conflict of Interest Code for Senators. Changes include a new rule of conduct (section 7.3) that explicitly prohibits harassment and violence, which states that senators shall "refrain from engaging in conduct that constitutes harassment and violence" (Senate Ethics Officer 2021). The Senate Ethics Officer is also no longer permitted to conduct a preliminary review or inquiry into complaints related to harassment or violence and must instead refer them to a trained external investigator.

Another positive development is that the new policy strengthens the Senate's data collection provisions in cases of harassment and violence. Data are to be disaggregated based on the number of occurrences and where they occurred, whether they relate to sexual harassment or non-sexual harassment and violence, the types of professional relationships of all parties, the time it took for a resolution to be reached, and the number of occurrences that fall under the prohibited grounds of discrimination in the Canadian Human Rights Act. These categories include sex, race, age, sexual orientation, gender identity, disability, and marital/family status. Anti-harassment training is also now mandatory for all staffers and senators.

Problem Representations: Gender- and Intersectional-Based Gaps

Despite these improvements, the new policy includes a number of significant gaps, which I argue will have negative consequences, especially for marginalized people who work inside the Senate. To identify its limitations, I first consider how the policy defines the problem it purports to address; or, as Bacchi asks: "What kind of problem is being represented?" ([1999] 2008, 199). A focus on how "problem representations" are lodged within policies, and their discursive constructions or "frames," allows researchers to identify the ways in which gender, race, and other social inequities are (un)addressed. What policymakers propose to do in a policy is usually based upon what they believe needs to be changed (199).

Gender and intersectional policy research are useful to apply here as they seek to illuminate how gaps and invisibilities embedded within public policies might have differential impacts based on race, gender, and other axes of difference. Shortcomings might include the perpetuation of a myth of gender/race neutrality and a lack of recognition of the limited access to power and resources for those who are marginalized (McPhail 2003). Existing research on anti-violence policies points out that such policies are prone to be ineffective if they do not take into consideration how women's lives differ from men's lives and how intersecting factors of race, Indigeneity, age, disability, and sexual orientation shape a person's risk exposure to harassing and violent behaviour (Hankivsky and Cormier 2011, 218).

Unfortunately, the Senate's 2021 policy does not explicitly define or situate violence as a uniquely gendered or raced problem. Instead, an appendix (Appendix A) has been added to the policy that offers examples of violence based upon gendered and other power differentials, such as "making fun of an employee because of gender identity"; sexist, racist, homophobic, or transphobic remarks; making "gender-related comments based on someone's physical characteristics, mannerisms, or conformity to sex-role stereotypes"; or verbal abuse based on someone's gender or sexual orientation (Senate of Canada

2021, 28). Although these individual examples are helpful in identifying gender and/or intersectional motivated violence, there is no mention in the policy of the underlying structural causes of violence, which are rooted in heteropatriarchal and colonial systems of power. As Crenshaw (1991, 1250) observes, the elision of "difference" in framing the problem of violence against women is problematic since it means that Indigenous, Black, and racially marginalized women will be less likely to have their needs met compared to white women. Including a preamble or mission statement in the policy that acknowledges how underlying inequities related to gender, race, ability, and other intersectional factors would help ensure that the policy is not gender- and race-blind in its application. This finding is similar to one identified by Collier and Raney in chapter 13 on provincial and territorial legislatures in this volume.

The 2021 policy also does not address a significant power imbalance between senators and their staffers that arises from several pre-existing, interlocking Senate rules. Due to parliamentary privilege, the Senate has a right to regulate its own affairs, while individual senators are afforded various immunities and rights, including the right to freedom of speech during parliamentary proceedings.[15] Moreover, senators are not "employees" of the Senate and cannot technically be fired from their jobs. Combined with the appointed nature of their positions, these unique privileges afford senators one of the most secure and protected jobs of any politician (or employee) and make the Senate one of the most hierarchical political institutions in the country.

In addition to its 105 senators, the Senate employs over 430 employees in the Senate Administration and approximately 260 employees in individual senators' offices (Senate of Canada 2019, iii). These employees are much less protected compared to senators. Although some employees are covered under collective agreements (legislative clerks), others are not. Staffers in senators' offices are also often employed on short-term (or "determinate") work contracts. Prior to 2022, for example, senators' political staffers could only be hired on employment contracts that were not to exceed twelve months; in 2022, the maximum length of a determinate contract was extended to twenty-four cumulative months. These employment rules leave determinate employees who work in senators' offices potentially vulnerable to abuse, as they must be reliant upon the "good word" of the senator whose office they work in for their future employment. Temporary workers may not want to report harassment out of fear of losing their job or not having their contract extended.[16]

In fact, these employment conditions were cited by some of former senator Meredith's victim/survivors as reasons why they were reluctant to file a claim under the existing 2009 anti-harassment policy. Speaking anonymously to the Senate Ethics Officer, one former Meredith staffer reported that she was "afraid to report his actions out of fear of being dismissed 'given the senator's history of firing his staff'" (Senate Ethics Officer 2019, 22). Another Meredith employee reported that her anxiety was so severe that Senate security once had to call an ambulance for her while she was having heart palpitations during a panic attack at work (21).

Policy Winners (Senators) and Losers (Victim/Survivors)

The Senate's 2021 anti-harassment policy also grants additional, new authority to those who already have the most power: senators. Feminist institutionalist research is useful to assess these institutional dynamics as it highlights how gendered power asymmetries can be reinforced or dismantled through various institutional rules and norms. As Chappell (2006, 223) argues, most political institutions are embedded with a "logic of gendered appropriateness," which serves to reinforce male dominant norms and privileges through various and interlocking formal and informal rules. Identifying how new rules are layered on top of, or "nested" within, pre-existing rules allows us to consider how new gendered rules may be used in everyday practice and which actors they are most likely to empower (or disempower) once implemented (Mackay 2014).

Drawing on feminist institutionalist research, we can observe how the Senate's new harassment and violence policy empowers senators in numerous ways. Although it includes provisions for an impartial third party to oversee claims, the policy gives senators final oversight over how independent investigations will be used to determine the outcome of cases. When the responding party of a claim is a senator's employee, the investigator is to prepare two reports: a summary and a final report. The summary report is to include recommendations to "eliminate or minimize the risk of a similar occurrence" (Senate of Canada 2021, 12). This report is then sent to the CIBA steering committee and a Workplace Committee to determine which of the recommendations will be taken up; this step is separate from any disciplinary action that may be taken.[17]

The final report details the nature of the allegation and sets out whether the conduct in question constitutes harassing or violent behaviour. When the responding party is a senator's employee, the final report is sent to the CIBA steering committee – comprised of senators – which determines whether any remedial, corrective, or disciplinary measures are needed. Further, the CIBA steering committee has been given the authority to "accept or reject the investigator's final report in whole or in part" (Senate of Canada 2021, 13). In cases involving a senator's employee, the Senate's 2021 policy thus empowers a panel of senators to override the contents of the independent investigator's findings as it sees fit.

In cases where the responding party is a senator, the investigator is to again prepare similar summary and final reports as discussed above, with a copy of the summary report sent to both parties, the CIBA HRRH Subcommittee, and the Workplace Committee. An additional step from above, however, provides that the independent Senate Ethics Officer (SEO) is to receive a copy of the final report detailing the nature of the allegations. The SEO then considers the report and *may* recommend disciplinary measures to the Senate's Ethics Committee (CONF). However, it is the Ethics Committee – comprised again of senators – that determines whether and what disciplinary action will be taken against a senator. Ultimately this process means that politicians will remain the final arbiters of what, if any, sanctions may be imposed upon their fellow politicians when they engage in violence or harassing behaviour.

In cases where it recommends suspension or expulsion, the Ethics Committee makes a recommendation to the Senate as a whole.[18] At the same time, although the Ethics Committee could recommend the most serious consequence of all – that a senator be expelled – no senator has ever been expelled in the chamber's history. Suspensions have occurred but are relatively rare, with the most recent example being the suspension of Senator Lynn Beyak in February 2020 when she failed to complete anti-racism training after posting anti-Indigenous statements to her website. Senators are further able to evade disciplinary action by resigning prior to a potential expulsion vote, which allows them to retain significant job perks, including their honourable title and pension for life.[19] The ability of senators to evade punishment for sexist/racist actions has occurred twice in the last five years.[20]

The 2021 policy's confidentiality provisions are also likely to shield senators' identities from public view when they commit violence or harassment. While confidentiality is absolutely necessary to protect the identities of victim/survivors, the policy binds both the responding *and* principal parties to strict confidentiality adherence, with the threat of discipline against either party for violating these provisions. Section 1.6.1 of the policy states:

> All matters under this Policy (e.g., notice of an occurrence, conciliation, investigation, etc.) are to be treated confidentially. Information in relation

to matters under this Policy may only be disclosed in accordance with this Policy or as required by law. Unauthorized disclosure of information may be *subject to disciplinary action*. (Senate of Canada 2021, 3–4; emphasis added)

Further problematic is that the new policy does not prohibit the use of non-disclosure agreements (NDAs) by the Senate, which can be imposed upon employees for a range of reasons, including when they have been harassed or experienced violent behaviour. In her criticisms of the new policy, Senator Marilou McPhedran noted that the policy's confidentiality provisions effectively impose a non-disclosure agreement "on every single participant in the process, from the very beginning through to the end" (Chen 2021, 12). One staffer who was harassed referred to these new provisions as amounting to the "weaponization of confidentiality" in the Senate (McPhedran 2021).

Existing Senate rules related to committee business will further aid in concealing senators' harassing/violent behaviours. In handling claims that it receives from the impartial third party (via the SEO), the Senate's current committee rules stipulate that, by default, Ethics Committee meetings are to be held *in camera*, while in practice, many meetings of the powerful Internal Economy (CIBA) Committee are also held *in camera*.[21] Thus, even in cases where a senator has been found to have harassed or committed violence against someone, decisions taken by these committees are likely to occur behind closed doors and away from the public eye.

Victim/survivors have also not been given the right to know the outcome of their claims in terms of disciplinary actions taken (or not). The policy states that disciplinary measures imposed upon responding parties are to "remain confidential and – unless disclosure is required for their implementation – are not to be shared with the principal party" (Senate of Canada 2021, 13).[22] As a result, victim/survivors may never know whether their perpetrator has been punished and, if they have, what action was taken against them. Future victim/survivors are thus potential policy "losers" in this regard and are likely to be disincentivized to rely upon a process that might punish them for speaking about their abuse, allows senators to determine sanctions against their colleagues in secret, prohibits them from knowing whether their perpetrator has been punished, and prevents them from knowing whether their employer (the Senate) has imposed a fair and just remedy for the abuse they experienced in their place of work.

These confidentiality measures also raise questions about democratic accountability in the Senate. We can observe some of these inadequacies by comparing the transparency provisions in the anti-harassment policy to the Ethics and Conflict of Interest Code for Senators, which deals with non-harassing behaviour. The Ethics Code is overseen by the Senate Ethics Officer (SEO), who conducts inquiries into senators' potential misconduct. All inquiry reports are published on the SEO's website and name the senator involved (https://seo-cse.sencanada.ca/en/reports-and-inquiries/).[23] By contrast, the Senate's new harassment and violence policy allows individual claims involving senators (as perpetrators) to remain hidden from public view, with public transparency not a requirement.[24] As a result, the public is likely to never know whether a public official serving in Canada's Senate has harassed their colleagues or fellow employees and, if they have, what punishment they received for their harassing conduct. This transparency "double standard" is likely to send a troubling message to victim/survivors and to citizens more broadly that harassing behaviour is less in need of public scrutiny compared to other unethical behaviour in the Senate, such as when senators accept free trips abroad or receive improper gifts.

A final advantage the new policy affords to senators relates to their individual parliamentary privileges. Rather than place limits on members' freedom of speech that might benefit victim/survivors, the new policy reasserts parliamentary privilege as an important historical rule, stating:

> The Senate – and, subject to the Senate's authority, its committees – have the exclusive authority to regulate their own proceedings. Individuals taking part in parliamentary proceedings are covered by parliamentary privilege in order to enable the Senate and senators to fulfill their constitutional role without undue interference, obstruction or fear of external retribution. This privilege is fundamental to parliamentary democracy and allows senators to express themselves fully. (Senate of Canada 2021, 2)

The reassertion of parliamentary privilege leaves several existing practices and norms in place that are likely to disadvantage victim/survivors. For example, despite concerns raised by some senators that bullying and racist behaviours have occurred in committee meetings, the new policy explicitly states that parliamentary proceedings do not fall under its purview and are protected by parliamentary privilege (Senate of Canada 2021, 7).[25] If a senator feels that they or someone else has experienced sexism, or racist or homophobic language or conduct, they must continue to bring the matter to the attention of the committee chair or the Speaker, who will decide on the matter. Senators' past practices of asserting parliamentary privilege in order to avoid participating in investigations relating to cases of harassment/violence also remain unaddressed. Finally, the policy does not limit members' freedom of speech in cases where a vote of suspension or expulsion is required on the Senate floor.[26] This oversight means that any senator(s), including a responding party or a potential ally, could "debate" cases of harassment in full public view without fear of reprisal or prosecution. At the same time, employees will not have the same opportunity to lay out the facts of their claim publicly while under the protection of similar free speech immunities.

"Fixing" the Upper House: Implications for Action

To sum up, the Senate's new harassment and violence prevention policy offers some improvements over the older 2009 policy. It broadens the scope of behaviour covered, strips power from party whips, and introduces an impartial investigator who must have anti-violence training. At the same time, it also includes several serious shortcomings. Due to unreconciled power differentials, those with the most power within the institution – senators – have considerable oversight over sanctioning decisions and remain protected by strict confidentiality and parliamentary privilege. Conversely, those who are at a structural disadvantage within the workplace – women, Black, Indigenous, and 2SLGBTQQIA+ employees, as well as those working under precarious employment contracts – are not fully protected by, nor will they likely be incentivized to use, the new policy. As a result, it is likely that harassment and violence will remain problems within Canada's upper house, which could lead victim/survivors to seek safer employment elsewhere. These policy shortcomings pose risks to core democratic principles, weakening the Senate's representative and accountability functions in Canada's legislative process.

The results in this chapter also raise questions about the link between women's descriptive and substantive political representation (Childs and Withey 2006; Childs and Krook 2009). As one of only three (approximately) gender-equal upper houses in the world, the Canadian Senate offers researchers a unique opportunity to evaluate the impact of women's increased presence on gender equality outcomes inside legislatures. The Senate's adoption of an anti-harassment policy that contains fairly serious flaws highlights the challenges feminist critical actors (women and men) face in their efforts to redesign institutions in more equitable, inclusive ways. In this case study, white, heteronormative, and hegemonically masculine norms and rules proved difficult to dislodge, even in a legislature that has an *equal number of women and men legislators*. As Mackay (2014, 551) argues, the "stickiness of old rules (formal and informal) about gender ... and the way newness functions as a gendered liability provides a powerful explanation for why it is so hard to make gender reforms ... stick." The prevalence of GBV-P in political institutions like Canada's Senate is thus a stark reminder of how gender equity remains elusive, even in a firmly established democracy. I conclude this chapter by offering several recommendations that all legislative bodies ought to consider in their adoption of anti-harassment rules.

Implications for Action

1 Legislatures need strong, effective, and transparent rules of conduct with serious and explicit consequences laid out for those who perpetrate violence.
2 Legislatures should create fully independent offices to oversee harassment/violence investigatory and grievance processes. Decisions should not be subject to review by politicians.
3 Investigations into politicians' behaviours involving harassment and violence should be publicly disclosed (while protecting the identities of victim/survivors); non-disclosure agreements in cases of harassment and violence should be prohibited.
4 Human Resource Directorates inside legislatures should provide guidance to politicians on best practices for staff, monitor contracts, and have the authority to intervene in cases where abuses of power occur.
5 Legislatures should conduct workplace gender and diversity sensitivity analyses. These analyses should include how various rules and norms, such as parliamentary privilege, inhibit the full inclusion and participation of women, Black, Indigenous, people of colour, and queer people who work there.
6 Additional research is needed on the role of critical actors inside legislatures in advocating for anti-harassment rules and policies.

NOTES

1 A previous version of this chapter was awarded the 2022 Jill Vickers Prize for the best paper presented on gender and politics at the Canadian Political Science Association annual conference. This research was supported by a James R. Mallory Grant from the Canadian Study of Parliament Group. I thank Toronto Metropolitan University Master in Public Policy and Administration student Evangeline Holtz-Schramek for her excellent research assistance.
2 Women who spoke out include senators (for example, Hon. Marilou McPhedran and Hon. Josée Verner) and staffers. In 2013, former Senate staffer Pascale Brisson filed a sexual harassment complaint against Senator

Colin Kenny, while Senator McPhedran established a confidential email address to provide support to victim/survivors of sexual harassment within the Senate.
3   At the time of writing, women held 48 per cent of seats in the Senate.
4   Senators are appointed by the governor general on the advice of the prime minister and serve until the age of seventy-five.
5   The collapse of the Senate's "duopoly" (Liberal/Conservative dominance) was precipitated by two events: in 2014 Justin Trudeau expelled all Liberal senators from his caucus; and in 2015, as prime minister, he adopted a more independent process to recommend individuals to the governor general for the Senate. As of November 2023, seventy-nine of ninety-four senators sat outside of a traditional party caucus. Despite the elimination of most Senate party caucuses, many senators continue to vote along partisan lines. See Godbout (2020).
6   The term "victim/survivors" (rather than "victims" or "survivors") is used throughout the chapter and is intended to capture the reality that those who experience violence may identify as a victim, as a survivor, or as both, depending on their individual histories, circumstances, and identities.
7   2SLGBTQQIA+ refers to those who identify as two-spirit, lesbian, gay, bisexual, transgender, queer, questioning, intersex, androgynous, and asexual. "Two-spirit" is a term used by some Indigenous people to reflect the complex (and non-binary) nature of gender roles and identities in Indigenous communities.
8   Although first reported in the media as an "affair," the Senate Ethics Officer's first inquiry report concluded that, on at least one occasion, Meredith allegedly had non-consensual sex with a minor, which would constitute sexual assault. Meredith denies all allegations. After charges were laid against him in 2022, senators voted to request that the governor general strip him of his honourable title.
9   As per Senate rules, both inquiries were initiated at the request of other senators; see Senate Ethics Officer (2019).
10 A "statement of regret" is not the same as an apology. See Ahmed (2021) on the potential harm of non-apology "apologies."
11 The subcommittee was comprised of five senators: three men and two women. The chair of the committee was a woman (Senate of Canada 2019, 7).
12 CIBA also recommended that the Senate refer questions of parliamentary privilege and potential revisions to the Ethics Code to two additional committees to report back to the Senate no later than 30 April 2020.
13 Section 28(1) of the Regulations (Bill C-65) specifies that an investigator must be trained in investigative techniques; have knowledge, training, and experience relating to harassment and violence in the workplace; and have knowledge of the Canadian Human Rights Act.

14 The 2009 policy stipulated that the respondent and/or the complainant may show cause why a person should not serve as an investigator or panel member, in which case a replacement may be appointed.
15 Parliamentary privilege is a set of historical rights and immunities granted to parliaments collectively and members individually in the exercise of their parliamentary duties. See Raney and Collier (2022) for a gendered analysis of parliamentary privilege in Canada and the United Kingdom.
16 While hiring and firing decisions of political staffers in the Senate are undertaken by the Human Resources Directorate, they are made under the direction of the employing senator. One senator reported that she was once asked by a lending bank to vouch for the long-term employment of a staffer who had applied for a mortgage (Interview with the author, March 2021).
17 The Workplace Committee includes staffers. When the responding party is an employee of the Senate Administration, the decision-making authority is the director or manager responsible for the employee.
18 In instances where remedial or corrective action is to be taken, the CIBA sub-committee is the decision-making authority.
19 Honourable titles are more than mere formalities; they allow senators to remain representatives of the institution through various community and speaking engagements while retired. Members are entitled to a pension after serving more than six years in the Senate.
20 As discussed earlier, Senator Don Meredith resigned prior to an expulsion vote in 2017; facing a possible expulsion vote for her anti-Indigenous statements, Senator Lynn Beyak resigned in 2021. Both retain their honourable titles and collect full pensions.
21 In fall 2020, CIBA announced that it would make its proceedings more open to the public; however, it is unclear whether this change would apply to harassment cases.
22 Disclosure would occur should a senator be asked to apologize or face expulsion/suspension, the latter of which requires a floor vote.
23 The Ethics Code prohibits activities such as improperly accepting gifts or various other financial conflicts of interest.
24 By comparison, the British House of Lords publishes reports in all cases where peers are accused of harassment, bullying, or sexual misconduct, with redactions to protect the identity of victim/survivors.
25 The Rules of the Senate define privilege as an "allegation that the privileges of the Senate or its members have been infringed"; these must be decided upon by the Senate.
26 This provision is unlike the policy in the British House of Lords, which limits debate on motions to sanction peers for misconduct in similar cases.

REFERENCES

Ahmed, Sara. 2021. "Apologies for Harm, Apologies as Harm." *Feminist Killjoys* (blog), 27 January 2021. https://feministkilljoys.com/2021/01/27/apologies-for-harm-apologies-as-harm/.

Bacchi, Carol Lee. (1999) 2008. *Women, Policy and Politics: The Construction of Policy Problems*. London: Sage Publications.

CBC News. 2016. "A Chronology of the Senate Expense Scandal." *CBC News*, 13 July 2016. https://www.cbc.ca/news/politics/senate-expense-scandal-timeline-1.3677457.

Chappell, Louise. 2006. "Comparing Political Institutions: Revealing the Gendered 'Logic of Appropriateness.'" *Politics & Gender* 2 (2): 223–35. https://doi.org/10.1017/S1743923X06221044.

Chappell, Louise, and Georgina Waylen. 2013. "Gender and the Hidden Life of Institutions." *Public Administration* 91 (3): 599–615. https://doi.org/10.1111/j.1467-9299.2012.02104.x.

Chen, Alice. 2021. "Senate Staff Reps Say They Want New Harassment Policy to Go Ahead as Dissenters Stand Firm." *The Hill Times*, 22 March 2021.

Childs, Sarah, and Mona Lena Krook. 2009. "Analysing Women's Substantive Representation: From Critical Mass to Critical Actors." *Government and Opposition* 44 (2): 125–45. https://doi.org/10.1111/j.1477-7053.2009.01279.x.

Childs, Sarah, and Julie Withey. 2006. "The Substantive Representation of Women: The Case of the Reduction of VAT on Sanitary Products." *Parliamentary Affairs* 59 (1): 10–23. https://doi.org/10.1093/pa/gsj003.

Collier, Cheryl N., and Tracey Raney. 2018a. "Canada's Member-to-Member Code of Conduct on Sexual Harassment." *Canadian Journal of Political Science* 51 (4): 795–815. https://doi.org/10.1017/S000842391800032X.

– 2018b. "Understanding Sexism and Sexual Harassment in Politics: A Comparison of Westminster Parliaments in Australia, the United Kingdom, and Canada" *Social Politics: International Studies in Gender, State & Society* 25 (3): 432–55. https://doi.org/10.1093/sp/jxy024.

Crenshaw, Kimberle. 1991. "Mapping the Margins: Intersectionality, Identity Politics, and Violence Against Women of Color." *Stanford Law Review* 43 (6): 1241–99. https://doi.org/10.2307/1229039.

Donovan, Kevin. 2015. "Teen Alleges Two-Year Affair with Senator Don Meredith." *The Toronto Star*, 17 June 2015. https://www.thestar.com/news/gta/teen-alleges-two-year-affair-with-senator-don-meredith/article_9cdad59e-1fcf-5ff6-bf9d-9b2c0d3f8709.html.

Godbout, Jean François. 2020. *Lost on Division: Party Unity in the Canadian Parliament*. Toronto, ON: University of Toronto Press.

Government of Canada. 2020. *Work Place Harassment and Violence Prevention Regulations*. SOR/2020-130. Canada Labour Code. Last amended 1 July

2021. Ottawa, ON: Minister of Justice. https://laws-lois.justice.gc.ca/PDF/SOR-2020-130.pdf.

Hankivsky, Olena, and Renee Cormier. 2011. "Intersectionality and Public Policy: Some Lessons from Existing Models." *Political Research Quarterly* 64 (1): 217–29. https://doi.org/10.1177/1065912910376385.

Krook, Mona Lena. 2018a. "Violence against Women in Politics: A Rising Global Trend." *Politics & Gender* 14 (4): 673–75. https://doi.org/10.1017/S1743923X18000582.

– 2018b. "Westminster Too: On Sexual Harassment in British Politics." *The Political Quarterly* 89 (1): 65–72. https://doi.org/10.1111/1467-923X.12458.

Lowndes, Vivien. 2020. "How Are Political Institutions Gendered?" *Political Studies* 68 (3): 543–64. https://doi.org/10.1177/0032321719867667.

Lum, Zi-Ann. 2020. "Senate to Pay $498K to Harassment Victims after Years-Long 'Crisis.'" *Huff Post*, 14 October 2020. https://www.huffpost.com/archive/ca/entry/don-meredith-senate-harassment-compensation_ca_5f87487fc5b6c4bb54723f9a.

Mackay, Fiona. 2014. "Nested Newness, Institutional Innovation, and the Gendered Limits of Change." *Politics & Gender* 10 (4): 549–71. https://doi.org/10.1017/S1743923X14000415.

McPhail, Beverly A. 2003. "A Feminist Policy Analysis Framework: Through a Gendered Lens." *The Social Policy Journal* 2 (2–3): 39–61. https://doi.org/10.1300/J185v02n02_04.

McPhedran, Marilou. 2021, 30 March. "Speech to the Senate of Canada by Hon. Marilou McPhedran." *Debates of the Senate*, vol. 152, no. 34, 43rd Parliament, 2nd Session (Hansard), 1233–5. Ottawa, ON: Senate of Canada. https://sencanada.ca/en/content/sen/chamber/432/debates/034db_2021-03-30-e#71.

Puwar, Nirmal. 2004. *Space Invaders: Race, Gender and Bodies Out of Place*. Oxford: Berg Publishers.

Raney, Tracey. 2021. *Addressing Violence and Harassment in Canada's Senate: Critical Actors and Institutional Responses*. A Report Prepared for the Canadian Study of Parliament Group. https://cspg-gcep.ca/pdf/addressing_violence_and_harassment_senate-e.pdf.

Raney, Tracey, and Cheryl N. Collier. 2022. "Privilege and Gendered Violence in the Canadian and British Houses of Commons: A Feminist Institutionalist Analysis." *Parliamentary Affairs* 75 (2): 382–99. https://doi.org/10.1093/pa/gsaa069.

Restrepo Sanín, Juliana. 2022. "Violence against Women in Politics as an Unintended Consequence of Democratization." *International Feminist Journal of Politics* 24 (1): 16–39. https://doi.org/10.1080/14616742.2021.2014343.

Senate Ethics Officer. 2019, 28 June. *Inquiry Report under the* Ethics and Conflict of Interest Code for Senators *Concerning Former Senator Don Meredith*.

Ottawa, ON: Office of the Senate Ethics Officer. https://seo-cse.sencanada.ca/en/reports-and-inquiries/inquiry-reports/.
– 2021. "Summary of Provisions on Harassment and Violence." Office of the Senate Ethics Officer. https://seo-cse.sencanada.ca/en/code/summary-of-provisions-on-harassment-and-violence/.
Senate of Canada. 2009. *The Senate Policy on the Prevention and Resolution of Harassment in the Workplace*. Ottawa, ON: Senate of Canada. https://sencanada.ca/content/sen/committee/402/inte/rep/rep08jun09-e.pdf.
– 2019. *Modernizing the Senate's Anti-Harassment Policy: Together Let's Protect Our Healthy Worklife*. Report of the Subcommittee on Human Resources. Ottawa, ON: Senate of Canada. https://sencanada.ca/content/sen/committee/421/CIBA/Reports/CIBA_37RPT_E.pdf.
– 2020. *Policy on the Prevention and Resolution of Harassment in the Senate Workplace*. Third Report of the Standing Committee on Internal Economy, Budgets and Administration. Ottawa, ON: Senate of Canada. https://sencanada.ca/en/committees/report/80596/43-1.
– 2021. *Senate Harassment and Violence Prevention Policy*. Fourth Report of the Standing Committee on Internal Economy, Budgets and Administration. Ottawa, ON: Senate of Canada. https://sencanada.ca/content/sen/committee/432/CIBA/Reports/CIBA_RTP5_POL_HVP_E.pdf.
Verge, Tania. 2022. "Too Few, Too Little? Parliaments' Response to Sexism and Sexual Harassment." *Parliamentary Affairs* 75 (1): 94–112. https://doi.org/10.1093/pa/gsaa052.
Waylen, Georgina. 2014. "Informal Institutions, Institutional Change and Gender Equality." *Political Research Quarterly* 67 (1): 212–23. https://doi.org/10.1177/1065912913510360.

13 Provincial and Territorial Legislature-Based Sexual Harassment Policies for Elected Members: Variation in Approaches but Commonality in Ineffectiveness

CHERYL N. COLLIER AND TRACEY RANEY

In 2015, the Canadian House of Commons made history by passing the first federal-level sexual harassment Code of Conduct for elected legislative members in any Westminster parliament in the world. The move was lauded by some international non-governmental organizations, noting that it was one of only four examples of national parliaments addressing sexual violence between elected parliamentarians (Inter-Parliamentary Union 2016), even though the Canadian code itself had significant limitations in its effectiveness (Collier and Raney 2018a). However, the problem of sexual harassment inside legislatures is not limited to the federal level in Canada. Even though researchers have identified historical Canadian substate instances of violence against women in politics, including sexual harassment (Collier and Raney 2018b; Krook 2020), there has been scant attention paid to provincial and territorial legislative gender-based violence in politics (GBV-P) policy responses,[1] some of which pre-date the Canadian federal milestone.

Examples of Canadian substate level GBV-P have been reported more regularly in the media both before and after #MeToo, illustrating that the scope of the problem is widespread and that no province or territory is immune. In 2007, Prince Edward Island member of the Legislative Assembly (MLA) Cynthia Dunsford filed a complaint against Deputy Health Minister Rory Beck following a sexual harassment incident in a Charlottetown bar. Beck was subject to a reprimand and took a leave of absence when the incident was leaked to the media (CBC News 2007). In 2016, Liberal member of the National Assembly (MNA) Gerry Sklavounos stepped down from the Quebec Liberal caucus following accusations that he had sexually assaulted a woman on two separate occasions (Canadian Press 2016). That year also saw revelations of two sexual harassment cases in Manitoba's legislature, including the case of former New Democratic Party (NDP) minister Stan Struthers, who was named "Minister Tickles" because of his propensity towards inappropriate touching (Kavanagh 2018).

Since #MeToo, additional allegations have surfaced. In New Brunswick, Speaker Chris Collins was suspended from the Liberal caucus in 2018 after sexual harassment allegations were levelled against him by a former employee of the Legislative Assembly (Bissett 2018). That same year, Iqaluit mayor Madeleine Redfern faced backlash after referring to some Inuit leaders in her community as "sexual predators" during testimony to the House of Commons Standing Committee on the Status of Women (Frizzell 2018). The year 2018 also saw attention to earlier (2015) sexual misconduct allegations against two sitting Alberta NDP MLAs (French 2019), and in Ontario, sexual harassment allegations brought Progressive Conservative (PC) leader Patrick Brown's provincial political career to an abrupt end during the lead-up to a provincial election his party would eventually win (although he would later go on to become mayor of the city of Brampton). In 2019, British Columbia Speaker Darryl Plecas shared a confidential memo to an all-party legislative committee regarding allegations of "#MeToo types of concerns" from a witness, noting that the allegations had not been properly investigated (Zussman 2020).

Clearly the problem of GBV-P is shared at the substate level in Canada, much as we have seen in other jurisdictions worldwide and in Canada at the national level. It is the purpose of this chapter to look at some of the substate legislative responses to GBV-P to fill a gap in the existing Canadian literature and in the literature on sexual harassment in subnational legislatures, where little attention has been paid. Specifically, our chapter comparatively chronicles and evaluates provincial and territorial legislature-based sexual harassment policies that cover *elected members* of Parliament. It is important to assess these policies, particularly in the wake of the #MeToo movement, which shone a brighter light on the need for sexual harassment prevention strategies in a variety of public workspaces. The existence and effectiveness of "workplace" sexual harassment policies inside legislatures also impacts democratic health, since legislatures that have traditionally been hostile to diverse participants – women and other minorities – and have ineffective sexual harassment policies to which these same diverse participants are often the targets, are ultimately less likely to be fully representative of, and responsive to, its citizenry. GBV-P, including sexual harassment, exists to exclude women and other minorities from participation in public life.[2] Its tacit acceptance perpetuates democratic deficits. Thus, robust and effective solutions to GBV-P are essential to promoting more inclusive and equitable democracies.

Provincial and Territorial Sexual Harassment Policies   267

This chapter finds that, despite the window of opportunity opening in the Canadian context in the wake of #MeToo, not all substate governments have enacted legislative member-to-member sexual harassment policies as a potential solution to GBV-P. It also argues that those policies that do exist vary substantially in their attention to gender-based violence, with many falling far short of the mark in terms of attention to and effectiveness in responding to *gendered* and *intersectional* power differentials inside legislative spaces. As a result, our comparative jurisdictional scan across Canada reveals a patchwork of legislative responses to GBV-P, leaving those who are the most likely to be targeted by it – women – unevenly protected across the country. We conclude by suggesting ways that provincial and territorial legislatures can do better to make parliaments safer and more open to diverse representatives, particularly women.

The chapter begins by briefly setting the stage for the comparative analysis and explains the legislative context of the thirteen provincial and territorial Westminster legislatures in Canada. We also highlight some of the institutional "challenges" in creating sexual harassment policies for legislative members in parliamentary spaces. The chapter then sets out the theoretical feminist institutionalist discursive framework used in the analysis of existing provincial/territorial sexual harassment policies to help ascertain their potential effectiveness as GBV-P solutions from a gendered perspective. Following this discussion, the chapter describes the discourse and content methodology for the comparative analysis and then applies this approach to provincial and territorial sexual harassment responses to date. It concludes with some suggestions for how substate legislatures can improve those responses – using a gender-based lens – in the future.

Comparative Provincial/Territorial Cases

While there is much variation between the ten provincial and three territorial substate governments in Canada with respect to their economies, political cultures, and geographic sizes, they are remarkably similar in their legislative structures. Even though the provinces have more constitutional jurisdictional power in the Canadian federal landscape than the territories, each follows a cabinet-parliamentary Westminster model adhering to the principles of responsible government. Each is unicameral in the modern political era (Quebec being the last to remove its upper house in the 1960s). The only significant structural difference between the thirteen Canadian substate legislatures is the lack of partisanship in two of the territories – Nunavut and the Northwest

Territories. Each of these territories operates on a consensus-based system, but still appoints a cabinet and Speaker, and has a Board of Internal Economy or a "similar committee" that administers substate legislative budgets and governs internal operational rules (Thomas and White 2016, 370). Thus, the foundation for legislature-based workplace sexual harassment policies for and between elected members in each of the substate legislatures in Canada is arguably quite similar and has the potential to follow similar templates.

At the same time, scholarship on federalism suggests that the substate level of government inside federations offers legislatures opportunities to diverge in governance practice to suit the particularities of their communities.[3] Thus, provinces, territories, state, and local governments may sometimes act as "laboratories" of democracy, where innovative policies can be enacted more readily than at the national level, and meso-level successes can be emulated through policy learning.[4] So, despite the foundation for similar rules and codes of conduct in provincial and territorial legislative assemblies, the opportunity to experiment and improve policy responses also exists.

Yet, there has been some resistance to, and hesitancy in, adopting harassment and sexual harassment policies and/or codes of conduct for elected members of parliamentary legislatures, including at the federal level. Even though harassment and violence have a long history in Canadian and other Westminster legislatures (Collier and Raney 2018b), legislatures have avoided enacting harassment and sexual harassment policies and processes for case investigation, adjudication, and sanctions until quite recently. One reason for this lack of action is the view of the legislative workplace as being "exceptional" in that elected members are not directly hired or managed by superiors but are instead beholden to the will of the people via periodic free and fair elections. Thus, these spaces are not workplaces like any other and cannot easily adopt workplace sexual harassment processes common in other areas of employment. The "exceptional" status of Westminster legislatures is bolstered by parliamentary privilege, an ancient set of rules that apply to legislatures allowing them to regulate their internal affairs without external influence (for example, the Crown). As Raney's chapter 12 in this volume on the Senate indicates, parliamentary privilege extends to individual members, providing them with various rights and immunities during parliamentary proceedings, such as protecting their freedom of speech or freedom from intimidation. Although the courts have imposed limitations on the scope of parliamentary privilege in various rulings over time, the constitutional-historical basis of parliamentary privilege is what allows legislatures to self-regulate the conduct of their

Figure 13.1. Elected women in provincial and territorial legislatures, 2022

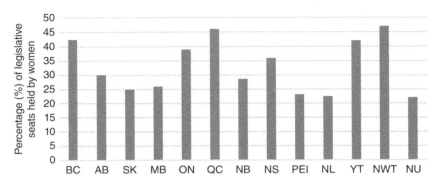

Notes: (1) Data reflects numbers as of 1 November 2022. (2) AB = Alberta; BC = British Columbia; MB = Manitoba; NB = New Brunswick; NL = Newfoundland and Labrador; NS = Nova Scotia; NU = Nunavut; NWT = Northwest Territories; ON = Ontario; PEI = Prince Edward Island; QC = Quebec; SK = Saskatchewan; YT = Yukon. (3) Data from provincial and territorial legislatures and elections offices.

members through the imposition of various punishments (for example, suspension or expulsion), as well as to protect the rights of members to freedom of speech during debates and committee hearings (Collier and Raney 2018b; Raney and Collier 2022). Due to its far-reaching consequences, some legislatures have had difficulty reconciling parliamentary privilege with harassment and violence policies that may offer some element of external oversight and/or place limits on members' speech, including the Canadian House of Commons itself.

The increasing numbers of women-identified legislators elected to public office over time has drawn more attention to the problem of GBV-P and has helped put pressure on some federal and provincial legislatures to look for solutions, as some politicians want to be seen as responsive to this problem. Although five of the thirteen substate jurisdictions have seen women reach or surpass the 40 per cent mark, women have yet to reach parity in any Canadian legislature. Others have been slower to reach these levels, as we see in Figure 13.1, with the lowest numbers located in Nunavut (22 per cent), Prince Edward Island (23 per cent), and Newfoundland and Labrador (23 per cent).

The disparity in electoral success rates for women in Canada's provinces and territories may explain some of the reticence in enacting sexual harassment policies, although the widespread attention to the #MeToo movement – particularly in late 2017 – across the country and worldwide likely mitigates it.

Discursively Assessing Provincial and Territorial Sexual Harassment Policies

A common approach used to evaluate the potential effectiveness of new policies, rules, and codes of conduct to ameliorate the problem of GBV-P in legislatures has been to adopt a feminist institutionalist analytical approach (see Lovenduski 2014; Krook 2020). Feminist institutionalism (FI) analyses institutional rules and norms – both formal and informal – using a gendered lens, understanding that most historical institutional legacies in legislatures are built upon an assumption of white maleness as the norm (Chappell 2006). This assumption makes it particularly difficult to "re-gender" institutions to ensure gender equity, particularly from an intersectional approach that also recognizes women's unique experiences across racial, ability, sexuality, age, and cultural matrices. FI scholars have pointed to several challenges to making institutions more gender equal, including existing institutional norms, both formal (for example, codes of conduct) and informal (norms and expectations that promote aggressive styles of debate). Thus, when new gender equality rules are adopted, they must rest upon, and interact with, older rules that have historically reinforced white, male-dominated norms (see Mackay 2014; Waylen 2014; Chappell and Waylen 2013). "Re-gendering" legislative institutions (that is, making them more gender equal) is seen as a critical aspect of ensuring legislatures are safe workspaces for gender-diverse people, particularly with respect to ensuring the effectiveness of policy/code of conduct solutions aimed at ending workplace harassment.

One way that FI scholars have begun to analyse the level of attention to re-gendering inside institutions has been through discursive analysis. Discursive analysis is also a common and useful policy analysis tool since policy discourse and content word choice is intentional and clearly reveals important levers of policy action that are supported (or not) by policymakers (see Rein and Schön 1991; Collier 2012). Not surprisingly, policy discourse is also highly gendered. Studying policy content and discourse can tell us much about whether gender, race, and other axes of marginalization are central or peripheral to policy problematization and/or prescribed solutions (Bacchi 2000, 2009). Discourses also shape institutions, as institutions are not fixed but always in a state of "reproduction" and, along with ideas, "occupy a central place in the process of institutional change" (Berthet and Kantola 2021, 8).

This chapter uses a discursive FI approach to analyse sexual harassment policies in the provinces and territories in Canada for the first time. To do so, we further draw in part on our previous analysis of the sexual harassment MP-to-MP Code of Conduct in the Canadian House of Commons, as well as on a more recent discursive analysis of sexual harassment policy debates in the European Parliament (Collier and Raney 2018a; Berthet and Kantola 2021). As such, the chapter identifies and assesses discursive elements of each substate policy/code to identify how the problem is framed. Does the policy/code use parliamentary privilege to assert self-policing of administrative Boards of Internal Economy (or equivalent, comprised of other elected legislators) over cases of GBV-P, or does it involve independent arbitration utilizing external sexual harassment investigative/interpretative expertise? Does the policy/code include language that would penalize GBV-P survivors who are found to have falsely accused someone of GBV-P, which may discourage use of the policy/code and suppress harassment reports? The comparative analysis will also establish the timing of each policy/code creation to situate it comparatively to the steps taken by the House of Commons to address this problem and to the #MeToo movement.

The discursive analysis then assesses the presence or absence of specific gender content by conducting content analyses of each enacted provincial or territorial sexual harassment policy for elected members. This analysis includes identifying the extent of the use of the words "sexual harassment" inside each policy/code as well as the appearance and attention to "gender," "women," "power," and "race." Attention to "power" is key with respect to fully understanding that sexual harassment is, at its core, an abuse of power. As Berthet and Kantola argue, sexual harassment discourses that clearly identify "abuse of gendered power" are more likely to propose new rule solutions to the problem that are pro–gender equality and reflective of a deeper understanding of the roots of GBV-P (2021, 20).

Discursive Comparative Analysis

As Table 13.1 shows, not all Canadian provinces have enacted specific harassment/sexual harassment policies or codes of conduct governing interactions between elected legislative members, yet all three territories have. At the time of writing, Alberta, New Brunswick, and Prince Edward Island (PEI) had not fully enacted sexual harassment policies or codes for their elected MLAs, although all but PEI had established committees to review existing sexual harassment practices with a view to extending these to legislators between 2018 and 2019. Notably, all of these provinces recently conducted elections (between

Table 13.1. Provincial and territorial legislature member-based sexual harassment policies

Province/Territory	Member policy	Date enacted	Type/Title	Privilege? / BOIE or equivalent role?	False claims clause?	Independent arbiter?
British Columbia	Yes	8 July 2021	Policy – Respectful Workplace Policy	No, but policy doesn't cover "interactions between members in the context of parliamentary proceedings"/No	Yes	No – but Independent Respectful Workplace Office manages process and investigates; external investigator can also be used
Alberta	No	n/a	–	–	–	–
Saskatchewan	Yes	1 April 2018	Code of Conduct – Code of Conduct for Members of the Legislative Assembly of Saskatchewan: Anti-Harassment Policy	No/Yes – BOIE	Yes	No – but external investigator can be used
Manitoba	Yes	6 March 2019	Policy – Respectful Workplace Policy: Addressing and Preventing Sexual Harassment, Harassment and Bullying	No/No – Non-political adjudication – Clerk/Speaker	Yes	No – but all MLA complaints use external investigators reporting to Speaker
Ontario	Yes	7 June 2018	Code of Conduct – Members Code of Conduct on Harassment	No/No – Role of Clerk and Speaker	Yes – but sanctions not mentioned	No – but external investigator can be used
Quebec	Yes	4 June 2015	Policy – Politique relative à la prévention et à la gestion des situations de harcèlement au travail	No/No – Role of Whip and Speaker	Yes	No – but external investigator is used
New Brunswick	No	n/a	–	–	–	–
Nova Scotia	Yes	20 May 2016	Policy – Nova Scotia House of Assembly Policy on the Prevention and Resolution of Harassment in the Workplace	No/Yes (Committee on Assembly Matters)	Yes	No – but external investigator can be used

Jurisdiction	Policy/Code	Date	Title	Oversight Body	Applies to MLAs	Independent Investigator/Mediator
Prince Edward Island	No	n/a	—	—	—	—
Newfoundland and Labrador	Yes	1 April 2020	Policy – Harassment-Free Workplace Policy Applicable to Complaints against Members of the House of Assembly	Yes/Yes (Standing Committee on Privileges and Elections)	Yes	No – but Office of the Citizen Representative does all investigations and provides harassment-specific support
Yukon	Yes	12 June 2019	Policy – Yukon Legislative Assembly Respectful Conduct	No/Yes (Member Services Board)	Yes	No – but independent investigator used in all formal complaints
Northwest Territories	Yes	2019	Policy – Workplace Harassment Policy & Code of Conduct (work together)	Yes (Code)/Yes (Board of Management)	Yes (Code)/ No (Policy)	No – but independent mediation and/or arbitrator can be brought in
Nunavut	Yes	20 September 2010	Policy – Workplace Harassment Policy	No/Yes (Management and Services Board)	No	No – but independent mediation and/or arbitrator can be brought in

Notes: (1) BOIE = Board of Internal Economy; MHA = member of the House Assembly; MLA = member of the Legislative Assembly. (2) For policies and codes from the various provinces and territories, see Assemblée nationale du Québec (2015); British Columbia (2021); Legislative Assembly of Manitoba (2019); Legislative Assembly of Ontario (2018); Legislative Assembly of Saskatchewan (2018); Newfoundland and Labrador (2019); Northwest Territories (2019a, 2019b); Nova Scotia (2016); Nunavut Legislative Assembly (2014); Yukon Legislative Assembly (2019). (3) The Newfoundland and Labrador legislature specifically amended its MHA Code of Conduct to enact a stand-alone harassment policy for legislative members. PEI has a policy for employees but not MLAs specifically. Equal Voice notes that New Brunswick has a policy but that it is "not available" (2022, 26).

2019 and 2020), which, along with the COVID-19 pandemic, may partially explain policy delays.

Of the remaining provinces and territories, three had enacted sexual harassment policies for elected members prior to the heightened attention to the issue via the #MeToo movement: Nunavut (2010), Quebec (2015), and Nova Scotia (2016). Notably, Nunavut enacted its Workplace Harassment Policy prior to the House of Commons, making it the first jurisdiction in Canada to do so. Seven provinces and territories subsequently enacted policies around or in the wake of the #MeToo movement: Saskatchewan (2018), Ontario (2018), Manitoba (2019), Yukon (2019), Northwest Territories (2019), Newfoundland and Labrador (2020), and British Columbia (2021). This timeline indicates that several Canadian legislatures were in some ways responsive to the #MeToo movement or at least suggests recognition on their part that they needed to be perceived publicly as being responsive to the events of fall 2017.

When we turn to the sexual harassment discourse in each of the ten enacted substate policies, the majority (seven) are self-governing (MLAs/MHAs governing themselves) with adjudication administered by the Board of Internal Economy (or equivalent) in each case. However, only two of the nine policies or codes specifically mention "privilege" of elected members in their policies/codes: Newfoundland and Labrador (policy) and the Northwest Territories (code, but not policy). This finding differs from the House of Commons, which made concerted efforts to ensure that parliamentary privilege was protected. Explicit efforts to maintain parliamentary privilege (effectively ensuring the self-policing of cases of MP-to-MP sexual harassment) in the 2015 MP Code of Conduct could very likely usurp or muddy the effectiveness of the policy to curb sexual harassment, as opposed to protecting the privacy and freedom of speech of elected members who may engage in sexually harassing behaviour. This problem potentially also exists in the two substate examples (Newfoundland and Labrador, and Nunavut).

Despite it not being mentioned explicitly in most policies, we also find that parliamentary privilege – a very old rule – remains a stumbling block for serious action in dealing with sexual harassment across most Canadian legislatures. This finding supports that found in Raney's chapter 12 in this volume, which also indicates that parliamentary privilege has posed a barrier to more meaningful action dealing with GBV-P in the Senate of Canada. Many substate policies appear to have ruled out the need for external oversight over sexual harassment cases, instead following the historical tradition of allowing politicians – mostly white men – to continue to police the behaviours of fellow politicians. Further problematic is that this self-regulation often occurs behind closed doors, away from the public eye.

When those in power are able to essentially "police themselves," they are less likely to challenge existing power differentials that victimize women and other minorities. Since women remain under-represented in most Canadian legislatures, the committees that oversee these new codes (for example, Boards of Internal Economies) will further be largely drawn from a pool of mostly white men, who will have the power to interpret, rewrite, or potentially ignore them.

Table 13.1 also shows that nine of the ten substate sexual harassment member-based policies/codes include a clause that would identify and potentially punish complainants who are found to have made false, "vexatious," or "bad faith" sexual harassment claims. These "false claim" provisions were often flagged as potential grounds for sanctions that (if proven) would be incurred by the sexual harassment complainant/survivor. From a gender perspective, the inclusion of these clauses perpetuates a long-standing myth that women and other victims of sexual violence and harassment often fabricate their claims, even though incidents of false reporting are in reality quite low. We have argued elsewhere that these clauses can have a chilling effect inside sexual harassment policies and codes that further discourage reporting, which is already quite low to begin with (Collier and Raney 2018a). The fact that these clauses are replicated in the provincial and territorial policies and codes in such high numbers is troubling and may discourage targets of violence from coming forward.

Finally, Table 13.1 illustrates whether independent arbiters or investigators are used to guide the formal processes of sexual harassment policies and codes for legislative members in the provinces and territories. The results in Table 13.1 show that arbitration is largely left to the legislative assemblies themselves, often via member-staffed administrative committees (that is, Boards of Internal Economies or equivalent), but that often independent investigators are used to gather evidence regarding sexual harassment claims. In six of the provinces/ territories with sexual harassment policies, independent investigators *can* be used, but the language does not mandate that independent investigations be conducted. Mandated independent investigation only appears in the Manitoba, Quebec, Newfoundland and Labrador, British Columbia, and Yukon policies. Independent investigation utilizing outside experts in sexual harassment processes can help ensure that investigations are conducted fairly and are sensitive to gender-based and intersectional power dynamics.

276   Cheryl N. Collier and Tracey Raney

Gender-Based Comparative Content Analysis

Table 13.2 displays the results of the content analysis for the ten provincial and territorial member-based sexual harassment policies/codes. The analysis tracks the usage of particular language that can signal a deeper understanding and consideration of gender-based causes of GBV-P – particularly sexual harassment – as well as each policy/code's attention specifically to *sexual* harassment as opposed to *general* harassment. Policies with more numerous references to "sexual harassment" indicate more attention to GBV-P (although this finding admittedly narrowly defines GBV-P as only including sexual harassment) than ones with minimal use of the term. In Table 13.1, we saw early indications of minimal content involving "sexual harassment" language, where sexual harassment only appeared in the title of one of the policies/codes under review: Manitoba's Respectful Workplace Policy: Assessing and Preventing Sexual Harassment, Harassment and Bullying. Even in Manitoba, however, sexual harassment is not the sole focus of the policy, which covers general harassment (including bullying) more broadly, much as is the case with policies and codes in other Canadian substate jurisdictions.

Perhaps not surprisingly, Manitoba (which includes sexual harassment in its policy title) also has the highest tally of twenty-three uses of the term "sexual harassment." The only other significant usage is found in Saskatchewan, with fourteen mentions of the term. The Northwest Territories sees four uses of the term across two documents – its Code of Conduct for MLAs and its specific Workplace Harassment Policy document. Nunavut only uses the term twice, and Newfoundland and Labrador, Yukon, British Columbia, and Quebec (French equivalent language)[5] use it once. Ontario and Nova Scotia do not explicitly use the term "sexual harassment" in their code and policy, respectfully. Ontario uses "harassment," including "sexual conduct," twice in its document, while Nova Scotia uses "harassment that is sexual in nature" once. The fact that most of the ten (seven) jurisdictions fail to mention sexual harassment more than twice raises questions regarding each legislature's commitment to preventing gender-based harassment most often experienced by women-identified elected members at the hands of their male-identified colleagues.

Policy and code use of the concept "gender" is also alarmingly low in most cases, with Manitoba again registering the highest number at five instances, followed by Newfoundland and Labrador and the Northwest Territories at three. Notably, neither Nova Scotia's nor the Yukon's policies use the term at all. The lack of attention to gender is

Table 13.2. Provincial and territorial sexual harassment policy content analysis

Province/Territory	Sexual harassment	Gender	Women	Power	Race/Diversity
British Columbia	1	1	0	0	1
Saskatchewan	14	1	0	0	1
Manitoba	23	5	0	0	2
Ontario	2 (sexual conduct)	2	0	0	0
Quebec	1	1	1	0	1
Nova Scotia	1 (sexual in nature)	0	0	0	0
Newfoundland and Labrador	1	3	0	1	1
Yukon	1	0	0	0	0
Northwest Territories	4	3	0	3	2
Nunavut	2	2	1	1	4

Note: Calculations made by the authors from published texts of harassment/sexual harassment member-based legislative policies. French equivalent words are used for the Quebec policy.

also problematic inside substate policies and codes aimed at curbing "gender-based" harassment. Only two of the ten policies/codes under review mention "women" or "woman" at all: Quebec and Nunavut. Interestingly, both of these policies were two of the earliest on record and may reflect less attention to gender binary language or a move away from a feminist understanding of sexual and gender-based violence that includes and considers the fact that women are most often victimized by sexual harassment and sexual violence.

Further problematic is that only three policies/codes include language about power and power differentials – a key cause of GBV-P and sexual harassment. The Northwest Territories' policy had the most references to power at three instances; Newfoundland and Labrador and Nunavut's policies referenced it once, respectively.

Intersectionality was addressed through the use of the concepts "race" and/or "diversity" in seven of the ten cases. Nunavut – where the majority of the provincial population identify as Inuit – used this frame the most with four mentions; Manitoba and the Northwest Territories at two mentions; Newfoundland and Labrador, Saskatchewan, British Columbia, and Quebec mention the concept only once. Notably, all three jurisdictions that failed to directly address "race" or "diversity" inside their policies – Ontario, Nova Scotia, and Yukon – also failed to mention "women" or "power" in their policy language. Nova Scotia additionally does not mention "gender" at all in its sexual harassment policy.

Summary Observations

The comparative analysis of Canadian provincial and territorial elected member-based sexual harassment policies and codes of conduct reveals a patchwork of approaches to the problem of GBV-P in the country that, for the most part, pay only cursory attention to key aspects of gender-based violence. Our analysis finds that, even though attention to the #MeToo movement appears to have at least partially motivated provincial and territorial legislatures to enact some sexual harassment protections inside the legislative workplace, to date just ten of the thirteen jurisdictions under review have some form of harassment/sexual harassment policies/codes in place for elected parliamentarians. While in 2022 two of the remaining three jurisdictions had begun investigation into enacting member-based sexual harassment protections of their own, it is unclear when or if these will come to fruition. Some provinces have yet to respond to this global movement at all. Should Canadians' attention to the #MeToo movement wane, the window of opportunity for this action may close.

Our comparative analysis also raises questions about the effectiveness and value of the sexual harassment policies that have thus far been enacted in Canada's provinces and territories. Despite the potential for the substate legislatures to lead as "laboratories of experimentation," many followed a similar trajectory to that of the House of Commons and failed to substantively address gendered and intersectional power differentials and male-dominated institutional cultures. Only one of the nine studied here mentions sexual harassment in its title – unlike the House of Commons code, which was specifically created to address sexual harassment between MPs. The absence of gender-specific language in these codes and policies raises serious questions about the commitment levels of provincial and territorial legislatures to (1) gain a fulsome understanding of the problem; (2) properly investigate and adjudicate incidents of sexual harassment; and (3) ultimately create safe spaces for less powerful elected members of legislatures across the country. The lack of attention to "sexual harassment" specifically inside the policies and codes themselves was highlighted by the fact that most of the ten documents barely used the words "sexual harassment" in the text of the policies. The two that did were both policies enacted in the prairie provinces in the wake of #MeToo: Saskatchewan and Manitoba in 2018 and 2019, respectively.

Discourse/content analyses of the policy texts further revealed a common willingness to accept rape mythology that blames women for bringing forward claims of sexual harassment deemed to be vexatious, false, or in bad faith. All ten substate sexual harassment policies and codes included some reference to this language. This reference will not encourage women to robustly use the policies to help root out sexist and hostile sexually harassing behaviour and may essentially render the policies moot in helping curb this specific form of GBV-P and ensuring safe and hospitable work environments for elected women and minority members of legislatures. Our analysis also illustrates a very narrow understanding of the scope of GBV-P at the provincial/territorial level – one that is focused almost entirely on sexual harassment, when sexual harassment is included at all.

While parliamentary privilege is not mentioned directly in more than two of the sexual harassment policy documents under review, the potential for privilege to curb the protections in the policies and codes themselves is evidently still strong, particularly since most jurisdictional policies and codes fall under a Board of Internal Economy, Board of Management, or equivalent jurisdiction. Even though independent investigatory processes are available in most jurisdictions that have adopted a relevant policy, legislatures across Canada have largely clung to their parliamentary privilege power to self-police the "bad" behaviour of their members. Since most elected officials across Canadian legislatures remain predominantly white, cisgendered men, the potential for these codes and policies to "re-gender" legislative spaces in more equitable, inclusive ways is low. Three jurisdictions reserved the arbitration role for the non-partisan/neutral Speakers of the legislature – Manitoba, Ontario, and Quebec – but Speakers are ultimately chosen from among member ranks and are not entirely independent in their roles. They are also usually white men.

The content analysis of all ten existing sexual harassment policies and codes raises additional questions about the effectiveness of these new rules to curb or challenge sexual harassment and GBV-P inside the legislatures for elected members. Gender-based understandings of power imbalances that permit and perpetuate GBV-P arguably require – at the very least – the use of the terms "gender" and "power" inside and alongside the definitions of sexual harassment (and harassment) and the processes to identify, investigate, and alleviate these problems. Our analysis shows that gender was mentioned only up to five times in one document under review – in Manitoba – and had fewer mentions in every other province and territory, with Nova Scotia and the Yukon avoiding the term "gender" altogether. The concept of power as being at the heart of GBV-P and sexual harassment was not included in the sexual harassment texts of more than three jurisdictions under review – Newfoundland and Labrador, Northwest Territories, and Nunavut. As Berthet and

Kantola argue, utilizing the discourse of the "abuse of gendered power" inside legislatures strongly indicates understanding and framing of a key explanation for sexual harassment in the first place. Without this recognition, it is unlikely that sexual harassment policies will disrupt existing institutional norms and values enough to re-gender parliamentary legislatures to move closer towards gender equity (2021, 10).

In the end, it is beyond the scope of this comparative analysis to establish exactly why Canada's provinces and territories differ in their sexual harassment policies and codes of conduct for legislative members. At the same time, this comparative study also reveals a pattern of shared absences and gaps, including the embrace of the false myth that victims falsely report sexual violence, the lack of explicit gendered language or gendered understandings of power, as well as legislatures' willingness to protect and police themselves as opposed to involving outside gender-based expert arbitration of formal complaints. All of these blind spots indicate that there is much that can be improved with respect to territorial and provincial legislative responses to sexual harassment and GBV-P across the country. In a country where women's descriptive representation remains consistently low, anti-harassment policies have the potential to create safer political workplaces that can help bolster the participation and inclusion of marginalized people in politics. Our results suggest that the approach taken to address GBV-P in Canada's legislatures is unlikely to have a significant impact on increasing women's political representation or inclusion in the democratic process.

Implications for Action

We suggest the following three main actions for provincial and territorial legislatures to begin to improve their sexual harassment member-based policies and codes of conduct:

1 That each Canadian province and territory conduct a review of existing member-based harassment and sexual harassment policies (or a launch of new policies/codes where one is not in place) by consulting outside sexual harassment and violence against women in the workplace experts to begin with a fulsome understanding of gender-based violence and sexual harassment that includes consideration of long-standing gendered and intersectional power disparities inside legislatures;
2 That an independent office with expertise in investigating and *adjudicating* sexual harassment and violence against women be

established in each province and territory tasked with administering and adjudicating new sexual harassment policies and codes of conduct for elected members of the legislatures;
3 That each policy and code of conduct be subject to regular review and that statistics on the use of the policies or codes be published and widely available for transparency to provincial and territorial constituents.

Acknowledgment

Thanks to Linda Coltman for her research assistant contributions to this chapter.

NOTES

1 For an examination of state-level sexual harassment legislation in the United States, see Mahoney et al. (2020). Equal Voice released a report on sexual harassment policies in the Canadian provinces and territories in 2022 alongside a survey of members of the legislative assemblies (Equal Voice 2022).
2 Krook uses the terminology "violence against women in politics" (2020, 4).
3 See, for example, Oates (1972); Kotsogiannis and Schwager (2006). For a counter argument to this thesis, see Wiseman and Owen (2018).
4 Policy learning is simply "adjusting understandings and beliefs related to public policy," understanding that policymakers can learn from successes and failures of others, which can then help them improve policy content over time (see Moyson, Scholten, and Weible 2017, 162).
5 Words used for the content analysis of the Quebec sexual harassment policy include "harcèlement sexuel," "le sexe," "femmes," "puissance," "la race," and "la diversité."

REFERENCES

Assemblé nationale du Québec. 2015. *Politique relative à la prévention et à la gestion des situations de harcèlement au travail.* https://assnat.qc.ca/PolitiqueHP.
Bacchi, Carol. 2000. "Policy as Discourse: What Does It Mean? Where Does It Get Us?" *Discourse: Studies in the Cultural Politics of Education* 21 (1): 45–57. https://doi.org/10.1080/01596300050005493.
– 2009. *Analysing Policy: What's the Problem Represented to Be?* Frenchs Forest, NSW: Pearson Australia.
Berthet, Valentine, and Johanna Kantola. 2021. "Gender, Violence, and Political Institutions: Struggles over Sexual Harassment in the European

Parliament." *Social Politics: International Studies in Gender, State & Society* 28 (1): 143–67. https://doi.org/10.1093/sp/jxaa015.
Bissett, Kevin. 2018. "N.B. Speaker Asked to Apologize after Probe into Harassment Allegations." *The Globe and Mail*, 27 July 2018. https://www.theglobeandmail.com/politics/article-new-brunswick-parties-split-on-committee-decision-in-speaker/.
British Columbia. 2021. *Legislative Assembly of British Columbia Respectful Workplace Policy*. https://www.leg.bc.ca/content/CommitteeDocuments/42nd-parliament/LAMC/2021-07-08/LAMC_Respectful-Workplace-Policy.pdf.
Canadian Press. 2016. "Woman Accusing Quebec Liberal of Sex Assault Speaks Out." *Toronto Star*, 21 October 2016. https://www.thestar.com/news/canada/2016/10/21/woman-accusing-quebec-liberal-of-sex-assault-speaks-out.html.
CBC News. 2007. "MLA's Harassment Complaint Botched, Crane Says." *CBC News*, 26 September 2007. https://www.cbc.ca/news/canada/prince-edward-island/mla-s-harassment-complaint-botched-crane-says-1.646083.
Chappell, Louise. 2006. "Comparing Political Institutions: Revealing the Gendered 'Logic of Appropriateness.'" *Politics & Gender* 2 (2): 223–35. https://doi.org/10.1017/S1743923X06221044.
Chappell, Louise, and Georgina Waylen. 2013. "Gender and the Hidden Life of Institutions." *Public Administration* 91 (3): 599–615. https://doi.org/10.1111/j.1467-9299.2012.02104.x.
Collier, Cheryl N. 2012. "Feminist and Gender-Neutral Frames in Contemporary Child-Care and Anti-Violence Policy Debates in Canada." *Politics & Gender* 8 (3): 283–303. https://doi.org/10.1017/S1743923X12000323.
Collier, Cheryl N., and Tracey Raney. 2018a. "Canada's Member-to-Member Code of Conduct on Sexual Harassment: Progress or Regress?" *Canadian Journal of Political Science* 51 (4): 795–815. https://doi.org/10.1017/S000842391800032X.
– 2018b. "Understanding Sexism and Sexual Harassment in Politics: A Comparison of Westminster Parliaments in Australia, the United Kingdom, and Canada." *Social Politics: International Studies in Gender, State & Society* 25 (3): 432–55. https://doi.org/10.1093/sp/jxy024.
Equal Voice. 2022. *Combatting Sexual Harassment in Canada's Legislative Assemblies*. https://equalvoice.ca/wp-content/uploads/2022/05/Public-Release-2022-Key-Findings-EN-1.pdf.
French, Janet. 2019. "Alberta Party Proposes Code of Conduct for MLAs in Wake of Sexual Harassment Investigations." *Edmonton Journal*, 31 March 2019. https://edmontonjournal.com/news/politics/alberta-party-proposes-code-of-conduct-for-mlas-in-wake-of-sexual-harassment-investigations.

Frizzell, Sara. 2018. "Iqaluit Mayor Faces Backlash after Calling Out Some Male Inuit Leaders as Sexual Predators." *CBC News*, 10 October 2018. https://www.cbc.ca/news/canada/north/iqaluit-mayor-madeleine-redfern-sex-harassment-travel-1.4851984.

Inter-Parliamentary Union (IPU). 2016. *Sexism, Harassment and Violence against Women Parliamentarians*. IPU Issues Brief, October 2016. http://www.ipu.org/pdf/publications/issuesbrief-e.pdf.

Kavanagh, Sean. 2018. "'Enough Is Enough': Speaker Works on Changes to Harassment Policy." *CBC News*, 19 October 2018. https://www.cbc.ca/news/canada/manitoba-legislature-speaker-myrna-driedger-harassment-policy-1.4870427.

Kotsogiannis, Christos, and Robert Schwager. 2006. "On the Incentives to Experiment in Federations." *Journal of Urban Economics* 60 (3): 484–97. https://doi.org/10.1016/j.jue.2006.04.008.

Krook, Mona Lena. 2020. *Violence against Women in Politics*. New York: Oxford University Press.

Legislative Assembly of Manitoba. 2019. *Respectful Workplace Policy: Addressing and Preventing Sexual Harassment, Harassment and Bullying*. https://www.gov.mb.ca/legislature/resources/pdf/rwp_policy.pdf.

Legislative Assembly of Ontario. 2018. *Report of the Speaker's Panel to Establish a Members' Code of Conduct on Harassment*. https://collections.ola.org/mon/2018/04/345424.pdf.

Legislative Assembly of Saskatchewan. 2018. *Anti-Harassment Code of Conduct*. https://www.legassembly.sk.ca/mlas/codes-of-conduct/anti-harassment-code-of-conduct/.

Lovenduski, Joni. 2014. "The Institutionalization of Sexism in Politics." *Political Insight* 5 (2): 16–19. https://doi.org/10.1111/2041-9066.12056.

Mackay, Fiona. 2014. "Nested Newness, Institutional Innovation, and the Gendered Limits of Change." *Politics & Gender* 10 (4): 549–71. https://doi.org/10.1017/S1743923X14000415.

Mahoney, Anna Mitchell, Meghan Kearney, and Carly Meagan Shaffer. 2020. "#MeToo in the State House." In *Politicking While Female: The Political Lives of Women*, edited by Nichole M. Bauer, 158–80. Baton Rouge: Louisiana State University Press.

Moyson, Stéphane, Peter Scholten, and Christopher M. Weible. 2017. "Policy Learning and Policy Change: Theorizing Their Relations from Different Perspectives." *Policy and Society* 36 (2): 161–77. https://doi.org/10.1080/14494035.2017.1331879.

Newfoundland and Labrador. 2019. *House of Assembly Standing Committee on Privileges and Elections Final Report to the House of Assembly on the Development of a Legislature-Specific Harassment-Free Workplace*

Policy. https://assembly.nl.ca/business/electronicdocuments
/PECFinalReportToHOAOnDevelopmentOfLegSpecificHFWPApril2019.pdf.
Northwest Territories. 2019a. *Code of Conduct for Members of the Legislative Assembly of the Northwest Territories.* https://www.ntassembly.ca/sites
/assembly/files/td_509-183.pdf.
– 2019b. "Workplace Harassment Policy." In *Members' Handbook, Northwest Territories Legislative Assembly*, Section 6. 19th Legislative Assembly. https://
www.ntassembly.ca/sites/assembly/files/images/legislative_assembly
_members_handbook_-_november_2022.pdf.
Nova Scotia. 2016. *Nova Scotia House of Assembly Policy on the Prevention and Resolution of Harassment in the Workplace (Policy).* 19 May 2016. https://
nslegislature.ca/sites/default/files/pdfs/people/harassment-policy.pdf.
Nunavut Legislative Assembly. 2014. "Workplace Harassment Policy." In *Legislative Assembly of Nunavut Members Handbook on Administrative and Financial Matters*, 1–23. https://assembly.nu.ca/library/GNedocs/2014
/002246-e.pdf.
Oates, Wallace E. 1972. *Fiscal Federalism.* New York: Harcourt Brace Jovanovich.
Raney, Tracey, and Cheryl N. Collier. 2022. "Privilege and Gendered Violence in the Canadian and British Houses of Commons." *Parliamentary Affairs* 75 (2): 382–99. https://doi.org/10.1093/pa/gsaa069.
Rein, Martin, and Donald Schön. 1991. "Frame-Reflective Policy Discourse." In *Social Sciences and Modern States: National Experiences and Theoretical Crossroads*, edited by Peter Wagner, Carol Hirschon Weiss, Björn Wittrock and Helmut Wollmann, 262–89. Cambridge: Cambridge University Press.
Thomas, Paul, and Graham White. 2016. "Evaluating Provincial and Territorial Legislatures." In *Provinces: Canadian Provincial Politics*, 3rd ed., edited by Christopher Dunn, 363–97. Toronto, ON: University of Toronto Press.
Waylen, Georgina. 2014. "Informal Institutions, Institutional Change, and Gender Equality." *Political Research Quarterly* 67 (1): 212–23. https://doi
.org/10.1177/1065912913510360.
Wiseman, Hannah Jacobs., and Dave Owen. 2018. "Federal Laboratories of Democracy." *University of California Davis Law Review* 52 (2): 1119–91. https://lawreview.law.ucdavis.edu/issues/52/2/Articles/52-2_Wiseman
_Owen.pdf.
Yukon Legislative Assembly. 2019. *Yukon Legislative Assembly Respectful Conduct.* https://yukonassembly.ca/sites/default/files/inline-files
/respectful-workplace-policy.pdf.
Zussman, Richard. 2020. "Former Speaker Claims 'Me Too' Allegations at B.C. Legislature Not Properly Investigated." *Global News*, 11 December 2020. https://globalnews.ca/news/7516494/former-speaker-claims-me-too
-allegations-at-b-c-legislature-not-properly-investigated/.

Conclusion: Canadian Experiences of Gender-Based Violence in Politics – Key Learnings, Action Items, and Avenues for Further Research

CHERYL N. COLLIER AND TRACEY RANEY

This edited volume centres its collective examination of gender-based violence in politics (GBV-P) on the Canadian experience, drawing attention to the various places and ways in which such violence is perpetrated against survivors who occupy a range of political spaces. Using the #MeToo movement as an entry point into broader and more diverse discussions about violence and harassment that includes Black, Indigenous, 2SLGBTQQIA+,[1] and women of colour, the chapters demonstrate how widespread this problem is in Canadian politics, the extent to which the problem interrupts democracy, and the challenging social, political, and structural changes that are needed to address it. Chapters examined the growing problem of online GBV-P by introducing a novel continuum, focused on gradations of experiences of online gender-based political violence, alongside investigating Canadian politicians' exposure to online GBV-P in the 2015 federal election against a global comparative backdrop. The volume foreshadows a worrying trend towards image-based sexual violence transnationally and in other countries, offering a cautionary warning for Canadian decision-makers. The prevalence of online threats and harassment against political candidates in the 2021 federal election suggests that this problem is likely to become more serious and that solutions are urgently needed to address it (Samara Centre for Democracy 2021).

The impact of media coverage was scrutinized through experimental testing of the perceived chilling impact of one high-profile GBV-P case on women's willingness to run for office. Mainstream national print coverage of GBV-P was analysed pre- and post-#MeToo, and the treatment of women and men political actors through hostile humour in political cartooning was examined in the "frontier masculine" province of Alberta. The scope and nuance of what GBV-P means in Indigenous communities was highlighted, illustrating that silence in all political spaces, including inside Indigenous communities, is exacerbated by ongoing colonialism and interrelated intergenerational trauma. A deep, qualitative case study of one municipal politician's experiences of GBV-P on the campaign trail showed how vulnerable and unprotected some women-identified political actors can be and how motherhood can be weaponized through a deliberate gendered disinformation campaign to attack and undermine women's leadership aspirations. Political staff experiences were also investigated, showing that those with the least power in political institutions often suffer the most and have the least recourse to justice and reparations. Systemic causal relationships to GBV-P were shown to be routinely ignored and accountability scarce in the aftermath of several recent incidents involving elected perpetrators of GBV-P. Orientation sessions and training for incoming Canadian members of Parliament (MPs) were exposed as largely inadequate, alongside those of their UK parliamentary counterparts. And so-called policy and code of conduct solutions also fell well short of the mark in both the appointed Senate and in the elected halls of the provinces and territories.

Collectively, the chapters here demonstrate that we can learn much from Canada in comparative context; they also make a strong case for continuing research as well as for a comprehensive action agenda to help reduce incidents of GBV-P in this country and elsewhere. Despite Canada's international status as a champion of anti-sexual harassment codes of conduct and women's rights generally, these chapters collectively prove that much work needs to be done to tackle GBV-P in Canada. Addressing anti-violence policy gaps, eliminating accountability loopholes, creating effective policies to address violence in online spaces, and attending to the ways in which violence is differentially experienced by Indigenous, Black, 2SLGBTQQIA+, and women of colour in politics are, in our estimation, crucial steps in creating more inclusive, equitable, and *representative* democratic spaces.

In this concluding chapter, we revisit the core research questions that have guided the work of the volume. Drawing upon the contributions of our authors, we have also pulled together and consolidated a list of action items for advocacy to end GBV-P in Canada and beyond. Finally, we make the call for more Canadian-based data collection and research in this important area to keep us firmly on the road towards positive gender equity in the political sphere.

Canadian Political Actors and Their Experiences of GBV-P

Who Are the Political Actors?

Chapters in this volume make a strong case for widening our consideration of who we include in our grouping of "political actors" and what we consider to be "political spaces," particularly taking into account an intersectional lens that includes Black, persons of colour, persons across the gender spectrum, persons with disabilities, as well as Indigenous actors. Major and Stirbys (chapter 7) argue convincingly that an understanding of "political space" for Indigenous peoples ranges broadly from elected halls to bureaucratic offices to community settings and to organizations, local communities, and families. The lack of visibility and prominence of women-identified Indigenous political actors in these spaces is a direct result of ongoing and systemic colonial practices and genocide, and will not be reconciled until, at the very least, Indigenous women are fully included and respected in all these settings.

Political actors also include journalists and other media gatekeepers who frame "accepted" portrayals of women politicians and appointed political staff. The media – through national print-based dailies, inside published political cartoons, and online news sources – have strong agenda-setting and discourse-setting powers. Those who call out GBV-P help raise awareness and can publicize strategies to combat exposure to GBV-P, including counter-speech. Those who tacitly or overtly reinforce sexism and violent depictions of women (and men) are a large part of perpetuating the problem and normalizing GBV-P in Canada as well as on the global stage.

Political actors also include vulnerable political staff, both men- and women-identified, who experience harassment and intersectional gender-based violence in their positions of limited to no power, underscored by precarious employment contracts that render them overtly beholden to their political bosses. As Cloutier's original survey study in chapter 9 shows, women and men staffers are reticent to report incidents of GBV-P; this reticence is even more the case with men-identified staff, who often ignore the violence itself or are embarrassed to mention it at all. As Thomas and Pruysers's chapter 4 indicates, the gendered dimensions of men as targets of violence are an avenue for future exploration.

How Do Canadian Actors Uniquely Experience GBV-P?

Existing GBV-P research tells us that partisanship heightens and deepens experiences of political violence, particularly during electoral contests (Krook 2020). This reality remains true in Canada, yet we also see disturbing cases of GBV-P in non-partisan electoral contests, such as in Canadian municipalities without formal political parties. Graham (chapter 8) argues that, despite suggestions to the contrary, municipal politics are not more open and accessible to women politicians. In the absence of partisanship, electoral contests can be riddled with incidents of GBV-P. At the municipal level, partisan structures are mostly absent,[2] as are other mechanisms to potentially support victims of GBV-P, especially during political campaigns.

The types of violence on the continuum described by Krook (2020) do well to describe cases of GBV-P included in this volume, although work by Lalonde (chapter 3) draws more attention to the nuances and scope of what sexual violence is in the online realm, including non-consensual dissemination of intimate images along with AI-assisted "deepfakes" and "deepnudes." Major and Stirbys (chapter 7) also draw our attention to Indigenous women's routine and all too common exposure to GBV-P, not only from Indigenous and non-Indigenous men but also from Indigenous and non-Indigenous women – all tied to colonial intergenerational violence that has stripped away the important historic place that Indigenous women used to occupy inside traditional Indigenous societies.

What Does Gender-Based Violence Tell Us about the State of Democracy in Canada?

As the chapters in this volume illustrate, gender-based violence in all its forms has a detrimental impact on democratic participation in Canada. Our volume started with excerpts from the exit speech passionately shared by former NDP MP Mumilaaq Qaqqaq. The federal legislature was a toxic environment for MP Qaqqaq, and she chose to remove herself from a workplace she had every right to work in, yet never made her feel welcome or safe. Celina Caesar-Chavannes, a Black women MP in the Liberal caucus, also resigned her seat to sit as a backbencher in Parliament until she left politics altogether – another example of how racism, sexism, and harassment force women, particularly racialized women, out of the formal political sphere. Thomas and Pruysers's chapter 4 finds that, while voters might not penalize women who are subject to GBV-P, the effects of the violence on individual women candidates and legislators can be a significant barrier to their participation. When women are forced to leave politics in order to safeguard their own well-being and safety, it reduces their opportunity to have their voices, opinions, and identities heard and reflected in the political process.

Allowing perpetrators of GBV-P to remain involved in the political process while facing no serious consequences for their actions additionally weakens democratic accountability. Gerrits's chapter 10 outlines how, both before and after #MeToo, incidents of GBV-P federally have not been sufficiently dealt with, leaving some perpetrators unaccountable for their actions. Of the known cases reported in the media, some of those who have committed GBV-P remain in public office today. Across online spaces and in-person legislative workplaces, a common theme is the extent to which GBV-P remains a clear problem, crowding out those who are already on the margins, with insufficient steps taken to hold those who perpetrate it accountable for their actions. Democratic dialogue and processes are impoverished when the cost of participating in these spaces is higher for some compared to others. Insufficient, weak rules to address GBV-P likely mean that many more instances remain under-reported and hidden from the public. They also send a message to citizens that violence and harassment are the "norm" and will be tolerated in Canada's democratic spaces. Canada's reputation as a global leader and supporter of gender-equality rights is hard to square with the reality of everyday and persistent GBV-P in all political spaces. The #MeToo movement has shone a bright spotlight on these challenges to democracy, yet there is still far to go to even the democratic playing field so that true representational intersectional gender parity can be achieved.

What Does the Canadian Case Tell Us about How GBV-P Should Be Tackled Globally?

Canada was one of the first countries in the world to address sexual harassment between elected members when it adopted its MP Code of Conduct on sexual harassment in 2015. Yet, as this book documents, this issue has yet to be sufficiently addressed across the country. As a federation, federal, provincial, territorial, and municipal governments have responded in different ways to the problem of GBV-P. As chapter 13 by Collier and Raney shows, some provinces and territories have produced anti-violence codes of conduct, but others have not. These policy inconsistencies leave women vulnerable to varying degrees of abuse and show that a one-size-fits-all approach is not sufficient. Policy advocates and decision-makers at multiple levels of government will need to respond to this problem in ways that are unique to their own political cultures and institutional needs. The widespread and ubiquitous nature of GBV-P across all jurisdictions in Canada demonstrates how gender inequality and violence are deeply rooted in this well-established democracy. Combined with a relatively low percentage of women in its federally elected legislature (at 30 per cent today), full gender equity remains an elusive goal for Canada's democracy. Global parliamentarians and activists seeking to implement their own solutions should be cautious in importing Canada's solutions, where much work remains to be done, into their jurisdictions.

Canada's colonial history and its relationship with Indigenous peoples have additional relevance for similar settler societies as they come to terms with GBV-P in their own jurisdictions. As a settler society, Canada has a long and troubled relationship with its founding peoples. Despite federal inquiries, including the 1996 Royal Commission on Aboriginal Peoples, the 2015 Truth and Reconciliation Commission, and the 2020 Missing and Murdered Indigenous Women and Girls Inquiry, Canada continues to fail to make significant and meaningful strides towards reconciliation and decolonization. Thus GBV-P persists in disturbing and systemic ways for Canada's Indigenous peoples, and that experience has not been well-documented in existing traditional research spaces. It is possible that these experiences are entirely unique – tethered to the specific genocidal state actions taken against Indigenous Canadians historically. Further comparative research between Canadian Indigenous experiences of GBV-P and colonial-based Indigenous GBV-P in other settler societies would help establish shared transnational patterns (for example, based on patriarchal and colonial practices of violence) and highlight the ways in which different countries have perpetrated this violence by specific and troubling means. As Major and Stirbys's contribution in chapter 7 shows here, solutions to GBV-P in settler societies must include Indigenous women's perspectives to assist in the broader goal of meaningful reconciliation.

Suggested Action Items to Help Combat Canadian GBV-P

Each chapter considered several potential avenues for action for their particular case studies, examples, and/or inadequate responses to Canadian incidents of GBV-P. Chapter authors raised overlapping/ overarching themes of common approaches to solving the varied manifestations of the problem of Canadian GBV-P. These include (1) more data collection and research; (2) stronger accountability measures; (3) independent GBV-P expertise; and (4) allyship and survivor supports. We highlight each of these actionable categories below.

More Data Collection and Research

A common theme in the volume was raised regarding the lack of current, available data and research on GBV-P broadly and in Canada specifically. The solution should include data collection regarding the causes of the problem, how it has changed (or not) over time, and how it compares across different diversity axes, and so on. Bardall and Tenove (chapter 1) note the paucity of comparative research on incidents of technologically facilitated online harassment in different countries and the need to develop standardized research methods and measures to aid in our comparative learning. Wagner and Young (chapter 2) also point to the need for more research and specifically call on the federal government to take the lead in "ramping up research capacity" on various forms of online GBV-P. New research would help facilitate evidence-based policymaking in the area. Lalonde (chapter 3) calls out the lack of data in identifying the growing problem of image-based sexual violence and its likely occurrence in Canada, even though other countries, including Australia and the United States, conduct national-level surveys to help understand image-based sexual violence in those countries. Thomas and Pruysers (chapter 4) call for future research on the extent to which men are subjects of GBV-P, as well as on public perceptions of such instances of violence. Overall, better data collection and research on Canadian experiences of GBV-P can aid the argument for more advocacy to find solutions.

Stronger Accountability Measures

Several chapter authors reference the need to improve accountability for perpetrators of GBV-P through a variety of means, including calling out and naming the problem more regularly and ensuring that perpetrators are made to answer or are sanctioned for their transgressions. Accountability also requires space to name systemic and cultural underpinnings of, particularly, intersectional GBV-P. Major and Stirbys (chapter 7) devote many of their proposed solutions to increased accountability for GBV-P against Indigenous peoples. This accountability includes the implementation of the ninety-four Calls to Action of the Truth and Reconciliation Commission and an end to cultural genocide through recognition and attention to the cultural, health, security, and justice needs of Indigenous women and girls. Accountability can also leverage existing human rights tools, both nationally and internationally, as well as bring attention to the elimination of colonization as "gendered oppression." Graham (chapter 8) also calls for greater accountability from those who administer elections due to the prevalence of GBV-P during the writ period. Accountability in this instance includes an examination of processes for "addressing unethical, discriminatory, and/or acts of gender-based violence" within the campaign cycle.

Chapters that cover sanctions and policies aimed at addressing elected officials who perpetrate GBV-P raise the current inadequacy of existing accountability processes and structures. Gerrits (chapter 10) argues that this accountability must shift the focus away from treating perpetrators as individual "bad apples" and focus instead on the culture and norms that perpetuate and facilitate GBV-P in the first place. Raney (chapter 12) adds that the public needs to be aware of investigations into senators who commit GBV-P so that public accountability to the Canadian people can be achieved. Transparent procedures and outcomes (that protect the identities of victims) are also needed for public office holders in provincial and territorial legislatures. Despite the global attention to gendered violence and harassment ushered in by the #MeToo movement, strong accountability mechanisms that enforce anti-violence rules and norms and that hold perpetrators responsible for their actions remain elusive in Canadian politics. Non-existent or weak accountability mechanisms that deal with GBV-P highlight the persistence of white, heteronormative male-dominated norms in politics and political institutions, and targets of violence are likely to have little faith that their abuse will be taken seriously by those in power. Insufficient GBV-P accountability mechanisms are thus highly problematic from a gendered and raced lens, as women, 2SLGBTQQIA+, and BIPOC[3] should not be subjected to toxicity or violence simply because they inhabit a historically white, cis-gendered, heterosexual, male-dominated workspace.

Independent GBV-P Expertise to Develop Effective Solutions and Responses

Chapter authors readily identify the importance of gender-based intersectional knowledge that is not clouded by partisanship to name, understand, and properly address incidents of GBV-P in Canada. Gender-based violence expertise needs to be involved at all stages, from receiving reports of GBV-P, to training people on what the problem is, to how to recognize and support survivors and adjudicate incidents, and, ultimately, in establishing sanctions and/or reparations. Intersectional lenses and diverse voices are crucial to solutions. Solutions must involve all women, not invisibilize or hide experiences of GBV-P, and importantly, cannot victim-blame or assume victims are responsible for solving the problem itself. Avoidance of victim-blaming is emphasized by Lalonde, Raney, and Collier and Raney (chapters 3, 12, and 13, respectively), along with Cloutier (chapter 9), whose collective research suggests that, without independent GBV-P expertise, policy solutions and codes of conduct are unlikely to be effective. Independent expertise and oversight are also a common call in chapters on media reports of GBV-P. Reist (chapter 6) argues that, not only should editors call out GBV-P inside political cartoons, but newspapers should incorporate a diverse, intersectional group of cartoonists instead of the current dominance of white, cis-gender males in these roles. Goodyear-Grant (chapter 5) notes that professional journalism standards and education of journalists can go a long way in ensuring that coverage of GBV-P is thoughtful and avoids harmful sexist stereotypes.

Allyship and Survivor Support

Finally, authors collectively point to the need for widespread allyship and support of survivors of GBV-P as a good initial step towards eradicating GBV-P. Survivors cannot adequately address this problem alone. GBV-P is a structural and systemic problem that will need all actors – from government, civil society, non-governmental organizations (NGOs), media owners and editors, social media conglomerates, and so on – to be aware of the problem and be part of the solution. Bardall and Tenove (chapter 1) point to legal and legislative actors as key players in creating lasting answers to the problem of GBV-P, aided by civil society. Wagner and Young (chapter 2) share this sentiment and note how important civil society is in curbing online GBV-P and that NGOs and human rights activists can and should lead the charge towards finding solutions. Major and Stirbys (chapter 7) call for allies to ensure that Indigenous women are given leadership roles and decision-making authority to counteract their forced invisibility in political spaces. Graham (chapter 8) encourages "organized and resourced groups" to call out GBV-P when they see it and to put pressure on leaders to address the problem through "institutionalized forms of allyship."

All of these collective action items are important takeaways for advocates interested in advancing an agenda that gets us closer to ending gender-based violence in Canada and beyond. These, alongside the individual solutions suggested by each author at the end of each chapter, may not encompass the entirety of potential effective next steps on GBV-P in this country, but they represent a good start to help operationalize and continue the positive energy surrounding the #MeToo movement. There is clearly much work to do.

Concluding Thoughts and Calls for More GBV-P in Canada Research

In the end, the chapters that make up this volume tell us much about Canadian experiences of, and potential ways to combat, GBV-P across the country. The case to address GBV-P across the gender spectrum by relying on evidence-based, intersectional research is strongly made here. More research can and should be advanced, and we encourage others – including government and policy actors – to continue to investigate the unique experiences of GBV-P in Canada and the comparative avenues for learning to which this research ultimately can contribute.

There is certainly more we can learn about men-identified experiences of GBV-P across the gender spectrum, something that Reist's chapter 6, for example, starts to uncover through her examination of frontier masculinity in the province of Alberta, which shows how the inability of Premier Ed Stelmach to strongly mirror this "ideal" political persona arguably left him more open to hostile humour rooted in GBV-P. Future research questions might consider how variations of masculinity impact experiences of, and solutions to, this kind of violence, as well as to racialized and Indigenous GBV-P experiences of male-identified political actors. Our volume was unable to fully investigate these questions, but we argue that they are germane for future research agendas to understand the scope of violence against political actors along all spaces on the gender continuum.

Our book also does not fully investigate experiences of GBV-P in the province of Quebec. How does language identity politics impact experiences of GBV-P, if at all? Quebec as a province has traditionally been more open to feminist analysis of the provincial state, yet feminist and gender-based attention to policy solutions for GBV-P inside the legislative assembly was not reflective of this potential, save for the earlier adoption of member of National Assembly (MNA) policies on sexual harassment. The #MeToo movement arguably unfolded in a unique way in Quebec relative to the rest of the country, with a fresh wave of allegations of sexual harassment and assault emerging in 2020 by employees of Ubisoft, a video game company. More attention to these questions would be fruitful in the context of Quebec politics.

While our volume breaks important ground by including a theoretical challenge to the scope of GBV-P from an Indigenous perspective, more could and should be included that incorporates these important experiences and pays attention to decolonization as a core solution to ending Indigenous GBV-P in all spaces. As one of the first, single-country case studies on GBV-P in the world, we view this volume as contributing to ongoing national and global discussions, rather than as a final word, on gender-based violence in the political realm. We look forward to other scholars and anti-violence advocates continuing this research and equity agenda, and moving us ever closer to ending GBV-P in Canada and elsewhere in the years to come.

NOTES

1 2SLGBTQQIA+ refers to those who identify as two-spirit, lesbian, gay, bisexual, transgender, queer, questioning, intersex, androgynous, and asexual. "Two-spirit" is a term used by some Indigenous people to reflect the complex (and non-binary) nature of gender roles and identities in Indigenous communities.
2 The city of Vancouver, BC, is one exception where parties exist municipally.
3 BIPOC refers to Black, Indigenous, and people of colour.

REFERENCES

Krook, Mona Lena. 2020. *Violence against Women in Politics*. London: Oxford University Press.
Samara Centre for Democracy. 2021. "*SAMBot Federal Election Day: September 20, 2021.*" www.samaracentre.ca/articles/sambot-federal-election-day-september-20-2021.

Contributors

Gabrielle Bardall has worked in over sixty countries worldwide for a variety of United Nations (UN) agencies and international organizations, including the UN Development Programme, UN Women, and the International Foundation for Electoral Systems (IFES). A specialist in gender and security, she has published and taught about online violence against women in politics for over a decade. Gabrielle holds degrees from McGill University, Sciences-Po Paris, and l'Université de Montreal. She received the American Political Science Association's Congressional Fellowship and the Pierre Elliott Trudeau Doctoral Scholarship for her work in the area of violence against women in politics. She is a fellow with the Center for Democracy and Technology.

Meagan Cloutier is a PhD candidate in political science at the University of Calgary. She researches the gendered nature of politics as work and is interested in the challenges political staffers face at work, with a specific interest in harassment and gender-based violence in politics.

Louise Cockram is a PhD candidate at Carleton University in Ottawa, ON. Her work focuses on the orientation of newly elected members of Parliament (MPs) in Canada and the United Kingdom.

Cheryl N. Collier is dean of the Faculty of Arts, Humanities, and Social Sciences and professor of political science at the University of Windsor. She researches in the areas of comparative women's movements, Canadian federal and provincial childcare and anti-violence against women policy, federalism, feminist institutionalism, and violence against women in politics. She has published in a variety of journals, including the *Canadian Journal of Political Science, Politics & Gender, Social Politics,* and *Parliamentary Affairs*.

Bailey Gerrits is the Mila Mulroney Research Chair in Women, Policy and Governance Leadership at St. Francis Xavier University and teaches in the Public Policy and Governance Program. Her research investigates the stories we tell about gender-based violence and how they contribute to ending or facilitating the violence. Current projects focus on Canadian parliamentary discourse, newspapers, and police social media storytelling. Dr. Gerrits earned her PhD in political studies from Queen's University in 2019. She has published in several peer-reviewed journals, including *Feminist Media Studies*; *Politics, Groups and Identities*; and the *Canadian Journal of Communication*.

Elizabeth Goodyear-Grant is a professor of political studies and director of the Canadian Opinion Research Archive (CORA) at Queen's University. Her research and teaching focus on elections and voting behaviour, political representation and marginalization, political communications, women and gender, as well as Canadian politics more broadly.

Kate Graham researches, writes, speaks, and teaches about politics in Canada. She completed her PhD in political science at Western University and teaches at Western and Huron University College. She is the creator and host of Canada 2020's *No Second Chances*, a top-rated podcast about the experiences of women in Canada's most senior political roles. Kate herself has been actively involved in politics, including running for leader of the Ontario Liberal Party in 2020.

Dianne Lalonde is a PhD candidate in political science at Western University. Her research explores the politics of identity and structural oppression. Her dissertation work is on the harms of cultural appropriation. Dianne is also a research and knowledge mobilization specialist at the Learning Network housed in the Centre for Research and Education on Violence against Women and Children, Western University. The Learning Network is a knowledge mobilization initiative committed to ending gender-based violence through evidence-informed resources and meaningful collaborations.

Rebecca Major, a Métis and non-status Mi'kmaq from New Brunswick, is the inaugural Northern Vision Development (NVD) research chair in Northern Governance and an associate professor at Yukon University. She holds a PhD from the University of Saskatchewan's Johnson Shoyama Graduate School of Public Policy; an MA from the University of Saskatchewan in Indigenous studies; an Honours BA from the

University of Saskatchewan in Indigenous studies and history; as well as an Indigenous Governance and Politics Certificate, Department of Political Studies, University of Saskatchewan.

Scott Pruysers is an associate professor of political science at Dalhousie University. His research focuses on questions of participation and representation in party and electoral politics. His research has appeared in national and international journals such as the *Canadian Journal of Political Science, Party Politics, Political Research Quarterly,* and *Politics & Gender*. His newest co-authored book, *The Political Party in Canada*, was published by UBC Press in 2022.

Tracey Raney is a professor in the Department of Politics and Public Administration at Toronto Metropolitan University (formerly Ryerson University). She studies women and politics, feminist institutionalism, sexual misconduct in legislatures, and gender-based violence in politics. Her research has been published in several leading journals and edited books, including *Parliamentary Affairs, Social Politics, Canadian Journal of Political Science,* and *Nations and Nationalism*.

Rissa Reist is a PhD candidate in political science at the University of Alberta. Her research considers how political humour responds to settler-colonial violence in Canada. Her goal is to understand how Canadian political humour marks some acts of violence as inappropriate but others as normal and acceptable. She holds master's degrees in political science and political communication from the University of Alberta and the University of Leeds. She has a passion for education, barrier removal, and humanizing experiences, especially the experiences of those at the margins of society.

Cynthia Niioo-bineh-seh-kwe Stirbys, PhD (University of Ottawa), is Lithuanian and Saulteaux-Cree from Treaty 4, Saskatchewan. Having a background in Indigenous health, Dr. Stirbys has worked in areas including social determinants of health, governance, policy regarding mental health and addictions, gender-based analysis, and research ethics. Dr. Stirbys has an MA in conflict studies, Saint Paul University/ University of Ottawa, and an Honours BA in economics and a minor in business, Carleton University. Currently, Dr. Stirbys is an assistant professor at the School of Social Work at the University of Windsor.

Chris Tenove is research associate and assistant director of the Centre for the Study of Democratic Institutions at the School of Public Policy

& Global Affairs, University of British Columbia. His research focuses on challenges that digital technologies pose to democracy and human rights. He has published peer-reviewed articles and book chapters on topics such as disinformation, electoral interference, online harassment of public figures, and international criminal justice. Dr. Tenove was previously a postdoctoral researcher at the University of Toronto's Centre for Ethics. He received his PhD in political science from the University of British Columbia and an MA in rhetoric from the University of California, Berkeley.

Melanee Thomas is a professor in political science at the University of Calgary. Her research addresses the causes and consequences of gender-based political inequality, with a particular focus on political attitudes and behaviour. Her objectives are to identify how Canadians think about themselves in politics; explain how this thinking is structured by gender, sexism, and racism; and then develop potential solutions that ameliorate and strengthen our democratic politics. Her work appears in *Politics & Gender*, *Electoral Politics*, *Political Behaviour*, *Political Communication*, and the *Canadian Journal of Political Science*.

Angelia Wagner is an adjunct professor in the Department of Political Science at the University of Alberta. Wagner specializes in Canadian politics, gender and politics, political communication, and political representation. She co-edited *Gendered Mediation: Identity and Image Making in Canadian Politics* (UBC Press, 2019). She has published articles in journals such as the *Canadian Journal of Political Science*; *Feminist Media Studies*; *International Journal of Press/Politics*; *Journal of Political Marketing*; *Journalism Practice*; *Politics, Groups, and Identities*; and *Women Studies in Communication*. Wagner is a former journalist, working at newspapers in Alberta and Saskatchewan.

Tayler Young is a law student at the University of Alberta. Before pursuing a law degree, Young completed a master's degree in political science at the University of Alberta. Her thesis investigated online gender-based violence against women in Canadian politics and the role of symbolic annihilation in this phenomenon.

Index

abusive discourse, 27, 47, 49, 51–5, 58–9, 69
anti-harassment training, 16, 198, 212, 229–30, 232–42, 252
apologies versus non-apologies, 260n10
artificial intelligence, 68
assimilation, 157–8

backlash, 7, 12, 33–4, 36, 38, 115, 131, 140, 142–3, 160, 177, 266
Beyak, Lyn (former senator), 255
Bill C-65, 189, 233, 250–1
Blackridge Strategy, 178–9
Board of Internal Economy, 197, 212, 233, 268, 274, 279

Chief Human Resources Officer, 190, 197, 233
City of London, 176, 178, 181
civility, 46–7, 50, 177
coding scheme, 114, 116, 118–19
colonialism, 9, 57, 124, 143, 151, 153, 154–6, 160, 164, 213, 285
colonial trauma, 154
colonization, 11, 135, 152–3, 156–8, 160–1, 165–6, 291
community, 55, 132, 152–61, 166, 171, 177, 182–4, 195, 236, 266, 287

comparative research/approaches, 7, 11, 15, 25, 28–9, 32–3, 35, 37–8, 52, 267, 271, 278, 280, 285–6, 290–1, 294
confidentiality, 222, 255–6, 258
content analysis, 31, 116, 131, 136, 271, 276, 278–9
counter-speech, 14, 27, 40, 101–2, 287
Cox, Jo, 46, 112

deadnaming, 55
deepfakes, 53, 65–9, 72, 74, 76, 78, 288
deepnudes, 53, 288
delegitimizing discourse, 27, 48, 50–1, 55, 59
democracy, 3–4, 6, 9, 46–7, 58, 89, 130, 139, 154, 173–4, 183, 189, 211, 222, 257, 259, 268, 285, 289
descriptive representation, 6, 10, 173, 258, 280
diaspora, 32–3, 38
discipline, 8, 213, 239, 255; disciplinary actions, 254–6; sanctions, 255–6, 268, 275, 291–2
discourse analysis, 29, 131, 136, 138, 248, 278

disinformation, 13, 15, 26, 33, 38, 66, 286

Elders, 154, 157
employment conditions, 254; precarious employment, 258, 287
experiments, 55, 89–90, 95, 101, 268
external oversight, 269, 274

Facebook, 29, 39, 47, 75, 178–9, 217, 221
family incest, 160–1
Farahi, Amir, 178–9
federalism, 268
feminist institutionalism, 270
forms of gender-based violence/abuse/discrimination, 5–7, 9, 13–15, 25–7, 29–31, 33, 36–7, 47, 52, 56, 58, 65–7, 69–70, 74, 77, 88, 90, 92, 94, 119–20, 137–8, 142, 151, 158, 160–2, 164, 212, 223, 288, 291
Franco, Marielle, 46
frontier masculinity, 9, 115, 131–2, 134–6, 139–43, 294

gender-based violence (GBV), 3–4, 5–8, 10, 12–13, 16, 17n2, 26, 36–7, 39, 45, 57, 65–6, 72, 77, 87, 93, 109–10, 116, 119, 121, 123, 152, 172, 175, 181, 184, 189, 211, 229, 231–2, 246–7, 265, 267, 277–8, 280, 285, 288, 292–4. *See also* forms of gender-based violence/abuse/discrimination
gendered and intersectional power differentials, 267, 278
gendered coverage, 92, 94
gendered logic of appropriateness, 254
gendered mediation, 89, 91–4, 120
gendered news, 92
gender quotas, 7, 115

gendertrolling, 52–3
geography (of online GBV-P), 33
governance (traditional), 3, 152, 154, 157, 176, 184, 211, 268

harassment: experience(s) of, 9, 15, 29, 87, 111, 113, 153, 171, 174, 188–9, 191–200, 203n4, 204n12, 204n20, 256, 276, 287; frequency of, 30, 111, 174, 188, 192–3, 201; online, 3, 9, 29–32, 35, 45, 87–8, 91, 111, 139, 174, 189, 191, 198, 285, 291; perpetrators of, 192, 198, 257; reporting, 190, 192, 195, 197, 234, 275; witnessing, 193–4, 201; at work, 87, 111, 118, 121, 188–90, 192–201, 204n12, 214, 223, 229–34, 236, 238–9, 246, 250, 270
Harper, Stephen, 196–7
homophobia, 32, 35, 57
hostile humour, 131–4, 136–9, 142–3, 285, 294

image-based sexual violence, 14, 35, 53, 65, 285, 291
impacts: of colonization on Indigenous women, 152–3; of GBV-P, 6, 14–15, 26–7, 29, 34–6, 37, 58, 183, 198, 252; of image-based sexual violence, 66, 69, 73–8; of sexual harassment policies in legislatures, 266
impoliteness, 46, 49
incest, 160, 166
incivility, 26–8, 30, 34, 46, 52, 91, 97
Independent Complaints and Grievances Scheme (ICGS), 229, 236
Indian Act, 154, 157, 165
Indian residential school (IRS), 154–60, 165
Indigenous feminism, 151–2
Indigenous people(s), 3–4, 6, 11, 15, 28, 34, 57, 71, 109, 122, 133, 135–6,

143, 151–66, 253, 258, 285–8, 290–1, 293–4
intersectionality, 124, 152–3, 155, 277

Kwan, Jenny, 45, 120, 189

laboratories of experimentation, 278
leadership, 12, 29, 31, 36, 51, 131, 137, 139–40, 142, 155, 159–60, 164, 166, 174, 197, 216–7, 229, 238–9, 242, 286, 293
lynching, 53

McKenna, Catherine, 87–8, 91, 95–6, 110, 120
media effects, 91, 93–4
members of Parliament (MPs), 6, 16, 45, 51, 90, 111–12, 120, 188–91, 194–8, 214, 218, 221, 229–42, 247, 253, 278, 286; as employers, 190
members of the House of Commons, 190, 212, 233, 247
Meredith, Don (former senator), 247–9, 254
#MeToo, 10–14, 16, 65–6, 75, 78, 109–21, 151, 171–2, 180, 190–1, 211–14, 218, 220–3, 233–5, 238, 246–7, 250, 265–7, 269, 271, 274, 278, 285, 288–9, 292–4
misgendering, 55
misinformation campaign, 175, 181, 183
missing and murdered Indigenous women and girls (MMIWG), 158, 160, 162, 164–5, 166
mixed methods, 28, 191
motives, 6, 25–7, 29, 37
MP Code of Conduct, 233, 236, 274, 289
municipal politics, 172, 180, 287

negativity (spectrum), 29–30

news coverage, 51, 90, 92–4, 110–12, 114–15, 121, 122
news media, 50, 88, 93, 109, 112, 115, 122, 124, 214–16
newspapers, 14, 93, 113, 131–2, 137, 144, 292
non-consensual distribution of intimate images (NCDII), 65–72, 75, 77
non-disclosure agreement (NDA), 256, 259
Notley, Rachel, 15, 46, 50, 90, 115, 119–20, 130–1, 134, 137–41, 143

Obama, Barack, 53
Oger, Morgane, 55, 67

panic button, 45, 120
parliamentary privilege, 253, 257–9, 261n15, 268, 274, 279
paternalism, in colonialism, 155–6
patriarchy, 112, 119, 153, 157–8, 165
physical violence, 8, 109, 138–9, 153, 156, 214
Policy on Preventing and Addressing Harassment, 190, 192, 229
political/editorial cartoons, 9, 15, 115, 131, 133–4, 136–7, 139, 144, 287, 292
political humour, 132–4, 142–4
political staff, 3, 188–92, 203n1, 253, 286–7
politicians, 4–6, 9, 12, 25–6, 30, 32–8, 45–9, 51–5, 57–9, 65, 67, 69, 73, 75, 89, 91–4, 96–8, 100–2, 109–10, 112–15, 117–18, 120–2, 124, 139, 143, 188–9, 196, 198, 211–14, 220–3, 231, 241, 246, 248, 253, 255, 259, 269, 274–5, 285–7
print news, 109, 113, 119
provinces, 16, 115, 267–8, 270–1, 274–5, 278, 280, 286

psychological GBV-P, 90–1, 93–4, 100–1

reconciliation, 156, 162–4, 166, 290
Redford, Alison, 15, 46, 115, 131, 137–8, 140–1, 143
re-gendering, 270
relationships, 27, 35, 77, 136, 152–4, 156, 162, 166, 286
residential school (for Indigenous children), 154–60, 165
revenge porn, 69, 77, 78n1
Ridley, Virginia, 170–2, 177–83

sanctions, 255–6, 268, 275, 291–2; sanctioning, 248, 258
semiotic reversal, 101–2
semiotic violence, 8, 55, 70, 102n4
Senate Ethics Officer (SEO), 249, 251, 254, 255, 257
Senate of Canada, 246–7, 274
sentiment analysis, 28
sexual double standards, 73–4, 77
sexual harassment policies and codes, 268, 271, 275–6, 278–81
sexual objectification, 70, 74
sexual privacy, 70
sexual violence, 8, 14, 26, 35, 45, 53, 55, 65–6, 69–70, 76, 78, 117, 214, 221, 265, 277, 280, 285, 288, 291
Singh, Jagmeet, 51, 216
social media platforms, 39, 53, 56, 76, 164, 172, 188

Stelmach, Ed, 15, 131, 137–8, 141–2, 294

targets (of GBV-P), 10, 14, 65, 93–4, 196
technology-facilitated violence, 45, 65, 74
territories, 16, 115–16, 267–71, 274–80, 286, 289
tolerable discourse, 47–50, 55, 58–9
Truth and Reconciliation Commission (TRC), 156, 162, 165–6
Twitter (now X), 29, 32–3, 47, 50, 54, 74, 111

unelected chambers, 247

Van Meerbergen, Paul, 176–9, 181, 184
viral attacks, 30

WhatsApp, 29, 233
whisper-network, 195
Workplace Harassment and Violence Prevention Policy, 229–30, 233, 234, 238–9
Workplace Harassment and Violence Prevention Program, 190
worldviews, 163

X (formerly Twitter), 29, 32–3, 47, 50, 54, 74, 111

Milton Keynes UK
Ingram Content Group UK Ltd.
UKHW010814150624
444079UK00002B/14